PLACES

A Directory of Public Places for Private Events & Private Places for Public Functions

Seventh Edition

A Tenth House Enterprises, Inc. Publication

PLACES

A Directory of Public Places for Private Events
& Private Places for Public Functions

Copyright © by Tenth House Enterprises, Inc.
1978, 1979, 1980, 1982/83, 1984/85, 1986/87, 1989/91

Seventh Edition

Library of Congress No: 856 44113
ISBN: 0-960 3310-6-9
ISSN: 0895-4682

Authors/Publishers: Hannelore Hahn
Tatiana Stoumen

Produced and Typeset by:
Robert Sturmer of WordCraft Publishers and Consultants

Graphic designs by: Morris Berman Studio, Inc.

Design consultant: David Ebin

Special thanks to Margaret Parker and Ann Wright who contributed many hours towards making this book better.

For information, address:
Tenth House Enterprises, Inc. Caller Box 810, Gracie Station, New York, N.Y. 10028

To order a copy of PLACES send a check or money order for $24.95 which includes postage, tax and handling. For speedy and/or out-of-state delivery, we recommend UPS (add $2.00; give street address, not P.O. Box).

Checks or money orders to be made out to
Tenth House Enterprises, Inc. and mailed to:
Caller Box 810
Gracie Station
New York, N.Y. 10028
(212) 737-7536

Printed by Promotion Graphics

LOOKING FOR PENN STATION

*On the Occasion of
The Publication of the
Tenth Anniversary Edition*

Dear Friends and Subscribers,

The year when **PLACES** was first issued, 1978, seems like very long ago. The world has changed so. Yet, the more rapid the changes, the greater the need on the part of human beings to commemorate and bless their personal and professional passages.

Rites of Passage, is what **PLACES** is intrinsically about. For if human beings did not care about marking their weddings, anniversaries and special birthdays, there would be no need for **PLACES** at all.

Certainly, the way an individual or corporation chooses to celebrate its special occasions says a lot about who they are and what they ascribe value to.

So what is it, in the past ten years, that people across the board have been looking for when faced with commemorating and celebrating a Rite of Passage?

They are all looking for things that seem to have been lost.

If nothing else were said on the subject, this one thing holds true: Human beings, in this rapidly changing world, are looking for something that no longer exists.

Everyone is searching for Penn Station.

The great architectural essayist, Ada Louise Huxtable, said, "We can never again afford a nine-acre structure of superbly detailed travertine anymore than we could build one of solid gold. It (Penn Station) is a monument to the lost art of magnificent construction, other values aside." *

But other values not aside— what is everyone seeking and hoping that their chosen space, its rooms, its very walls will express?

Dignity and Continuity.

To these words we can add: character, style, nobility, elegance, beauty, aesthetics, timelessness, endurance— values which when pitted against present day economic expediency, have been enormously eroded.

They say Rome was not built in a day, but Penn Station, which was erected in 1910, was destroyed only fifty-six years later; its 90-foot columns and classical figures, eagles and ornaments pulverized and buried as fill in the Secaucus, New Jersey Meadows. No trace remains.

And, I venture to say, no one prefers what went up instead.

In this, its Tenth Anniversary edition, by far the most comprehensive in its history, **PLACES** has assembled hundreds of locations across the country which are imbued with the spirit, the ambiance, the dignity and the values which human beings deep down feel are their right to have at the most important moments and transitions in their lives. It is to be noted moreover that, in so doing, **PLACES** contributes importantly towards the structures' maintenance and economic stability. For, without a shadow of a doubt, all these vulnerable and venerable structures have been endangered and people everywhere have needed help in their fight for their preservation and restoration.

Thus, **PLACES**, having now come of age, doubly serves. Helping not only to lead the searcher to his or her appropriate location, it looks to play its part in raising the consciousness of many to the importance of enduring values— not only those of our architectural environment, but of our earth, *our habitat.*

The staff of **PLACES** and I bid you to accept our directory in the spirit of its cover: a glass raised... a toast offered... warm thanks... and appreciation to all subscribers such as yourself, who have helped establish this directory as the first and foremost in the field.

Hannelore Hahn
Publisher, **PLACES**
Spring, 1989

* *Will They Ever Finish Bruckner Boulevard (Macmillan 1963) p. 45*

i

CONTENTS

NEW YORK CITY PARTY PLACES

NEW YORK CITY GENERAL LISTINGS

A U X I L I A R Y   S E R V I C E S / C L A S S I F I E D   S E C T I O N (see center of book)

GREATER NEW YORK METROPOLITAN REGION

PLACES/U.S.A.

NEW YORK CITY

PARTY PLACES

BALLROOMS

By Maximum Capacity

New York Academy of Sciences	125
Columbia University/Earl Hall Center	150
Assembly Hall	150
Jewish Center of Bayside Hills (Queens)	200
Temple Isaiah (Queens)	200
Workmen's Circle Building	200
Lamb's Theater	220
Art Deco Ballroom	325
St. John's Hall	350
Sam & Esther Minskoff Cultural Center	400
Temple Torah (Queens)	400
Marc Ballroom	450
Sutton Place Synagogue	450
Temple Beth Sholom (Queens)	450
Fordham University (Rose Hill Campus) (Bronx)	500
Manhattanville College (Westchester)	500
Flushing Jewish Center (Queens)	600
Queens College Student Union (Queens)	850
The Ballroom at Windows on the World	1000
Manhattan Center	1200
Oyster Bay & Crystal Palace (Queens)	1500
Grand Soho Ballroom	2000
Former German Opera House in Brooklyn (Brooklyn)	2500
Jacob K. Javits Convention Center of New York	2500
Roseland	3450

Art Deco Ballroom   (212) 737-7536
(West 80's)
New York, NY

This rose and grey ballroom has its own stage, tables, chairs and large kitchen. Located in a synagogue, both kosher and non-kosher food may be served.
Dance floor
Guest capacity: up to 325

Assembly Hall   (212) 737-7536
(East 80's)
New York, NY

This ballroom offers a two-story high room, mirrors, chandeliers and a raised platform.
Guest capacity: 120/150 with dancing in 60 ft. x 23 ft. space
Note: Not available during June, July and August.

The Ballroom at Windows on the World   (212) 938-0032
Contact: Serge M. Baret, Director, Sales & Marketing
1 World Trade Center 106th fl.
New York, NY 10048

Guest capacity: 1000 for receptions; 600 for meetings; 550 for a sitdown dinner
1350 feet up into the air, 40,000 sq. ft. of space available for down to earth business meetings or floating parties.

Manhattan Center   (212) 279-7740
311 West 34th Street
Contact: Steve Honey
New York, NY 10001

Concert hall/ballroom/auditorium, recording studio, hall, Green Room
Guest capacity: 1200 theater-style/800 dance in 95 ft. x 95 ft. Grand Ballroom; 200 theater-style/120 for a dance in 28 ft. x 61 ft. hall
Proscenium stage, computerized lighting and sound system, 40' domed ceiling; world-renowned acoustics; food may be served by caterer of your choice
Building constructed by Oscar Hammerstein, Sr. in 1906; Grand Ballroom built by Scottish Rites.
Suggested uses: meeting, concert, performance, party

Marc Ballroom   (212) 924-4085
27 Union Square West
Contact: Mr. Julie Fleitman, Manager
New York, NY 10003

Ballroom
Guest capacity: 450
Stage, piano, dance floor; food may be served
Suggested uses: all special events are possible

Oyster Bay & Crystal Palace   (718) 545-8402
                    (718) 545-2990
3101 Broadway
Astoria, NY 11106
Contact: Banquet Manager

Main ballroom, meeting rooms
Guest capacity: 50/1000
Suggested uses: meeting, dinner, christening, wedding

Roseland
(212) 247-0200

239 West 52nd Street
New York, NY 10019

Contact: Hillary Ginsberg,
Director of Sales

Recently renovated ballroom/arena, lounge, restaurant, parking lot
Guest capacity: 3450 maximum capacity; 2000 on dance floor plus 700 spectator seats; 1600 cabaret-style/2000 theater-style; 250 standard exhibit booths can be accommodated on first floor (additional capacity on dance floor and Downstairs Lounge). 196' x 95' arena area (including Terrace Restaurant) 15' x 23' stage extension available, 112' x 55' dance floor, complete theatrical lighting and disco equipment, music and address systems, 50' long bandstand, street level loading facilities, 15' ceiling to chandelier, 2 stand-up bars plus rolling bars; on premises kitchen food may be served or bring caterer of your choice
Suggested uses: dance, exhibit, lecture, dinner, show

Also see: DISCOS/SUPPER & VIDEO CLUBS
Former German Opera House in Brooklyn
Grand Soho Ballroom
HOTELS
Lavish Jewish Community Center
SOCIAL HALLS

BOATS & BARGES

*P*rivate boat activity in the New York harbor has increased many-fold, ever since the 1976 Bicentennial and the 1986 Statue of Liberty Centennial. This may also be due to the increased worldwide interest in the outdoors and the fact that New York City waterfront access has been made more available due to popular demand. Close to 100 boats may be chartered during the peak season which is usually between April and October. Some of the boats are winterized and are available all year round. The listing of boats below is divided into the following categories: Classic Motor Yachts; Modern Motor Yachts; Turn-of-the-Century Passenger Steamboats; Sailboats, Schooners, Tug Boats, Chinese Junks, etc., Ferries, Sightseeing Boats, Dinner Boats, Aircraft Carriers. Call (212) 737-7536 for updates.

CLASSIC MOTOR YACHTS

(This description refers to motor yachts built in the 20's, 30's and 40's)

Al Capone's Yacht
(212) 737-7536

This magnificently restored yacht, in the spirit of the 1920's, is a floating English manor house.
Capacity: 200 (10 seated in formal dining room) on 136 ft. yacht

Elegante
(212) 737-7536
105 ft.
Capacity: 75

Enticer   (212) 737-7536

Sister ship to the presidential yacht Sequoia. Museum-quality restoration of brass, wood and fittings to the 1930's original style. The luxury of an expensive, antique private yacht. This 85' Mathis Trumpy features a covered salon and aft-deck of 55' and a 60' observation and sundeck.

Capacity: 60; sleeps 6 (for corporate cruises)

Berthed in New York City and Stamford, CT from May to November; Boca Raton from December to April. Not available on weekends in the summer.

Mariner III   (212) 737-7536

Richly paneled in polished teak with fixtures of brass and bevelled lead-crystal windows hand-crafted in Paris, this 122' luxury yacht with fully air-conditioned interior offers 5 state rooms and an entertainment center complete with stereo, TV and VCR. Available for day or week charters, business meetings and dockside entertaining May through October. Also available for long-term charters.

Capacity: 85

The Presidents   (212) 737-7536

Five American presidents used this 93 ft. deluxe yacht. From 1945 to 1970 it was refurbished by Presidents Truman, Eisenhower, Kennedy, Johnson and Nixon.

Capacity: 50

Salisa M   (212) 737-7536

110 ft.

Capacity: 30 seated/80 buffet

MODERN MOTOR YACHTS

Amazon Honeymoon/Incentive   (212) 737-7536
Getaway

This 150 ft. yacht sailing under a British flag was designed for the South American climate to cruise in places where normally no other ships could travel. Eleven-day Amazon cruises have been planned by the same persons who planned the voyages of Jacques Cousteau and Malcolm Forbes. The yacht's two canoes are used for excursions in the jungle under the guidance of an experienced guide.

Cost includes roundtrip airfare to and from Manaus, Brazil where this 14-man crew ship is docked.

Capacity: sleeps 20 in comfortably "English-style" surroundings

Amberjack V (212) 737-7536

This flexible dinner cruise 127' vessel has boarding points in Manhattan and New Jersey. Dancing and entertainment on upper deck.

Capacity: 225
Rental fee: $2,500 for 3 hours

Binghampton Too! (212) 737-7536
65 ft.
Capacity: 20

Cajun Princess (212) 737-7536
100 ft.
Capacity: 75

Charmed (212) 737-7536
42 ft.
Capacity: 12

Cloud 9 (212) 737-7536
65 ft.
Capacity: 42

Entrepreneur II (212) 737-7536

This newly built 130 ft. luxurious vessel offers three levels. The upper deck has an open-air sundeck for dancing and a glass-enclosed lounge with piano bar. The main salon is located on the main deck, as is the dining salon. The aft deck is also suitable for dining and dancing with banquette seating around its perimeter.

Capacity: 149 maximum/84 seated

Berthed in New York City from May to November, it is ideal for both corporate and private entertaining. Breakfasts, luncheons and evening events.
Resident caterer

Evviva (212) 737-7536
58 ft.
Capacity: 20

Family Ties (212) 737-7536
93 ft.
Capacity: 45

Firebird (212) 737-7536
65 ft.
Capacity: 35

Genie (212) 737-7536
110 ft.
Capacity: 70

Imperator (212) 737-7536
142 ft.
Capacity: 100

Jabiru (212) 737-7536
65 ft.
Capacity: 40
Resident caterer

Klondike VIII   **(212) 737-7536**
90 ft.
Capacity: 150

Klondike Princess   **(212) 737-7536**
110 ft.
Capacity: 150

Marco Polo   **(212) 737-7536**
93 ft.
Capacity: 80

Misti Star   **(212) 737-7536**
43 ft.
Capacity: 18

Mykonos   **(212) 737-7536**
50 ft.
Capacity: 20

Natanya II   **(212) 737-7536**
105 ft.
Capacity: 90

Paco Rabanne   **(212) 737-7536**
167 ft.
Capacity: 250

Raconteur   **(212) 737-7536**
70 ft.
Capacity: 35 seated on Main Deck; 49 buffet-style
Resident caterer

Sea Hunter III   **(212) 737-7536**
60 ft. excursion boat
Capacity: 35

Spirit of New York   **(212) 737-7536**
166 ft.
Capacity: 600

Wings of a Dove   **(212) 737-7536**
63 ft.
Capacity: 35

TURN-OF-THE-CENTURY PASSENGER STEAMBOATS

Hudson River Side Wheeler   **(212) 737-7536**
Foot of Fulton Street, East River
New York, NY

Modern 125 ft. replica of a Hudson River side wheeler with three
  decks: galley and snack bar below, carpeted saloon deck,
  open-air third deck with bandstand and dance floor.
Capacity: 200/400 (smaller parties may book a portion of the
  saloon deck and separate their section from the general
  public)

continued on next page

Rental fee: $5,000 for 4 hours for entire boat
Air-conditioned for summer, heated for winter

Recreated Nostalgic Steamboat   (212) 737-7536
Foot of Fulton Street, East River
New York, NY

This 150 ft. steamboat with etched glass clerestory windows has two enclosed fully heated and air-conditioned decks. Open-air deck with bandstand and dance floor.
Capacity: 600

SAILBOATS, SCHOONERS, BARGES, TUG BOATS, CHINESE JUNKS, ETC.

Anne Kristine   (212) 737-7536
South Street Seaport
New York, NY

Built in 1868 and traditionally rigged and fitted in the manner of a 19th century sailing vessel, this 95 ft. boat also has radios, radar and a satellite navigation system as well as magnetic steering compass and sextant. Beautifully restored by the present captain and his family and in continuous service for 119 years, it is available only from mid-September through May.
Capacity: 30/40 on deck; sleeps 15

Aquilla Marina   (212) 737-7536
120 ft. schooner
Capacity: 70

Argo   (212) 737-7536
60 ft. houseboat
Capacity: 35

Bargemusic, Ltd.   (212) 737-7536
Fulton Ferry
(foot of Cadman Plaza West)
Brooklyn, NY
Barge
Capacity: 150 in 102 ft. x 30 ft. space
Large fireplace, wood panelled decor; food may be served by caterer of your choice.
Offers a panoramic view of the East River and Lower Manhattan skyline and the Brooklyn Bridge.
Suggested uses: meeting, conference, private party for corporate non-profit organizations as well as for individuals, film, fundraiser, location shoot, wedding

The Blue Moon   (212) 737-7536
45 ft. fishing boat
Capacity: 12

Bring Sailing Back, Inc.   (212) 825-1976
c/o Petrel   Contact: Rosemarie Bechtold
Battery Park
New York, NY 10004

Capacity: 35 during the day; 30 during the evening
Catered buffet and open bar by caterer of your choice.
Sails out of Battery Park
Suggested uses: class, meeting, party, reception, wedding, baptism, photographing advertisements on yawl, fundraiser, private charter, public sail

---

Dolly Madison   (212) 737-7536
65 ft. excursion boat
Capacity: 175 people

The Freedom   (212) 737-7536
76 ft. schooner
Capacity: 70

Lehigh Valley Railroad Barge   (212) 737-7536
(New York Harbor)
New York, NY

Listed on The National Register of Historic Places, the original
  interior cargo space (30 ft. x 90 ft. x 11 ft.) and the captain's
  quarters of this 1914 wooden barge feature spectacular views
  and a warm and versatile ambiance.
Guest capacity: 250
Food may be served by the caterer of your choice.
All special events are possible including location shoots.
Note: Available May through October.

The Marschallin   (212) 737-7536
This 55 ft. Finnish-built schooner is primarily available for TV,
print work and film but its 120 horsepower diesel engine
makes it available also for world cruising.

James J. Minot   (212) 737-7536
New York, NY
1919 restored tugboat
Up to 4 couples can travel on the James J. Minot around harbor
  or Manhattan Island.

The Mon Lei   (212) 545-8211
Chesapeake Bay and China   Contact: Alen York
Sea Towing Company
1040 Avenue of the Americas
New York, NY 10018
Chinese junk
Capacity: 100 on 60 ft. vessel
Junk is 128 years old. Reminiscent of a Buddhist temple, the
  bulkheads and hull are decorated with authentic storytelling
  scrolls.
Note: Only available for private parties dockside.

Peking   (212) 964-7633
Pier 16, Foot of Fulton amd   Contact: Mr. Brook Lapin
South Street, East River
New York, NY

Built in Germany in 1911, this 377' long x 47' wide x 170' x 7"
  high ship spent her entire active career transporting nitrate
  from the west coast of South America for the manufacture of
  fertilizer in Europe. Purchased by a British nautical boys'
  school in the 1930's, this second largest sailing ship is now
  moored permanently at the South Street Seaport Museum.
Capacity: 180/200 tented seated dinner; 800 for dockside cocktail receptions
Rental fee: $1,000 minimum/$5,000 maximum; $12.50 per per-
  son
Dance floor; bring your own caterer
Available May through October.
Suggested uses: cocktail reception, buffet dinner, concert,
  presentation

Pioneer   (212) 669-9405
Pier 16, Foot of Fulton and   Contact: Cathy Pascale,
South Street, East River   Sales Manager
New York, NY

Sail past the Statue of Liberty and around the New York Harbor
  for 2 to 3 hours on a 100 year-old sailing schooner.
Capacity: 40
Food may be served by caterer of your choice.

Prelude   (212) 737-7536
60 ft. sailboat
Capacity: 15

Queen Elizabeth 2/Cunard Line   (212) 880-7500
New York, NY   Contact: David Morris,
                   Vice-President, Sales

This last great trans-Atlantic liner entered service in 1969 as a
    13-story floating luxury liner.
Capacity: 70/600
Note: There are 16 possible dates for special event rentals
    dockside when this vessel is in the Port of New York. Dates
    have to be confirmed. Hours are from 11:30 to 2:30 p.m. only.

FERRIES, SIGHTSEEING BOATS, DINNER BOATS, AIRCRAFT CARRIERS

Captree Spray and Moonchaser   (516) 661-5061
Long Island Ferry Boat at   (516) 669-6917
Captree Boat Basin (near   Contact: Caroline Bauer
 Robert Moses beaches, east of Jones Beach)
West Islip, NY 11795

Capacity: 263 per vessel
Bar, enclosed lounge, dance floor, band facilities, sun deck
Boat can sail anywhere in the Great South Bay and up and down
    Fire Island for a 4-hour charter from early spring through the
    fall. Daily excursions in summer. Fall schedule available.
Suggested uses: dinner/champagne cruise, alumni reunion, sales
    meeting, company outing, wedding, bar mitzvah
Note: Bookings are made a year in advance for weekends.
    Mailing address is P.O. Box 204, West Islip, NY 11795.

Circle Line Sightseeing Yachts   (212) 563-3201
Pier 83 (foot of West 43rd Street)   Contact: Bill Cotter
New York, NY 10036

Capacity: 300/500
Note: Boats are only available for a 4-hour evening charter
    mid-March through mid-November.

The Floating Hospital   (212) 685-0193
New York's Ship of Health   (212) 736-0745
275 Madison Avenue
New York, NY 10016

This 822-ton ship, located on Pier 84 at 44th Street and the
    Hudson River, is committed to the health care of the needy
    and the poor. The vessel can comfortably accommodate large
    numbers for social functions dockside. Available May
    through September.
Capacity: 300/500
Rental fee: $2,000 for a 4-hour minimum

Intrepid   (212) 737-7536
Pier 86 (West 46th Street at the Hudson River)
New York, NY

Capacity: 700/800 seated; 2500/3000 standing
Runway/deck
During WWII the Intrepid carried 103 aircraft and about 3300
    men. Functions can be coordinated with special exhibit of
    antique airplanes and films of 20th century history and tech-
    nology.
Food may be served only by approved caterers.
Suggested uses: business or social function, location shoot

Staten Island Ferry   (212) 806-6900
New York City Department of   Contact: Joseph Notto,
Transportation, Bureau of Ferry &   Commissioner
General Aviation Operations
Battery Maritime Building
New York, NY 10004

Capacity: 1500
Available for charter throughout the year.
Call for information.

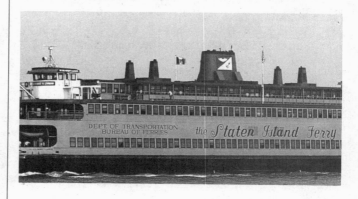

Take a Deck for Your Wedding   (212) 737-7536
(Pier 11)
New York, NY

This 130 ft. dinner boat is available for small and large groups.
Capacity: 469 seated on entire boat; 200 seated on one deck
Note: Resident caterer must be used if only one deck is rented.
    For entire boat you may bring your own caterer.

World Yacht Enterprises   (212) 929-7090
Pier 62
West 23rd Street & Hudson River
New York, NY 10001

The following three restaurant yachts are available year-round,
    day or night. The Empress of New York, capacity: 500; The
    Riveranda, capacity: 400; The Cabaret, capacity: 250

OTHER THINGS THAT MOVE

HORSE-DRAWN CARRIAGES & WAGONS

Horse-Drawn Carriages and Wagons   (212) 737-7536
New York, NY

Largest working collection in the U.S. of antique horse-drawn
    conveyances. Enameled exterior/velvet interior *victorias* and
    vis-a-vis in various colors; antique farm vehicles, closed
    carriages, such as *landaus, rockaways, delivery wagons, a
    hearse, an omnibus, sleighs,* etc. Also an extraordinary assort-
    ment of tack and equipment from throughout the world.
Suggested uses: corporate event, promotion, sales incentive,
    wedding, location shoot
Transport arrangements throughout the New York area.

HOT AIR BALLOONS

Air Pirate Balloon Academy   (201) 439-3531
Lamington Road   Contact: Jack Grenton
Bedminster, NJ 07921

Various balloon adventures for up to 13 people

PRIVATE RAILROAD CARS

Approximately 100 vintage railroad cars are privately owned in
    the U.S. and available for private charter. These may be Coach
    or Parlor cars suitable for daytime travel, Sleeper cars with
    overnight rooms, Diner or Lounge cars for meal and beverage
    service, as well as a combination of the categories named
    above. Some cars include special features such as rear obser-
    vation platforms and/or domed sections which afford scenic
    views.
Generally speaking, private cars can go wherever Amtrak goes,
    anywhere in the U.S., with trips into Canada and Mexico as
    additional possibilities.
Because of the variety of equipment and incidental charges en
    route, it is impossible to quote a uniform rate for private car
    charter. A very rough rule of thumb might project 35 cents per
    passenger per mile during the day; 50 cents per passenger per
    mile at night. Meal and beverage service, which is often
    included is, of course, in addition to the equipment/mileage
    fees.
Suitable for transportation to major sporting events, college
    reunions, family excursions, conventions, executive enter-
    tainment, honeymoons.
Open house/reception may also be scheduled when trains are in
    station.
Call PLACES at (212) 737-7536 for further information.

Art Deco Private Railroad Cars　　(212) 737-7536

New York, NY and Washington, DC

Built in the 1940s and formerly operated between New York and Florida, these streamlined stainless steel cars, now privately owned and completely refurbished, may be chartered along any route on the Amtrak system for special occasions, business presentations, sporting events, etc.

Guest capacity: 48 seated in Lounge/Observation Car; 48 seated in Dining Car; additional lounge or dining cars are available for larger groups.

Appropriate for use as a 4-hour round-trip dinner train, for example, from New York to Philadelphia, Pennsylvania. Also suitable for a mystery murder party on board.

The Blue Ridge, A Mansion on Rails　　(212) 737-7536

Morristown, NJ

Originally built for the Norfolk and Western Railroad in 1914, and later rebuilt into a business car, this private railroad car offers a dining room, a lounge, 3 state rooms and an open platform.

Guest capacity: 8 seated in dining room; 8/10 seated in lounge; 6 sleeping accommodations

Suggested uses: wedding or honeymoon, cocktail or dinner party, family reunion, business meeting en route to a convention or sporting event

Also see: Have Murder will Travel

BREWERIES

Soho Brewery　　(212) 737-7536

(Soho)
New York, NY

This three-level German-style beer hall produces its own brew both on tap and in bottles.

Guest capacity: up to 500 in main hall and mezzanine; 80 seated in third floor Ocean Grill

CHILDREN'S BIRTHDAY PARTIES

Aerobics West
131 West 86th Street
New York, NY 10024

(212) 787-3356
Contact: Grace Desimone

Gymnasium houses half court basketball and swimming pool.
Guest capacity: 60 maximum
Rental fee: $150 includes one hour use of gym plus one hour use of pool
Available for children's birthday parties and other special events.

Aviation Hall of Fame of New Jersey (201) 288-6344
Teterboro Airport
Teterboro, NJ 07608

Contact: H. V. Pat Reilly,
Executive Director or
Dottie Usherson, Assistant

Arrange for a 1-hour birthday party with cake, punch, souvenirs and a junior pilot's certificate at the 100-foot air-traffic control tower at Teterboro Airport where children play with deactivated switches and buttons, make radio contact with the nearby working tower.
Rental fee: $40 for 7 children/$2.00 for each additional child

CAROUSELS (In New York City Parks)

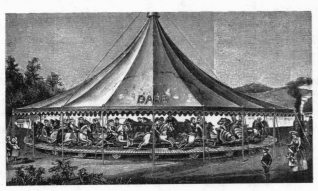

Central Park, Manhattan
65th Street (mid-park)

(212) 879-0244

Flushing Meadows, Corona Park, Queens
111th Street and 54th Ave.

(718) 592-6539

Children's Museum of Manhattan (212) 765-5904
314 West 54th Street
New York, NY 10019

Contact: Linda Koebner,
Director of Development

For $7 per child the museum offers its exhibits (things to see and events to participate in) as well as art materials and 2 staff persons to direct an art activity. Guests get to take their party-made handwork home as favors. Parents must provide all the food and table decorations, or for $13 per guest space will include a birthday cake, favors from the gift shop, soft drinks and decorations. Backyard is available.
Space is available for 15 to 30 youngsters ages 4 to 11 from 2:30 to 5 p.m.

Dainty Tea Parties for Older Children (212) 737-7536
New York, NY

Young ladies and gentlemen between the ages of 7 and 13 are invited to a dress-up sitdown tea party with lace table cloth, silver and fine porcelain. Room is decorated with balloons. Puppet show, theatrical performance and other entertainment is provided.
Guest capacity: 40

Gymnastic Birthday Parties
(Soho)
New York, NY

(212) 737-7536

In a 12,000 sq. ft. skylit and windowed space, children are divided into groups of 7 per instructor and participate in floor exercises, rings, balance beam, trampoline, etc. Popcorn parties on the trampoline are a favorite. Younger children use scaled down gymnastic equipment. Ages 3 and up.

continued on next page

Birthday parties may also include Karate— Tae Kwon Do parties with all children participating and demonstration by instructors. Ballet— with all children participating and "dancing." Ages 6 and up.

All parties are 1½ hours long which includes an hour for the activities and half an hour for for refreshments provided by the hosts. The cost is $15 per person with a minimum charge of $150. Parties may be scheduled on Saturday and Sunday at 1:30 and 3:30 p.m. Other days and times are available by special arrangement.

Kids Yummy Hats　　　　　　　　　　　(212) 737-7536
New York, NY

A nutritious alternative to the sugar overload at many children's birthday parties is offered by Jitka, a caterer/mother, who stuffs cowboy hats with festive and nourishing goodies, finger sandwiches in amusing shapes, fruits, juice, raisins, toys and surprises. She will also bring along a robot to deliver a birthday message and a wizard as well as other entertainers.

KITE FLYING
(In New York City Parks)

THE BRONX
Pelham Bay Park, Orchard Beach,
Van Cortlandt Park

BROOKLYN
Prospect Park, Long Meadow, Nethermead

MANHATTAN
Central Park, Sheep Meadow

QUEENS
Flushing Meadows, Corona Park

Mostly Magic　　　　　　　　　　　　(212) 737-7536
(Little Italy)
New York, NY

This nightclub/theater in lower Manhattan offers a magician or clown experienced in performing for children, plus an inscribed birthday cake, beverages and party favors are provided on Saturday afternoons.
Rental fee: $250 for 25 children over 5 years of age
Note: At least one adult guardian must be in attendance.

Museum of Broadcasting　　　　　　　(212) 752-4690
1 East 53rd Street　　　　　　　　　　Contact: Education
New York, NY 10022　　　　　　　　　　　　　　Department

The guest of honor can choose a program that was on television the day he or she was born or find out about shows that were favorites before the child's time.
Rental fee: $40 to $60 for up to 40 people
Space is available Tuesday through Saturday mornings and on Mondays from 9:30 a.m. to 5 p.m.
Note: Refreshments are not allowed.

Nancy Drew Parties for Older　　　　(212) 737-7536
Children
New York, NY

Children between the ages of 7 and 13 receive costumes to act out favorite plots from Nancy Drew and other mystery stories.
Guest capacity: 40

The New York Aquarium　　　　　　　(718) 266-8624
Boardwalk & West 8th Street　　　Contact: Education Hall
Brooklyn, NY 11224

Birthday children are treated to fascinating marine animals through role-playing, handling of artifacts, slides and discussion, as well as a mini-tour. Program is tailor-made to the children's ages. Each guest will also make his or her own fish print to take home. Tables and chairs are provided but party giver must supply party fare and favors.
Guest capacity: 15 children maximum (ages 5 and over) and 4 adults
Rental fee: $110 plus $1.25 per person
Note: Space is only available weekends September through mid-May.

Prospect Park Birthday Tents　　　　(718) 965-6507
New York City Department of　　Contact: Special Events
Parks　　　　　　　　　　　　　　　　　　Department
Litchfield Mansion
Prospect Park
Brooklyn, NY 11215

Children's birthday party tents available for rent in Prospect Park.

Soho Children's Shows　　　　　　　　(212) 737-7536
(Greene Street)
New York, NY

Late Sunday afternoon children's entertainment
Guest capacity: 50

Staten Island Children's Museum　　(718) 273-2060
1000 Richmond Terrace　　　　Contact: Karen Spinelli,
Staten Island, NY 10301　　　Birthday Party Coordinator

For children 4 to 10 years old this museum will make a room available with a performance stage. A staff member will take children through the current exhibit and conduct an art workshop. All details pertaining to refreshments, etc., are left up to the parents.
Guest capacity: 15

Rental fee: $50 for the use of room and services of staff member, plus $2 per child. A $35 family membership fee is also required.

SWEET 16's (Popular Places)

Automat: The Only One Left in America
Beach Boys & Girls
The Big Kitchen New York Party/Streets of New York
Club Paradise
DISCOS
40's & 50's Nostalgia
Large Private Party and Meeting Facility Overlooking Harbor
Live Swing & Jazz
LOFTS
No Strings Attached
Puttin' on the Hits
Rehearsal/Party Site
Thea's Studio
Used Cars

13th Street Theatre Repertory   **(212) 675-6677**
50 West 13th Street   Contact: Edith O'Hara
New York, NY 10011
Guest capacity: 75 in theater; 30 in lobby
Bring your own birthday cake and refreshments to be served in lobby. See show either before or after party. Children's shows every Saturday and Sunday at 1 and 3 p.m.
Rental fee: $10 for lobby plus $3.00 per person charge for show
Note: Another theater is available for regular theatrical events.

The U.S.S. Ling   **(201) 487-9493**
Submarine Memorial Association   **(201) 342-3268**
P.O. Box 395   Contact: Office
Hackensack, NJ 07602
Birthday parties for children ages 5 to 10 are held in museum and gift shop. Party includes a nautical birthday cake, captain's hat for the birthday child, guided tour of the U.S.S. Ling, a WWII vessel moored in Hackensack, New Jersey, tablecloth, napkins, glasses, forks, candles and punch. Each child receives a pin and patch as a souvenir.
Guest capacity: 20
Rental fee: $35 for 6 children plus $2.50 for each additional child. $2.50 for each adult and additional charge for cake if larger than 7 inches. $10 non-refundable advance deposit required. Party is tax-deductible.
Note: Birthday parties are arranged for weekdays only.

Young at Art   **(212) 595-3902**
122 West 83rd Street   Contact: Susan Striker,
New York, NY 10024   Director
Offers creative birthday parties for children ages 1 through 12 in gaily decorated party room as well as garden area. Parties are supervised by certified art teachers and children draw, paint, paste and sculpt during the event. They also decorate their own birthday cake and make their own party favors. This facility can also provide professional videotaping or a photo album.
Guest capacity: 6/45

Also see: James J. Minot (tugboat)
New York City Fire Museum
Participatory Art Parties
Spoke the Hub Dancing (Brooklyn)

DISCOS/SUPPER & VIDEO CLUBS

Classic Comeback

*T*his category changes rapidly. Clubs open and close and open again. This is also a section which usually offers larger spaces than average. Bear in mind that, in most cases, Friday and Saturday evenings are prime nights for the general public and some of these clubs will not be available then for private functions (always inquire anyway). However, these clubs welcome renting their spaces during the day and on "off" nights. In addition to dancing, consider renting them for luncheons, product displays, fashion shows, etc.

continued on next page

By Maximum Capacity

Soho Art Deco	100
Live Swing & Jazz	150
Where Barbara Streisand First Sang	150
Alibi	200
Turn-of-the-Century and High Tech	200
Beach Boys & Girls	225
El Morocco	300
Juke Box N.Y.C.	300
New York's Alternative Night Club	300
Surf Club	350
Westside Club with Large Dance Floor	350
Ah! The English	400
Casual Dance Club	400
Art Nouveau Downtown	450
West Village with View	450
Club Paradise	500
Down Home/Uptown	500
179 Varick	500
Regine's	500
Sounds of Brazil	500
Video Nightclub in Chelsea	500
Classic Comeback	600
Contemporary Japanese/American	600
Nirvana Club One	600
House Party/Dinner Club	700
Reggae	700
Cat Club	800
Classic Nightclub	800
Disco with Roof Deck	1000
High Tech Disco	1000
Midtown Club	1000
Unexpected Times Square Space	1000
Club House Club	1200
Ritz	1500
Emerald City	1800
Disco in a Former Church	2000
Merlin's	2000
Used Cars	2000
Opulance Inside a Stone Fortress	2500
Large and Attractive	3000

Ah! The English   (212) 737-7536
(Chelsea)
New York, NY
Classic Victorian setting with dark wood paneling, overstuffed sofas, crystal chandeliers and diminutive engravings
Guest capacity: 400

Alibi   (212) 219-2207
St. John's Lane (Canal & Beach)   Contact: Victor Giganti
New York, NY 10013
Located in a Tribeca alley, this is a true lower Manhattan hideaway.
Guest capacity: 200

Art Nouveau Downtown   (212) 737-7536
(Tribeca)
New York, NY
This night club is fashioned after the art nouveau style of the 1930's. Its lobby-like design offers a dance floor, stage, sound system, bar and VIP room.
Guest capacity: 30/450 (some built-in seating)

Beach Boys and Girls   (212) 737-7536
(Soho)
New York, NY
Hawaiian surfers decor with sand on the floor and sharks
Guest capacity: 225
Dance floor, stage
Suitable for all kinds of parties including sweet 16's.

Casual Dance Club   (212) 737-7536
(West 72nd Street)
New York, NY
This club features rock and roll.
Guest capacity: 400

CAT Club   (212) 505-0090
76 East 13th Street   Contact: Manager
New York, NY 10003
Guest capacity: 400 seated/800 maximum
24 ft. x 17 ft. stage
Suggested uses: performance, fashion show, party
Note: Space is available anytime on Sundays, Wednesdays and Thursdays, after 10 p.m. on other days.

Classic Nightclub   (212) 737-7536
(East 60's)
New York, NY
Ballroom, rehearsal space, conference room, reception area, workshop/banquet space
Guest capacity: 1000 cocktail seating on 2 levels; 380 lower level/150 upper level formal seating

Club House Club   (212) 737-7536
(East 60's)
New York, NY
Guest capacity: 600 seated/1000 buffet/1200 cocktails
Suggested uses: fashion show, product display

Club Paradise   (212) 737-7536
(Waverly Place)
New York, NY
Located in the West Village, this spot offers a sophisticated tropical decor along with a dance floor, sound system and stage.
Guest capacity: 500
Full catering is available.
Suggested uses: party, fashion or trade show, fundraiser, etc.

Contemporary Japanese/American   (212) 737-7536
(Soho)
New York, NY
This three-level restaurant offers room for dancing as well.
Guest capacity: 300 seated/450 buffet/600 cocktails

Disco in a Former Church   (212) 737-7536
(West 20's)
New York, NY
Guest capacity: 2000 standing on all 3 floors
Fireplaces, kitchen; food may be served by caterer of your
    choice

Disco with Roof Deck   (212) 737-7536
(West 19th Street)
New York, NY
Guest capacity: 1000 first floor; 300 second floor; 200 on roof
    deck

Down Home Roadhouse   (212) 737-7536
(West 50's)
New York, NY
This 2-floor nightclub/restaurant, which specializes in music
    with American roots, is available during the day for business
    lunches and special events. Excellent sight lines.
Guest capacity: 250 seated/500 standing

El Morocco   (212) 750-1500
307 East 54th Street   Contact: Amy Hornwood
New York, NY 10022
Famous 1930's night club
Guest capacity: 300 upstairs and downstairs; 200 downstairs

High Tech Disco   (212) 737-7536
(Chelsea)
New York, NY
Two-floor disco with roof garden
Guest capacity: 750 downstairs; 250 upstairs; 100 on roof

House Party/Dinner Club   (212) 737-7536
(Fifth Avenue in the 20's)
New York, NY
This former neo-classical bank building offers a 3-floor house
    party stage/set-like atmosphere with a living room and bar
    downstairs, a dining room upstairs and a billiard room and
    bedroom on the top floor.
Guest capacity: 700; 100 seated in dining room
Note: Space is only available Sunday through Wednesday even-
    ings and every day during the day.

Juke Box N.Y.C.   (212) 737-7536
(East 30's)
New York, NY
Guest capacity: 300

Large and Attractive   (212) 737-7536
(West 18th Street)
New York, NY
This split-level club is both large and good looking.
Guest capacity: 3000

Live Swing & Jazz
(212) 737-7536

(West 70's)
New York, NY

This new supper club creates the way it used to be in the 30's and 40's.
Guest capacity: 150 seated/270 cocktails; 35 seated/50 cocktails in private room

Merlin's
(212) 737-7536

(West 50's)
New York, NY

Futuristic 26,000 sq. ft. nightclub with a 2000 sq. ft. dance floor, a VIP room and projected holographic images suggesting a subterranean moonscape.
Guest capacity: 2000

Midtown Club
(212) 737-7536

(East 40's)
New York, NY

2-floor club with dance floor
Guest capacity: 500 on each floor
Resident caterer

New York's Alternative Night Club
(212) 737-7536

Houston Street (Soho)
New York, NY

Host to art openings, readings, experimental films, dance parties and performance works of all kinds, this club offers two spaces—an upstairs theater-gallery showing the work of area artists and a downstairs floor for improvisational music. Also a bar and restaurant facilities.
Guest capacity: 300 on both floors
Suggested uses: record release parties, pre-release record listening parties and other arts related promotional evenings

Nirvana Club One
(212) 486-6860
(212) 486-6868
(212) 486-6869
Contact: Manager

1 Times Square
(42nd Street,
16th & 17th floor)
New York, NY 10036

Guest capacity: 130 seated/600 standing
Space is a club with an East Indian flavor.
View of Times Square.

No Strings Attached
(212) 737-7536

(East 20's)
New York, NY

Sophisticated 1940's club with black and pink decor
Guest capacity: 900 total in club; 125 seated in restaurant; 75 seated in Champagne Room
State-of-the-art sound and lighting, video projection capabilities

One City Block-Long Disco
(212) 737-7536

(West 50's)
New York, NY

Guest capacity: 1800
4000 sq. ft. dance floor, disc jockey, sound and theatrical lighting systems, bars; food may be served
Space houses the largest display of fiber-optics in the City.
Note: Space is not available Saturday evenings.

179 Varick
(212) 691-2388
Contact: Manager

179 Varick Street (Soho)
New York, NY 10013

Rock and Roll 50's and 80's dance club
Guest capacity: approximately 500

Opulence Inside a Stone Fortress
(212) 737-7536

(Chelsea)
New York, NY

Large enough to shelter two freight trains, this immense railroad terminal/warehouse was built in 1891 at the edge of New York's waterfront. Now transformed into a truly fascinating space, it captures the imagination by contrasts: a huge crystal chandelier opposite massive brick walls and steel beams; Chippendale chairs and antique sofas overlooking 700 feet of leftover railway track; 15,000 sq. ft. of state-of-the-art sound/light systems and dance floor adjacent to former grain and coal bins now small casbah cavern-like rooms for privacy. A study in opposites.
Guest capacity: 20/2500
Suggested uses: all manner of special events including fashion shows

Reggae
(212) 226-7691
Contact: Manager

285 West Broadway (Tribeca)
New York, NY 10013

Guest capacity: 75 seated/700 standing

Regine's
(212) 688-0516

502 Park Avenue (59th Street) Contact: Banquet Manager
New York, NY 10022

Ballroom (Crystal Room), dining room (Panache Room)
Guest capacity: 100/400 Sunday through Thursday; 100/220 in Crystal Room; 50/80 in Panache Room
Food may be served only by caterer on premises unless kosher.

Ritz   (212) 737-5536
119 West 11th Street
New York, NY 10003
Ballroom
Guest capacity: 1500
Stage, balcony

Soho/Art Deco   (212) 737-5536
(Prince Street)
New York, NY
This lair-like hideaway features black leather couches as well as audio-visual screens and equipment.
Guest capacity: 100
Resident caterer

Sounds of Brazil   (212) 243-4940
204 Varick Street (Tribeca)   Contact: Manager
New York, NY 10014
Guest capacity: 200 seated/500 standing
Decorated in tropical motif featuring paintings and sculpture from Haiti, African musical instruments and gourds and Jamaican thatched huts.

Surf Club   (212) 410-1360
415 East 91st Street   Contact: Manager
New York, NY 10128
Guest capacity: 60 seated/350 standing

Turn-of-the-Century and High Tech   (212) 737-5536
(West Village)
New York, NY
This space features a circular oak bar and dance floor.
Guest capacity: 200
Note: Space is only available Monday and Tuesday evenings and Saturday until 11:00 p.m.

Unexpected Times Square Space   (212) 737-5536
(West 40's)
New York, NY
Guest capacity: 1000
This light and airy space is suitable for large midtown parties, fashion shows, product displays, bar mitzvahs, etc.

Video Nightclub in Chelsea   (212) 737-5536
(West 21st Street)
New York, NY
This sleek, contemporary nightclub features 34 video screens in the main room. Pictures are projected from a control booth that resembles a network news operation. Screens flash several videos at once as the vee-jay mixes images.
The club's sophisticated video capabilities are also appropriate for diverse trade shows, private parties and fundraisers particularly on Monday nights.
Guest capacity: 500 in downstairs and 500 in upstairs party rooms

West Village with View   (212) 737-5536
(Horatio Street)
New York, NY
This 5000 sq. ft. open space offers a large glass exposure towards the Hudson River with beautiful sunsets and night views.
Guest capacity: 250 upstairs; 150 downstairs
Sound system, fully equipped bar

Westside Club with Large Dance Floor   (212) 737-5536
(West 70's)
New York, NY
Guest capacity: 200 seated/350 maximum
Resident caterer

Where Barbara Streisand First Sang   (212) 737-5536
(West 8th Street)
New York, NY
Elegant supper club
Guest capacity: 150 seated

Also see: Classic Comeback
              Used Cars

GALLERIES

The Alternative Museum   (212) 966-3680
17 White Street (Church Street)   Contact: Gail Strickler,
New York, NY 10013   Special Events Manager
Guest capacity: 100/125 seated, 150 cocktails in 2500 sq. ft.
    space
Rental fee: $1,200 to $1,500 tax-deductible donation
Columns, 20 ft. tin ceiling; caterer must be chosen from approved list
Suggested uses: wedding

The Arch   (212) 737-7536
(Soho)
New York, NY
Wide arched windows give a special note to this contemporary gallery.
Guest capacity: 80 seated/120 cocktails

Artists Space   (212) 226-3970
223 West Broadway   Contact: Andrea Pedersen
New York, NY 10013
Guest capacity: 200 amidst contemporary art

Broome Street Gallery   (212) 737-7536
(Broome Street)
New York, NY

This 2000 sq. ft. gallery space located on the ground floor offers track lighting, a sound system and a full kitchen.
Guest capacity: up to 150

The Colorful Gallery   (212) 737-7536
(Soho)
New York, NY

Specializing in Mexican/Latin contemporary art, this 3200 sq. ft. space offers one main room and two smaller rooms for special functions.
Guest capacity: 125 seated/150 buffet/250 cocktails
Note: Space is available every evening and all day Sunday and Monday.

Contemporary Gallery   (212) 737-7536
(Soho)
New York, NY

This new two-level space offers 4500 sq. ft. on its lower level for private functions. Contemporary art serves as backdrop.
Guest capacity: 150 seated/250 cocktails in two adjoining rooms.

Hispanic Art Gallery   (212) 737-7536
(Soho)
New York, NY

Guest capacity: 150 seated/300 standing in main gallery; 70 seated/200 standing in second space; 1500 standing when three spaces are combined
Arena stage, sound system, hardwood floors, elevator, working kitchen, piano
Suggested uses: meeting, performance, banquet, fashion show, reception, wedding
Note: Smoking is not allowed in exhibition area.

Intimate West 57th Street Gallery   (212) 737-7536
New York, NY
Conveniently located between Fifth and Sixth Avenues, this light and airy space is one of the few midtown galleries available for private events. The 15 ft. x 28 ft. gallery offers blond oak

floors, 66 ft. wall space, track lighting on an interestingly shaped angular ceiling with two skylights. Also available are 20 chairs and 40 floor pillows.
Guest capacity: 50 seated/75 standing
Suggested uses: music recital, poetry reading, small reception, wedding
Note: Space is available every evening and all day Sunday and Monday. Not available during August.

L-Shaped Gallery   (212) 737-7536
(West 57th Street)
New York, NY
This 1200 sq. ft. L-shaped third floor gallery has a wall length of 100 ft. and is available for exhibitions of contemporary art as well as parties and lectures.
Guest capacity: 100 seated/150 standing

Midtown Gallery   (212) 737-7536
(West 57th Street)
New York, NY
This contemporary gallery has white walls and hardwood floors.
Guest capacity: 200 standing

Soho 20   (212) 226-4167
469 Broome Street   Contact: Patricia Sands,
New York, NY 10013   Director
Guest capacity: 150 in 35' x 35' space; 75 seated
Rental fee: negotiable
Refreshments may be served.
Space is a feminist art gallery.
Suggested uses: class, exhibit, lecture, meeting, low-key performance, reception

GARDENS, TERRACES AND OTHER INDOOR LOCATIONS WITH OUTDOOR ACCESS

Azure-Tiled Roof Garden with Penthouse   (212) 737-7536
(Soho)
New York, NY
This 3500 sq. ft. air-conditioned penthouse has access to a 7000 sq. ft. azure-tiled roof garden.
Guest capacity: 150 seated indoors; 400 outdoors

Botanical Garden in Queens   (212) 737-7536
Flushing, NY

Known for its wedding garden and delicate white gazebo, this location may also be used for wedding receptions. These are held in what is simply called the auditorium, a brick-walled room whose windows overlook the lawns. Two sets of double doors open to a patio.
Guest capacity: 80 seated with dancing/100 buffet (150 with patio); 100 standing in Wedding Garden
Serving kitchen

Brooklyn Botanic Garden   (212) 737-7536
Brooklyn, NY

The spectacular new Steinhardt Conservatory has opened a new chapter in the Brooklyn Botanic Garden. Graceful pavilions and rejuvenated gardens create a joyful haven.

The newly built Palm House, a Victorian greenhouse, is an exact duplicate of the original crystal conservatory and faces lily pools. The Spencer Terrace, which may be tented, looks into the Conservatory which may be lighted up at night.

Guest capacity: 250 seated/300 cocktails indoors year-round in Palm House; 600 cocktails around outdoor lily pools, 250 seated/300 cocktails in Japanese teahouse; 250 with dancing on Spencer Terrace; 110 seated/100 seated with dancing/200 cocktails in Rotunda

The Rose Garden may only be used for wedding ceremonies.
Resident caterer as well as a kosher caterer

Eighty Acres on the Waterfront   (212) 737-7536
Staten Island, NY

Opened in 1833 as a sailors' retirement home, this National Historic Landmark offers numerous historic buildings for private functions such as the Beaux Art-style Great Hall with 35 ft. ceilings and Palladian windows with its lower level Gallery with tiled flooring and fireplace, Memorial Hall/Seamen's Chapel for inter-denominational

Great Hall

wedding ceremonies and concerts (with a reception space downstairs); The Visitor's Center Harbor Room; the Governor's House, a 19th century Victorian home with two front parlors, dining room and a kitchen. All have a magnificent view of the Bay of New York and Manhattan skyline.

This site's vast park land offers many areas for tented affairs: the Gazebo area (20,000 sq. ft.) is shaded and centrally located; the West Lawn (50,000 sq. ft.) is near Duck Pond; the East Meadow (79,000 sq. ft.) can accommodate major events like clambakes, etc.; the South Meadow (117,000 sq. ft.) is available for concerts or festivals and has a professional stage.

Guest capacity: 350 seated/500 cocktails in Great Hall; 150 seated/250 cocktail in Great Hall Gallery; 205 seated (60 seated in lobby) in Memorial Hall; 40 seated/50 standing in Harbor Room; 40 seated/75 buffet in Governor's House; many more in tents outdoors

Resident caterer

Suggested uses: business meeting, conference, reception, corporate picnic, wedding, location shoot

English Rooftop Garden   (212) 737-7536
(Soho)
New York, NY

A 5000 sq. ft. English garden with lawns, trees, flower beds and rose covered brick walls sits atop a party penthouse.

Guest capacity: 200 in garden and penthouse

Former Farm/Now Beer Garden and   (212) 737-7536 Social Hall
(Queens)
Astoria, NY

When this social hall and beer garden was built in 1910, it took over a working farm. Located a few blocks from the Triboro Bridge, its *piece de resistance* is a secluded half block long beer garden with tables, benches and wonderful old linden, maple and elm trees.

Guest capacity: 800 in outdoor beer garden; 350 seated indoors

Former West Village Home of a   (212) 737-7536 Famous Chef
(West 12th Street)
New York, NY

This charming Greenwich Village townhouse features the unique James Beard kitchen and a greenhouse/dining room on its first floor which overlooks the garden; additional space and balcony on second floor

Guest capacity: 20 seated in greenhouse; 100 in whole house and garden

---

Garden/Upper West Side   (212) 369-6183
Columbus Avenue (bet. 89th & 90th St.)
New York, NY

This 18,000 sq. ft. community garden offers meandering landscaped paths and a terraced floral amphitheater.

Guest capacity: 180

Suggested uses: wedding ceremony

La Fête au Lac de Central Park   (212) 737-7536
New York, NY

This wonderfully restored boat house now offers a Buffet Court for private parties such as a permanently tented three-division area with dance floor.

The designers of the restoration have kept all manner of special events in mind including promotions, fashion shows, corporate picnics, dinner and luncheon meetings, banquets and, of course, weddings.

Rowboats, bicycles and roller skates are also available to the private party.

Guest capacity: 600 maximum when both tented areas and edge-of-water decks are used; 20/400 in Buffet Court (available March through November); up to 200 in boat house indoors year-round after 5 p.m.

Resident caterer as well as a resident kosher caterer

New York Botanical Garden   (212) 220-8774 (Baity)
Bronx, NY 10458   (212) 220-8774 (Beitz)
(212) 547-0511 (Friberg)

Contact: Jean Baity, Director of Special Events; Jean Beitz, Assistant Director of Special Events for location shoot in the Conservatory or Eric Friberg, Caterer, for Snuff Mill Restaurant Conservatory

Guest capacity: 800 cocktail reception in the Conservatory; 125 seated in House of Hanging Plants which is part of the Conservatory (500 seated if tent is erected outside); 120 seated/150 standing in Restaurant

A series of 11 greenhouses, or plant galleries, including a central palm court with a 90 ft. dome are part of the Enid A. Haupt Conservatory.

A terrace and garden are part of the Snuff Mill Restaurant which used to be an 18th century snuff mill and is an historic landmark. It overlooks the Bronx River and is particularly suitable for weddings.

Also see: Brownstone with Redwood Roof Deck
Colonial Dames
East Side Bistro at a Reasonable Price
Former Longshoreman's Bar/Now Silk Purse
Guess What's in My Backyard
Heights Townhouse (Brooklyn)
Italian Restaurant with Garden
Midtown Magnolia
Old Merchant's House
Penthouse with Roof Garden Overlooking Central Park
Prospect Park West Mansion (Brooklyn)
Studio Loft with Tented Roof
Times Square Restaurant with Roof Terrace

LOFTS FOR PARTIES

The following lofts represent spaces which are particularly appropriate for parties. Lofts that are primarily used for workshops and seminars are listed under the WORKSHOP/SEMINAR SPACES heading.

Amphitheatre Loft   (212) 737-7536
(East Village)
New York, NY
Cathedral windows, 16 ft. ceilings and a 1200 ft. dance floor make this 2500 sq. ft. space a find.
Guest capacity: up to 250

Caterer's Loft with Antiques   (212) 737-7536
(West 19th Street)
New York, NY
This caterer's loft is filled with antiques
Guest capacity: 50
Note: This location may be rented by outside caterers as well.

Caterer's Post-Modern Loft   (212) 737-7536
(West 20's)
New York, NY
This living loft with a 16 ft. cathedral ceiling and faux marble columns offers an open space for dancing.
Guest capacity: 30 seated/100 buffet
Full kitchen, sound system, bar area

Chelsea Loft   (212) 737-7536
(West 25th Street)
New York, NY
Presently used as an all-white photographer's studio. Fine floor-to-ceiling French windows and 15 ft. ceilings bespeak of a former time when it was a meeting salon which used gas lamps for lighting.
Guest capacity: 150 seated in 2300 sq. ft. space

East of Fifth Avenue Caterer's Loft   (212) 737-7536
(East 17th Street)
New York, NY
This caterer's loft offers 2000 sq. ft. of space
Guest capacity: 40 seated/50 cocktails

Genuine Soho Artist's Loft   (212) 737-7536
(Broadway & Prince)
New York, NY

Located in a 1904 landmark building designed by Ernest Flagg, this 1900 sq. ft. loft offers a romantically wrought iron decorated window area that spans 35 feet.
Guest capacity: 60/100 with flexible seating and dancing; 125 standing

Plants, paintings on walls. Two self-service and two freight elevators open directly into space for deliveries.

Good wood floors, north light, air-conditioning, open kitchen; food may be served by caterer of your choice

---

Loft with a Classic Touch   **(212) 737-7536**
(Soho)
New York, NY

The Japanese interior decorator/owner has given this space a unique mix of European and Oriental touches.
Guest capacity: 50 seated/125 standing

Masterview   **(212) 737-7536**
(West 30's)
New York, NY
Ground floor space
Capacity: 200 seated/350 standing in 7000 sq. ft. space

Mission West   **(212) 737-7536**
(Chelsea)
New York, NY

This 3000 sq. ft. L-shaped space is owned by a French painter and offers 38 feet of windows. White walls and bleached floors.
Guest capacity: 60 seated/200 reception

Nancy's Studio   **(212) 737-7536**
(West 20's)
New York, NY

Just off Fifth Avenue, this 5000 sq. ft. all-white space on the second floor offers a huge kitchen.
Guest capacity: up to 150

New York Views   **(212) 737-7536**
(Union Square)
New York, NY

The outstanding feature of this freshly refurbished photographer's loft is the marvellous view of the Twin Towers and other New York highrises which glow in sunlight during the day and are lit up at night. Windows face both east and south.
Oak floors, newly renovated kitchen
Guest capacity: 50
Suggested uses: social, photo shoot

The Party Loft   **(212) 737-7536**
(15th Street)
New York, NY

Exclusive designer interior on lower Fifth Avenue offering muted modern touches.
Guest capacity: 40 seated/75 buffet/85 cocktails
Raised carpeted platform for leisure seating. Piano, sound system, dance floor, serving bar, two powder rooms
Resident caterer

Studio Loft
(212) 737-7536
(Fifth Avenue & 20th Street)
New York, NY

A: Photo by Abner Symons

This 2000 sq. ft. studio on the 5th floor is available for various social purposes.
Guest capacity: 150
Piano, full sound system, maplewood floors, mirrors, skylight, windows overlooking Fifth Avenue
This space is also suitable for workshops, classes, showcases, staged readings, auditions, rehearsals, videotapings and benefits.

Stylistic Loft
(212) 737-7536
(Tribeca)
New York, NY

This 3000 sq. ft. loft is in the style of the American Crafts Movement of the early part of this century.
Guest capacity: under 40
Note: Also suitable for location shoots.

Thea's Studio
(212) 737-7536
(West 70's)
New York, NY

Guest capacity: 150 in 2800 sq. ft. studio space
Sound system, light wood floors, track lighting, 2 mirrored walls, 21 large windows, lots of sunlight
Suggested uses: rehearsal, seminar, audition, party, sweet 16, location shoot

Theater Loft
(212) 737-7536
(West 19th Street)
New York, NY

This tasteful space offers wall-to-wall carpeting, theatrical lighting, a stage, plus contemporary art and sculpture on display pedestals which may be moved as necessary.
Guest capacity: 70 seated/100 cocktails
Suggested uses: product display, meeting, conference, sweet 16, dance party

Touch of Art Deco
(212) 737-7536
(Soho)
New York, NY

This 2500 sq. ft. loft belongs to a German painter who keeps it light and lean. Open kitchen.
Guest capacity: 50 seated/150 reception
Note: Weddings are not allowed.

Tropicana Loft   (212) 737-7536
(Greenwich Village)
New York, NY

A zebra skin rug and leopard upholstered chairs, a bar for
margueritas and palm trees give a resort-style ambiance to this
1500 sq. ft. loft.
Guest capacity: 70

West Village Caterer's Loft   (212) 737-7536
(Horatio Street)
New York, NY

A catering firm has decorated this 35 ft. x 35 ft. ground floor
space plus an additional 15 ft. x 35 ft. reception area to serve
private functions. Floor-to-ceiling windows, cream and black
decor, full lighting and sound system.
Guest capacity: 60 seated/100 cocktails
Resident caterer

Where Size is Not a Problem   (212) 737-7536
(Soho)
New York, NY

Located in a newly renovated gallery building, this large
space offers maple floors, track lighting, air-conditioning
and kitchen facilities.
Guest capacity: 350 seated/800 standing

Also see: Calligraphy School and Recording Studio in Noho
Dance Center

LOUD DANCE PARTIES

Bond Street Loft   (212) 737-7536
(Bond & Lafayette)
New York, NY

Self-contained artist's loft in a former 2-story industrial building.
Guest capacity: 100 in 1300 sq. ft. loft; 200 in conjunction with
1200 sq. ft. roof deck
Suggested uses: dance party

D-Photo Studio   (212) 737-7536
(Fifth Avenue & 13th Street)
New York, NY

2000 sq. ft. light and airy space
Guest capacity: approximately 200 standing; 125 seated
Kitchen, bar

Gusto House   (212) 737-7536
(East 4th Street)
New York, NY

Guest capacity: 175
Sound system with mixing board
Suggested use: dance party

Hi-Tech Bar   (212) 737-7536
(West 80's)
New York, NY

This bi-level bar looks like a bachelor's loft.
Guest capacity: 35/100 in 1000 sq. ft. space
Oak bar, state-of-the-art tape system, track lighting, TV monitor.
Good for amplified music; outside caterers welcome.
Note: Space is usually only available Monday through Friday
from 5:30 to 9:30 p.m. and weekend afternoons.

MC Loft   (212) 737-7536
(West 29th Street)
New York, NY
Artist's studio with large sci-fi murals
Guest capacity: 125 in 2400 sq. ft. space
Space is near the docks of the Hudson River.
Suggested use: dance party

Rehearsal/Party Site   (212) 737-7536
(Tribeca)
New York, NY
Theater with 3 studios
Guest capacity: 250 for a party in 1920 sq. ft. space; 60 in theater
Dance floor, 2 pianos, ballet barre, bar area, d.j. system, professional lighting and sound system; 8' x 10' bandstand, movable walls
Suggested uses: rehearsal, theater showcase, party

Three Versatile Floors   (212) 719-2733
(West 40's)
New York, NY
When not in use for Broadway dance and theater rehearsals, this three-floor space is available for a variety of functions, including benefits, dance parties, art shows, etc.
Guest capacity: 75 on each floor (2000 sq. ft.); over 200 on all three floors
Elevator, 2 bathrooms on each floor

Also see: Amphitheatre Loft

MUSEUMS AND OTHER MAJOR PUBLIC BUILDINGS

American Museum of Natural History (212) 737-7536
Central Park West at 79th Street
New York, NY 10024

Receptions and dinners under a 94 ft. blue whale preceded by private viewings of selected exhibitions. Thirty-nine other exhibition spaces are available.
Guest capacity: 50/1000 sitdown dinner; 100/3000 cocktail reception in Hall of Ocean Life; 650 cocktails in Hall of Meteorites, Minerals and Gems
Rental fee: by corporate contribution
Food may be served only by caterer on premises.

Suggested uses: corporate meeting, reception, dinner, promotion, audio-visual presentation, fashion show, photography or film location shoot
Note: Fundraising and private functions are not allowed.

The Anchorage/Brooklyn Bridge   (212) 737-7536
Brooklyn, NY
Eight stories (50 feet high), nearly a city block square and weighing 120 million pounds, this stone structure holds down the ends of four suspension cables that bear the entire weight of the Brooklyn Bridge roadway.
Its 14,500 sq. ft. indoor space, which is

divided into eight rooms, is available for special events and parties.
Guest capacity: 600 seated/1215 cocktails
Note: Of special interest are the 375 million year old fossils of sea creatures which are embedded in the limestone walls.

The Asia Society   (212) 737-7536
(Park Avenue, corner of East 70th Street)
New York, NY

Located on Park Avenue and designed by architect Edward Larrabee Barnes, this eight-story rose-hued granite building offers a distinctive setting for board meetings, corporate conferences, receptions, dinners and the like.
Guest capacity: 258 in auditorium/theater and connecting reception rooms; 10 to 100 for meetings/200 for banquets and receptions in penthouse; 150 in outdoor garden terrace
Caterers may be chosen only from approved list.
Note: Private and fundraising events are not allowed. Private gallery tours and Asian music, theater and dance performances may be tailored to each event.

Brooklyn Museum   (212) 737-7536
200 Eastern Parkway
Brooklyn, NY

Since this magnificent museum cannot move to Manhattan, the people of Manhattan must come to Brooklyn.
Housed in an historic Beaux Arts building designed at the turn-of-the-century by McKim, Mead & White, this grand museum's facilities are available for a wide range of purposes. Its diadem is the third floor Court. This 10,000 sq. ft. area has a peaked glass roof, stone arches and a floor of glass bricks which is illuminated from below for evening events. The museum's renowned collection of Egyptian and ancient art surrounds the Court. Other areas available for special events are the museum's grand lobby, renovated in the 1930's in the art deco style; the first floor

Hall of the Americas, with its permanent display of outstanding art from Africa, Oceana and the Americas; the museum's fifth floor offers a rotunda and galleries filled with paintings; and the Outdoor Sculpture Garden, which besides sculpture is decorated with architectural fragments from New York City building's surrounded by flowers and large trees. This space can be tented.
Guest capacity: 1200 dinner and dancing/2000 cocktails in third floor Court; 250 dinner/1000 cocktails in Grand Lobby; 600 cocktails in Hall of the America's; 200 dinner/500 cocktails in Outdoor Sculpture Garden
Note: Space is only available to corporate members who may be bussed to and from the museum.

Delegates Dining Room/United   (212) 737-7536
Nations
(44th Street & First Avenue)
New York, NY

This renowned world forum overlooks the East River and is open to the public.
Guest capacity: 400 seated/350 seated with dancing/ 1000 reception in Delegates Dining Room; 10/180 seated in private dining rooms
Note: If event is in the afternoon, it can be combined with a tour of the United Nations.

Equitable Center Dining Room   (212) 554-2168
787 Seventh Avenue (52nd Street)
New York, NY 10019

This corporate dining room on the fiftieth floor is occasionally made available to outside corporations and organizations upon approval.
Guest capacity: 300 seated in corporate dining room; 300 cocktails on forty-ninth floor
Resident caterer

Five-Story Corporate Atrium   (212) 737-7536
(West 50's)
New York, NY

This cathedral-like new space is decorated with a huge mural by
Roy Lichtenstein called *Mural With Blue Brush Strokes.* Its
convenient midtown location makes it an important space for
grand receptions.
Guest capacity: 500 sitdown/1000 standing

Grand Central Station   (212) 340-4916
(East 42nd Street &   Contact: Public Affairs
Vanderbilt Avenue)
New York, NY

Main Level, Waiting Room, Lower Level, Balcony
Guest capacity: several thousand persons for Main Level and
Lower Level; exact capacity depends on use
Food may be served by caterer of your choice
Suggested uses: fundraiser, promotion, press party, location
shoot, etc.
Note: Private railroad cars may be rented for trips along the
Hudson to Poughkeepsie and beyond. Mailing address is
Metro North Commuter Railroad, 347 Madison Avenue, 13th
fl., New York, NY 10017.

Hayden Planetarium   (212) 737-7536
Central Park West & 81st Street
New York, NY

Guest capacity: 650 in Sky Theater; 300 sitdown dinner/400
buffet/800 cocktails in Guggenheim Space Theater on first
floor
Rental fee: by corporate contribution
Dance floor, audio visual equipment
Suggested uses: corporate evenings offer special planetarium
Sky Show and laser light shows as well as sales meetings,

product introductions, cocktails or dinners. Custom designed
shows may be arranged.
Resident caterer

International Design Center   (718) 937-7474
29-10 Thompson Avenue   Contact: Liz Bruder,
Long Island City, NY 11105   Special Events Coordinator

This premiere centralized marketplace for the design and interior
furnishings industry was architecturally transformed from the
EverReady battery factory and the Chiclet Chewing Gum
factory. Center Two, a nine-story central atrium with light and
sound bridges suspended across the span, lends itself to
parties, dinners, lectures and audio-visual presentations.
Center One contains two atria that are approximately 9000 sq.
ft. each. Center Four, a 30,000 sq. ft. flexible unfinished space,
is appropriate for large exhibits, conventions and fashion
shows.
Guest capacity: 250 to 350 seated dinner/over 1000 cocktails in
Center Two (together cocktails for 8000 are possible); 500
seated/2000 cocktails in Center Four
Kitchen; food may be served by caterer of your choice

The Jewish Museum   (212) 860-1872
1109 Fifth Avenue (92nd Street)
New York, NY 10028

Auditorium (Gallery 5)
Guest capacity: 250 auditorium-style
Stage, platform, PA system, kosher food and beverages only may
be served by caterer of your choice
Suggested uses: luncheon, reception, dinner meeting
Note: Museum exhibitions are available for viewing.

Lincoln Center for the Performing   (212) 737-7536
Arts
140 West 65th Street
New York, NY 10023

Auditoriums, meeting rooms, board rooms and large reception
areas are part of the Lincoln Center complex and may be used
for meetings, conferences, receptions and major functions.
Guest capacity: 25/600
Special functions may be combined with performances, tours
and special *Meet the Artist* events.
Food may be served

Metropolitan Museum of Art   (212) 570-3773

Fifth Avenue & 82nd Street   Contact: Manager for Social
New York, NY 10028   Events or Vice-President of
                                                       Development

Great Hall, Temple of Dendur, American Wing Courtyard, Blumenthal Patio, Medieval Sculpture Hall
Guest capacity: 1000 for a reception in Great Hall; 350 seated/800 cocktails in Temple of Dendur; 200 seated/500 cocktails in American Wing Courtyard; 100 seated/250 cocktails in Blumenthal Patio; 250 seated/400 cocktails in Medieval Sculpture Hall
Note: The museum is only available to corporate sponsors of the museum and/or its events.

Metropolitan Opera House   (212) 737-7536

(Broadway & 65th Street)
New York, NY

Guest capacity: 150 seated/cocktails in Allegro Cafe/Adagio Buffet; 550 seated/450 seated with dancing/1000 cocktails in Avery Fisher Hall-Grand Promenade; 350 seated/250 seated with dancing/500 cocktails in Metropolitan Opera-Grand Tier
Resident caterer
Note: Grand Tier guests must hold tickets for that day's performance of the opera.

Museum for the Artistry of the   (212) 737-7536
Handmade Object

(West 50's)
New York, NY

Designed by the New York architectural firm of Fox & Fowle, this recently re-opened museum is organized around a dramatic 40 ft. high stair/atrium. One of the museum's four levels is a multi-use area available for private functions amidst the splendor and artistry of handmade objects.

Guest capacity: 30 seated downstairs; 600 standing throughout the galleries

Museum Devoted to the History of   (212) 737-7536
New York City

103rd Street & Fifth Avenue
New York, NY

Three floors of this museum rent for special functions.
Guest capacity: 300 sitdown dinner/800 cocktail reception on first and second floors combined; 248 in auditorium
Rental fee: $10,000 contribution for dinner and/or cocktail reception for over 50 guests $5,000 for under 50; $3,000 for auditorium; non-profit organizations and public agencies are charged a small administrative fee.

The Museum of Modern Art   (212) 708-9680

11 West 53rd Street   Contact: Special Events
New York, NY 10019

Having undergone major expansion, this museum can now offer special events use of its numerous recently redesigned museum areas to corporate members.
These include the glass-enclosed Garden Hall, outdoor Sculpture Garden, two restaurants overlooking the Garden as well as the two auditoriums for films or meetings.
Guest capacity: 1000 maximum for a standup reception
Approved list of caterers.
Note: An annual membership contribution of $10,000 entitles member to use the facilities for as many events as museum's schedule allows.

National Academy of Design   (212) 369-4880

1083 Fifth Avenue (89th Street)   Contact: Public Information
New York, NY 10128

This turn-of-the-century mansion was erected in 1906 and extensively refurbished with home-like exhibition galleries by Ogden Codman, Jr. in 1915.

Guest capacity: 60/200 for dinner (depending on number of rooms used); 250/500 for cocktails

Suggested uses: formal dinner party, corporate reception, fashion show, location shoot

Note: Weddings and smoking are not allowed.

New York City Fire Museum   (212) 737-7536

(Soho)
New York, NY

One of the most comprehensive collections of fire memorabilia in the country is located in a renovated Beaux Arts-style firehouse built in 1904. Exhibits highlight the vehicles and tools of fire fighting from Colonial America to the present, including the pageantry of fire fighting in the days of the volunteers. The museum includes an outdoor courtyard.

Guest capacity: 300 standing (seated functions are inappropriate because of museum displays on both floors)

Suggested uses: fun party, financial district reception, children's birthday party, sweet 16

New York Hall of Science   (212) 737-7536

(Queens)
Corona, NY

This museum offers 30,000 sq. ft. for various social functions. It is set on 22 acres of parkland.

Guest capacity: 500 seated/750 cocktail/buffet; 300 in 6000 sq. ft. Great Hall

Great Hall offers blue stained glass wall and an 80 ft. tower. It is suitable for wedding ceremonies and receptions.

Food may be served by caterer of your choice. Ample parking.

Suggested uses: meeting, conference, wedding, photo/film shoot, picnic

The New-York Historical Society   (212) 873-3400

170 Central Park West (77th Street)   **ext. 69**
New York, NY 10024   Contact: Alexandra Lester, Special Events

Auditorium, art galleries

Guest capacity: 326 seated in auditorium; 180 dinner-dance/200 sitdown/600 to 800 reception using two gallery floors

Food and beverages may be served only by approved caterers.

Special events may be coordinated with private viewing of galleries.

Note: Use of galleries is a benefit of membership. Special rates for use of auditorium by non-profit groups. Private parties and fundraising are not allowed.

The New York Public Library   (212) 930-0730

Fifth Avenue & 42nd Street,   Contact: Paul Goren or Kelley
Room 205 New York, NY 10018   Smith, Special Events

Astor Hall, The Celeste Bartos Forum (Room 80), The McGraw Rotunda, Trustees Room

Astor Hall has a vaulted ceiling of veined white Vermont marble; The Celeste Bartos Forum is a recently restored turn-of-the-century cast iron solarium with a 30 ft. glass dome, soaring pillars and walls of rare yellow and grey marble; The McGraw Rotunda is marble with wall panels illustrating the history of the written word; the Trustees Room has teak floors, French

doors and four gold and silk Flemish tapestries from the 17th century.
Guest capacity: 250 sitdown dinner/800 reception in Astor Hall; 50/400 sitdown dinner or reception in the 6400 sq. ft. Celeste Bartos Forum; 300 standup reception in The McGraw Rotunda; 110 sitdown dinner/200 reception in Trustees Room
The Celeste Bartos Hall is also suitable for lectures, concerts and film showings.

New York State Theater   (212) 737-7536
(Lincoln Center for the Performing Arts)
New York, NY

This famous theater which is part of the Lincoln Center complex offers a magnificent and contemporary Promenade.
Guest capacity: 675 seated dinner with dance floor/700 cocktails

NEW YORK ZOOLOGICAL SOCIETY

Bronx Zoo   (212) 220-5090
185th Street & Southern Blvd.   Contact: Special Events
Bronx, NY 10460   Department

The Bronx Zoo offers JungleWorld, a magnificent tropical rain forest.
Guest capacity: 150 cocktails, 100 for a seated dinner, up to 1000 can spend an evening under the stars with tent in Wild Asia or Astor Court

Central Park Zoo   (212) 439-6531
64th Street & Fifth Avenue   Contact: Special Events
New York, NY 10021   Department

The Central Park Zoo can accommodate up to 100 guests for cocktails and 60 for a seated dinner year-round in the Tropic Zone, a tropical skylighted building, or up to 500 with tent in the Central Garden. The setting offers a spectacular view of the Manhattan skyline in addition to the animals.

The New York Aquarium   (718) 265-3428
West 8th Street & Boardwalk   Contact: Special Events
Brooklyn, NY 11224   Department

The New York Aquarium, at Coney Island, can offer affairs in the Main Exhibit Hall, then on to a private dolphin and sea lion show. It is available year-round for 100 to 200 guests.

Note: Benefits are not allowed in any of the above locations.

One of New York's Great Theological   (212) 737-7536
Institutions
(Broadway & 120th Street)
New York, NY

Built in the English Gothic style with its historic buildings facing a quad, this outstanding theological institution offers both spacious and elegant facilities indoors and out.
Guest capacity: 150 seated/200 cocktails in Reception Hall; 150 seated in Banquet Room; 175 seated in Chapel (flexible seating); 600 in Garden; 20 rooms for overnight accommodations
Resident caterer
Suggested uses: reception, luncheon, banquet, meeting, conference, concert, art show, party, wedding

One of New York's Most Beautiful   (212) 737-7536
Interior Spaces
(Chelsea)
New York, NY

Established by the Episcopal Church as its first seminary in the U.S., this English Gothic Revival-style complex was designed by Charles Coolidge Haight. Comprising several secluded city blocks, this seminary, whose numerous buildings face a park-like inner quad, offers a grand dining room for weddings and

other receptions. The Great Hall is vaulted by a superb coffered ceiling supported by bracketed beams made of cast iron covered with oak veneer. Its north wall is filled with colored glass windows. Twelve brass chandeliers suspended from long chains and walls of oak wainscotting enhance its beauty, plus a huge fireplace. A carved oak musican's gallery overhangs its raised east end.
Guest capacity: 250 seated in Great Hall Refectory; 150 seated in Auditorium

The Pierpont Morgan Library   (212) 737-7536
(East 30's)
New York, NY

Built in 1906 by Charles McKim of McKim, Mead & White, this library was constructed to house the book, manuscript and art collection of Pierpont Morgan. The interior of the library is particularly distinguished by the ceiling murals of H. Siddons Mowbray and the rich array of wood and marble surfaces. The Rotunda is a replica of the rotunda in the Villa Pia in the Vatican and is richly adorned with ceiling murals and plaster work illustrating the literary arts. The East Room is filled with tiers of bookcases and decorated with 16th century Flemish tapestry. Murals of female muses, symbols of the zodiac and Roman deities are on the cove ceiling.
Guest capacity: 350 for a reception in the Rotunda; 150 seated in meeting room; 50 seated in East Room
Resident caterer
Note: Required corporate contributions: $5000 for a reception in Rotunda; $10,000 for a reception plus a dinner in the meeting room; $15,000 for a reception and East Room dinner. Weddings, dancing, fundraising and promotional activities are not allowed. Space is available only on Monday, Tuesday, Wednesday or Thursday evenings; weekend events will only be considered for a corporate East Room dinner.

Radio City Music Hall   (212) 246-4600
1260 Avenue of the Americas   Contact: Sales Department
(50th Street)
New York, NY 10020

An elegantly restored American landmark, guests can be accommodated in Art Deco Grand Lounge, Grand Foyer or First Mezzanine.
Guest capacity: 200/800 in Grand Lounge; 300/800 in Grand Foyer; 300 in First Mezzanine for dinner dance, banquet or cocktail reception
Available for both private and corporate parties. Group rate tickets to Radio City Music Hall stage show, in combination with cocktail reception or dinner may be arranged.
Suggested uses: cocktail reception, benefit dinner dance or concert, fashion show, press party

The Winter Garden   (212) 945-2600
(World Financial Center)   Contact: Melissa Coley,
New York, NY   Special Events Manager

The process of building The World Trade Center in the 1970's involved the excavation of millions of tons of rock, sand and stone. This enormous mass was used as landfill to create the 92-acre Battery Park City site in downtown Manhattan. It is on this newly created site that the $1.5 billion World Financial Center has been built.
Guest capacity: 300 to 1000 seated/2000 cocktails
The centerpiece of the complex is the 45,000 sq. ft. Winter Garden, a glass and steel latticework structure reminiscent of London's nineteenth century Crystal Palace. A grand marble staircase sweeps down through its center, beyond which sixteen palms rise 45 feet, to frame a spectacular vista of the waterfront.
The Winter Garden's vaulted glass ceiling is 120 feet high.
Rental fee: $15,000
Note: This space is only available to charities. Not available in December.

RESTAURANTS FOR PRIVATE FUNCTIONS (Some With Private Rooms)

Antique Storefront/Now Restaurant   (212) 737-7536
(East 90's)
New York, NY

This antique storefront turned restaurant, located in a landmark building on the upper East Side, has all the charm and ambiance of a cafe on the French countryside.
Guest capacity: 26
Suggested uses: wedding rehearsal dinner, birthday party, graduation celebration, intimate gathering

Authentic Old New York   (212) 737-7536
(Chelsea)
New York, NY

Housed in an 1889 building, this restaurant possesses the charm of the "attractive, refined saloons" that O'Henry described in his short stories of the early 1900's. Its second and third floors featuring paneled mahogany wainscotting, lace curtained windows, floor length velvet draperies and working fireplaces are entirely reserved for private functions.
Guest capacity: 120 seated/200 cocktails on second floor; 80 seated/150 cocktails on third floor

Automat: The Only One Left In   (212) 737-7536
America
(Midtown)
New York, NY

Conceived in 1911 and refurbished in art deco style with etched glass and mirrored columns, its unique little automat windows can serve up any food desired, as well as a complete dinner through the cafeteria line and served by a staff of waiters or waitresses.
Guest capacity: 175 seated/400 buffet style
Suggested uses: all special events are possible including a dance, bar mitzvah or reunion

Century-Old Former Theatrical Club   (212) 737-7536
(West 30's)
New York, NY

Four private dining rooms
Guest capacity: 75 in Lambs Room (can hold 130 when combined with adjoining Lincoln Room); 36 in Bull Moose Room; 20 in Lillie Langtree Room
Richly decorated with genuine antiques and completely restored, this spacious two story site had its beginnings in 1885 as the

continued on next page

Men's Grill of the Lambs Club and emanates an ambiance of 19th century American and English theater as well as New York City history.

Working fireplaces. Historic memorabilia.

Resident caterer

Note: Closed last two weeks of August.

East of the Rhine   (212) 737-7536
(East 40's)
New York, NY

Situated in a brownstone restaurant which makes one feel transported to an aristocratic hunting lodge, this exquisite space is embellished with an American stained glass window, trompe l'oeil pilasters, tapestry covered chairs and touches of whimsical opulence.

Two additional opulently decorated rooms are also available.

Guest capacity: 30 seated/70 cocktails in Music Room; 18 at rectangular table in the golden-hued Marie Antoinette Room; 14 seated at round table in navy blue tapestried King Boris Room

East Side Bistro at a Reasonable Price (212) 737-7536
(East 46th Street)
New York, NY

Secluded on a side street near the United Nations, this entire restaurant space in a small century-old house is available for private functions. A garden is in the back.

Guest capacity: up to 50 seated/80 cocktails inside

Elegant and Cuban   (212) 737-7536
(West 50's)
New York, NY

This long established Cuban restaurant will create Caribbean dishes, with decor to match, mariacchis and green parrots.

Guest capacity: 100 with dancing

Former Church/Now Inn   (212) 737-7536
(Financial District)
New York, NY

On a crooked street formerly trod by seafaring men, presently located in World Trade Center country, this Greek chapel has been transformed into a three-floor dining and party facility complete with serving bars, fireplaces and handsome oak panelling.

Guest capacity: 150 with dancing/250 cocktails on second floor; 50 seated in basement party room

Former German Opera House in   (212) 737-7536
Brooklyn
(Park Slope)
Brooklyn, NY

Built in 1892, this restored restaurant facility offers a 20,000 sq. ft. ballroom with 45-foot ceilings. Most events, however, take place in smaller and less spectacular rooms.

Guest capacity: 2000 seated in ballroom (2500 with balcony seating); 250/400 in Chopin Room with dancing; 75 seated in Queens Room with dancing; 300 seated in Beer Garden

Resident caterer, kosher food is available

Note: The ballroom is only available for events of a minimum of 500 guests and is also used for film shoots.

Former Longshoreman's Bar/Now   (212) 737-7536
Silk Purse
(West 20's)
New York, NY

Three brownstones near the water's edge in Chelsea combine to make this family-owned tavern-restaurant sparkle like the Waterford crystal in its cabinets.

Guest capacity: 150 maximum; 20/40/60 in three private rooms; 150 standing/100 with dancing in main room

Along with wood-burning fireplaces to take the chill off nippy nights, it offers French doors opening onto a rear patio for warm weather outdoor celebrations.

Guess What's in My Backyard   (212) 737-7536
(East 70's)
New York, NY

In the garden behind this upper East Side restaurant is a massive rock that is a glacial remnant and was a famous picnic spot for couples a century ago. This combined with a waterfall gives a most satisfying and unique country atmosphere to this city trysting place.

Guest capacity: 90 seated indoors/160 indoors and out; 150 cocktails indoors/200 indoors and out

Her English is Too Good, She Must Be Foreign   (212) 737-7536
(West 30's)
New York, NY

Red velvet drapes and crystal chandeliers transform this Ninth Avenue former fish market into tongue-in-cheek formality.
Guest capacity: 50

Herald Square Greenhouse   (212) 737-7536
(West 34th Street)
New York, NY

This glassed-in greenhouse-style restaurant has access to an outdoor roof garden. Great views of of the Empire State Building and other surrounding skyscrapers from the 25th floor.
Guest capacity: 40 seated in glassed-in greenhouse; 60 in additional indoor space; 100 cocktails on roof garden
Resident caterer
This space is available days, evenings and weekends.

Italian Cafeteria-Style   (212) 737-7536
(West 70's)
New York, NY

This restaurant is particularly popular for corporate and organizational receptions.
Guest capacity: 300 in entire restaurant; 60 for private dining

Italian Restaurant with Garden   (212) 737-7536
(West 50's)
New York, NY

Classic Italian restaurant of long standing.
Guest capacity: 200 seated indoors; 75 seated in garden

Knight of Malta Room   (212) 737-7536
(50's off Fifth Avenue)
New York, NY

Situated on the second floor of an established Italian restaurant, this 16th century-style room was once part of the personal townhouse of Stanford White.
Totally private with an extraordinary floor-to-ceiling French burled walnut fireplace, this formal room gives an aura of the way things should be when one has occasion to gather for a special event.
Guest capacity: 20 to 55 seated/90 cocktails
Piano, separate bar area

Kozy and Kosher   (212) 737-7536
(East 80's)
New York, NY

The ground floor of a brownstone on the upper East Side is a cozy spot for those who wish to eat kosher Italian cuisine. Specialties are fish and pasta.
Guest capacity: 60 seated
Rosewood piano

Large Restaurant in Flat Iron District   (212) 737-7536
(East 18th Street)
New York, NY

A 20 ft. ceiling hovers over 9600 sq. ft. of dining room and bar.
Guest capacity: 350 seated/600 cocktails
Professional sound and PA system, dance floor

Meeting of East and West   (212) 737-7536
(East 50's)
New York, NY

Combining continental and oriental atmosphere, this two-floor restaurant offers a glass-enclosed atrium garden upstairs and a bar and private dining facility downstairs.
Guest capacity: 120 seated
Note: An additional possibility is the use of an adjacent public atrium for events up to 500 persons.

Near Lincoln Center   (212) 737-7536
(West 70's)
New York, NY

This private room is like a glass-roofed winter garden.
Guest capacity: 45 seated
Suggested uses: luncheon, dinner, shower, rehearsal dinner, etc.

Neo-Classic French Bistro with Art Gallery   (212) 737-7536
(East 16th Street)
New York, NY

A 14 ft. ceiling and moderne decor enhance the art on the walls and the food on your plate.
Guest capacity: 115 maximum
Note: Restaurant will open on Sundays for private parties and weddings.

Newspaper Spoof (212) 737-7536
(East 42nd Street)
New York, NY

This high energy, black and white restaurant in the Daily News
building features replicas of newspaper print on its walls.
Guest capacity: 190 seated/250 cocktails
Suggested uses: bar mitzvah, sweet 16, alumni and other organizational parties, etc.

Putting on the Ritz (212) 737-7536
(Murray Hill)
New York, NY

This large dining room on Park Avenue offers a classy and
substantial aura.
Guest capacity: 185 seated

Reminiscent of Noble Crossings (212) 737-7536
(South Street Seaport)
New York, NY

Admirably designed like the interior of a 1930's ocean liner, this
seaport restaurant is a special place for private functions. It
offers a panoramic view of New York Harbor.
Guest capacity: 25/400

Restaurant/Cabaret/Theater (212) 737-7536
(Chelsea)
New York, NY

After an eventful decade in Soho where it led the revival of the
cabaret in New York, this restaurant/theater offers expertise
and experience in creating unique party themes and scouts
fresh entertainment.
Guest capacity: 50/300

Fully equipped theater, complete sound and light system, d.j.,
Americas's oldest tapas bar, resident award-winning chef
Suggested uses: organizational meeting during the day, cocktail
party, banquet, press conference, fashion show, wedding

Site of Cornelius Vanderbilt's Private (212) 737-7536
Railroad Station
(East 30's)
New York, NY

The original Vanderbilt hotel is now an apartment co-op on Park
Avenue, but its corner restaurant still has its original tiled
vaulted ceilings from the time it was a chic Rathskeller. One
large copper wall panel now blocks the direct entrance into
the former hotel's lobby. Frequented by Teddy Roosevelt and
Enrico Caruso, the Rathskeller's flooring roofs the private
railroad station's stop below where Mr. Vanderbilt enjoyed a
private entrance to his own hotel.
Guest capacity: 120 seated/200 cocktails; 20 seated in private
room

Tavern on the Green (212) 737-7536
(Central Park West & 67th Street)
New York, NY

Guest capacity: 250 seated/500 cocktails in glass-enclosed Crystal Room; 250 seated/400 cocktails in Rafters Room; 150
seated/250 cocktails in Chestnut Room; 100 seated/200 cocktails in Terrace Room; 80 seated/150 cocktails in Park Room
and garden; 80 seated/90 cocktails in Pavilion Room; 1000
seated/2000 cocktails in whole restaurant

Theater District Restaurant (212) 737-7536
(East 50's)
New York, NY

Casually elegant, this new restaurant accented with burnished
wood is geared for private events.
Guest capacity: 75 seated in Hemingway Room (150 if mezzanine is used); 250 seated/500 cocktails in entire restaurant

Three Restaurants in Rockefeller Plaza   (212) 737-7536
(Fifth Avenue & 50th Street)
New York, NY

Three of New York's finest locations for special events overlook the ice rink in winter and a garden in summer.
Guest capacity: 60 to 180 seated in each of three restaurants; 1500 reception with buffet when all three restaurants are combined
Resident caterer

Times Square Restaurant with Roof Terrace   (212) 737-7536
(West 40's)
New York, NY

This contemporary bi-level restaurant offers a stainless steel bar along with roof terrace access.
Guest capacity: 140 in dining room/90 at bar on first level; 40 seated/60 standing in cafe on second level; 100 on roof terrace

Two Midtown Sister Restaurants Run by Two Brothers   (212) 737-7536
(East 50's)
New York, NY

These two elegantly Northern Italian restaurants each offer tinted mirrors and elaborate wall sconces. One of these locations will rent out the entire restaurant as well.
Guest capacity: 50 in each of two private rooms; 150 in entire restaurant

Two Townhouses are Better Than One   (212) 737-7536
(East 60's)
New York, NY

The beguiling decor of this townhouse restaurant offers two separate private function areas: the modern Champagne Room with a balcony, raised platform and grand piano along with the Salum and Terrace which offers a Mediterranean look.
Guest capacity: 32 seated/80 cocktails in the Champagne Room; 90 seated/150 cocktails in the Salum and Terrace
Note: This location makes both a wedding ceremony and reception possible.

Via Veneto's Veranda   (212) 737-7536
(East 70's)
New York, NY

This roofed indoor/outdoor space offers a surprisingly large social space.
Guest capacity: 250 seated inside/150 seated outside; 500 cocktails

Victorian Weddings   (212) 737-7536
(Wall Street area)
New York, NY

Since 1938, this famous location has hosted every notable figure in the worlds of finance, politics, art, theater, society, science and literature. Its genteel past and recently restored decor elevates any special occasion.

Guest capacity: 150 seated on main floor; 150 seated downstairs; 100 in Front Room; 75 in Club Room; 12 in Board Room
Ample 24-hour parking; resident caterer
Suggested uses: corporate receptions, meetings and product displays. Perfect for weekend weddings.

Village Restaurant with Private Room   (212) 737-7536
(Waverly Place)
New York, NY

This popular village restaurant offers a handsome private party space done in turn-of-the-century mood.
Guest capacity: 150 seated/200 standing
Piano
Also available for location shoots.
Note: Outside caterers are welcome.

Yorkville Tea Room   (212) 737-7536
(East 85th Street)
New York, NY

English chintz and family heirlooms decorate this cozy shoppe/restaurant on a quiet side street. Perfect for small christenings, bridal showers and birthday parties.
Guest capacity: 25

Also see: Art Deco Penthouse Restaurant
Blue Plate Special/Diner Parties
Down Home Road House
Greenhouse/Penthouse Restaurant
Large Private Party and Meeting Facility Overlooking Harbor

SOCIAL SPACES

Billy Rose Diamond Horseshoe Club   (212) 737-7536
(West 46th Street)
New York, NY

This famous 1930's nightclub is currently a versatile space which
allows itself to be both glamorous and utilitarian.
Guest capacity: 400 seated/600 cocktails
12 ft. deep stage (for dance band)
Suggested uses: fashion show, benefit, prom, flights of fancy

Caterer-Owned Private Party Space   (212) 737-7536
(West 21st Street)
New York, NY

This caterer-owned location is only open to private parties.
Guest capacity: 50 to 450; 180 seated dinner
Bar, dance floor, separate elaborate indoor swimming pool
Suggested uses: bar mitzvah, sweet 16, birthday, etc.

The Colonial Dames   (212) 737-7536
(East 60's)
New York, NY

This Upper East Side special function space is in a cut-stone
house which is maintained by the Colonial Dames of
America. A back door leads to a secret garden whose apple
trees and tidy lawn are an entirely unexpected benefit. Wedding ceremonies may take place in the garden.
Guest capacity: 200 auditorium-style/150 sitdown dinner/75 to
100 dinner dance indoors
Galley kitchen; food may be served by caterer of your choice

Community House in Queens   (212) 737-7536
Forest Hills, NY

This substantially built and comfortable century-old location has
working fireplaces, a balcony and decorative oak details.
Guest capacity: 160 seated/250 cocktails; 200 seated in adjacent
gymnasium
Stage
Food may be served by caterer of your choice.
Suggested uses: meeting, performance, benefit, wedding

Duplex with Greenhouse and   (212) 737-7536
Balconies
(West 80's)
New York, NY

This eclectic penthouse apartment on Manhattan's West Side
offers a glass-enclosed balcony for orchids and roses and a
light and sunny living/dining room below.
Guest capacity: 30 seated/60 cocktails

East Side Party Space   (212) 737-7536
(East 77th Street)
New York, NY

This adaptable modern space with curved walls and multi-level
ceilings features a 17 ft. curved oak bar, dance floor and sound
system (with optional disco lights), trees, baskets of plants,
modular sofas, carpeting, air-conditioning and coat check.
Guest capacity: 40 to 100 seated with dancing/up to 150 cocktails
with dancing
Full kitchen; food may be served by caterer of your choice
Suggested uses: wedding, wedding reception, cocktail/dinner
party, corporate special event, conference, breakfast meeting,
fashion show, exhibit

Former Bread Factory/Now Film   (212) 737-7536
Studio
Long Island City, NY

This long loaf of a loft offers a 90-foot long unobstructed view
of Manhattan through 20-foot high windows. Its hardwood
floor and soundproof structure make this location perfect for
large dinner dances.
Guest capacity: 300 seated/1000 standing
Resident caterer
Note: Located at the foot of the Queensborough Bridge. Ample
parking.

Photo by: Dianne Baasch Maio

Former Chapel   (212) 737-7536
(West 85th Street)
New York, NY

A vaulted ceiling and stained glass windows along with brass
handeliers embellish this former chapel. Its attractive interior can be used for all manner of events, both social and
educational.

Guest capacity: 140 seated
Platform stage
Additional uses are memorial services and interfaith ceremonies.

Former New York Wool Exchange   (212) 737-7536
(Tribeca)
New York, NY

This wonderfully remodeled three-tiered space is being made
available entirely for special events use. Built in 1896 as New
York's trading center for wool and fur, its *piece de resistance*
are arched windows that are 26-feet high and 34-feet wide.
Guest capacity: 90 seated in Main Room; 35 seated on Balcony;
35 seated in downstairs room; 250 for cocktails in entire space
Suggested uses: wedding, fashion show, corporate meeting,
reception, benefit

Georgian Suite   (212) 737-7536
(East 77th Street)
New York, NY

Private foyer on the ground floor of an upper East Side apartment
house sets the stage for the culinary skills of a French chef.
Guest capacity: 100 seated with dancing/200 cocktails
Arches separate dinner and dancing sections; formal decor
Dance floor; food may be served only by resident caterer
Suggested use: formal social event
Note: Space is usually not available on Sundays and is closed
July and August.

Grand Soho Ballroom   (212) 737-7536
(Lafayette Street)
New York, NY

Designed in 1885 by Albert Wagner to house printing and
lithography companies, this red brick Romanesque Revival
edifice occupies one entire block. A 10,000 sq. ft. white-
columned street floor ballroom has been artfully created.
Guest capacity: 2000

Great Cast Hall   (212) 737-7536
(Soho)
New York, NY

This museum hall near Cooper Square in the Village offers a 6200 sq. ft. exhibit hall with shining oak floors, 14 ft. high ceilings and classical columns. White casts of life-size sculpture of the human form and 19th century paintings lend a traditional art motif to an untraditional space.
Guest capacity: 200 seated/300 cocktails
Partial kitchen, air-conditioning, ample parking

La Belle Epoque   (212) 737-7536
(West 12th Street)
New York, NY

Decorated in la belle epoque, the French period between 1895 and 1905, with authentic mirrors, globe light sconces, pewter-topped bars, etc., this social space also offers a 60 ft. long mezzanine balcony taken from a French bistro with wrought iron balustrade from which to watch the elegance below. French doors open onto the balcony.
Guest capacity: 125/150 seated; 150/175 standing
Full kitchen

Midtown Magnolia   (212) 737-7536
(West 50's)
New York, NY

Hidden from the street, this ground floor space contains a living and dining area, 18 ft. ceilings, two terraces, a baby grand piano, and eclectic furnishings graciously arranged by its Southern owner. Dancing is allowed.
Guest capacity: 50

Old Merchant's House   (212) 737-7536
(East 4th Street)
New York, NY

The only 19th century house in Manhattan which has survived intact with its original furniture and family memorabilia. Its family room and kitchen on ground floor are occasionally available for private functions by appointment.
Guest capacity: 12 seated/80 cocktails
Rental fee: $1,500 tax deductible contribution
Small garden

Place for Refined Sociability   (212) 737-7536
(West 40's)
New York, NY

This unique hideaway came into being at the time when Robert Benchley, Douglas Fairbanks, Christopher Morley, Maxfield Parrish, Cole Porter, Charles Scribner, Otis Skinner, Booth Tarkington, and others were the shining lights on the city's cultural scene. Modeled after the original idea of an English club where "peer could meet peer," this charming social oasis, one that now welcomes women as members, features a comfortable drawing room, a library and a downstairs dining room.
Guest capacity: 60 cocktails on both floors; 40 cocktails in drawing room; 32 seated at long table in dining room
Suggested uses: book party, small celebration, wedding, rehearsal dinner

Society for Art History   (212) 737-7536
(East 50's)
New York, NY

Situated in a 100-year-old neo-Renaissance villa in midtown, this private society devoted to the city's art history makes special function areas available.
Guest capacity: 100 seated/150 buffet/200 cocktails
Air-conditioned
Note: Space is only available on Friday, Saturday and Sunday after 6 p.m.

Solidaridad Humana **(212) 260-4080**
107 Suffolk Street Contact: Dr. Louis
New York, NY 10002 Rodriguez-Abad

This former school building built in 1897 offers a gymnasium, auditorium, cafeteria and gallery room
Guest capacity: 500 in 7500 sq. ft. gymnasium; 300 in auditorium; 50 in gallery room
Suitable for benefits and receptions for non-profit community and arts organizations. Also film and photo shoots.

Special Function Room of a Ballet School **(212) 737-7536**
(19th Street & Broadway)
New York, NY

This 35 ft. x 80 ft. carpeted space boasts two walls of windows overlooking quaint rooftops. Formerly the space of one of America's great choreographers, special functions can be quite elegant.
Guest capacity: 75 seated/125 cocktails
Kitchen

Also see: Advertising Trade Association/Graphic Design Gallery
Central Park West Special Function Site

THEME PARTIES

The Big Apple Circus **(212) 391-0760**
Damrosch Park, 62nd Street &
Amsterdam Avenue
New York, NY 10023

Up to 1500 guests may combine a circus show followed by a private party under the big tent mid-November through early January.
Mailing address is: 220 West 42nd Street, 17th fl., New York, NY 10036.

The Big Kitchen New York Party/Streets of New York **(212) 737-7536**
The World Trade Center
New York, NY

Streets of New York Buffets is a theme which expresses the culinary tastes of New York City's neighborhoods. Included are Jewish, Italian, Creole, Chinese, the Fulton Market experience, etc. Live music for dancing.
Guest capacity: 200/400

Suggested uses: company party, fundraiser, fashion show, bar mitzvah, sweet 16, private party, etc.
Note: In-house kosher caterers are also available. Private transportation to and from The World Trade Center may be arranged to either of these spaces. Free parking.

Blue Plate Special/Diner Parties **(212) 737-7536**
(West 40's)
New York, NY

This is the last of a chain of family-owned diners which dotted the furthest rim of the West Side facing the once busy piers. Decor is 1960's.
Guest capacity: 75 banquet-style with dancing/125 meeting-style in downstairs room; 300 in entire diner
Dance floor
Free and ample 24-hour parking.

Diamonds are Forever
(212) 737-7536
(Central Park South)
New York, NY

You can't strike out at this elegant yet comfortable baseball/sports bar and restaurant which doubles as New York's only sports art gallery. Just west of Fifth Avenue, it offers a dance floor, video, sound system and screening facilities.
Guest capacity: up to 250 in entire restaurant
Suggested uses: all corporate and private events
Note: Sports figures are available to make guest appearances upon special request.

40's & 50's Nostalgia
(212) 737-7536
(Soho) New York, NY

Studded with mementos of movie stars and big bands which may be bought and taken home, this sentimental restaurant evokes memories of prom nights of yesteryear. Corsages are in.
Guest capacity: 100
Suggested uses: corporate lunch or dinner, anniversary, class reunion, birthday party and other special occasions

Have Ferry Will Cook
(212) 737-7536
Staten Island, NY

A *haute cuisine* Belgian chef will meet his guests on the Manhattan side and transport them via Staten Island Ferry to his Staten Island restaurant. Food and drinks are served as soon as the Ferry pushes off the dock and continues on land one block from the Ferry Terminal.
Guest capacity: 65 seated

Have Murder Will Travel
(212) 737-7536
New York, NY

Comedy murder mysteries are acted out to groups who may also request that a special script for them be written. This company, which is permanently stationed in a Soho cocktail lounge, will travel anywhere.
Special feature is Murder on the Amtrak. Groups of at least 54 persons may rent an Amtrak coach which will serve as a murder mystery stage while guests travel to and from their destination at regular railway fares.

Heart of Broadway
(212) 737-7536
(West 46th Street)
New York, NY

This performance/party space is particularly suited for custom-scripted performances for special occasions such as surprise birthday parties, anniversaries, roasts, etc. It is professionally equipped with state-of-the-art lighting and sound, director's booth, 20 x 20 ft. stage with curtain and piano, dressing room, as well as a 25 inch VCR TV, complete bar, and lounge with comfortable leather couches.
It is also appropriate for producer showcases, backers auditions, late night cabaret and concerts, and performances with an audience.

Knockout Parties
(212) 737-7536
(under the Brooklyn Bridge)
Brooklyn, NY

This 11,000 sq. ft. arena can have a stage or boxing ring as well as tables for dining and a dance floor. The genuine five decade old boxing environment is a unique mood for all manner of special events such as large benefits and corporate affairs.
Guest capacity: 1100 seated in arena; 500 seated in gymnasium
Space is also suitable for fashion shows and location shoots.
Convenient parking.

Largest Pool Hall in Manhattan   (212) 737-7536
(West 20's)
New York, NY

This 15,000 sq. ft. space is the new home to what is considered
   to be the fastest growing participatory sport in the U.S. Guests
   have access to 21 pool tables and 2 billiard tables.
Guest capacity: 200
Rental fee: $500 per hour (3 hour minimum)
Sound and PA system, carpeting, air-conditioning
Note: Available only Sunday through Wednesday until 8:30 p.m.

Magic   (212) 737-7536
(West Village)
New York, NY

A buffet-style meal with drinks precedes an evening of magic
   and comedy performed in a professional theater by a variety
   of magicians and comedians.
Organizational speech-making and ceremonies may be inter-
   woven with the entertainment.
Guest capacity: 65

Mystery Murders   (212) 737-7536
(Chelsea)
New York, NY

Mystery games are the filet mignon of this Chelsea restaurant
   which specializes in arranging mystery themes for
   special events.

Unsuspecting
guests may sud-
denly be involved
in a staged murder
and in solving the
crime before the
evening is over.
Some of the
themes are: murder
in the boardroom;
murder in the
publishing in-
dustry, murder of
a newspaper
reporter, murder
on Broadway, etc., as well as old radio shows in which the
audience is involved in a quiz or showing of classic mystery
films.

Guest capacity: 60 seated/100 cocktails
Note: Special weekend murder mysteries may be arranged in
   country inns and one trip annually is made to a castle in
   England.

Participatory Art Parties   (212) 737-7536
(East Village)
New York, NY

The art work in this 800 sq. ft. ground floor gallery is in the
   category of "multi media constructions" which look as though
   they were found in a jungle or on a sunken ship. Created by
   the resident artist for fun, buttons may be pushed and pedals
   stepped on which in turn make the constructions move and
   emit sound and light. "The Electric Eel" and "The Screaming
   Dinosaur" are two favorite constructions. Available for adult
   receptions and children's birthday parties.
Guest capacity: 50 seated/over 100 cocktails
Note: The artist/owner will also create additional decor to express any theme.

Puttin' on the Hits   (212) 737-7536
(Lower Fifth Avenue)
New York, NY

This fun audience-participation club is based on an idea that's
   already popular in Japan. You choose a selection from the
   diversified Song Menu, get up on stage (with or without your
   friends as "back-up") and it's "lip-synch or swim"!
Guest capacity: 175 seated/500 cocktails
Suggested uses: private or corporate party, luncheon, sweet 16,
   bar mitzvah, birthday, anniversary

Salvaged from the Wrecker's Ball   (212) 737-7536
Parties
(Cooper Square area)
New York, NY

This two-floor showroom filled with intriguing examples of
   architectural antiques, stained glass windows, gargoyles, pillars and columns, fireplace mantels, pedestal sinks and tubs
   and other splendid items from buildings of historic or architectural interest are arranged in an informal manner which
   invite browsing.
Guest capacity: 200 standing
Suitable for cocktail parties only by corporate and non-profit
   groups.
Note: Non-profit and corporate groups are particularly welcome.

Side Shows by the Seashore   (718) 372-5159
1205 Boardwalk (at West 12th Street)   Contact: Dick Zigun
Coney Island, NY 11224

This museum, located in a former 1930's penny arcade, houses Coney Island memorabilia such as side show banners of midgets, flesh eating fish, snake charmers, sword swallowers, tatooed men, etc. Also a collection of antique rolling chairs, bumping cars and spook house cars. Fully equipped stage.

Guest capacity: 150 seated

Food may be served by caterer of your choice.

Suggested uses: surprise birthday party, alumni party, sweet 16, etc.

Sports and Polo   (212) 737-7536
(East 80's)
New York, NY

This location offers state-of-the-art video and screens plus room for dancing.

Guest capacity: 200

Tapas Party   (212) 737-7536
(Chelsea)
New York, NY

Originally Spanish, now international, tapas are Mediterranean hors d'oeuvres served in the style of dim sum.

Renowned chef Felipe Rojas-Lombardi's repertoire includes hundreds of variations served on an unending array of little plates.

Guest capacity: 60 in dining room; 40 in lounge; 250 maximum

Available for a minimum of three-hour periods day or evening.

Transit Exhibit   (718) 643-3227
New York City Transit Authority   Contact: Sybil Morgan,
370 Jay Street, Rm. 816   Special Events Department
Brooklyn, NY 11201

Vintage subway cars are located in an unused subway station with a 600 ft. mezzanine and 600 ft. platform on two levels in Brooklyn.

Suggested uses: cocktails and dancing

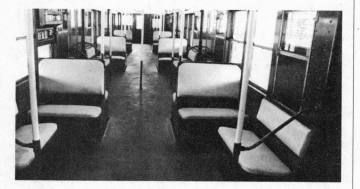

Tropical Lounge   (212) 260-6183
(St. Mark's Pl.)
New York, NY

If Tarzan were alive today, he'd feel right at home in this jungle paradise. Shrunken heads, coconuts and palm trees all add to the tropical motif. There's even a "crashed" Cessna airplane in the garden.

Guest capacity: 60/100 indoors; 200 outside in garden; 20 on patio

Note: Dancing is not allowed.

Used Cars   (212) 737-7536
(West 20's)
New York, NY

Your dance party will be a gas as you jitterbug amidst the vintage MGs, GMs and other 50's memorabilia.

This five-story, 100,000 sq. ft. entertainment complex, with the world's only indoor drive-in movie theater, 2 private party/meeting rooms, and Malt Shoppe, is a unique choice for sweet 16's and birthday parties as well.

Guest capacity: 100/2000

Citroën-Kegresse, 1928-29

Also see: **BOATS & BARGES**
Elegant and Cuban
HORSE-DRAWN CARRIAGES & WAGONS
HOT AIR BALLOONS
PRIVATE RAILROAD CARS
Three Restaurants in Rockefeller Plaza
(ice skating parties)
Video Nightclub in Chelsea

TOWNHOUSES/MANSIONS

Baronial Mansion Reborn   **(212) 737-7536**
(Second Avenue near 15th Street)
New York, NY

Having endured hard times, this mansion which was built by an English baron in the 1860's has recently undergone a million dollar renovation and is ready for all types of events. Its diadem is the second floor double ballroom with gilded wall moldings.

Guest capacity: 125 seated/200 cocktails in double ballroom; additional rooms on first and third floor

Resident caterer

Note: Available only Sunday and Monday evenings as well as Monday through Friday during the day.

Brownstone Flower Shop   **(212) 737-7536**
(Gramercy Park)
New York, NY

This charming street level shop in a Gramercy Park-style brownstone is reminiscent of Liza Doolittle and all fair ladies.

Guest capacity: 45

Suggested uses: author's reception, bridal and baby shower, luncheon, etc.

Brownstone with Redwood Roof Deck **(212) 737-7536**
(West 80's)
New York, NY

An atrium-style living room is but one of many features of this three-floor townhouse which has been finely restored in a contemporary manner on the inside and boasts a circa 1890 facade. Terrace plus roof deck.

Guest capacity: 100

Note: Also available for photo and film shoots.

Fabbri Mansion   **(212) 737-7536**
(East 90's)
New York, NY

Built in 1914 by Grosvernor Atterbury for the great granddaughter of Cornelius Vanderbilt, this landmark Italian Renaissance town mansion offers numerous fine rooms, including the original Renaissance studio library of the Ducal Palace of Urbino and a courtyard. It is presently used as a religious retreat house.

Guest capacity: 80 seated/250 standing

Suggested uses: dignified party, concert, location shoot

Gallery Floor on the Upper East Side   **(212) 737-7536**
(East 70's)
New York, NY

Charles Dana Gibson, creator of the Gibson Girl, lived in this townhouse designed by Stanford White. It is now owned by a foundation and frequently exhibits works of art.

Guest capacity: 60 seated/200 cocktails

Note: Available any day after 5 p.m. and all day on Sunday.

Greenwich Village Federal-Style   **(212) 737-7536**
Townhouse
(West Village)
New York, NY

Built in 1845, this historic landmark features a contemporary, multi-level interior.

Guest capacity: 50 buffet/70 cocktails

Garden, kitchen; food may be served by caterer of your choice

Suggested uses: wedding, cocktail party

Heights Townhouse   **(212) 737-7536**
(Brooklyn Heights)
Brooklyn, NY

Built in 1842, the beautifully restored parlor floor ballroom is 70 feet long with 17 ft. ceilings. There are twin black marble working fireplaces, etched-glass sliding mahogany doors, Tiffany chandeliers and sconces, gleaming wood dance floor, a dramatic staircase and an outdoor paved Japanese Maple-lined garden. Two concert pianos, sound system, various musical instruments and fine art and furniture are included. Private bride's room.

continued on next page

Guest capacity: 25/150 buffet-style with dancing
Spacious kitchen; bring your own caterer
Located approximately ten miles from Wall Street, this
    townhouse offers spectacular views of the Manhattan
    skyline from the Promenade nearby.
Suitable for wedding ceremonies and receptions, bar mitzvahs,
    christenings, conferences, dinner meetings, exhibits as well
    as location shoots.

Italian Renaissance Mansion   (212) 737-7536
(East 90's)
New York, NY

Built in 1914, this marvelous location rents out its third floor as
    an elegant party ballroom.
Guest capacity: 200 seated/300 cocktails

Landmark Club House   (212) 737-7536
(Park Slope)
Brooklyn, NY

Operated continuously as a
    private club since 1889, this
    historic location was
    designed in the Venetian
    Gothic style by New York's
    architect Francis H. Kimball
    who was inspired by the
    famous *Ca d' Oro* on
    Venice's Grand Canal.
Guest capacity: 120 seated with
    dancing
Resident caterer

Murray Hill Townhouse   (212) 737-7536
(East 37th Street)
New York, NY

This private brownstone in the heart of New York's historic
    Murray Hill combines the elegance of 1881 with every con-
    venience of the 20th century.
Its beautiful decor includes crystal chandeliers, parquet floors, a
    grand piano and a graceful staircase connecting the two
    reception floors.
Guest capacity: 75 for wedding receptions and buffet dinners; up
    to 100 guests for cocktail parties.
It is well suited for corporate functions and business meetings
    and rents for location shoots as well.

Park Slope Townhouse of a Caterer   (212) 737-7536
Brooklyn, NY

The ground level floor of this totally renovated townhouse offers
    14 ft. ceilings, track lighting and the clean look of a Soho gallery.
Guest capacity: 100 seated/80 seated with dancing/150 cocktails
    in 2000 sq. ft. space
Professional kitchen; resident caterer
Note: This space, particularly the kitchen, is available for loca-
    tion shoots.

Prospect Park West Mansion   (212) 737-7536
Brooklyn, NY

Built by William Childs, the manufacturer of Bon Ami soap and
    powder, this fine mansion is decorated with Tiffany glass and
    also offers a garden.
Guest capacity: 80 seated/120 cocktails indoors; 50 seated in garden.

Second Floor of a Historical Building   (212) 737-7536
(West 12th Street)
New York, NY

Situated on a quaint residential Village block, the entire second
floor of this 1850 townhouse is available for special occasions. Having its own private entrance, it is decorated with
English country chintz and country pine antiques and has a
warm yet elegant ambiance.

Guest capacity: 25 seated/35 buffet/50 cocktails

Fireplace, original floors have been refinished, accessible parking

Resident caterer

Suggested uses: dinner or cocktail party, location shoot

Staten Island, Too   (212) 737-7536
Staten Island, NY

Built in 1876 as the original Staten Island Savings Bank and later
used as a speakeasy for the Vanderbilts and Barrymores, this
landmark three story Victorian building is located in
Stapleton, Staten Island's most nostalgic neighborhood, five
blocks from the ferry.

Completely restored, its former bank vaults are now used as wine
cellars. French Victorian windows and doors, 18-foot ceilings, oak flooring and a glass-enclosed veranda are also
included.

Guest capacity: 30 seated/125 cocktails upstairs; 50 seated/325
cocktails upstairs and downstairs

Full kitchen; outside caterers are welcome

Townhouse Filled with Flowers   (212) 737-7536
(East 30's)
New York, NY

Built in 1849 and redesigned with the knowing hand of one of
the great culinary food experts and television personalities,
this "mille fleurs" townhouse is fully staffed and every care
is taken for the comfort of its guests.

Guest capacity: 80 seated/60 seated with dancing in Atrium
Room; 20 in each of three additional private rooms

Skylights, 25 ft. atrium, audio-visual equipment

Resident caterer

Note: Corporate functions on weekdays. Occasional private
functions, such as a small wedding, may take place on
weekends.

Traditionally Irish   (212) 737-7536
(Fifth Avenue in the 80's)
New York, NY

This extremely gracious house offers Waterford crystal, lace
curtains and fine antiques.

Guest capacity: 50 seated, 100 buffet/cocktails

Resident caterer

Two Park Avenue Mansions   (212) 737-7536
(East 60's)
New York, NY

Designed by McKim, Mead & White, these two landmark mansions offer elegant spaces for dinners, receptions and weddings.

Guest capacities: 70 seated/125 cocktails in one mansion; 110
seated in winter or 175 in summer on patio in the second

Upper East Side Art Center   (212) 737-7536
(East 60's)
New York, NY

Located in two adjacent landmark townhouses that retain many
of the original architectural details, this museum space, which
includes five galleries on two floors, offers an environment
for entertaining as well as viewing art.
Guest capacity: 250 cocktails or buffet
Rental fee: $500 (non-profit groups), $1,000 (private groups);
fee is tax-deductible
Note: Available any evening after 5 p.m. Music is limited to
chamber quartets. Dancing is not allowed.

Upper East Side Club/Mansion   (212) 737-7536
(East 70's)
New York, NY

This location hosts geographers, oceanographers and other explorers of challenging areas of the world. It also is suitable for
weddings and other receptions.
Guest capacity: 120 seated/250 cocktails
Resident caterer

Upstairs, Downstairs   (212) 737-7536
(West Village)
New York, NY

In a three story former artist studio, the present owner, a caterer,
shows his knowledge about what makes a space work. There
are 2700 sq. ft. on each of two floors. The downstairs floor
can seat as many as 135 guests together, which is unusual for
a townhouse. This floor also features a red oak dance floor,
16-foot ceilings, working fireplaces, skylights, chandeliers,
stained glass windows, a pool table, custom designed lighting

and two baby grand pianos. Upstairs is perfect for wedding
ceremonies. Connecting both floors is a grand staircase for
memorable entrances.
Guest capacity: 135 seated/250 buffet downstairs; 75 upstairs

Wedding Present for a Former   (212) 737-7536
President
(East 60's)
New York, NY

Sarah Delano Roosevelt gave one half of this facility to her son,
Franklin, on the occasion of his wedding. Both Franklin
Delano Roosevelt and Eleanor lived in one of the two floor-
through Upper East Side brownstones while Sarah Delano
Roosevelt occupied the other half. Now newly refurbished,
both halves are available for weddings, meetings and recep-
tions.
Guest capacity: 60 seated/75 standing in two largest rooms; 245
in whole house; 5 smaller rooms for 25 seated/35 standing are
available on two separate floors
Kitchen
Note: Space is not available during the summer.

Also see: The Colonial Dames
Victorian Weddings

VIEWS

Art Deco Penthouse Restaurant   (212) 737-7536
(United Nations area)
New York, NY

This glass-enclosed top floor of an East Side residential hotel offers great flexibility in its uses plus a magnificent view.

Guest capacity: 120 seated with dancing/135 buffet/175 cocktails

Suggested uses: meeting, fashion show, fundraiser, bar mitzvah, reunion, brunch, shower, wedding

Resident caterer

Classic Comeback   (212) 737-7536
(Rockefeller Center)
New York, NY

The crown jewel of the 1930's, is artfully brought into the 1980's, with Aubergine silk, silver lame, cherry stained wood, a revolving dance floor and spectacular views. This is where Beatrice Lillie and Noel Coward sang impromptu duets.

On the same floor, the Pavilion Room is also available, as well as the Pegasus Room and the Radio City Suite on the 64th floor.

Guest capacity: 300 seated with dancing/350 seated without dancing, 500 cocktails with dancing/600 cocktails without dancing in main room on 65th floor; 150 seated/250 cocktails in Pavilion Room; 300 seated/450 cocktails in Pegasus Room; 90 seated/150 cocktails in Radio City Suite (slightly smaller capacity with dancing)

Department Store Penthouse Transformed   (212) 737-7536
(Chelsea)
New York, NY

Located on the penthouse floor of a landmark building which housed the Siegel-Cooper Department Store in 1896, the grandest department store of the Gilded Age and also the largest building in New York City at that time. Designed by the German-trained architectural firm Delemos and Cardes, The Big Store, as it was known at the turn of the century, opened with an estimated 150,000 people in attendance. It had 31,000 employees. It also featured a famous fountain that

continued on next page

49

contained a 70 ft. high reproduction of Daniel Chester French's famous female figure of The Republic. Meet me at the Fountain, was a popular phrase for the turn-of-the-century generation which congregated in the store also known as the Ladies Mile.

It was indeed the Bloomingdale's of its time, but changing neighborhoods led to the sale of the building's fixtures only twenty years later. After World War I, the building was used as a military hospital and J. C. Penney and other companies used it as a warehouse.

Guest capacity: 12 in private dining room; 150 seated in gallery; 350/400 maximum on entire floor

Currently an exhibition and performance gallery, this 7000 sq. ft. top floor is also available for parties, recitals, ceremonies, dance performances, film screenings, concerts and fashion shows.

Additional features are 30 ft. ceilings, skylights, an upper balcony that can be converted into a stage, a private dining room with adjoining library and separate kitchen, an observation room atop a spiral staircase with views of the Manhattan skyline, a greenhouse and an outdoor garden.

Corporate and organizational events as well as wedding ceremonies and wedding receptions are welcome.

Film and Party Studios   (212) 737-7536
(Lafayette Street)
New York, NY

Set atop a Romanesque Revival building which occupies an entire block, these film studios also serve as fine special function spaces. All have excellent views. The seventh floor studio/ballroom offers 7000 sq. ft., walls of arched windows, skylights, white columns and a gleaming wood floor, plus reception foyer.

The ninth floor offers 4000 sq. ft. with two walls of windows, 12 ft. vaulted ceilings, plus stairway to rooftop garden.

The 800 sq. ft. penthouse is topped with a glass roof and its doors and windows open to the roof garden.

Guest capacity: 400 seated/750 cocktails in seventh floor studio; 200 seated/500 cocktails on ninth floor; 75 seated/150 cocktails in the penthouse studio

Great Idea with View   (212) 737-7536
(West 60th Street)
New York, NY

The transformation of this former restaurant into an exclusive private party facility is, indeed, a great idea. Its 43rd floor

location offers one of the best views of Central Park and of the city.

Guest capacity: 150 with dancing; 10/75 in four smaller rooms

Resident caterer

Suggested uses: executive meeting/luncheon during day; weddings and other private functions in evenings and on weekends

Greenhouse/Penthouse Restaurant   (212) 737-7536
(Upper West Side)
New York, NY

Located on top of a Columbia University building, this former greenhouse offers views of the Palisades and the Hudson River.

Guest capacity: 165 seated in entire space; 150 in Main Dining Room; 50/60 in Greenhouse Dining Room

Resident caterer

Suggested uses: all private parties, especially wedding receptions

Note: Closed last two weeks of July and first two weeks of August.

International Penthouse   (212) 737-7536
(United Nations area)
New York, NY

Conference center, lounge, rooftop terrace

Guest capacity: 350 seated for dinner/450 to 500 cocktails in 2nd floor conference center; 70 sitdown dinner/70 to 90 buffet/ 100 to 300 cocktails on rooftop terrace

Overlooks East River and the U.N.

Full kitchen; food may be served by caterer of your choice including kosher caterers

Suggested uses: all special events are possible including a meeting, cocktail lunch or dinner, party or wedding

Large Private Party and Meeting   (212) 737-7536
Facility Overlooking Harbor
(South Street Seaport)
New York, NY

Located atop the historic Fulton Market building, this seaport facility offers dramatic views of the Brooklyn Bridge, ships in the harbor and the glistening towers of lower Manhattan. In addition, thirteen hand-built authentic boats decorate the high atria of this large and airy space. Wrap-around outdoor terrace spanning 2000 sq. ft. overlooks Seaport.

Guest capacity: This 23,000 sq. ft. space can hold 600 seated/ 700 reception in B.W. Room; 300 seated/800 reception in O.R.G. Room; 1500/2000 when both spaces are combined

Suggested uses: meeting, gala corporate or social event, benefit, lunch, bar mitzvah, fashion show, wedding, etc.

Note: Kosher catering is available.

The Loft   (212) 737-7536
(Gramercy Park area)
New York, NY

Exquisite turn-of-the-century antiques are artfully arranged into numerous private islands giving this 7000 sq. ft. space on lower Fifth Avenue a spacious yet intimate interior.

Guest capacity: 200 seated, 240 buffet/cocktails

Thirty-nine tall windows offer dramatic views of the Empire State, Con Edison, Metropolitan Life and Chrysler buildings lit up at night. Concert grand piano; catering is available.

Long Island City: The New Frontier   (212) 737-7536
Long Island City, NY

With a view of Manhattan, this 9000 sq. ft. eclectic warehouse is available for elegant parties. A 30 ft. x 60 ft. space has been recently opened upstairs with columns, mirrored arches and a stenciled floor.

Guest capacity: 200 seated/500 cocktails downstairs; 25/100 seated upstairs

Raised platform for live performances, skylight, state-of-the-art lighting, chandeliers, kitchen

Roof garden

Penthouse with Roof Garden Overlooking Central Park   (212) 737-7536
(West 70's)
New York, NY

Light and airy with numerous skylights, this location offers a
    spectacular view of Central Park.
Guest capacity: up to 50
Concert piano, roof garden

Private Penthouse of a Restaurateur   (212) 737-7536
(Chelsea)
New York, NY

Light, airy penthouse with spectacular mid-Manhattan view.
Guest capacity: 80 seated/125 cocktails
Parquet floors, professional sound system, piano, track lighting,
    video equipment
Resident caterer

Private Space   (212) 737-7536
(Rockefeller Center)
New York, NY

Delft-tiled fireplaces, warm woods and midtown views make
    this private club a gracious location for dinners and recep-
    tions.
Guest capacity: 125 seated/200 cocktails
Resident caterer

Two Floors in Rockefeller Center   (212) 737-7536
(Avenue of the Americas & 50th Street)
New York, NY

Entirely devoted to private functions, two floors in the Time-Life
    Building offer spectacular views and a variety of spaces.
Guest capacity: 300 for a fashion show/425 seated with danc-
    ing/800 cocktails on 48th floor; 50 to 80 seated in each of
    several private rooms on 47th floor
Resident caterer

The World Trade Center   (212) 737-7536
New York, NY

The Observation Deck Party
A quarter-of-a-mile above New York City, this enclosed deck
    on the 107th floor of The World Trade Center is available
    for private parties and offers Streets of New York Buffets,
    open bars and live music.
Guest capacity: 300 seated/1000 buffet
Suggested uses: company party, fundraiser, wedding, etc.
Note: In-house kosher caterers are also available.

NEW YORK CITY

GENERAL LISTING

ATRIUMS

*S*ome *of the most welcome urban places are the indoor sitting areas in corporate buildings, most of which are not available for private functions. The few which are available are: 805 Third Avenue and the Five-Story Corporate Atrium. The following list of atriums, though not available for private functions, are restorative public rest stops for sitting, thinking, reading, meeting a friend and people watching. Most also offer food as well as cultural performances.*

AT&T Headquarters
550 Madison Avenue
(55th & 56th St.)

Chemcourt
277 Park Avenue
(47th & 48th St.)

Citicorp Center
53 East 53rd Street
(Lexington Ave.)

Continental Insurance
180 Maiden Lane
(Wall Street area)

805 Third Avenue
(50th St.)

875 Third Avenue
(53rd St.)

IBM Headquarters
590 Madison Avenue
(56th & 57th St.)

900 Third Avenue
(54th & 55th St.)

Olympic Tower
645 Fifth Avenue
(51st St.)

Park Avenue Atrium
466 Lexington Avenue
(45th & 46th St.)

Park Avenue Plaza
55 East 52nd Street
(Madison & Park Aves.)

Winter Garden

Philip Morris
120 Park Avenue
(42nd St.)

7 World Trade Center
(World Financial Center)

Trump Tower
725 Fifth Avenue
(56th & 57th St.)

Whitney Museum Downtown
2 Federal Reserve Plaza

Also see: Five-Story Corporate Atrium
Winter Garden

AUDITORIUMS (Seating 500 or more)

Manhattan Center

Edison Theater	500
Educational Alliance	500
Eighty Acres on the Waterfront (Staten Island)	500
International Center	500
James Weldon Johnson Community Center, Inc. (outdoor recreation area)	500
La Guardia Memorial House	500
Midtown Location for Business & Professional Presentations	500
New York Hall of Science	500
Parson's School of Design	500
People's Institutional A.M.E. Church (Brooklyn)	500
Reformed Church of Staten Island	500
St. Hilda's and St. Hugh's School	500
Universalist Church	500
Flushing Jewish Center (Queens)	600
Brooklyn YWCA	605
Roberto Clemente State Park (Bronx)	630
Sutton Place Synagogue	645
St. Michael's Episcopal Church	650
Diocese of the Armenian Church of America	660
East Harlem Arts & Education Complex	667
International House	670
Circle in the Square (Uptown)	680
New York Academy of Medicine	687
New York City Mission Society, Mission Town House	716
The Concord Baptist Church (Brooklyn)	750
Hayden Planetarium	800
Central Park West Special Function Site	867
Symphony Space, Inc.	885

The Community Church of New York	900
92nd Street YM-YWHA	916
American Museum of Natural History	994
Borough of Manhattan Community College	1000
Congregational Church of North New York (Bronx)	1000
Oyster Bay & Crystal Palace (Queens)	1000
Salem Community Service Council, Inc.	1000
Savoy Manor (Bronx)	1000
Alice Tully Hall/Lincoln Center for the Performing Arts	1096
Co-operative Auditorium	1100
College of Mount St. Vincent (Bronx)	1200
Manhattan Center	1200
Town Hall	1500
United Methodist Parish in Bushwick (Brooklyn)	1500
New York City Passenger Ship Terminal	2000
Former German Opera House in Brooklyn	2500
Avery Fisher Hall/Lincoln Center for the Performing Arts	2738
City Center 55th Street Theater	2932
Roseland	3400
Huge and Remarkable	500/3500
Cathedral Church of St. John the Divine	4000
Metropolitan Opera Association/Lincoln Center for the Performing Arts	4000
Felt Forum/Madison Square Garden Center	4600
Radio City Music Hall	5874
Jacob K. Javits Convention Center of New York	3600/35,000

American Museum of Natural History and the Hayden Planetarium   **(212) 737-7536**

Central Park West at   Contact: Marilyn Badaracco,
79th Street   Manager, Office of Guest Services
New York, NY 10024

Auditorium, 6 theaters, board room, classrooms, exhibit space
Capacity: 996 in auditorium; 650 in Sky Theater; 600 in Naturemax Theater; 300 in Guggenheim Space Theatre; 299 in Henry Kaufmann Theater; 154 in Harold F. Linder Theater; 80 in People Center; 50/75 in classrooms
Stages, audio-visual equipment in all locations, IMAX motion picture system
Resident caterer
Suggested uses: conference, lecture, symposia, workshop, audio-visual/multi-media presentation, stockholders/board/annual meeting, etc.
Note: Fundraising is not allowed.

Co-operative Auditorium   (212) 777-5530

551 Grand Street   Contact: Edward Ward
New York, NY 10002

Auditorium, rehearsal space
Capacity: 1100
Rental fee: $900 during day; $1,125 Monday through Thursday night; $1,300 for Friday evening; $1,500 for Saturday evening; $1,200 for Sunday evening; $1,550 for wedding and reception; $1,350 for reception only
30' x 20' stage, platform, piano, dance floor, kitchen; food may be served
Suggested uses: banquet, lecture, meeting, party, reception, wedding

Educational Alliance   (212) 475-6200 ext.220

197 East Broadway   Contact: Sylvia Lefkowitz
New York, NY 10002

Auditorium/gymnasium, theater, rehearsal space, classrooms, conference room, art and photography gallery
Capacity: 500 in auditorium
Rental fee: $27.50 minimum on a weekday; varies with day, hours and size of room
Stage, platform, piano, dance floor, motion picture projector, slide projectors, sound equipment, kitchen; food may be served
Suggested uses: all special events are possible

International Center   (212) 737-7536

345 East 46th Street   Contact: Deena Lee
New York, NY 10017

Auditorium, conference rooms, exhibit space, lounge, roof terrace
Capacity: 500
Rental fee: varies with space and time
Platform, dance floor, PA system, full kitchen; catering facilities available
View of East River from roof terrace
Suggested uses: all special events are possible

La Guardia Memorial House   (212) 534-7800

307 East 116th Street   Contact: Peter Pascale
New York, NY 10029

Auditorium/gymnasium, classroom, lounge
Capacity: 500 in auditorium; 50 in classroom; 100 in lounge
Rental fee: maintenance charge
Stage, kitchen; food may be served
Suggested uses: concert, class, exhibit, lecture, meeting

Manhattan Center   (212) 279-7740

311 West 34th Street   Contact: Steve Honey
New York, NY 10001

Concert hall/ballroom, recording studio, hall, Green Room
Capacity: 800 dance/1200 theater-style in 95' x 95' Grand Ballroom; 120 for a dance/200 theater-style in 28' x 61' hall
Proscenium stage, computerized lighting and sound system, 40' domed ceiling; world renowned acoustics; food may be served by caterer of your choice
Building constructed by Oscar Hammerstein, Sr. in 1906. Grand Ballroom built by Scottish Rites.

Midtown Location for Business &   (212) 737-7536
Organizational Presentations

(West 40's)
New York, NY

Auditorium/exhibition center, conference rooms, exhibit space, reception area
Capacity: 500 in auditorium; as few as 50 in smaller conference rooms
Proscenium stage, platforms, runway, audio/electrical technicians, lighting grid, control booth, screen
Suggested uses: catered breakfast, luncheon, cocktails, stockholder's meeting, dance, fashion show, press conference, commencement exercise, testimonial, location shoot

New York Academy of Medicine   (212) 737-7536

2 East 103rd Street   Contact: Dr. Cheryl Vinckus,
New York, NY 10029   Administrative Assistant, Office of Medical Education

Auditorium, meeting rooms
Capacity: 687 in auditorium; 50/190 in meeting rooms
Resident caterer
Note: This location will rent only to medically-related non-profit organizations.

Savoy Manor   (212) 585-3500

120 East 149th Street   Contact: Jerome Green,
Bronx, NY 10451   Manager

Auditorium, rehearsal space, conference room, meeting room, exhibit space, reception area, chapel
Capacity: 100/1000
Stage, platform, piano; space can cater for up to 1000 or bring your own
Suggested uses: meeting, dance, party, wedding, church service, gospel show

Also see: ARMORIES
            BALLROOMS
            HOTELS
            LIBRARIES
            MEETING ROOMS/CONFERENCE ROOMS/AUDITORIUMS (Seating 499 or less)
            PERFORMANCE SPACES (CONCERT/ RECITAL)
            PERFORMANCE SPACES (DANCE/ THEATER)
            SCHOOLS
            STADIUMS

CHURCHES

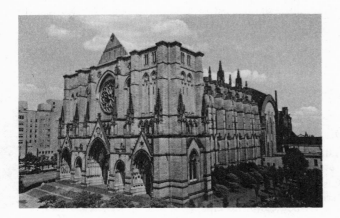

MANHATTAN

Cathedral Church of St. John the Divine   (212) 316-7497
(212) 316-7573
Amsterdam Avenue &   Contact: Arrangements Office
112th Street
New York, NY 10025

Synod Hall, Undercroft, 3 meeting rooms, exhibit space, museum, cathedral, chapel, 13 acres of grounds
Capacity: 4000 in cathedral; 500 in Synod Hall; 300 auditorium-style in Undercroft; 40/80 in meeting rooms
Rental fee: $350 minimum
Limited kitchen facilities; refreshments may be served by caterer on premises or bring your own
Suggested uses: concert, meeting, lecture
Note: For special events, such as banquets, receptions and performances, Synod Hall is the primary location. Review by clergy is necessary. Gothic cathedral is the world's largest.

Central Synagogue   (212) 838-5122
123 East 55th Street   Contact: Barry Kugel,
New York, NY 10022   Administrative Vice President

2 auditoriums, 2 catering halls
Capacity: 380 in Arnold & Marie Schwartz Auditorium; 450 in Beir Auditorium
Rental fee: reimbursement for out-of-pocket costs
Stage, piano, kitchen; food may be served
Suggested uses: concert, exhibit, lecture, meeting, performance, wedding
Note: Space is only available to philanthropic groups.

Christ Church United Methodist   (212) 838-3036
520 Park Avenue (60th Street)   Contact: Cynthia Redlo
New York, NY 10021

Auditorium, 2 meeting rooms
Capacity: 250 in auditorium; 50/60 in one meeting room, 30 in other meeting room
Rental fee: $150 minimum depending on day or evening used and location
Stage, piano, theatrical lighting, PA system, 2 kitchens; refreshments may be served
Suggested uses: auction, concert, class, dance, exhibit, lecture, meeting, performance, wedding
Note: Space is only available to non-profit groups.

Christ and St. Stephen's Church   (212) 787-2755
120 West 69th Street   Contact: Office
New York, NY 10023

Community room
Capacity: 165
Suggested uses: rehearsal, meeting, seminar
Note: Space is only available to non-profit groups.

Church of the Covenant   (212) 697-3185
310 East 42nd Street   Contact: The Office
New York, NY 10017

Parish hall, meeting rooms
Capacity: 120 in parish hall; 25 in meeting rooms
Stage, piano
Suggested uses: all special events are possible except a banquet, fair or promotion
Note: Space is only available to non-profit groups.

Church of the Holy Family   (212) 753-3401
315 East 47th Street   Contact: Receptionist
New York, NY 10017

Auditorium
Capacity: 300
Stage, piano, kitchen; food may be served

The Community Church of New York   (212) 683-4988
40 East 35th Street   Contact: Administrator
New York, NY 10016

Auditorium, assembly hall, chapel
Capacity: 900 in auditorium; 180 in assembly hall; 50 in chapel
Stage, platform, piano
Suggested uses: concert, lecture, meeting, wedding
Note: Space is only available to approved non-profit groups.

Diocese of the Armenian Church of America   (212) 686-0710
Contact: Center Manager
630 Second Avenue (34th Street)
New York, NY 10016

Auditorium, rehearsal space, 2 classrooms, conference rooms, exhibit space, reception area
Seating capacity: 660 in auditorium; 125 maximum in classrooms and conference rooms
Stage, concert piano, dance floor, kitchen; food may be served
Suggested uses: banquet, conference, seminar, social dance, wedding

Good Neighbor Church   (212) 369-0505
119 East 106th Street
Contact: Rev. D. Rosado
New York, NY 10029

Conference room
Capacity: 100/125
Rental fee: negotiable $100 donation to cover costs
Note: Space has limited availability. Political groups, smoking and alcoholic beverages are not allowed.

Madison Avenue Baptist Church   (212) 685-1377
30 East 31st Street
Contact: Michael B. Easterling,
New York, NY 10016
Pastor

Multi-purpose room
Capacity: 125
Proscenium stage, platform, piano
Suggested uses: auction, concert, class, exhibit, lecture, meeting, performance, rehearsal

New York Society for Ethical Culture   (212) 874-5210
2 West 64th Street
Contact: Jean Brown-Meehan,
New York, NY 10023
Administrator

Auditorium, study, library, reception area, social hall, ceremonial hall, patio
Capacity: 867 in auditorium; 100 seated in 19' x 10' x 29' Adler Study; 60 in 19' x 6' x 28' library; 285 in 50' x 65' social hall; 150 in 35' x 44' ceremonial hall
Rental fee: $700 to $800 for auditorium; $200 for Adler study or library; $400 to $450 for social hall; $300 to $400 for ceremonial hall and patio
14' x 30' stage, platform, Steinway Grand piano, dance floor, Wicks pipe organ, theatrical lighting, PA system, Tiffany stained glass windows, kitchen; food may be served only by caterer on premises
Suggested uses: conference, memorial service, committee meeting, wedding, etc.
Designed by Robert D. Kohn, who also designed Temple Emanuel and R. H. Macy's, the facility's stained glass windows are included in Stained Glass Windows of New York City.
Note: Applications should be made in writing and should outline the general purposes of the group, its community service aspects and programs, tax status, and the date, time and number of persons anticipated.

New York Society of the New Church (Swedenborgian)   (212) 685-8967
Contact: Secretary
112 East 35th Street
New York, NY 10016

Auditorium/Sunday school room
Capacity: 65
Rental fee: by contribution according to suggested scale
Stage, piano; food may be served on occasion
Small non-profit groups with compatible aims are encouraged.
Note: Smoking is not allowed.

Riverside Church   (212) 222-5900 ext. 339 or 446
490 Riverside Drive
Contact: Coordinator
(122nd Street)
for Building Use & Services
New York, NY 10027

Hall, conference rooms, theater, lounge
Capacity: 250 seated dinner/450 lecture-style in 62 x 86 sq. ft. Assembly Hall; 15/40 in conference rooms; 270 in theater; 90 seated dinner/150 lecture-style in 60 x 37 sq. ft. 9th floor Tower Lounge
Stage, kitchens; food may be served only by resident caterer
Stone floor and stained glass windows in Assembly Hall; medieval-style lounge has large fireplace and view of the Hudson River.
Note: Space is only available to non-profit groups. Liquor is not allowed.

St. John's Hall   (212) 564-9070 ext. 105
210 West 31st Street
Contact: Pastor
New York, NY 10001

Auditorium/ballroom/exhibit space, meeting rooms, Frieri Room, A.A Room
Capacity: 350 in approximately 100 x 60 sq. ft. auditorium space; 50/60 in meeting rooms; 50 sitdown in Frieri Room and in A.A. Room
Proscenium stage, piano, dance floor, kitchen; food may be served
Suggested uses: all special events are possible including a flea market, except a performance, promotion or wedding

St. Mark's Church in-the-Bowery   (212) 674-6377
Second Avenue & 10th Street
Contact: Nora Lugo
New York, NY 10003

Open sanctuary, parish hall
Capacity: 350 in sanctuary; 120 in parish hall; 40 x 80 sq. ft. of space is available
Rental fee: $1,650 weekly for sanctuary; no fee for parish hall except for a charge for a staff member to be present
Piano, hardwood dance floor
Suggested uses: music or dance performance, rehearsal in conjunction with performance
Note: Sanctuary is available for weekly blocks of time.
Parish hall is only available to community groups.

St. Michael's Episcopal Church (212) 222-2700
225 West 99th Street   Contact: Schedule Manager
New York, NY 10024
Church, concert/recital hall
Capacity: 650 in church; 150 in concert hall
Rental fee: $300 for entire church; $180 for concert hall
   (includes rehearsal time and security guards)
Stage, grand piano

St. Peter's Church (212) 935-2200
619 Lexington Avenue (54th Street)   Contact: Building/
New York, NY 10022   Projects Coordinator
Theater, music/rehearsal room, lounge/living room, sanctuary, studio
Capacity: 199 in theater; 70 in music room; 150 in lounge; 325 in sanctuary
Piano, kitchen; food may be served
Suggested uses: concert, class, exhibit, lecture, meeting, party, performance, reception, wedding, film showing, staged reading

Salem Community Service Council, (212) 678-2700
Inc.   Contact: Dr. Grissom,
Salem United Methodist Church   Pastor
2190 Seventh Avenue (129th Street)
New York, NY 10027
Auditorium, rehearsal space, sanctuary
Capacity: 1000 in sanctuary
Rental fee: $100 per hour for auditorium; sanctuary use is negotiable
Stage, platform, piano, motion picture projector, phonograph; food may be served

Sutton Place Synagogue (212) 593-3300
225 East 51st Street   Contact: Mrs. H. Janover,
New York, NY 10022   Executive Director
Sanctuary/auditorium, rehearsal space, ballroom, exhibit space, reception area, board room
Capacity: 645 auditorium-style (may be divided) in sanctuary; 200 for a dance/300 seated/450 auditorium-style in ballroom
Platform, piano, dance floor, kitchen; kosher food only may be served
Suggested uses: all special events are possible
Note: Space is not available on Friday night or Saturday afternoon.

Trinity Evangelical Lutheran Church (212) 737-7536
168 West 100th Street
New York, NY 10025
Undercroft, sanctuary
Capacity: 50 to 150 in social hall; 300 in sanctuary
Stage, kitchen; food may be served
Caterer on premises; outside caterer may also be used
Suggested uses: wedding, memorial service, meeting, family reunion, lecture, performance, party, location shoot
Note: Hard liquor and smoking are not allowed in this 100-year-old building.

United Nations Methodist Church (212) 661-1762
777 United Nations Plaza   Contact: Dr. Hawthorne
New York, NY 10017
Conference room, 2 meeting rooms
Capacity: 200 in conference room, 50 in each meeting room
Suggested uses: conference, meeting
Note: Space is only available to non-profit groups.

Universalist Church of New York (212) 595-8410
4 West 76th Street   Contact: Alexander Dyer,
New York, NY 10023   Business Manager
Auditorium/Gothic Sanctuary, hall, conference/classrooms, rehearsal space, gymnasium
Capacity: 500 in auditorium; 100 in hall; 12/75 in conference rooms; 150 in gymnasium
Stage, platform, piano, sound equipment; food may be served
Space is a landmark.
Suggested uses: all special events are possible including a location shoot

Washington Square Church (212) 777-2528
135 West 4th Street   Contact: Office Manager
New York, NY 10012
Auditorium/sanctuary, meeting parlor
Capacity: 250 in auditorium; approximately 50 in meeting parlor
Piano, kitchen; food may be served
Suggested uses: concert, class, lecture, meeting, performance, poetry reading

Also see: Columbia University, Millbank Chapel

BRONX

Church of God of Woodcrest Avenue (212) 992-4087
923 Woodcrest Avenue   Contact: Pastor Grant
Bronx, NY 10452
Capacity: 200
Note: Available only on Mondays, Tuesdays or Thursdays and only to non-profit groups.

Congregational Church of North New (212) 292-1950
York   Contact: Minister
411 East 143rd Street
Bronx, NY 10454
Auditorium/sanctuary, rehearsal space, conference room, gymnasium
Capacity: approximately 1000 in auditorium; 300 in gymnasium
Rental fee: negotiable
Stage, piano, motion picture projector, film strip projector; food may be served
Suggested uses: lecture, meeting, concert, class, sport event

BROOKLYN

Church of St. Ann and The Holy Trinity
(718) 834-8794
(718) 875-6960

St. Ann's Center for
Restoration and the Arts Inc.
157 Montague Street
Brooklyn Heights, NY 11201

Contact: Production Manager, The Arts at St. Ann's

Parish hall, sanctuary
Capacity: 200 in Parish Hall; 600 in sanctuary
Stage, platform, piano, dance floor; food may be served
Space is an 1847 landmark.
Suggested uses: all cultural and religious events are possible including an opera, ballet, dance or film showing except a promotion

The Concord Baptist Church
(718) 622-1818

833 Marcy Avenue
Brooklyn, NY 11216

Contact: Wyatt Logan

Auditorium, rehearsal space, conference room, exhibit space, lounge
Capacity: 750 in auditorium
Stage, platform, piano, motion picture projector, sound equipment, kitchen; food may be served

People's Institutional A.M.E. Church
(718) 574-4141

628 Madison Street
Brooklyn, NY 11221

Contact: Rev. James F. Leath

Auditorium, fellowship hall, rehearsal space, conference room, lounge/exhibit space
Capacity: 500 in auditorium; 150 in fellowship hall; 12 in conference room
Stage, platform, piano, kitchen; food may be served
Suggested uses: all special events are possible except a party
Note: Alcohol is not allowed.

St. James Cathedral-Basilica
(718) 855-6390
(718) 852-4002

Jay and Tillary Streets
Brooklyn, NY 11201

Contact: Sr. Honora Nolty

Assembly hall, 2 meeting/seminar rooms, exhibit space
Capacity: 350 in Cathedral Pavilion; 100 in Cathedral Center; 25 in smaller meeting room
Suggested uses: concert, meeting, exhibit of works by painters, photographers and graphic artists

St. John - St. Matthew Emanuel Community Center
(718) 768-0772

415 Seventh Street
Brooklyn, NY 11215

Contact: Ann Rodie, Coordinator

Auditorium, rehearsal space, sanctuary
Capacity: approximately 150 in auditorium; 350 in sanctuary
Rental fee: $50 per hour per room; space available for long term
Stage, platform, piano; food may be served
Suggested uses: concert, class, professional dance, exhibit, lecture, meeting, performance, reception, wedding

United Methodist Parish in Bushwick
(718) 574-6610

1139 Bushwick Avenue
Brooklyn, NY 11221

Contact: Rev. Smart

Sanctuary, rehearsal space
Capacity: 1500 in sanctuary
Rental fee: negotiable
Platform, pianos, sound equipment, pipe organ, kitchen; food may be served
Suggested uses: concert, banquet

QUEENS

Temple Beth Sholom
(718) 463-4143

171-39 Northern Blvd.
Flushing, NY 11358

Contact: Sol Solarsh

Auditorium, ballroom, classrooms, conference room, reception areas
Capacity: approximately 270 in auditorium; over 300 auditorium-style in ballroom with stage; 35 in classrooms; 80/100 in conference room with folding doors
Raised stage, 2 pianos, dance floor, 2 kitchens; food may be served by caterer of your choice upon approval
Suggested uses: all special events are possible

Temple Isaiah
(718) 544-2800

75-24 Grand Central Parkway
Forest Hills, NY 11375

Contact: Marcia Weinroth, Administrator

Auditorium/meeting room, ballroom, rehearsal space, classroom, conference room
Capacity: 75/100 in auditorium; 150/200 in ballroom; 25 in classrooms and conference rooms
Small stage, small platform, pianos, dance floor, kitchen; caterers available or bring your own
Suggested uses: all special events are possible

Temple Torah
(718) 423-1235
(718) 423-2100

54-27 Little Neck Parkway
Little Neck, NY 11362

Contact: Sam Klein

Ballroom and synagogue
Capacity: 400 seated in ballroom
Suggested uses: banquet, party

STATEN ISLAND

All Saints Church
(718) 698-1338

2329 Victory Boulevard
Staten Island, NY 10314

Contact: Rev. Joel E.A. Novey

Community room, reception area, grassy area, playground
Capacity: 50/250
Dance floor, kitchen; food may be served
Suggested uses: all special events are possible

Christ United Methodist Church   **(718) 442-3755**
   (718) 442-2023
1890 Forest Avenue
Staten Island, NY 10303   Contact: Rev. Jeffrey Oak
Auditorium, rehearsal space, conference room
Capacity: 300 in auditorium; 150 in conference room
Rental fee: minimum $75 donation plus minimal janitor fee for
   auditorium
Stage, piano, dance floor, kitchen; light refreshments may be served
Note: Space is only available to non-profit groups. Alcoholic
   beverages are not allowed.

Reformed Church of Staten Island   **(718) 442-7393**
    Contact: Pastor
54 Richmond Avenue
Staten Island, NY 10314
Auditorium/sanctuary, meeting room, open space
Capacity: 500 in auditorium; 50/200 in meeting room and open
   space
Rental fee: by donation
Stage, motion picture projector, phonograph

COMPANY PICNIC SITES

(New York City and Tri-State Area)

The company picnic, a recreational outing into the country, has become increasingly popular. The following sites were chosen because they allow day outings and offer numerous activities — tennis, swimming, volleyball, boating, barbecuing, etc. All are within a comfortable distance from New York City to assure getting back at a reasonable hour. Call (212) 737-7536 for updates.

Camp for Company Picnics   **(212) 737-7536**
(Sullivan County)
Glen Spey, NY
This camp can accommodate up to 2000 people on 200 acres for
   recreational day outings.
2 lakefront swimming areas plus a swimming pool, 4 mile lake
   for boating and fishing, 9 tennis courts, 6 basketball courts,
   10 volleyball courts, 3 full-sized soccer and football fields,
kick ball field, softball field, 6 handball courts, horseshoe
   areas, hiking, picnic area, numerous indoor areas
Social/athletic directors are on hand to organize games and
   special events.
Located 85 miles from New York City.
Note: Space is only available during May through end of June
   and late August through end of October.

Day Camp in Rockland County   **(212) 737-7536**
Stony Point, NY
Picturesque 33-acre grounds offer a variety of recreational ac-
   tivities including softball, tennis, basketball, boating, vol-
   leyball, hiking trails, picnic tables and 3 swimming pools.
Capacity: 500
Available spring, summer and fall. Twenty-eight miles from
   New York City.
Resident caterer

Gateway National Recreation Area
Headquarters
Floyd Bennet Field
Brooklyn, NY 11234
Any group seeking to utilize facilities for special activities belong-
   ing to the Gateway National Recreation Area must make applica-
   tion for a permit by contacting the Area Manager of each unit.
   Events must be free of charge. Tours and various other group
   events are also regularly held by the individual units.

Jamaica Bay Unit   **(718) 338-3829**
    Contact: Area Manager
Canarsie Pier — available for cultural events which are free of
   charge to the public.
Floyd Bennet Field — its several aircraft hangars are available
   for various special events.

continued on next page

Sandy Hook Unit　　　　(201) 872-0115
Contact: Area Manager

Fort Hancock — historic fort on picturesque site offers magnificent view of Manhattan. Oldest operating lighthouse nearby is a national historic landmark.

Historic Fort Hancock — museum and theater

Staten Island Unit　　　　(718) 351-8700
Contact: Area Manager

Conference rooms, beach area, grassy area, ball fields, tennis courts, parking lot

Capacity: 20/70 in conference rooms

Hudson Guild Farm　　　　(212) 737-7536
Andover, NJ

Located on 500 acres of scenic northern New Jersey land, this site offers hiking, stream and pond fishing, picnicking, boating, canoeing, swimming, handball, basketball, softball, shuffleboard, a nearby golf course and winter sports.

Capacity: 25/125 in Barn Recreation Hall; unlimited capacity outdoors; overnight accommodations in 6 buildings

Open year-round, this location is 55 miles from New York City.

Just a Ferry Ride Away　　　　(212) 737-7536
Staten Island, NY

This grand location comprises 80 acres of lawns which overlook New York Harbor and the New York skyline. Company picnics may be coordinated with volleyball, horseshoes, games and races, clambakes, etc. Harbor rangers are at hand to conduct nature walks as well as children's activities. In addition, picnics may coincide with major cultural entertainment such as The New York Philharmonic and pop concerts scheduled for summer evenings. The South Meadow has a professional stage.

Capacity: 20 to 5000 divided between 20,000 sq. ft. Gazebo area; 50,000 sq. ft. West Lawn; 79,000 sq. ft. East Meadow; and 117,000 sq. ft. South Meadow

Resident caterer. For events such as barbecues and clambakes, recreational activity staff is on site.

Le Camp　　　(914) 356-5005 (camp)
175 West Clarkstown Road　　(201) 767-0237 (Hamilton)
Spring Valley, NY 10977　　Contact: Mary Ann Hamilton

This camp offers 11 acres, 2 pools, tennis courts and ball fields, roller skating/hockey rink, 2 roofed pavilions

Capacity: 500

Offers a greased pig contest and clambakes.

Available most dates during the spring and fall and every weekend July 1 through August 26.

In-house catering

Located 17 miles from the George Washington Bridge in Rockland County.

New Jersey Corporate Picnic Site　　(212) 737-7536
Newfoundland, NJ

This recreation complex is a 58-acre mountain estate in Morris County. Facilities include tennis and volleyball courts, heated swimming pools, miniature golf course, as well as 2 quarter-mile mountain coaster rides, water bumper boats, a restaurant and cocktail lounge.

Located 35 miles from the George Washington Bridge.

Note: Also available for weddings, mainly outdoors.

Ranch Resort　　　　(212) 737-7536
(Catskills)
Kerhonkson, NY

Located in the rolling hills of the Catskills, this 200-acre preserve breeds and trains Arabian horses.

Capacity: 150 rooms plus 10 private rooms are available for overnight

Suitable for picnics, boating, hiking, horseback riding, fishing, tennis and swimming.

Located 90 miles from New York City.

Suntan Lake　　　　(212) 737-7536
Riverdale, NJ

This 48-acre recreation complex includes a 3-acre pool, paddle boats, miniature golf, basketball and volleyball courts, and picnic pavilions.

Capacity: 5000

Available May through October.

Located 30 miles from New York City.

Twenty-Acre Estate　　　　(212) 737-7536
Huntington, NY

Located on the border of Nassau and Suffolk Counties, these private grounds for fishing, boating, riding corrals, athletic fields, hiking trails, playgrounds, a miniature golf course, 5 swimming pools and a dance pavilion. It is great for barbecues and clambakes.

Capacity: 250/2500

Resident caterer

Located 30 miles from New York City.

Also see:　CONFERENCE CENTERS
New York City Parks (Picnic Sites)

CONFERENCE CENTERS

(New York City and Tri-State Area)

This section offers a choice of facilities that provide various types of settings for conferences, from formal to rustic, for corporations and/or non-profit groups who will stay for the day or longer. Many offer overnight accommodations. Listings outside of New York City are no further than 2½ hours away. Call (212) 737-7536 for updates and conference centers nationwide.

North Shore Conference Center

Alley Pond Environmental Center   **(718) 229-4000**
228-06 Northern Boulevard   Contact: Kim Estes,
Douglaston, NY 11363   Adult Services Director
Auditorium
Capacity: 100
Note: Space is usually only available to community groups.

Appel Farm Arts and Music Center   **(609) 358-2472**
Elmer, NJ 08318   Contact: Shawn Timmons,
Conference Center Director
Conference center with overnight accommodations for 30 to 150 persons.
Auditorium, 5 conference/classrooms, various outdoor areas, exhibit space, reception areas, dining hall, practice rooms, dormitories
Capacity: 250 in auditorium; 40/100 in conference rooms; 200 in dining area
Stage, platform, piano, fireplace, dance floor, space's food only may be served
Located approximately 120 miles from New York City.
Suggested uses: all special events are possible including a sport event

Arden Homestead   **(914) 351-2171**
Arden, NY 10910   Contact: Richard F. Kopacz,
Manager
Opened in the Fall of 1985, it is surrounded by 540 private acres, miles of footpaths and a lake. As the former home of E. Roland and Gladys Harriman, it is ideal for small-scale executive meetings.
Capacity: 35 in comfortable wood-paneled living room/library; 17 overnight suites for single or double occupancy
Located 48 miles from New York City.
Available to educational, governmental and business organizations.

Arden House   **(914) 351-4715**
Harriman, NY 10926   Contact: Richard F. Kopacz,
Manager

In 1950, when Dwight D. Eisenhower was Columbia University's 13th President, W. Averell and E. Roland Harriman gave their magnificent country estate to Columbia University as a gift to be used for conferences by educational, government and business groups.

continued on next page

Auditorium, 9 meeting rooms, dining room, dining terrace, indoor and outdoor recreational facilities
Built in 1909, the estate sits atop a 1300 ft. ridge and commands a stunning view.
Capacity: 125 in auditorium; 80 bedroom suites are available for overnight accommodations
Located 149 miles from New York City.

Bard College   (914) 758-6822 ext.125

Annandale-on-Hudson,   Contact: William Beckman,
NY 12504   Director of Operations

Auditorium, performance/lecture halls, conference space, rehearsal space, exhibit space, reception area, studio spaces, game room, dining room
Six-hundred acres with one mile of river frontage
Capacity: 400 in auditorium; 150 in performance/lecture halls; 25/75 in conference room; 600 in reception area; 25/75 in studio spaces
Located 100 miles north of New York City.

Bear Mountain Inn   (914) 786-2731

Bear Mountain State Park   Contact: Sales Department
Bear Mountain, NY 10911

Complete conference center with overnight accommodations.
Sixty single rooms can accommodate 132 persons double occupancy; daytime conference center can accommodate 500. Various meeting rooms.
Rental fee: $113.50 single/$102.50 double per person includes three meals and meeting room
Located approximaely 50 miles from New York City.
Note: Space is also available for banquets and weddings.

Caldwell College Conference Center   (201) 228-4424

Caldwell, NJ 07006   ext. 266
    Contact: Director of College Services

Comfortable seminar rooms, lecture rooms and quiet lounges are available at the conference center of this 100-acre college campus in suburban west Essex County. Access to campus TV studio, computer center and college library. Dining room and cafeteria.
Capacity: 20/400
Overnight accommodations are available.
Located approximately 20 miles from New York City.

Caumsett Mansion   (718) 520-7240

Queens College Center for Environmental   (516) 421-3526
Teaching and Research   Contact: Dr. Philip White,
Caumsett State Park   Director
Huntington, NY 11743

Georgian style mansion built in 1925. Former home of Marshall Field III.
Surrounded by 1600 acres of forests, meadows, pond and beach.

Capacity: 150/200 for a meeting during the day; 60 persons overnight
Located approximately 38 miles from New York City.
Note: Space is only available for a limited number of environmentally related conferences or workshops.

College of Mount St. Vincent   (212) 549-8000

Riverdale, NY 10471   Contact: Maureen Russell

Auditorium, Assembly Hall
Capacity: 1200 in auditorium; 400 in South Hall
Rental fee: $700 to $1200 for auditorium; $200 for Hall
Stage
Suggested uses: concert, meeting, lecture
Note: Space is available on a limited basis and occasionally available for summer conferences with an overnight capacity of 350.

Deerpark Farms Resort   (914) 754-8357

Galley Hill Road   Contact: Romeo or Hanni
Cuddebackville, NY 12729   Moncheur, Managing Owners

Resort can accommodate 250 during the day, 150 overnight.
Auditorium, rehearsal space, ballroom, 10 classrooms, 2 conference rooms, exhibit space, reception area, lounge, dining rooms, game rooms, tennis courts, heated swimming pool, whirlpool spa
Stage, piano, 2 fireplaces, 3 dance floors, kitchen; space's food only may be served
Suggested uses: all special events are possible including a seminar, workshop or family reunion

De Seversky Conference Center   (516) 626-1600

Northern Boulevard   Contact: Lawrence Q. Mahoney,
Old Westbury, NY 11568   Managing Director

Conference center with overnight accommodations for 26 persons double occupancy.
3 meeting rooms
Capacity: 75 in Ballroom; 20 in Library; 20 in Terrace Room
Platform, piano, fireplace, winding staircase, dance floor, kitchen; food may be served only by resident caterer
Located approximately 25 miles from New York City.
Suggested uses: class, lecture, meeting or wedding

Edith Macy Conference Center   (914) 945-8000

Chappaqua Road   Contact: Stacey McGee
Briarcliff Manor, NY 10510

Nestled on a hilltop on 400 lush wooded acres, this facility was specifically designed for small business meetings and training sessions. There are 5 well-equipped soundproof meeting rooms, a 200-seat amphitheater and 46 guest rooms.
Recreational activities include an exercise room, outdoor swimming pool and jogging trails.

English Country Estate (212) 737-7536
(Dutchess County)
Amenia, NY

Impeccably staffed, this award-winning conference site will take up to 30 executives per day and overnight. Complete audio-visual facilities. Indoor and outdoor pools.

Fairleigh Dickinson University (201) 593-8920
Florham-Madison Campus Contact: Pat Wessel,
Madison, NJ 07940 Special Events Manager

This 177-acre campus is the site of the former Twombly estate, owned by Florence Vanderbilt Twombly and Hamilton Twombly.
Lenfell Hall is located in the 100-room mansion now used as the college administration building. The Hall was once the Grand Ballroom of the estate.
Capacity: 200 seated; adjoining gardens may also be used for special functions
Located approximately 47 miles from New York City.
Food may be served only by resident caterer.

Former Shaker Mill/Now Inn (212) 737-7536
Canaan, NY

Built in 1824 of stone, with walls a yard thick and 40 feet high, this former grist mill is located in the Berkshire foothills. Totally restored by a renowned innkeeper who is also a carpenter, this rustic inn welcomes conferences and seminars for the day and for a month or longer.
Capacity: 50 for the day and overnight
Resident caterer
Located 135 miles from New York City.

Frost Valley YMCA (914) 985-2291
P.O. Box 97 Contact: Conference Registrar
Oliverea, NY 12462

45 cabins, 10 lodges, conference hall, meeting rooms, dining hall, athletic grounds; cross-country skiing is available
This 4500-acre center includes the Forstmann Center which is made up of three lodges: The Castle has 12 luxurious bedrooms, Margetts Lodge has 8 bedrooms and Huessey Lodge has 13 bedrooms, a lounge, bedrooms and a fireplace. The Gladys & Roger Straus Estate in adjoining valley, with 9 bedrooms, lounge and fireplace, serves as an additional conference site.

Capacity: 300 in conference hall; 700 in dining hall
Suitable for weekend retreats, professional workshops and reunions.
Originally founded in 1901 as Camp Wawayanda for Boys, Frost Valley moved to its present location, 125 miles from New York City, nearly three decades ago with the purchase of the Julius Forstmann Estate. Stone buildings have been renovated.

Greenkill Conference Center (914) 856-4302
Hugenot, NY 12746

This year-round conference center, 85 miles from New York City near Port Jervis, offers a variety of activities for up to 200 persons.

The Henry Chauncey Conference (609) 921-3600
Center Contact: Sales Office
Educational Testing Service
Princeton, NJ 08541

Complete conference center with 100 overnight accommodations for 200 persons single or double occupancy.
This 400-acre campus consists of two separate structures for meetings: a modern two-story complex with 11 meeting rooms, one of which can hold 200 persons, plus 2 suites; and a nineteenth-century house that has been reconverted to accommodate small executive groups.
Cocktail lounge, dining room, game room, 2 tennis courts, outdoor swimming pool, sauna, gymnasium, terraces; audio-visual equipment is available
Located approximately 50 miles from New York City.
Especially suitable for educational purposes and conferences; banquets and private receptions can also be arranged.
Note: Mailing address is CN6652, Princeton, NJ 08541-6652.

Holiday Hills (914) 855-1550
Pawling, NY 12564 Contact: Sales Department
Conference and vacation center with overnight accommodations for 180 persons.
Two dining rooms accommodate from 50 to 200; largest auditorium can hold 350; 12 meeting rooms, 7 lounge areas (with 4 fireplaces)
Donaldson Center has 24 air-conditioned rooms with twin beds; Cottage Row has 42 air-conditioned rooms with twin beds; The Inn has 15 rooms with twin or double beds
Eight tennis courts are situated on 550 acres which are suitable for a conference, training event, seminar, reunion or retreat. Audio-visual equipment. Fitness center. Extensive outdoor recreational facilities.
Overlooks Berkshire foothills and Green Mountain Lake.
Rates are reasonable at this center which is a branch of the YMCA of Greater New York and is 60 miles from New York City.

Hotel Thayer   (914) 446-4731

West Point, NY 10996   Contact: Sales Office

Located on the grounds of the U.S. Military Academy overlooking the Hudson River, this historic hotel reflects traditional comforts and elegance.

Located approximately 60 miles from New York City.

Capacity: 15/300 in meeting rooms; 170 in overnight guest rooms

Hudson River Conference Center   (914) 762-5600

321 North Highland Avenue   Contact: Sales Manager
Ossining, NY 10562

This elegant corporate conference center for up to 400 guests offers 20 breakout rooms.

Located approximately 35 miles from New York City.

The Institute on Man & Science   (518) 797-3783

Rensselaerville, NY 12147   (518) 797-5100
                                Contact: William Gifford

Situated 27 miles southwest of Albany, this primarily state and corporate conference facility features 2 estate houses and 2 modern residence facilities on estate property plus a modern central building.

Capacity: 160 in Guggenheim Pavilion auditorium; 75 in overnight guest rooms

Iona College   (914) 633-2359 (Lavery)

715 North Avenue   (914) 633-2491 (Quinn)
New Rochelle, NY 10801   Contact: Barbara Lavery,
                        Coordinator of Student Activities
                        or Richard Quinn (gymnasium)

Auditorium, classrooms, lounge, dining hall, faculty dining room, exhibit space, gymnasium

Capacity: 250 in auditorium; 15/40 in classrooms; 350 in lounge and dining hall; 50 in faculty dining room; 4000 in 180' x 120' gymnasium

Located about 30 miles from New York City.

Note: Space has limited availability except during the summer and January.

Italian Renaissance Villa Replica   (212) 737-7536

(Finger Lakes Wine Country)
Geneva, NY

Situated on a bluff overlooking Seneca Lake, this European-style resort and executive conference retreat is also ideal for a wedding or family reunion.

Built in 1911 for the millionaire malt manufacturer Byron Nester, this year-round resort surrounded by ten acres of landscaped grounds is a diminutive version of the Villa Lancellotti in Frascati outside of Rome. The resort is less than one hour from Rochester or Syracuse, and includes a terrace, formal garden, classical sculptures, and a 70 ft. pool and sailing facility.

Capacity: 50/75 for wedding receptions; 29 guest suites, each with a living/dining room and kitchen

Manhattanville College   (914) 694-2200

Purchase, NY 10577   Contact: Donna Messina,
                                    President's Office

Theater, ballroom, classrooms, reception space

Capacity: 120 in Little Theater; 500 in East Room; 20/120 in classrooms

Food may be served

Located approximately 35 miles from New York City.

Suggested uses: banquet, meeting, conference, performance, wedding

Marymount College   (914) 631-3200 ext. 209

Marymount Avenue   Contact: Carol Haber,
Tarrytown, NY 10591   Director of Conferences &
                                    Special Events

Auditorium, theater/concert hall, classrooms, conference rooms, exhibit space, lecture hall, lounges, dining room

Capacity: 900 in auditorium; 205 in lecture hall; 149 in theater; 25/50 in classrooms; 900 in dining room

Stage, piano; food may be served only by space's own caterer

Suggested uses: all special events are possible including a wedding reception

Located approximately 45 miles from New York City.

Note: Space rents out dormitories for overnight conferences in the summer.

Mohonk Lake Mountain House   (914) 255-1000

Mohonk Lake   (212) 233-2244
New Paltz, NY 12561   Contact: Libby Long,
                                    Sales Director

Complete meeting site for 300 persons with overnight accommodations for 500 persons.

Various sized meeting rooms, conference rooms, exhibit spaces and reception areas. Many of the rooms have fireplaces. A piano and dance floor are also on the premises. Private dining is available.

View of lake and the Catskill Mountains.

Facility was established in 1869 and is 90 miles from New York City.

New York Institute of Technology (516) 348-3244
(Suffolk County) Contact: Stephen M. Jones,
211 Carleton Avenue Special Assistant to the President
Central Islip, NY 11722

This park-like residential college campus is available in the
summer for use by outside groups.
Auditorium, dormitories, dining room
Capacity: 400 in auditorium; 1000 in dormitories
Indoor and outdoor recreation facilities include playing fields,
tennis courts, a nine-hole golf course, indoor swimming pool,
gymnasium and bowling alleys.
Computer facilities are available for education-related activities.

North Shore Conference Center (212) 737-7536
Glen Cove, NY Contact: Manager,
Conference Center Services

Complete conference center can accommodate 340 persons.
Located approximately 50 miles from New York City.
Space is a Long Island estate and manor house with 200 rooms
for overnight accommodations.

North Shore Historic House and (212) 737-7536
Planetarium
Centerport, NY

Corporate memberships of $100 to $2,000 or $50 to $1,000 for
non-profit organizations, depending on the number of people,
make this Vanderbilt property on Long Island available for
elegant conferences and receptions.
Capacity: 10 to 400 indoors; 250 seated in tented affairs outdoors
Located approximately 75 miles from New York City.
Note: Private functions are not allowed.

Omega Institute for Holistic Studies (914) 266-4301
Lake Drive R.D. 2 (914) 338-6030
Box 377 Contact: Director's Office
Rhinebeck, NY 12572

Situated on 80 acres near Rhinebeck, this rustic conference
center with overnight accommodations has many buildings
including 2 theaters, classrooms, dining hall, kitchen, organic
gardens and a lake.
Capacity: 150 and 250 in theaters; 400 in dining area; 150 in
double occupancy rooms with private or semi-private
bathrooms; 50 in camp-style dormitories with large
bathrooms for 8 people; 75 in camping facilities
Open to outside groups September 1 through October 15 and
May 15 through June 30. Located 85 miles from New York
City.

Reid Castle (914) 694-3425
Manhattanville College Contact: Dean of Special Programs
Purchase, NY 10577

Formerly the home of Whitlaw Reid, owner of the New York
Tribune, this French and English-style castle now serves as a
fully equipped modern conference facility for corporate and
community educational organizations.
Capacity: 150 in five separate rooms on two floors
Resident caterer
Located 20 miles north of New York City.

Rutgers University Continuing (201) 932-9144
Education Center Contact: Director
Clifton Avenue
New Brunswick, NJ 08903

Capacity: 100 maximum in seven conference and seminar
rooms; 36 overnight double-occupancy
Located between New York and Philadelphia.

Sacks Lodge (914) 246-8711
P.O. Box 28, Gold Kings Road Contact: Ann Sacks,
Saugerties, NY 12477 Owner

Conference room, exhibit space, 2 lounges, dining room
Capacity: 100/120 in conference room; 60/80 in each lounge;
100/120 in dining room
Piano, four fireplaces, dance floor, kitchen; food may be served
View of mountains.
This country lodge has 70 acres of lawn and hillside and is 90
miles from New York City.
Suggested uses: all special events are possible including an
indoor or outdoor wedding

The Sagamore (212) 737-7536
Bolton Landing, NY

Situated on its own 70-acre island, facing the Narrows, the finest
stretch of Lake George, this more than one hundred year-old
hotel has just had its interior totally modernized. Offering 351
guest rooms, most with separate sitting rooms, this grand
hotel also offers a complete conference center totalling
55,760 sq. ft. of function space.
Capacity: 1350 in Ballroom; 50/1350 in 9 separate rooms; 20 in
self-contained Hermitage Executive Retreat

Sarah Lawrence College (914) 337-0700 ext.412
Bronxville, NY 10708 Contact: Joan Bero,
Director of College Events

Concert hall, theater, 15 classrooms, multi-purpose exhibit
space, screening room, lecture hall
Capacity: 380 in Reisinger Concert Hall; 150 in theater; 20 in
classrooms; 150 in screening room; 77 in lecture hall
Proscenium stage, piano
Food service is available.
Located 15 miles north of New York City.
Note: Space is only available during the summer and has an
overnight capacity for 500.

Sterling Forest Conference Center (914) 351-4777
R.R. No. 1 (212) 873-8048
Sterling Lake Road Contact: Marketing Representative
Tuxedo, NY 10987

Complete conference center with overnight accommodations.
Auditorium, classroom, conference room, tennis courts, exhibit space, reception area, gymnasium, game room, terrace
Sixty-two rooms can accommodate 100 persons.
Rental fee: Overnight rates are $140 twin/$210 single; weekend rates are $130 twin/$185 single
Platform, dance floor, fireplace, kitchen; food may be served
View of lake. Facility is 30 miles from New York City.
Suggested uses: all special events are possible except an auction, professional dance or fair

SUNY at Old Westbury (516) 876-3203
Old Westbury, NY 11568-0210 Contact: Jackie Fagan

This State University's campus facilities include the Maguire Theater, Recital Hall amphitheater, conference halls and auditoriums.
Capacity: 400 in Maguire Theater; 330 in Recital Hall
Located 20 miles east of New York's Midtown Tunnel.
Note: Space is only available to non-profit groups.

Tarrytown House (914) 591-8200
Executive Conference Center Contact: Director of Sales
East Sunnyside Lane
Tarrytown, NY 10591

Complete conference center with overnight accommodations.
One-hundred-and-fifty rooms can accommodate 200 persons double occupancy.
Thirty-five conference rooms accommodate 5 to 200 persons; recreational facilities are on the premises.
Complete audio-visual equipment
Twenty-six-acre estate which was built in 1840 and was the home of Mary Duke Biddle overlooks the Hudson River and is 20 miles north of New York City.

Wainwright House (914) 967-6080
260 Stuyvesant Avenue Contact: Nancy Genn
Rye, NY 10580

Drawing room, 2 meeting rooms, library
Capacity: 120 theater-style in drawing room; 35/40 in three other rooms
Overnight accommodations for 38 persons.

Piano, fireplace, winding staircase, kitchen; food may be served by resident caterer only
Space was formerly a private home, modeled after a French chateau, with view of an inlet from Long Island Sound.
Suggested uses: concert, class, exhibit, lecture, meeting, retreat
Located 20 miles from New York City.

Ward's Castle (212) 737-7536
Port Chester, NY 10573

This castle-like cement structure has fireplaces in every room.
Capacity: 60 seated on two levels
Note: This location only rents for corporate meetings and corporate parties.

Where Front Porch Rocking is an Art (212) 737-7536
Cape May, NJ

Built in 1876 by Col. Henry Sawyer, a Civil War hero, who was traded for the son of Robert E. Lee in a prisoner of war exchange, this grand hotel is one of the renowned examples of restored Victorian architecture which has made all of Cape May a National Historic Landmark. A green awning shades the wonderful porch which wraps around the building where porch rocking winds down the pace of modern life. Offering home cooked Southern fare, the hotel is especially suited for conferences and seminars by non-profit organizations.
Capacity: 175 seated in main dining room; 90 in air-conditioned special meeting space; 40 in King Edward Bar; 40 in Reading and Writing Rooms; porches and garden; 72 sleeping rooms for overnight accommodations
Note: It is available for rent April through October.

**William Paterson College
Conference Center**
300 Pompton Road
Wayne, NJ 07470

(201) 595-3243
Contact: Director of
Conference Services

Meeting rooms, dining rooms
Capacity: 20/4500
Overnight accommodations are available.
Located approximately 20 miles from New York City.

NEW YORK CITY: DAY CONFERENCE LOCATIONS

Chase Development Center
33 Maiden Lane
New York, NY 10081

(212) 968-3200
Contact: Mindy Dutka,
Director of Sales

Located in the heart of the financial district, this corporate
conference center offers 16 conference rooms complete with
audio-visual equipment, additional breakout rooms and
dining facilities.
Professional conference planners are available.
Capacity: 10/150 seated

Corporate Retreat with Great View   **(212) 737-7536**
(East 50's)
New York, NY

Available in one of New York City's most prestigious buildings,
this quiet and completely private living room with marble
floors is furnished in a formal English style. Wall-to-wall
glass view over Manhattan.
Capacity: 12 meetings/40 cocktails
Resident caterer
Note: Management staff person is on hand to answer the telephone and serve breakfast and/or lunch.

Institute of International Education   **(212) 737-7536**
(U.N. area)
New York, NY

Impressive 12th floor conference and reception center overlook-
ing the East River and the U.N.
Capacity: 151 seated for dinner or conference/225 reception in
main room; 10/25 in three additional rooms
Audio-visual capabilities
Suggested uses: conference, meeting, reception
Note: Space is not available on weekends.

International Center   **(212) 737-7536**
(East 46th Street)
New York, NY

Auditorium, conference room, exhibit space, roof terrace,
lounge
Capacity: 20/500
Platform, PA system, kitchen; food may be served
Suggested uses: dinner, luncheon, class, exhibit, promotion,
reception, meeting, workshop

International House
500 Riverside Drive
(122nd Street)
New York, NY 10027

(212) 316-8400
(212) 316-8465
Contact: Conference Coordinator

Daytime conference center
Auditorium, conference/meeting rooms, recital room,
auditorium foyer, dining room
Capacity: 350 for meals/670 sitdown in auditorium (flexible
seating); 15/80 in conference rooms; 125 in auditorium foyer;
45 in dining room
Guest suites available for short stays.
In-house catering
Suggested uses: meeting, conference, reception, seminar, recital,
luncheon, dinner, staff retreat, interfaith ceremony, memorial
service

Limestone Townhouse   **(212) 737-7536**
(East 65th Street)
New York, NY

Built in the Italian Renaissance-style by the New York City
architects Trowbridge & Livingston, the former Benson B.
Sloan residence is presently the home of a non-profit organization. A marble staircase leads to two spacious rooms
divided by a foyer. The oak panelled reception room offers
large floor-to-ceiling arched windows. Across the hall, a
second room has walls of French limestone, a coffered ceiling
painted in the Italian Renaissance-style, a fireplace and a
Persian rug.
Capacity: under 100 seated/125 cocktails in both rooms; 40
seated in each room meeting-style
Additional accoutrements are a stately reception hall at the entry
level, a coat room, powder room and a kitchen
Suggested uses: corporate or organizational meeting, wedding

McGraw Hill Seminar Center

1221 Avenue of the Americas
(49th Street)
New York, NY 10017

Contact: Scott Stahl,
Manager of Conference
Services

Auditorium, banquet room, 5 conference rooms, lounge
Capacity: 277/320 in auditorium; 220 in banquet room; 25/80 in
  conference rooms (flexible seating)
Rental fee: varies according to profit or non-profit status
Resident caterer
Note: A written application for space rental is necessary. Space
  is not available on weekends. Private events and press events
  are not allowed. Meetings may not exceed one day.

Murray Hill Center

(212) 889-4777

205 Lexington Avenue (33rd Street)
New York, NY 10016

Contact: Sue Weiner
or Sue Mender

Three conference rooms are available with one-way mirrors,
  television and audio recording equipment as well as a separate
  research kitchen.
Capacity: up to 12 in each room
Suggested uses: training, observing customer reactions to new
  products, etc.

Park Avenue Society Building

(212) 737-7536

(East 70's)
New York, NY

This eight story granite building designed by Edward Larrabee
  Barnes is now an elegantly appointed state-of-the-art facility.
Capacity: 258 in auditorium; reception areas can handle small
  and large gatherings; 200 in penthouse; 10/100 in meeting
  rooms; 150 in terrace garden
Suggested uses: meeting, screening, reception
Note: Space is only available for corporate events.

Pride of Lions

(212) 737-7536

(East 70's)
New York, NY

Located above a countrified Upper East Side restaurant, this
  completely private space with separate entrance offers a bi-
  level room, a service bar/lounge, separate dining area and two
  wood burning fireplaces, plus a view onto a rock garden.
Capacity: 40 for a meeting/75 cocktails
Suggested uses: business meeting, social occasion
In-house catering

Wave Hill: A Public Garden & Cultural Center

(212) 549-2055
(212) 549-3200

675 West 252nd Street
(entrance is at 249th Street &
Independence Avenue)
Bronx, NY 10471

Contact: Susan Logan

Built in the early 19th century as a family estate for William
  Lewis Morris and lived in by conductor Arturo Toscanini,
  publisher William Appleton, writer Mark Twain and others,
  Wave Hill was a gathering place for thinkers and notables.
  Overlooking the Hudson and the Palisades, this 150-year-old
  New York City property is a 28-acre public garden. Its man-
  sion is a two-story fieldstone house designed in the Greek
  Revival style, with Armor Hall providing an excellent setting
  for indoor functions.
Auditorium/ballroom/concert hall, 3 conference rooms, patio,
  garden, exhibit space, reception areas, dining room
Capacity: up to 100
Piano, kitchen; food may be served by caterer of your choice
Suggested uses: concert, meeting, outdoor dance performance,
  educational and garden workshop, outdoor and indoor motion
  picture shooting and fashion photography, guided tour
Note: Space is available to non-profit groups and corporate
  members for a meeting, conference, lecture, etc. Individual
  private events such as weddings are not allowed.

World Trade Institute

(212) 466-4044

One World Trade Center
55th floor
New York, NY 10048

Contact: Conference Space
Manager

Thirteen conference spaces with blackboards, screens, podiums
  and microphones.
Capacity: 12/125 in individual or combined rooms

Also see: **CHURCHES**
HOTELS
SCHOOLS AND COLLEGES
Shingle/Stone Mansion at the Water's Edge (CT)
Y's

For COUNTRY CLUBS inquire at your local Chamber
of Commerce.

EXHIBITS, GREENMARKETS & STREET FAIRS/Outdoors

"EYES," 1986 Louise Bourgeoise
Photo by Petet Bellamy - Public Art Fund

EXHIBITS: Outdoors

Brooklyn Botanic Garden Fence Art   **(718) 622-4433**
Show
1000 Washington Avenue
Brooklyn, NY 11225

Central Park South Outdoor Art   **(305) 456-3576**
Exhibit   Contact: Brenda Bogoff
1965 S. Ocean Dr.
Hallandale, FL 33009

Children's Art Carnival at Lincoln   **(212) 234-4093**
Center   Contact: Betty Blayton-Taylor
62 Hamilton Terrace
New York, NY 10031

Creative Time, Inc.   **(212) 619-1955**
66 West Broadway   Contact: Executive Director
New York, NY 10007
This non-profit arts organization assists both visual and performing artists in the realization of temporary, site-specific work designed for public presentation. Three provocative indoor/outdoor urban locations are: The Brooklyn Bridge Anchorage (an unusual stone structure in Brooklyn), The Winter Garden (a new public indoor atrium space in Battery Park City in Manhattan), and Hunters Point (a landfill in Queens).

Gracie Square Art Exhibit   Contact: Laura C. Mayer
(contact in writing)
Box 14, 1642 Second Avenue
New York, NY 10028

Lincoln Center Plaza American   **(201) 746-0091**
Crafts Festival   Contact: Paul Weingarten
American Concern for Artistry
& Craftsmanship
P.O. Box 650
Montclair, NJ 07042

Promenade and Fine Arts Exhibition   **(718) 783-4469**
Brooklyn Arts and Culture Association   **(718) 783-3077**
The Brooklyn Museum
200 Eastern Parkway
Brooklyn, NY 11238

Public Art Fund, Inc.   **(212) 541-8423**
25 Central Park West, Room 25R   Contact: Project Director
New York, NY 10023
Reviews proposals for public art projects on an ongoing basis. Maintains a slide file on artists working in public spaces.

Washington Square Outdoor Art Show   (212) 982-6255
33 Fifth Avenue
New York, NY 10003

Also see: PARKS & PLAZAS

GREENMARKETS (Farmers Markets in New York City)

Council on the Environment   (212) 566-0990
51 Chambers Street, Room 228
New York, NY 10007
Greenmarket is the city dweller's way of supporting regional farmers while at the same time improving the freshness, taste and nutritional value of fruits and vegetables available in the City.

STREET FAIRS

Street Activity Permit   (212) 566-2506
Community Assistance Unit
51 Chambers Street, Room 608
New York, NY 10007
Contact: Apply at your local Community Board office. To find out where your Board office is located, or for general information such as dates, call or write the Community Assistance Unit above.

Some of the major Street Fairs in New York City (call for dates)

Amsterdam Ave.   (212) 595-3333
Amsterdam Ave. bet. 77th & 90th St.

Atlantic Antic   (718) 783-4469
Atlantic Ave. Brooklyn

Autumn Jubilee   (212) 684-4077
Second Ave. bet. 14th & 34th St.

Avenue of the Americas   (212) 732-0460
6th Ave. bet. 35th & 50th St.

Columbus Avenue Festival   (212) 595-3333
66th to 79th St.

Feast of St. Anthony   (212) 777-2755
Houston, Spring & Prince St.

Feast of San Gennaro   (212) 226-9546
Mulberry St.

Festa Italiana   (212) 242-6644
Carmine St. bet. 6th & 7th Aves.

Fifty Second Street Fair   (212) 759-9411
East to West on 52nd St.

Great July 4th Festival   (212) 732-0460
Water Street

Irish Fair   (212) 759-9411
Ft. of Brooklyn Bridge,
Cadman Plaza, Brooklyn

Irving Place   (212) 684-4077
Irving Pl. bet. 14th & 20th St.

Kids Arts in the Apple Festival   (212) 269-0320
(Battery Park City)

Lexington Avenue   (212) 684-4077
Lexington Ave. bet. 23rd & 34th St.

Lincoln Center for the Performing Arts   (212) 877-1800
Fountain Plaza, adjacent plazas, Damrosch Park

Lower Eastside Jewish Festival   (212) 475-6200
Rutger St. to Montgomery St.

Museum Mile   (212) 860-6868
5th Ave. bet. 86th & 105th St.

New York Is Book Country   (212) 794-2231
48th to 57th St.

Ninth Avenue Fair   (212) 581-7217
East to West on 9th Ave.

One World Festival   (212) 686-0710
35th St. & 2nd Ave.

Park Avenue Fair   (212) 684-4077
Park Ave. S. bet. 23rd & 32nd St.

Queens Day   (212) 520-3178
Flushing Meadow Park

Second Avenue Fair   (212) 517-7799
68th to 96th St.

Soho Festival   (212) 925-1928

Stuyvesant Park Festival   (212) 684-4077
Second Ave. bet. 15th & 16th St.

Tama Fair   (212) 684-4077
14th to 34th St.

Third Avenue Fair   (212) 517-7799
68th to 96th St.

Third Avenue Summerfest   (212) 684-4077
Third Ave. bet. 42nd & 57th St.

Turtlebay   (212) 684-4077
Second Ave. bet. 42nd & 53rd St.

Westchester County Fair & Exposition   (914) 968-4200
Yonkers Raceway
Yonkers, NY 10704

For ethnic festivals, Oktoberfests, etc. see:
SOCIAL HALLS

EXPOSITIONS/TRADE SHOWS

ARMORIES

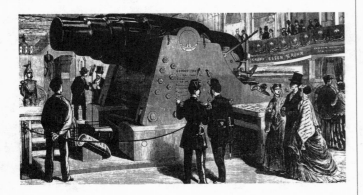

*R*equests for non-military use of State Armories should be directed to the individual Armory Officers in Charges and Control. Requests should be on the business or official letterhead of requesting organization or agency and should contain the following information:

Name and address of organization, agency or individual of the prospective lessee; the purpose, character and extent of the use; commercial, non-profit, charitable, governmental or youth activity; space to be used; day and hours of use, including moving in and out; admission charge, if any.

Manhattan: **(212) 439-0300**
643 Park Avenue
New York, NY 10021

Brooklyn: **(718) 493-0973**
1579 Bedford Avenue
Brooklyn, NY 11225

1492 Eighth Avenue   **(718) 788-3537**
Brooklyn, NY 11215   or **(718) 788-2666**

355 Marcy Avenue   **(718) 387-9102**
Brooklyn, NY 11206

Staten Island: **(718) 442-8400**
321 Manor Road
Richmond, NY 10314

Jacob K. Javits Convention Center of   (212) 737-7536
New York   Contact: Sales Department
(11th and 12th Avenues
between 34th and 39th Streets)
New York, NY 10001

Situated along the Hudson on Manhattan's west side and designed by architect I. M. Pei and Partners, this prime state-of-the-art convention and trade show facility is a stunning design of an assemblage of glass cubes that reflect the New York skyline by day and become spectacularly transparent by night.

It offers 1.8 million gross sq. ft. of trade show and exhibition space all under one roof and on two levels, over 100 meeting rooms, one exhibit hall with 410,000 sq. ft. of exhibit space and another with 230,000 sq. ft. Each hall is divisible into thirds. Outdoor exhibition space immediately adjacent.

Meeting rooms are of various sizes to accommodate groups from 35 to 3200. Larger rooms will accommodate from 7000 to 35,000.

On-site kitchens

Note: Mailing address is 655 West 34th Street, New York, NY 10001.

The Rotunda   **(212) 563-8000**
Madison Square Garden Center   Contact: Mark Albin
Pennsylvania Plaza (33rd Street)
New York, NY 10001
Exposition area: 50,000 sq. ft.

The World Trade Center/Mezzanine   (212) 737-7536
The Port Authority of New York   Contact: Public Services
and New Jersey   Coordinator
1 World Trade Center
New York, NY 10048

Capacity: 9000 sq. ft. on mezzanine

Suggested uses: art and small product-type exhibition; small trade show

---

Also see: HOTELS
PIERS
Used Cars

GALLERIES/EXHIBITION SPACES

Arsenal Gallery   **(212) 360-3423**
830 Fifth Avenue (3rd fl.)   Contact: Margaret Tsirantonakis
New York, NY 10021

Anyone can submit a portfolio from which a selection of artists to showcase will be made. Showings are usually of a four-week duration.

Note: Space is in the historic Arsenal Building in Central Park.

Bronx Museum of the Arts   **(212) 681-6000**
1040 Grand Concourse   Contact: Carmen Vega Rivera
Bronx, NY 10456

4 exhibit spaces, conference room, classroom, community room
Capacity: 350 in Gallery 2; 280 in Lower Gallery; 50/75 in conference room; approximately 100 in classroom; 10 in community room
Rental fee: varies with non-profit or for-profit status
Piano, bar, small kitchen; food may be served
Suggested uses: concert, class, exhibit, lecture, reception, promotion, workshop, fundraiser

---

City Gallery   **(212) 974-1150**
2 Columbus Circle   Contact: Elyse Reissman,
New York, NY 10019   Director

20' x 75' of space is available with 15' ceilings
Rental fee: none
Professional lighting, temperature controlled
Note: Free exhibit space is offered to non-profit arts organizations in New York City. Deadline for submitting proposals is June 1 and November 1 of each year. Request application guidelines. This space is in the former Huntington Hartford Museum.

La Galeria En El Bohio   **(212) 982-0627**
El Bohio Cultural   Contact: Emily Rubin
and Community Center   or Chino Garcia
605 East 9th Street
New York, NY 10009

Exhibit space
Capacity: 90' x 25' x 30' exhibit space with 12' ceilings

Wave Hill   **(212) 549-2055**
675 West 252nd Street   Contact: Assistant Administrator
Bronx, NY 10471

Glyndor House, the red brick former home of Mrs. Perkins, now has a new gallery space on the first floor. Exhibition space is also available in Wave Hill House
Capacity: 3 rooms have 15' x 20', 15' x 30', and 30' x 40' of space available

---

CLOCK TOWERS

The Institute for Art and Urban   **(212) 233-1096**
Resources, Inc.   Contact: Tom Finkelpearl
The Clocktower
108 Leonard Street
New York, NY 10013

Unique exhibition space for one-person shows in what used to be the old New York Federal Building. Lower gallery's walls are 10 ft. high. Tower gallery's walls are 20 ft. high. Total footage is under 3000 ft. Artists are encouraged to submit documentation and proposals for the showing of their work in writing to the offices at P.S. 1, 46-01 21st Street, Long Island City, N.Y. 11101. Space is open Thursday through Sunday, 12 to 6 p.m.

Also see: GALLERIES
         Mission West
         Three Versatile Floors

GYMNASIUMS/POOLS

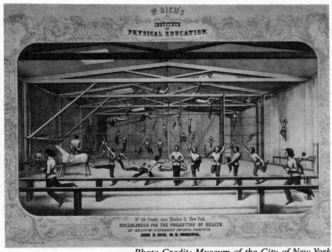

Photo Credit: Museum of the City of New York

Childrens Aid Society (212) 369-1223
DunLevy Milbank Community Center Contact: Louis von
14-32 West 118th Street Fickling
New York, NY 10026

Gymnasium, lounge, olympic size swimming pool
Capacity: 250 in gymnasium; 100 in lounge
Rental fee: $200 per hour minimum
Portable stage, piano, 2 kitchens; food may be served
Note: Space is only available from 9 p.m. to 3 a.m.

Hunter College of the City (212) 772-4782
University of New York Contact: Charles Brown,
695 Park Avenue Athletic Office
New York, NY 10021

5 new gymnasiums, 2 swimming pools, racquet ball courts,
  dance studio
Capacity: 2300

Suggested uses: conference, fashion show, antique show, sport
  clinic
Note: Food and dancing are not allowed.

Top of the One Club (212) 595-5121
20 West 64th Street Contact: Manager
New York, NY 10023

Capacity: 300 indoors and outdoors in summer; 200 indoors in
  winter
Lounges, 20 ft. x 40 ft. pools, sundecks with 360 degree unobstructed views, kitchens; food may be served
Suggested uses: private party, cast party, sweet 16, birthday, bar
  mitzvah
Note: Space is available Tuesday day and evening; weekends
  only after 7 p.m.

Also see: Aerobics West
  Bronx House (Bronx)
  Caterer-Owned Private Party Space
  CONFERENCE CENTERS
  Congregational Church of North New York
    (Bronx)
  East Harlem Arts & Education Complex
  Educational Alliance
  Gymnastic Birthday Parties
  Lenox Hill Neighborhood Association
  Manhattanville Community Centers, Inc.
  Sam & Esther Minskoff Cultural Center
  Murphy Center at Asphalt Green
  New York City Parks (borough numbers)
  Parker Meridien New York
  Regina Center (Brooklyn)
  Roberto Clemente State Park (Bronx)
  SCHOOLS
  United Nations Plaza Hotel
  Universalist Church
  Y's

HOTELS

Algonquin Hotel   **(212) 840-6800**
59 West 44th Street
New York, NY 10036
Stratford Suite
Capacity: 30 seated/75 standing in 3rd floor Stratford Suite; 170 rooms for overnight accommodations
Space is traditionally known for literary and book critic functions, theater and press conferences.

Barbizon   **(212) 715-6920/6982** (overnight)
140 East 63rd Street   **(212) 737-7536**
New York, NY 10021   **(meetings and banquets)**
Rousseau Room, 8 banquet/conference rooms, exhibit space, reception area
Capacity: 500 on whole mezzanine; 85 classroom/150 theater/175 cocktail-style in Rousseau Room; 100 seated in Carot Room which has 1232 sq. ft. of exhibit space with reception area; 360 rooms for overnight accommodations
1581 sq. ft. stage, 3 pianos, dance floors, kitchen; food may be served
Note: Plans are being made to remodel this hotel to be an "urban spa."

Berkshire Place   **(212) 753-5800** ext. 7127
21 East 52nd Street
New York, NY 10022
3 meeting rooms (The Ambassador, The Senator, The Madison); executive board room
Capacity: 20/50 persons in meeting rooms; 10 in executive board room; 415 rooms plus penthouse for overnight accommodations

---

The Carlyle   **(212) 570-7106**
35 East 76th Street   **(212) 570-7107**
New York, NY 10021   Contact: Ruth Trager,
                          Director of Banquet and Sales
2 meeting banquet rooms
Capacity: 200 reception-style, 120 sitdown dinner in 66' x 20' Versailles Suite; 250 reception-style/170 sitdown dinner in 67' x 25' Trianon Suite; 250 rooms for overnight accommodations
Both rooms can be divided.
2 dance floors, 2 pianos, kitchen; space's food only may be served
Suggested uses: corporate meeting, reception, social party

The Day's Inn   **(212) 581-8100**
440 West 57th Street (at the Coliseum)
New York, NY 10019
Embassy Room, Renaissance Room, Imperial Room, Mandarin Room, Medallion Room, Marco Polo Room, Coliseum Room
Capacity: 650 auditorium-style in Embassy Room and Imperial Room (can open into one room); 250 auditorium/200 banquet/100 classroom-style in Renaissance Room; 200 auditorium-style in Imperial Room; 40 in other rooms; 600 rooms for overnight accommodations

---

Doral Tuscany   **(212) 686-1600**
120 East 39th Street   Contact: Susan Krasner,
New York, NY 10016   Director of Catering
Renaissance Suite, Sienna Room
Capacity: 75 seated in Renaissance Suite; 25 seated in Sienna Room
120 rooms for overnight accommodations

Gramercy Park Hotel   **(212) 475-4320**
2 Lexington Avenue   Contact: Tom O'Brien
New York, NY 10010
Auditorium, rehearsal space, lounge, conference room, ballroom, exhibit space, roof garden
Capacity: 12/150 seated; 500 maximum standing; 350 rooms for overnight accommodations
Platform, piano, dance floor, kitchen; food may be served
Suggested uses: all special events are possible including a meeting or display, except a concert or fair

Grand Bay Hotel
(212) 765-1900
(800) 237-0990

Equitable Center
152 West 51st Street
New York, NY 10019

Capacity: 20/30 for banquet and meetings in each of 2 rooms; 178 rooms including 52 suites for overnight

Grand Hyatt New York
(212) 883-1234
(800) 228-9000

Park Avenue at Grand Central Station
New York, NY 10017

34-story mirrored hotel

Regency Room on Mezzanine Level has 1400 sq. ft. and can accommodate 150 for a reception/120 banquet/180 theater/80 school room and 40 conference-style.

20 meeting rooms are on Conference Level, 4th floor, ranging from 490 sq. ft. to 1260 sq. ft. with 8 ft. ceilings, accommodating 120/315 for a reception, 70/180 theater, 50/125 banquet, 35/90 school room and 30/80 conference-style.

5 ballrooms are on Ballroom Level, 5th floor, ranging from 3200 sq. ft. to 18,950 sq. ft. accommodating 800/1800 for a reception, 320/1800 banquet, 460/1760 theater and 225/1180 school room-style.

These facilities can function as exhibit spaces.

20 meeting/sleeping rooms on the 14th floor can accommodate 15/20 persons conference style; 1407 rooms for overnight accommodations.

Atrium-lobby, glass-enclosed restaurant

Halloran House
(212) 755-4000

525 Lexington Avenue (49th Street)
New York, NY 10017

Stuyvesant Room on lobby floor can accommodate 250 theater, 170 school room, 250 banquet-style and 300 for a reception in 80' x 35' space

6 meeting rooms on the 2nd floor can accommodate from 32/220 school room, 50/350 banquet, 50/450 theater and 75/700 reception style. Smallest is 25' x 24' x 16'; largest is 135' x 32' x 14'.

The Garden Room and Fountain Room on the 16th floor are 48' x 39' x 12' and 51' x 32' x 12' respectively. Garden Room can accommodate 28 school room, 50 theater, 90 banquet and 150 reception-style; Fountain Room can accommodate 80 school room, 100 banquet, 125 theater and 200 reception-style; terrace outside of Fountain Room accommodates 75 reception-style; 642 rooms for overnight accommodations

Audio-visual equipment on premises

The Harley of New York
(212) 490-8900

212 East 42nd Street
New York, NY 10017

Contact: Carlotta Spindel, Director of Catering

793 rooms, 7 third floor meeting rooms, ballroom

Capacity: 40/300; 170 for dinner dance in ballroom (Knickerbocker Suite); 790 rooms for overnight accommodations

On-site parking is provided by this 41-story hotel.

The Helmsley Palace
(212) 888-7000

Madison Avenue & 50th Street
New York, NY 10020

4 modern meeting rooms, 2 historic meeting rooms, Grand Ballroom, 4 lounges, 3 restaurants

Capacity: 10/200 in modern meeting rooms; 15/150 in historic meeting rooms; over 300 in Grand Ballroom; 650 rooms for overnight accommodations

This 55-story hotel with 650 rooms and suites is entered through the historic cobblestone courtyard of the 100 year-old neo-Italian Renaissance landmark Villard Houses, which is part of this luxury hotel.

Hotel Plaza
(212) 546-5486 (overnight)
(212) 737-7536
(meetings and banquets)

Fifth Avenue & 59th Street
New York, NY 10019

Various rooms and foyers including Grand Ballroom

Capacity: 800 in Grand Ballroom; 550 for a banquet/750 for a reception in Baroque Room; 80 in State Suite; 30 in Blue Room; 20/500 in other rooms; 800 rooms for overnight accommodations

Hotel Ritz Carlton
(212) 757-1900

112 Central Park South
New York, NY 10019

This British-style hotel overlooks Central Park and has a working fireplace in restaurant.

Capacity: 100 seated in Park Suite; 30 in Board Room; 231 rooms for overnight accommodations

Hotel Tudor
(212) 986-8800

304 East 42nd Street
New York, NY 10017

Classroom/meeting room

Capacity: 100 in basement level meeting room (Cameo Room); 30 on 2nd floor Carriage Room; 400 rooms for overnight accommodations

Rental fee: $250 for Cameo Room; $150 for Carriage Room

Space's food only may be served.

Suggested uses: banquet, class, social or professional dance, lecture, meeting, party, reception, wedding

Inter-Continental New York
(212) 755-5900 or
(800) 327-0200 (overnight)
(212) 737-7536 (meetings and banquets)

111 East 48th Street
New York, NY 10017

Formerly the Barclay, this hotel offers 17 meeting/banquet rooms.

Capacity: 10/100 meeting-style; 30/175 banquet-style; 686 rooms offer overnight accommodations

Loews Summit   (212) 752-7000

Lexington Avenue & 51st Street   Contact: John Esposito,
New York, NY 10022   Director of Catering or
          Irma S. Platt, Banquet
            Coordinator

Grand ballroom, 9 smaller banquet rooms
Capacity: 300 in 3850 sq. ft. Grand ballroom; 10/200 in smaller banquet rooms; 766 rooms for overnight accommodations

Lowell Hotel   (212) 838-1400 (overnight)
             (212) 737-7536 (meetings
28 East 63rd Street   **and banquets)**
New York, NY 10021
2 English-style rooms
Capacity: 100 maximum for cocktails and dinner when both the Pembroke and Park Room are combined; 30 meeting-style in Park Room; 75 cocktails in either room; 48 suites and 13 single and double rooms for overnight accommodations

Mayflower Hotel   (212) 265-0060

61st Street & Central Park West   Contact: Naomi Freistadt,
New York, NY 10023   Sales Department
Capacity: 50 for meetings in Plymouth Room, Mayflower Room and Suite #1203 respectively (100 when combined); 30/200 banquet-style; 377 rooms for overnight accommodations

The New York Hilton   (212) 586-7000 (overnight)
             (212) 737-7536 (meetings
Rockefeller Center   **and banquets)**
1335 Avenue of the Americas
(54th Street)
New York, NY 10019
Numerous ballrooms, suites, parlors and restaurants
Capacity: 40/3300 for a meeting, 30/2800 banquet-style; 1802 rooms and suites in hotel, 318 rooms for overnight in Executive Tower
Note: Penthouse East and Penthouse West on the 45th floor, each a duplex of 7500 sq. ft., offer skyline views through walls of glass for special corporate and private events. Kosher menu available.

New York Marriott Marquis   (212) 398-1900 (overnight)
             (212) 737-7536 (meetings
Broadway between 45th &   **and banquets)**
46th Streets
New York, NY 10036
This Times Square hotel offers 80,000 sq. ft. of meeting space.
3 ballrooms, 41 meeting rooms, 11 board rooms, 3 conference rooms
Capacity: 2550 in both the ballrooms (28,800 sq. ft. Grand Ballroom is divisible into 10 sections/22,500 sq. ft. ballroom/exhibit hall on 5th floor is divisible into 11 sections); 6,120 sq. ft. Junior Ballroom is divisible into 2 sections; 1871 rooms for overnight accommodations
The View, a 3-tiered revolving rooftop restaurant and lounge, is the only such facility in New York City.

Omni Park Central   (212) 247-8000

870 Seventh Avenue (56th Street)
New York, NY 10019
Ballroom, 8 suites
Capacity: 700 meeting-style/800 banquet-style in ballroom; 60/400 for meeting-style/40/300 banquet-style in suites; up to 1525 meeting-style/1260 banquet-style when rooms combined

Park Avenue Hotel   (212) 737-7536

(East 30's)
New York, NY
Park Avenue Room, Executive Suite, Murray Hill Room, roof garden
Capacity: 100 seated/150 standing in Park Avenue Room; 40 seated/70 reception in Executive Room; 30 seated in Murray Hill Room; 100 reception on roof garden; 151 rooms for overnight accommodations

Parker Meridien New York   (212) 245-5000 (overnight)
119 West 56th Street   (212) 737-7536 (meetings
New York, NY 10019   **and banquets)**
Conference rooms, banquet rooms, 2 squash and 4 racquetball courts, complete health club, rooftop swimming pool, sundeck, jogging track, patio
Capacity: 225 theater, 130 classroom, 160 banquet and 250 reception-style in Salon Vendome (ballroom); 190 theater, 110 classroom, 150 banquet, 220 reception-style in Salon Concorde; 138 theater, 70 classroom, 100 banquet, 170 reception-style in Salon Rivoli; 60 theater, 40 classroom, 40 banquet, 60 reception-style in Salon Castiglione; 125 theater, 90 classroom, 140 banquet, 175 reception-style in Penthouse North; 50 theater, 70 classroom, 80 banquet, 125 reception-style in Penthouse South; 700 rooms for overnight accommodations
This 600-room, 40-story hotel is operated by Meridien, an international hotel chain and a subsidiary of Air France.

The Peninsula   (212) 247-2200 (overnight)
700 Fifth Avenue (55th Street)   (212) 737-7536 (meetings
New York, NY 10019   **and banquets)**
The original Hotel Gotham has been magnificently restored with belle epoque and art nouveau design.
Capacity: 10/100 for special functions; 254 rooms for overnight accommodations

The Pierre   (212) 838-8000 (overnight)
61st Street & Fifth Avenue   (212) 737-7536 (meetings
New York, NY 10021   **and banquets)**
Grand Ballroom, Garden Foyer, Gold Room, Regency Room, Cotillion Room, Wedgwood Salon
Capacity: 250/750 for a meeting, 250/850 banquet-style in Grand Ballroom; 50/110 banquet-style in Garden Foyer; 20/60 for a meeting or banquet in Gold Room; 100/150 for a meeting, 50/150 banquet-style in Regency Room; 150/400 for a meeting, 150/360 banquet-style in Cotillion Room; 50/200 for a meeting, 30/150 banquet-style in Wedgwood Salon
Offers 196 rooms for overnight.

Roosevelt Hotel (212) 661-9600 ext. 7117

Madison Avenue & 45th Street
New York, NY 10017

Terrace Room, Oval Suite, Colonial Room, Grand Ballroom, meeting rooms, exhibit spaces, foyer, balcony
Capacity: 500 theater/250 classroom/400 banquet-style/700 for a reception in 86' x 48' with 23' ceiling Terrace Room; 200 theater/150 classroom/225 banquet/300 for a reception in 62' x 49 ½' with 23' ceiling Oval Suite; 250 banquet-style/450 for a reception in Colonial Room (can be divided); 1000 theater/450 classroom/750 banquet-style/1000 for a reception in 89' x 64' versatile Grand Ballroom; 300 for a reception in foyer; 12/120 in additional meeting rooms; 1060 rooms for overnight accommodations
Piano, dance floor

Royal Concordia (212) 838-7070

54th Street between 6th and 7th Avenues
New York, NY 10019

This hotel of 54 stories is the tallest in Manhattan.
Capacity: 10/140 for meetings and banquets; 500 rooms for overnight accommodations; 6 Royal Suites of 2500 sq. ft. each serve as entertainment facilities with either a billiard table or piano
Note: Scheduled opening date in mid-1989.

St. Moritz On-the-Park (212) 755-5800 or
(800) 221-4774 (overnight)
50 Central Park South (212) 737-7536 (meetings
New York, NY 10019 and banquets)

Quadrille Ballroom, Sky Garden, Terrace Penthouse, La Trianon
Capacity: 200 seated/400 reception in Quadrille Ballroom; 120 seated/150 reception in Sky Garden; 90 seated/100 reception in Terrace Penthouse; 50 seated/60 reception in Le Trianon; 800 rooms for overnight accommodations

Sheraton Centre Hotel & Towers (212) 581-1000

811 Seventh Avenue (52nd Street) ext. 6425
New York, NY 10019

6 ballrooms, 35 meeting rooms, exhibit hall
Capacity: 2400 theater style/3000 cocktail reception in main ballroom; 5 smaller ballrooms are each 3000 sq. ft.; meeting rooms hold 40/100; exhibit hall is 30,000 sq. ft.; 1800 rooms for overnight accommodations
Broadway-type stage, audio-visual facilities
The main ballroom is one of the largest in New York City.

United Nations Plaza Hotel (212) 355-3400

1 United Nations Plaza
New York, NY 10017

4 meeting/banquet rooms (Dag Hammarskjold, U Thant, Trygve Lie, Prez de Cuellar) limited exhibit space, lounge, Ambassador Grill restaurant, swimming pool
Capacity: 70 classroom/120 theater/100 banquet-style in Dag Hammarskjold Room; 15/25 for a meeting, 50 for a banquet in U Thant Room; 15/25 for a meeting, 50/60 for a banquet in the Trygve Lie Room; 442 rooms for overnight accommodations
Rental fee: varies from $200 to $600

6 ft. x 12 ft. platform, dance floor; food may be served
Suggested uses: all special events are possible including weddings in the Prez de Cuellar Suite with floor-to-ceiling windows on the 29th floor

Vista International New York (212) 938-9100

3 World Trade Center (overnight)
New York, NY 10048 (212) 737-7536 (meetings
and banquets)

829 guest rooms. Private function facilities are available in 3rd floor salons.
Theme parties available in International Ballroom:
(a) On The New York Waterfront in the 19th Century: huge murals of clipperships, yard arms and sails form the backdrop of a busy quay. Amidst an authentic wharf with loading crates, barrels and bundles, a buffet is laid out with shop fronts of yesteryear, fishmongers, bakers and butchers. A real seafaring pub dispenses wine and ale. Period costumed waiters and waitresses, etc.
(b) Nostalgic Subway Champagne Soiree: a 1922 vintage subway in mint condition with waiters dressed in black tie and tails serving chilled champagne takes guests on half-hour ride to Brooklyn Transit Museum for a sumptuous buffet amidst period subway cars.
(c) A Salute To the Good Ole U.S.A.: a Virginia Smokehouse, a Mississippi Riverboat and a Pennsylvania Dutch Farm House are used to create a setting for food displays from these regions; also a Covered Wagon of the 1800's and a chandeliered gazebo of the Roaring Twenties. Waiters and waitresses costumed in period style and entertainment from a variety of states and times.

Waldorf-Astoria (212) 872-4792/3 (Civitano)

Park Avenue & 50th Street (212) 872-4535/6
New York, NY 10022 (Reservations)
Contact: Thomas Civitano
Director of Sales, or Reservations

4 reception rooms
Capacity: 650/700 in Starlight Roof; 400/600 in Empire Room; 400/500 in Hilton Room; 250/300 in Palm Room

Westbury Hotel (212) 246-6440 (overnight)

69th Street & Madison Avenue (212) 737-7536 (meetings
New York, NY 10021 and banquets)
Contact: Sales

Built in the late 1920's by the family of an American polo player, this hotel offers 7 meeting/banquet rooms plus 300 rooms and suites for overnight accommodations
Capacity: 26/240 for meetings in suites ranging from 694 sq. ft. to 2190 sq. ft; 60/180 for banquets

Please Note : *For information on three additional hotels with an exclusive style of their own, call (212) 737-7536.*

LIBRARIES

MANHATTAN, BRONX, and STATEN ISLAND BRANCH LIBRARIES

The New York Public Library　　(212) 340-0899
Office of The Branch Libraries
455 Fifth Avenue (40th Street)
New York, NY 10016

The New York Public Library has 82 branches in Manhattan, The Bronx, and Staten Island. A number of the larger libraries have auditoriums and almost all have some form of meeting space, often the Children's Room, available for meetings during non-service hours. The capacities of these spaces vary greatly, from 15 to 275. Interested persons are asked to contact the individual branches.

Rental fee: A nominal fee is charged; for information, consult the branch librarian. All meetings must be without fee to the public and be related to a cultural, educational or civic purpose.

The brochure *It's Your Library* lists the names and addresses of all 82 branch libraries and is available through the Borough Offices, or at any of the branch libraries.

Also see:　Library and Museum of the Performing Arts
　　　　　　New York Public Library, 42nd Street branch

BROOKLYN BRANCH LIBRARIES

Brooklyn Public Library　　(718) 780-7700
Grand Army Plaza　　Contact: Ellen Rudley,
Brooklyn, NY 11238　　Public Information
Ingersoll Building (Grand Army Plaza)
Auditorium, conference room
Capacity: 100 in auditorium; 30 in Conference Room #214

The Brooklyn Public Library System administers 58 branch libraries in Brooklyn. A brochure listing names and locations of these libraries, with capacities ranging from 36 to 160, may be requested at the Central Library, Grand Army Plaza, or at any of the local branches. There is no rental fee.

QUEENS BRANCH LIBRARIES

Queens Borough Public Library　　(718) 990-0700
89-11 Merrick Blvd.
Jamaica, NY 11432
Auditorium, 2 meeting rooms
Capacity: 180 in auditorium; 50 in each meeting room.

Information on names and locations of these libraries, with capacities ranging from 25 to 200, as well as regulations governing the use of their facilities may be obtained at the above address or at any of the branches in Queens.

LOCATION SHOOTS

Many of the listings in **PLACES** *offer possibilities for both still and film photography. In addition,* **PLACES** *maintains a file of particular sites which are only available for still or film photography. For further information call* **PLACES** *at (212) 737-7536.*

MEETING ROOMS/CONFERENCE ROOMS/AUDITORIUMS
(Seating 499 or less)

New York Center for Psychoanalytic Training	10	Wave Hill Center for Environmental Studies	48/130
Small East Side	30	Dimele Center	140
Academic Review	5/40	Former Chapel	140
Corporate Retreat with Great View	12/40	Langston Hughes Community Library and Cultural Center	150
Michael Schulman Theater	40	Morris-Jumel Mansion	75/150
Business Communication Center	50	Riverdale-Yonkers Society for Ethical Culture	150
Village Brownstone	50	Sky Rink	150
New York Hall of Science	50/60	William Sobelsohn Associates	20/150
Museum of Broadcasting	40/63	Department of Cultural Affairs	120/154
Mercantile Library Association	65	Castillo Center	66/200
American Association of University Women	30/70	Community House in Queens	200
Gateway National Recreation Area	25/70	Flushing Jewish Center	200
AT & T Infoquest Center	72	Fraunces Tavern Museum	50/200
Historic Blackman House	50/75	Metropolitan Republican Club	200
Mechanics Institute	75	Ohio Theatr Center	200
Richmondtown Restoration	75	Studios 58 Playhouse	200
TRS Inc. Professional Suite	30/75	Taller Latino Americano	5/200
Women's City Club of New York, Inc.	75	Tiffany Hall	30/200
East Side International Community Center	35/100	New York Genealogical & Biographical Society	60/210
Eastern Christian Leasing Center	100	Grolier Club	100/225
La Guardia Memorial House	50/100	Jewish Community Center of Yonkers	20/225
Margaret Sanger Center	25/100	Oval Room	130/230
Theodore Roosevelt House	30/100	Hudson Guild	10/240
Yoga Center	45/100	Museum of the City of New York	248
America's Society	15/110	Jewish Guild for the Blind	250
College of Insurance	25/120	Jewish Museum	250
The Studio Museum in Harlem	30/120	Lenox Hill Neighborhood Association	15/250
Limestone Townhouse	40/125	The Asia Society	150/258
New York Academy of Sciences	20/125		
Catholic Kolping Society	50/130		

continued on next page

Association of the Bar of the City of New York	16/270
Adam Clayton Powell State Office Building	20/300
American Museum of Natural History	75/300
Brooklyn Museum	300
James Weldon Johnson Community Centers, Inc.	300
Japan Society	12/300
Lavish Jewish Community Building	40/300
Seaport Experience Theatre	150/300
East Harlem Arts & Education Complex	100/300
McGraw Hill Seminar Center	25/320
New York Blood Center	40/348
Workmen's Circle Building	12/350
Jewish Center of Bayside Hills	35/350
Advertising Trade Association/Graphic Design Gallery	125/400
Bronx House	350/400
Central Park West Special Function Site	100/400
City University of New York Graduate Center	40/400
French Institute	120/400
Hayden Planetarium	400
Hillcrest Jewish Center	30/400
Sam & Esther Minskoff Cultural Center	25/400
The New York Public Library/Celeste Bartos Forum	50/400
Manhattanville Community Centers, Inc.	50/450
Equitable Center Auditorium	490
Jacob K. Javits Convention Center of New York	35/499

Academic Review
(212) 724-6011

3 West 73rd Street
New York, NY 10023
Contact: Les Halpert, Educational Services Director

Classroom, conference room, meeting room
Capacity: 5/40
Rental fee: varies with function and number of people
Kitchen; food may be served
Suggested uses: class, lecture, meeting

Adam Clayton Powell State Office Building
(212) 870-4390
Contact: Irma Harvin

163 West 125th Street
New York, NY 10027

Conference room, meeting rooms, executive suite, plaza area
Capacity: 20/300 in conference and meeting rooms; 200/250 sitdown in executive suite
Piano; food may be served only by resident caterer
Suggested uses: lecture, conference, meeting, fashion show, banquet, wedding

Advertising Trade Association/ Graphic Design Gallery
(212) 737-7536

(East 20's)
New York, NY

Located just west of Gramercy Park on Park Avenue, this home of an advertising association is in the heart of one of the city's most stimulating neighborhoods—a newly burgeoning center of New York's advertising industry and its auxiliary creative services. This modern, elegant facility features two levels of continuous exhibition and meeting space, as well as facilities for formal dining or an informal buffet. Graphic design exhibitions serve as a backdrop.

Capacity: 125 seated/200 cocktails in Main Gallery or Lower Gallery; 400 cocktails in both galleries
In-house caterer
Suggested uses: seminar, conference, auction, exhibit, meeting, fundraiser, public relations event
Note: Private parties, except for weddings, are occasionally allowed.

American Association of University Women
(212) 684-6068
Contact: Executive Secretary

111 East 37th Street
New York, NY 10016

Meeting rooms, patio
Capacity: 70 upstairs; 30 downstairs
Kitchen; food may be served
Space is a brownstone
Suggested uses: meeting, small reception

American Museum of Natural History and the Hayden Planetarium
(212) 799-5350
Contact: Marilyn Badaracco, Manager, Office of Guest Services

Central Park West at 79th Street
New York, NY 10024

Auditorium, 6 theaters, board room, classroom, exhibit space
Guest capacity: 996 in auditorium; 650 in Sky Theater; 600 in Naturemax Theater (IMAX motion picture system); 300 in Guggenheim Space Theater; 299 in Henry Kaufmann Theater; 154 in Harold F. Linder Theater; 80 in People Center; 75 in classrooms
Stages, audio-visual equipment
Suggested uses: lecture, conference, board meeting, workshop, symposia, presentation
Note: Fundraising is not allowed.

Americas Society
(212) 249-8950

680 Park Avenue (68th Street)
New York, NY 10021
Contact: Bea Wolfe

Conference room, reception area
Capacity: 15/110
Platform, piano, kitchen; food may be served
Suggested uses: banquet, concert, lecture, meeting, reception
Note: Space is only available to groups having an inter-American purpose.

Association of the Bar of the City of New York
(212) 382-6638
(212) 382-6637
Contact: Eileen Riley, Director of Meeting Services

42 West 44th Street
New York, NY 10036

Meeting hall, reception room, 9 meeting rooms
Capacity: 270 seated in meeting hall; 200 in reception room; 16/60 in meeting rooms
Resident caterer
Note: Space is only available to corporations and non-profit organizations and only Monday through Thursday from 9 a.m. to 5 p.m., Friday from 9 a.m. to 10 p.m. and Saturday from 9 a.m. to 5 p.m.

AT & T Infoquest Center (212) 605-6907
550 Madison Avenue (56th Street) Contact: Dianna Maeurer
New York, NY 10022
Capacity: 72 in auditorium
Note: Space is only available to non-profit groups on Wednesday, Thursday and Friday evenings.

Business Communication Center (212) 737-7536
(East 34th Street)
New York, NY
This meeting space is on the 3rd floor of an East Side brownstone.
Capacity: 50 in 900 sq. ft. space
Audio-visual equipment; resident caterer
Suggested uses: lecture, meeting, seminar

Catholic Kolping Society (212) 369-6647
165 East 88th Street Contact: Manager
New York, NY 10128
Auditorium, beer hall
Capacity: 130 in auditorium; 50/60 in beer hall
Stage, piano, dance floor; food may be served
Suggested uses: all special events are possible except a fair or promotion

Central Park West Special Function Site (212) 737-7536
(West 60's)
New York, NY
This landmark building offers a variety of function spaces.
Guest capacity: 867 in auditorium; 60 in 19' x 10' x 29' study; 60 in 19' x 6' x 28' library; 285 in 50' x 65' social hall; 150 in 35' x 44' ceremonial hall
14 ft. x 30 ft. stage, platform, 3 Steinway Grand pianos, PA system, dance floor, Wicks Pipe Organ, theatrical lighting, kitchen; food may be served by preferred caterer or bring your own.
Suggested uses: conference, memorial service, committee meeting, wedding, etc.

Church Center for the U.N. (212) 661-1762
777 U.N. Plaza Contact: Lois Washington
New York, NY 10017
3 conference rooms
Capacity: 150 on 2nd floor; 60 on 10th floor; 50 on 12th floor
Note: Space is primarily available during the day to non-profit, tax-exempt groups affiliated with the U.N. Other non-profit groups may apply as well.
Suggested uses: seminar, memorial service

City University of New York Graduate Center (212) 737-7536
Dining Commons
33 West 42nd Street (18th fl.)
New York, NY 10036
Auditorium, meeting rooms, 4 dining/reception rooms
Guest capacity: 246 in auditorium (with adjacent lobby for receptions); up to 40 in meeting rooms; 10/400 in dining rooms
Audio-visual equipment

College of Insurance (212) 962-4111
101 Murray Street Contact: Judy Levi,
New York, NY 10007 Marketing Representative
Auditorium, conference room, classrooms
Capacity: 120 in auditorium; 50/60 in conference room; 25/45 in classrooms
Audio-visual equipment, small kitchen; food may be served
Suggested uses: meeting, seminar
Note: Space is available Monday through Friday usually only during the day.

Department of Cultural Affairs (212) 974-1150
2 Columbus Circle (58th Street) (212) 245-1257
New York, NY 10019 Contact: Ruth Burrell Brown
Auditorium, meeting room
Capacity: 154 in downstairs Mark Goodson Theater; 120 in 9th floor Gauguin Room
16mm and 35mm projectors, Dolby sound; food may be served by caterer of your choice in meeting room
Suggested uses: meeting, conference, reception, recital, reading, screening rooms, etc.
Lounge overlooks Central Park.
Note: Smoking is not allowed in the auditorium or foyer.

Dimele Center (212) 737-7536
(West 57th Street)
New York, NY
Workshop/seminar space; 9 soundproof breakout rooms with phones
Capacity: 140 lecture-style in 1000 sq. ft. of space
Sound system, a/v equipment, TV monitor, VCR, fully carpeted, wall of windows, plants
Space has 24 hour access.
Suggested uses: conference, self-help/psychology/growth workshop

East Side International Community Center, Inc. (212) 371-8604
Contact: Theodora Corsell
330 East 45th Street
New York, NY 10017
Rehearsal space, multi-purpose reception area, meeting room, playground
Capacity: 100 in reception area; 35/40 in meeting room
Dance floor, kitchen; food may be served

Equitable Center Auditorium   (212) 554-8890

787 Seventh Avenue (52nd Street)   Contact: Judy Gray
New York, NY 10019

Auditorium
Capacity: 490
State-of-the-art audio-visual technology, on-site TV studios, stage lighting, portable dance floor, orchestra shell, dressing rooms
Suggested uses: sales/stockholder meeting, lecture, training program, multi-site teleconference, product introduction, artistic performance
Programs and presentations may be broadcast by satellite around the world or taped and edited for later transmission.

Fraunces Tavern Museum   (212) 425-1778

54 Pearl Street   Contact: Andrea Laine,
New York, NY 10004   Public Affairs Associate

Auditorium/conference room
Capacity: 50/200
Cocktails and refreshments may be served.
Space is in a converted sail loft building and is part of museum complex.
Suggested uses: meeting, reception

Grolier Club   (212) 838-6690

47 East 60th Street   Contact: Eleanor Goetz,
New York, NY 10022   Office Manager

Exhibition hall
Capacity: 100/225 seated
Suggested uses: reception, lecture

Historic Blackman House   (212) 832-4540

Roosevelt Island Operating   Contact: Michael Rosa,
Corporation   Director and Counsel of
591 Main Street   Commercial Operations
Roosevelt Island, NY 10044

Situated on a parcel of land in the East River which was purchased from two Indian chiefs by Dutch Governor Wouter van Twiller in 1637, this 2-story clapboard farm house was built by the Blackman family in 1796. It is one of the oldest residences in the City. Recently renovated, the historic house contains six rooms plus a large porch.
Capacity: 50/75
Suggested uses: cocktail party, reception, conference, meeting

Hudson Guild   (212) 760-9808

441 West 26th Street   Contact: Dorothy Bond,
New York, NY 10001   Office Manager

Auditorium, rehearsal space, conference room, meeting rooms, exhibit space, reception area, gymnasium
Capacity: 139 in auditorium; 240 in reception area; 10/50 in meeting rooms
Suggested uses: all special events are possible except a fair, promotion, wedding or religious ceremony

Hunter College of the City University   (212) 772-4282 of New York   Contact: Banquet Department

695 Park Avenue
New York, NY 10021

Dining room, lounge
Capacity: 125 seated in Faculty Staff Dining Room and Lounge
Resident caterer
Suggested uses: reception, dinner, occasional wedding

Japan Society   (212) 832-1155

333 East 47th Street   Contact: Rental Program
New York, NY 10017   Administrative Officer

Auditorium, 3 conference rooms, reception room
Capacity: 275 in Lila Acheson Wallace Auditorium; 30/50 in conference rooms; 12/300 in reception room
Note: Space is only available to non-profit and government groups.

Jewish Guild for the Blind   (212) 769-6200

15 West 65th Street   Contact: Alan R. Morse
New York, NY 10023

Auditorium
Capacity: 250 (flexible seating; may be partitioned for smaller space)
Note: Space is only available to non-profit groups Tuesdays and Thursdays during the day October through May; June through September the space is available any weekday.

The Jewish Museum   (212) 860-1872

1109 Fifth Avenue (92nd Street)   Contact: Roberta Heyman,
New York, NY 10028   Assistant to the Director

Auditorium (Gallery 5)
Capacity: 250 auditorium-style
Stage, platform, PA system; kosher food and beverages only may be served by caterer of your choice
Suggested uses: luncheon, reception, dinner meeting
Museum collections are available for viewing.

John Jay College for Criminal Justice   (212) 489-3500

899 Tenth Avenue (56th Street)   Contact: Yvonne Williams
New York, NY 10019

This conference room features a circular conference table and rosewood furniture. It adjoins a private dining room and two terraces.
Capacity: 25 seated

Lavish Jewish Community Building   (212) 737-7536

(West 80's)
New York, NY

Built in the 1920's and thoroughly restored, this large center offers a great variety of function spaces.
Ballroom, conference room, 2 reception rooms, library, chapel

Capacity: 300 seated in 4000 sq. ft. ballroom; 40 seated in wood-panelled conference room; 200 seated lecture-style in 1400 sq. ft. main reception room; 150 seated lecture-style in 1100 sq. ft. small reception room; 1100 sq. ft. of space is available in Moorish-style chapel
Suggested uses: concert, conference, meeting, poetry reading
Note: Space is not available Friday evenings or during the day on Saturday.

Lenox Hill Neighborhood Association   (212) 744-5022
331 East 70th Street   Contact: Dallas Purdy,
New York, NY 10021   Executive Assistant

Auditorium, small conference rooms, gymnasium, swimming pool
Capacity: 250 in auditorium, 15/40 in each conference room; 400 in gymnasium
Note: Space is only available to non-profit groups. Neighborhood groups are welcome.

Manhattanville Community Centers,   (212) 491-3377
Inc.   (6 to 10 p.m.)
530 West 133rd Street   Contact: Nelson Resto
New York, NY 10027

Auditorium/gym, lounge
Capacity: 450 in auditorium; 50/75 in lounge
Stage, dance floor, kitchen
Rental fee: $350 minimum for gym (up to 5 hours); $150 for lounge
Suggested uses: meeting, reception, etc.

Mechanics Institute   (212) 840-7648
20 West 44th Street   Contact: Robert Kramek
New York, NY 10035

Various-sized classroom space
Capacity: 75 maximum
Rental fee: by donation
Note: This facility is open Mondays through Fridays, including evening hours. No smoking, no food service. Closed during July.

Mercantile Library Association   (212) 755-6710
17 East 47th Street   Contact: Joanna Bendheim
New York, NY 10017

Lecture/library room
Capacity: 65
Suggested uses: class, lecture, meeting, reception
Note: Space is only available in the early evening.

Sam & Esther Minskoff Cultural   (212) 737-6900
Center   Contact: Executive Director
164 East 68th Street
New York, NY 10021

Auditorium/lecture hall, rehearsal space, conference room, ballroom, exhibit space, classrooms, gymnasium
Capacity: 125 in auditorium; 400 in ballroom; 25 in each classroom
Small stage, piano, dance floor, catering facilities; kosher food only may be served

---

Morris-Jumel Mansion   (212) 923-8008
1765 Jumel Terrace   Contact: Susannah Elliott
New York, NY 10032

Built as a summer house in 1765 by Colonel Roger Morris, a retired British officer, it is Manhattan's oldest residence. Aaron Burr, third Vice-President of the United States, was married in the front parlor. The house was bought in 1903 by the City of New York and opened as an historic house and museum in 1904 under the auspices of the Washington Headquarters Association.
Capacity: 75/100 indoors; 125/150 with use of garden
Garden; food may be served by caterer on premises or by caterer of your choice
Suggested uses: luncheon, seminar, meeting, benefit, party, location shoot
Space is available to corporations, foundations, architectural and historical groups.

Museum of Broadcasting   (212) 752-4690 ext. 38
1 East 53rd Street   Contact: Director of Operations
New York, NY 10022

Auditorium, 2 screening rooms
Capacity: 63; 40 in each screening room
Complete technical facilities for video tape projection, ¾" x ½" advent screen

---

New York Academy of Sciences   (212) 838-0230
2 East 63rd Street   Contact: Matthew Katz,
New York, NY 10021   Meeting Services Director

Auditorium, 4 conference/lecture rooms, ballroom, 18' x 18' planted courtyard, exhibit space, reception area, library
Capacity: 20/125
16mm sound motion picture projector, slide projectors, overhead projector, sound system, portable lectern, kitchen; food may be served (kitchen and banquet staff available)
Space is a townhouse.
Suggested uses: banquet, meeting, reception
Note: Space is only available to non-profit groups, particularly those involved in science or medicine, on weekdays.

New York Blood Center   (212) 570-3000
310 East 67th Street   Contact: James Toner,
New York, NY 10021   Administrator

Auditorium, classroom/conference room
Capacity: 348 in auditorium; 40 in classroom
Rental fee: $700 minimum for auditorium; $150 minimum for 3 hour use of classroom
Stage, piano
Suggested uses: class, lecture, meeting

New York Center for Psychoanalytic   (212) 757-9200
Training
Contact: Administrator
1780 Broadway (57th Street)
New York, NY 10019

5 small meeting/consultation rooms
Capacity: 10 in largest room
Available by the hour or by the day for meeting or class.

New York Genealogical &   (212) 755-8532
Biographical Society
Contact: Marion Hartsoe,
122 East 58th Street   Assistant to Executive
New York, NY 10022   Director

Auditorium meeting room
Capacity: 210 in auditorium; 60 in meeting room
Rental fee: $125 donation for auditorium; $160 if food is served
Platform, sound equipment, kitchen; food may be served
Suggested uses: lecture, meeting
Note: Space is only available to historic, cultural and patriotic groups. Admission charges, fundraising and sales are not allowed.

Oval Room   (212) 466-8165
The Port Authority of New York   (201) 622-6600 ext. 8165
& New Jersey   Contact: Paul Brechbiel,
1 World Trade Center   Supervising Special Services
New York, NY 10048   Representative

Meeting room, reception area, lounge
Capacity: 7000 sq. ft. space consists of an outer reception area encompassing an interior room capable of being transformed into 3 separate rooms; 30/220 for a single room; 230 auditorium-style/198 for a luncheon/130 classroom-style
Complete audio-visual equipment; food may be served only by caterer on premises
Suggested uses: press conference, reception, luncheon, seminar, audio-visual presentation, product display

Michael Schulman Theater   (212) 777-3055
7 East 15th Street   Contact: Michael Schulman
New York, NY 10003

Studio
Capacity: 40 in 25' x 50' space
Suggested uses: class, lecture, reading, performance

Seaport Experience Theatre   (212) 737-7536
(South Street Seaport)
New York, NY

Unique theater-style auditorium set in the re-created ambiance of South Street circa 1800. Full multi-media capabilities, including over 100 projectors, for individual presentations. Stage can be set up and theater stylized for specialized use and/or in-house show, The Seaport Experience. Location allows for tie-ins with South Street Seaport restaurants for breakfast, lunch and dinner and all-day functions.
Capacity: 300 seated in theater; 150/200 cocktails or continental service in lobby
Suggested uses: all special events are possible

William Sobelsohn Associates   (212) 244-3900
352 Seventh Avenue (45th Street)   Contact: William Sobelsohn
New York, NY 10036

Classrooms/meeting rooms
Capacity: 20/150
Food may be served

Studio Loft with Roof Terrace   (212) 737-7536
(East 34th Street)
New York, NY

Situated on the 2nd floor of a two story building, this white-walled rectangular studio transforms into a flexible space. Its tented roof garden just one flight up is an added bonus for six months of the year.
Capacity: 75 seated/300 cocktails
State-of-the-art video, fully appointed kitchen; food may be served by caterer of your choice
Suggested uses: meeting, party, commercial usage
Note: Weddings are not allowed.

The Studio Museum in Harlem   (212) 864-4500 ext. 15
144 West 125th Street   Contact: Public Relations Director
New York, NY 10027

Fine arts museum
Capacity: 120 seated/200 standing in Main Floor Gallery; 30 seated/50 standing in Mezzanine Gallery; 50 seated/70 standing in 2nd floor workshop space
Hardwood floors, sound system, film/slide projection and video equipment
Suggested uses: meeting, lecture, concert performance, reception, location shoot

Studios 58 Playhouse, Inc.   (212) 581-7238
Wellington Hotel - Laurelton Room   Contact: Grace Bramson
55th Street & Seventh Avenue
New York, NY 10019

Rehearsal space/conference room/exhibit space
Capacity: 200
Steinway B Grand piano, professional lighting, excellent acoustics
Suggested uses: concert, class, exhibit, lecture, rehearsal, audition, recital

TRS Inc. Professional Suite   **(212) 685-2848**

7 East 30th Street   Contact: Charlie Friedman,
New York, NY 10016   Director

This 2-floor facility has numerous air-conditioned and carpeted rooms which are particularly suitable for workshops in the fields of holistic health, meditation, personal and spiritual growth.
Capacity: 30/75
Rental fee: $10 per hour minimum

Taller Latino Americano   **(212) 777-2250**

The Latin American Workshop, Inc.   Contact: Rental Coordinator
63 East 2nd Street
New York, NY 10003

Auditorium, 6 classrooms, exhibit space, lounge area, cafe, recording studio, editing room
Capacity: 150/200 seated in 1500 sq. ft. auditorium; 15 in each classroom
250 sq. ft. raised platform, professional hard oak dance floor, spot lights, PA system, kitchen; food may be served
Suggested uses: concert, meeting, dance rehearsal, cultural event, film showing, small party

Theodore Roosevelt House   **(212) 260-1616**

20 East 20th Street   Contact: John Lancos,
New York, NY 10003   Site Manager,
    or Catherine Gross, Secretary

Auditorium, library
Capacity: 100 in auditorium; 30 in library
Suggested uses: organizational/alumni association meeting

Tiffany Hall   **(212) 737-7536**

(East 30's)
New York, NY

Meeting hall, conference room
Capacity: 200 theater/144 classroom and banquet-style in meeting hall; 60 theater/45 classroom/30 banquet-style in board room
Rental fee: $125 per hour/$150 per hour weekdays after 5 p.m. for meeting hall; $50 per hour/$65 per hour weekdays after 5 p.m. for conference room. Four-hour minimum
Grand piano, state-of-the-art audio-visual equipment, slide and 16mm and 35mm projectors, wall-to-wall carpeting
Suggested uses: all special events are possible

Village Brownstone   **(212) 737-7536**

(West 13th Street)
New York, NY

Library, parlor room
Capacity: up to 50
Fireplaces, tall windows, small garden, kitchen; food may be served
Suggested uses: meeting, etc.

Women's City Club of New York, Inc.   **(212) 353-8070**

35 East 21st Street   Contact: Ellen Kramer
New York, NY 10010

Conference room
Capacity: 75
Suggested uses: class, lecture, meeting, reception

Workmen's Circle Building   **(212) 889-6800**

45 East 33rd Street   Contact: Mark Eckstein
New York, NY 10016

Auditorium, rehearsal space, conference room, ballroom, exhibit space, reception area, multi-purpose rooms
Capacity: 12/350; 200 banquet-style
Rental fee: by regular contract or single function
Platform, piano, dance floor, kitchen; food may be served

Bronx

Bronx House   **(212) 792-1800**

990 Pelham Parkway South   Contact: Marlene Goldstein
Bronx, NY 10461   (gym); Howard Martin,
    Director of Special Projects
    (all other spaces)

Auditorium, rehearsal space, conference room, roof garden, lounge, meeting rooms, gymnasium, swimming pool
Capacity: 350/400
Stage, platform, piano, dance floor, motion picture projector, PA system, kitchen; kosher or dairy food only may be served

Riverdale-Yonkers Society for Ethical **(212) 548-4445**
Culture   Contact: Mrs. Florence Keller,
4450 Fieldston Road   Secretary
Bronx, NY 10471

Meeting room, rehearsal space, exhibit space, terrace
Capacity: 150 in Society Meeting Room
Rental fee: $75 per hour during day; $200 from 8:30 to 11 p.m.
Piano
Suggested uses: concert, class (no desks), exhibit, lecture, meeting, performance, rehearsal

Brooklyn

Brooklyn Museum   **(718) 638-5000**

200 Eastern Parkway   Contact: Corporate Development
Brooklyn, NY 11238   Office

Lecture hall
Capacity: 300

Queens

Flushing Jewish Center
(718) 358-7071

43-00 171st Street   Contact: Ed Seligman or office
Flushing, NY 11358

Auditorium, rehearsal space, conference room, ballroom
Capacity: 200 in auditorium; 600 in ballroom
Stage, platform, dance floor; food may be served only by Glatt kosher caterer
Suggested uses: all special events are possible including a wedding or bar mitzvah except a fair

Hillcrest Jewish Center
(718) 380-4145

83-02 Union Turnpike   Contact: Eleanor Schaffer
Flushing, NY 11366

Auditorium, ballroom, classroom
Capacity: 400 in auditorium (flexible seating); 400 in ballroom; 30 in each classroom
Piano; kosher food only may be served and only by space's own caterer
Suggested uses: banquet, lecture, meeting, party, reception, wedding

Jewish Center of Bayside Hills
(718) 225-5301

211th Street & 48th Avenue   Contact: Herman Solowey
Bayside, NY 11364

Auditorium/ballroom, conference room, exhibit space, 3 classrooms
Capacity: 200 ballroom-style/300 seated in auditorium; 350/385 in conference room; 35 in each classroom
Stage, piano, dance floor, 2 kitchens; kosher food only may be served
Suggested uses: all special events are possible
Note: Space is only available to non-profit groups.

Langston Hughes Community Library and Cultural Center
(718) 651-1101

102-09 Northern Boulevard   Contact: Andrew Jackson, Executive Director
Corona, NY 11368

Auditorium/exhibit space
Capacity: 150
Rental fee: none during hours when open
Stage, kitchen; food may be served
Suggested use: meeting
Note: Space is only available to community groups.

Staten Island

Richmondtown Restoration
(718) 351-1617

441 Clarke Avenue   Contact: Marie Rachimiel,
Staten Island, NY 10306   Executive Secretary to Barnett Shepherd

Meeting room, exhibit space, historic buildings, pond
Capacity: 75 in auditorium in old Court House; 25 acres of grounds
Rental fee: varies with number of people and location
Platform, winding staircase, kitchen; food may be served
Suggested uses: exhibit, lecture, meeting, outdoor performance, promotion
Note: Space is only available upon approval of the Board of Directors and there are limitations due to the historic nature of the premises.

Westchester

Jewish Community Center of Yonkers
(914) 963-8457

122 South Broadway   Contact: Mr. Martin Greenberg,
Yonkers, NY 10701   Executive Director

Auditorium/exhibit space, theater, classrooms/meeting rooms
Capacity: 225 in auditorium; 125 in theater; 20/60 in classrooms
Stage, piano, kitchen; kosher food only may be served
Suggested uses: meeting, etc.
Note: Space is not available on Saturdays.

Also see: **AUDITORIUMS** (Seating 500 or more)
      CHURCHES
      CONFERENCE CENTERS
      Former Chapel
      HOTELS
      LIBRARIES
      PERFORMANCE SPACES (CONCERT/ RECITAL)
      PERFORMANCE SPACES (DANCE/ THEATER)
      SCHOOLS
      WORKSHOP/SEMINAR SPACES
      Y's

PARKS AND PLAZAS

NEW YORK CITY PARKS

*N*ew *York City parks comprise 26,176 acres of land in its five boroughs. Permits are issued free of charge for cultural and athletic activities. To obtain a special event permit, or to reserve a sporting facility (i.e. baseball field), call the Parks Department Office in the borough which pertains to the location of the event.*

Manhattan	(212) 408-0204
Bronx	(212) 430-1825
Brooklyn	(718) 965-8900
Queens	(718) 520-5911
Staten Island	(718) 390-8000

Note: Wedding ceremonies may be held in any park and do not need permits; wedding receptions must be held elsewhere.

If you wish to attend a special event that is free, call (212) 360-1333 any time of the day or night for a daily tape.

Conservatory Garden in Central Park   (212) 860-1330

(near 105th Street & Fifth Avenue)
New York, NY

Two elaborate French gates which were made in Paris for the Vanderbilt's in 1894 form the entrance to what is New York City's only formal garden. This six-acre site is also the one area in Central Park which is filled with flowers, crab apple trees, wisteria and 30,000 bulbs. Modeled after the great estate gardens of the 1920's and opened in 1937 on the site of Central Park's former greenhouses, it also offers two fountains and a water lily pond. This special site for wedding ceremonies is also suitable for special events by community or corporate groups. Not available for private receptions.

The Dairy   (212) 397-3156
Central Park Conservancy   (212) 397-3165
830 Fifth Avenue   Contact: Heidi Loefkin,
New York, NY 10021   Rental Coordinator

Restored to its 1870 Victorian Gothic charm, this delightful structure was originally designed by the architect Calvert Vaux, associate to landscape architect Frederick Law Olmsted, the creator of Central Park. Presently serving as the Visitor Information Center and located near the zoo and the Carousel, the Dairy's pastoral setting is a rare juxtaposition of repose and innocence in the middle of Manhattan.

Its 59' x 21' Great Hall and 20' high ceiling offer excellent acoustics. The decorative Loggia overlooking the ice skating rink adds a roofed outdoor space.

Capacity: 80 seated (additional guests may be accommodated in Loggia); 150 standing

Food may be served by caterer of your choice.

Prospect Park Picnic House   (212) 737-7536
Brooklyn, NY

Set in the Long Meadow, this 1920s building replaced an earlier open-air rustic wood shelter that stood on the same site to provide shelter for picnickers surprised by inclement weather. Its recent renovation provides a top floor which is available for special events.

Capacity: 175 seated
Rental fee: by permit and contribution
Stage, theatrical lighting

Also see: La Fete au Lac de Central Park

PICNIC AREAS

*P*icnicking is permitted in all the larger parks; barbecuing is *prohibited except where noted.*

The Bronx

Pelham Bay Park, Rice Stadium area, Bruckner Blvd. and Watt Ave. (barbecuing permitted); Orchard Beach.
Van Cortlandt Park, Shandler Recreation Area

Brooklyn

Manhattan Beach (barbecuing permitted)
Prospect Park, Picnic House, shores of Prospect Lake, Nethermead, Long Meadow

Manhattan

Central Park, Sheep Meadow, East Meadow, Pool Shores
Riverside Park, W. 93rd to W. 98th Sts., W. 147th to W. 152nd Sts.

Queens

Barbecuing is permitted in the following specified areas:
Alley Pond Park, between Springfield Blvd. & 76th Ave.
Cunningham Park, 193rd St. & Union Turnpike
Flushing Meadows Corona Park, between Jewel Ave. and Van Wyck Expwy.
Forest Park, Forest Park Dr. & Interborough Pkwy.
Kissena Park, Oak & Rose Aves.
Francis Lewis Park, between 147th St., Third Ave. and East River
Rockaway Beach, at Beach 17th, Beach 88th and Beach 98th Sts.

Staten Island

Clove Lakes, Willowbrook and Wolfe's Pond Parks
Note: Picnickers need to supply their own grills for use on grill slabs. Grilling, flames or fires of any sort are not permitted at sites without grill slabs and an adult must be present to supervise the fire.

Also see: COMPANY PICNIC SITES
Gateway National Recreation Area

NEW YORK STATE PARKS IN NEW YORK CITY

Clay Pit Ponds State Park Preserve   **(718) 967-1976**
83 Nielson Avenue   Contact: John Wood,
(Charleston section)   Park Supervisor
Staten Island, NY 10309
Preserve comprises most of the 250 acres. Programs relate mainly to environmental education. Interpretive programs with guided tours on trails.

Empire Fulton Ferry State Park   **(212) 858-4708**
New Dock Street   Contact: Assistant
Brooklyn, NY 11201   Regional Director
2-acre waterfront park with boardwalk comprised mainly of a lawn area with plants.
Overlooks East River and lower Manhattan skyline.
Suggested use: location shoot
Note: Permit is necessary for a location shoot. Weekend concerts and performances are open to the public. Space is only available during the spring and summer.

Harbor Park   **(212) 406-3434**
Seaport Line   Contact: Seaport Line
19 Fulton Street, Suite 406   Management
South Street Seaport
New York, NY 10036
This is New York City's designated New York State Urban Cultural Park. It includes Battery Park and South Street Seaport in Manhattan, Fulton Ferry/Empire Stores in Brooklyn, Snug Harbor Cultural Center in Staten Island, and the Statue of Liberty and Ellis Island.
Waterborne transportation is provided by the South Street Seaport's excursion boat, the Andrew Fletcher. Urban Park Rangers give historical interpretations on the maritime and immigration history on the harbor during the course of the tour.

Roberto Clemente State Park   **(212) 299-8750**
(State Park & Recreation   Contact: Richard Ortiz,
Commission for the City of New York)   Park Director or
West Tremont & Matthewson Road   Clarence Ware,
Bronx, NY 10453   Recreation Supervisor
Rehearsal space, conference room, promenade space, exhibit space, gymnasium with bleachers, swimming pool, playgrounds, basketball court, baseball field, picnic areas, outdoor concert areas
Capacity: 630 in gymnasium
Rental fee: none
Note: Space is only available for use with a permit.

URBAN GARDENS

Department of General Services   **(212) 233-2926**
Operation Green Thumb   Contact: Jane Weissman,
49 Chambers Street   Director
New York, NY 10007
City-owned lots throughout the five boroughs are leased to community groups for $1.00 a year to be developed into urban gardens, play areas or sitting areas. Technical assistance will be provided whenever possible. Shrubs, seeds, soil, tools and lumber will be provided to lease holding groups who qualify. Design consulting services provided on a long term basis. Groups with proven track records can apply for long term leases of 5 to 10 years.

Open Space Greening Program   **(212) 566-0990**
Plant a Lot Project
c/o Council on the Environment
51 Chambers Street, Room 228
New York, NY 10007

This program has resulted in close to 20 community parks/gardens due to the volunteer labor of love donated by New York City residents who wished to transform empty, rubble-strewn lots into lush neighborhood gardens. Some of these feature lily ponds, rose gardens, fruit trees, lawns, colorful seasonal plantings, wrought iron fences, gazebos, terraced amphitheaters, barbecue pits, teak benches, woodchip paths and arboretums.

Call for further information on both volunteer participation in this greening program or possible rental of a garden for a special function.

PLAZAS/MINI PARKS

*T*he following outdoor urban rest stops, which are primarily corporate-sponsored, are not available for rent, but are important spaces for sitting, thinking, waiting and people watching. Some have snack bars and offer cultural entertainment. Also waterfalls.

Bethune Senior Center   **(212) 862-6700**
1949 Amsterdam Avenue   Contact: Rosie Eugene
(157th Street)
New York, NY 10032
Mall
Piano
Food may be served
Space is usually available during the summer and during the day in the winter for free performances.

Burlington House   **(212) 752-5000** (Yodice)
1345 Avenue of the Americas   **(212) 581-7795** (Dine)
(55th Street)   Contact: Robert Yodice,
New York, NY 10019   Executive General Manager or
Nick Dine, Building Manager

Channel Gardens
Rockefeller Center
Fifth Avenue (50th Street)

Chase Manhattan Plaza
55 Water Street

Exxon Mini-Park
1251 Avenue of the Americas (50th Street)
535 Madison Avenue (54th Street)

Foley Square   **(212) 732-0414**
(near Municipal Building &   Contact: Joe Giovani or
Federal Courthouse)   Arthur Tisi
Capacity: 400/1000
Cobblestone plaza is available 7 days a week, 24 hours a day.
12 international food stalls
Suggested uses: performance, location shoot
Note: Mailing address is Plaza Cafe Catering Corporation, 133 Mulberry Street, New York, NY 10013.

Grand Army Plaza,
Fifth Ave. & Central Park South (59th Street)

Greenacre Park
217-221 East 51st Street

Hunters Point   **(212) 619-1955**
Long Island City, NY
A weedy hillside overlooking the East River and Manhattan

International Paper Plaza
1166 Sixth Avenue (46th Street)

Lincoln Center Plazas   **(212) 877-1800**
Lincoln Center for the   Contact: Leonard de Paur
Performing Arts, Inc.
140 West 65th Street
New York, NY 10023
Outdoor plazas with display fountain and reflecting pool
Stage, sound equipment

McGraw Park
1221 Avenue of the Americas (48th Street)

127 John Street   **(212) 943-9355**
Sage Realty   Contact: Richard Brook
New York, NY 10038

Paley Park
3 East 52nd Street

Plaza Esplanade
(World Financial Center & Battery Park City)

St. Andrew's Plaza
Foley Square (Center and Reade Street)

77 Water Street   **(212) 422-7277**
Sage Realty   Contact: Richard Brook
New York, NY 10005

Socrates Sculpture Park   **(718) 545-7142**
Hallets Cove
Long Island City

Vietnam Veterans Memorial Plaza
(Jeannette Park, lower Manhattan)

Wall Street Plaza
Water Street (Pine & Maiden Lane)

World Trade Center Plaza   **(212) 466-4233**
The Port Authority of New York   Contact: Sandra Ward,
and New Jersey   Public Services
1 World Trade Center   Coordinator
New York, NY 10048
Comprises 5 acres of outdoor space

Also see: ATRIUMS
           Botanical Garden in Queens
           Brooklyn Botanic Garden
           New York Botanical Garden
           PARTY PLACES/New York City

For PENTHOUSES, ROOF GARDENS and TERRACES see:
VIEWS

PERFORMANCE SPACES (CONCERT/RECITAL)

Abraham Goodman House   **(212) 362-8060**
Home of the Hebrew Arts School   Contact: Paula Mayo,
129 West 67th Street   Theater Manager
New York, NY 10023
Concert hall (Merkin Hall), recital hall, exhibit hall, music
   library, music practice studios, 2 dance studios
Capacity: 457 in Merkin Hall; 130 in recital hall
35' x 26' concert stage, platform, piano, dance floor, dressing
   rooms
Suggested uses: concert, rehearsal, recording, audition

Alice Tully Hall   **(212) 580-8700**
Lincoln Center for the   Contact: Delmar Hendricks,
Performing Arts, Inc.   Booking Manager
65th Street & Broadway
New York, NY 10023
Auditorium
Capacity: 1096
21'6 deep x 38' across back x 50' across front stage, piano,
   motion picture projector, sound equipment; food may be
   served only by caterer on premises

Avery Fisher Hall   **(212) 580-8700**
Lincoln Center for the   Contact: Delmar Hendricks,
Performing Arts, Inc.   Booking Manager
Lincoln Center Plaza
65th Street & Broadway
New York, NY 10023
Auditorium
Capacity: 2738
40'4 deep x 45' x 8 across back x 68' across front stage, piano,
   motion picture projector; food may be served only by space's
   own caterer

Bloomingdale House of Music   (212) 663-6021

323 West 108th Street   Contact: Director
New York, NY 10025

Auditorium, limited rehearsal space, lounge, reception room, classrooms, library, small garden
Capacity: 80 in auditorium
Rental fee: negotiable
Space is a townhouse.
Suggested uses: musically oriented events only are allowed
Note: Space has limited availability.

Brooklyn College   (718) 780-5296

Bedford Avenue & Avenue H   Contact: Richard Grossberg
Brooklyn, NY 11210

2 auditoriums
Capacity: 2482 in Whitman Hall (professional concert hall); 504 in Gershwin Hall
Rental fee: $2,650 for Whitman Hall; $1,100 for 5 hours in Gershwin Hall
Stage, platform, piano, 35mm motion picture projector, sound equipment, concert lighting
Suggested uses: concert, video taping and filming; light refreshments may be served

Cami Hall   (212) 841-9650

(formerly Judson Hall)   Contact: Richard E. Hansen,
165 West 57th Street   Manager or Dolores Hewlett,
New York, NY 10019   Assistant Manager

Concert hall
Capacity: 240
Rental fee: varies with day and time from $300 to $400; hourly rates vary from $24 to $36. Additional charge for other services and equipment.
Stage, platform, concert grand pianos, concert lighting
Suggested uses: auction, concert, class, exhibit, lecture, meeting, rehearsal, performance, promotion, audition

The Carnegie Hall Corporation   (212) 903-9600

Weill Recital Hall   Contact: Gilda Barlas
154 West 57th Street   Weissberger, Booking Manager
New York, NY 10019

Main Hall, recital hall, rehearsal space
Capacity: 2804 in Main Hall; 268 in recital hall
40' x 60' x 43' stage, piano and sound equipment in Main Hall; stage and piano in recital hall
Suggested uses: concert, lecture, meeting, performance

Greenwich House Music School   (212) 242-4770

46 Barrow Street   Contact: Dan Tucker,
New York, NY 10014   Assistant Registrar

Auditorium, rehearsal space, classroom, exhibit space, courtyard/garden
Capacity: 80 in Renee Weiler Concert Hall; 30 in classroom
Rental fee: $225 for auditorium and courtyard; varies per hour for rehearsal space and classroom
Stage, 2 pianos, harpsichord
Music oriented groups are particularly welcome.
Suggested uses: concert, chamber ensemble, class, exhibit, lecture, meeting, performance, reception

The Harlem School of the Arts   (212) 926-4100

645 St. Nicholas Avenue   Contact: Zoe Friedman,
(141st Street)   Program Coordinator
New York, NY 10030

Auditorium, rehearsal space, classroom, reception area, dance studios
Capacity: approximately 125 in auditorium
Stage, piano, kitchen; food may be served
Suggested uses: concert, class, lecture, meeting, performance, reception

Library and Museum of the Performing Arts   (212) 870-1613

                      Contact: Joan Canale
111 Amsterdam Avenue (65th Street)
New York, NY 10023

Auditorium, conference room, exhibit space
Capacity: 212
Rental fee: none if event is open to the public
Stage, piano, motion picture projectors, sound equipment; food may be served

Metropolitan Opera Association   (212) 799-3100 ext. 2203

                      Contact: Dan O'Leary,
Lincoln Center for the Performing   Assistant House Manager
Arts, Inc.
Lincoln Center Plaza
Broadway & 63rd Street
New York, NY 10023

Auditorium
Capacity: 4000
54' x 54' proscenium stage; food may be served only by space's own caterer

Museum of the City of New York   (212) 534-1672

103rd Street & Fifth Avenue   Contact: Education Department
New York, NY 10029

Auditorium
Capacity: 248

Radio City Music Hall   (212) 246-4600
1260 Avenue of the Americas   Contact: Sales Department
(50th Street)
New York, NY 10020
Auditorium, rehearsal space, reception areas, exhibit space
Capacity: 5874 in auditorium
144' x 66 ½' proscenium stage, piano, motion picture projector
   and screen, Dolby sound system, stage elevators, turntable,
   organ production and special events staff
Suggested uses: all special events are possible including a concert, performance or convention

Symphony Space, Inc.   (212) 864-1414
2537 Broadway (95th Street)   Contact: Patricia Sinnott,
New York, NY 10025   Booking Director
Auditorium, rehearsal space
Capacity: 885
Stage, platforms, pianos
Space is a non-profit community performing arts center.
Suggested uses: concert, dance, reading

Town Hall   (212) 997-1003
123 West 43rd Street   Contact: Phoebe Planick
New York, NY 10036
Concert hall
Capacity: 1500
Stage, piano
Space is a 68-year-old landmark listed in the National Register
   of Historic Places.
Suggested uses: recital, chamber music, concert, lecture, dance,
   children's show, graduation

Turtle Bay Music School   (212) 753-8811
244 East 52nd Street   Contact: Executive Director
New York, NY 10022
Concert hall
Capacity: 175
Rental fee: varies with function
Stage, piano, sound equipment, stationary spot lights
Suggested uses: meeting, recital, play

Bronx

Lehman College Center for the   (212) 960-8232
Performing Arts   Contact: Managing Director
Bedford Park Boulevard West
Bronx, NY 10468
Concert hall, theater
Capacity: 2310 in concert hall; 500 in theater

Brooklyn

Regina Center   (718) 232-4340
1258 65th Street   Contact: Fr. Zeni
Brooklyn, NY 11219
Auditorium, classroom, gymnasium
Capacity: 70 in auditorium; 500 in gymnasium
Rental fee: $50 to $1,600 donation
Stage, kitchen; food may be served
Suggested uses: auction, class, dance, lecture, meeting, party,
   performance, wedding

Long Island

Five Towns Music and Art   (516) 569-0011
Foundation   Contact: Mrs. Rena Sandler,
Broadway & Johnson Place   Executive Secretary
Woodmere, NY 11598
Auditorium, conference/music room
Capacity: 300 in auditorium (flexible seating); 40/60 in con-
   ference room
Stage, piano, dance floor; refreshments may be served
Suggested uses: all special events are possible except a banquet,
   professional dance, fair, promotion, reception or wedding

Also see: **AUDITORIUMS**
            BANDSHELLS
            Bargemusic, Ltd.
            CHURCHES
            Equitable Center Auditorium
            Lavish Jewish Community Building
            LIBRARIES
            Manhattan Center
            PARKS & PLAZAS
            PERFORMANCE SPACES
               (DANCE/THEATER)
            PIERS
            SCHOOLS & COLLEGES

BANDSHELLS

The Bronx

Poe Park   **(212) 822-4705**
East 192nd St. & Grand Concourse

Brooklyn

Asser Levy/Seaside Park   **(718) 783-3077**
Seabreeze Ave. & West 5th St.

Prospect Park   **(718) 788-0055**
11th St., Prospect Park West

Manhattan

Guggenheim, Damrosch Park,   **(212) 397-3159**
Lincoln Center
West 62nd St. & Amsterdam Ave.

Richard Rodgers, Marcus Garvey   **(212) 397-3135**
Park
122nd St. & Mt. Morris Park West (near Fifth Ave.)

Central Park Mall   **(212) 397-3120**
72nd St., midpark

Tompkins Square Park   **(212) 397-3109**
East 7th St. & Ave. A

Queens

Seuffert, Forest Park   **(718) 520-5990**
Forest Park Dr. near Woodhaven Blvd.

PERFORMANCE SPACES (DANCE/THEATER)

Acme Bar and Grill   **(212) 420-1934**
9 Great Jones Street   Contact: Sharon Bernard
New York, NY 10003
Performance/restaurant space
Capacity: 60 seated/100 cocktails
22' x 12' stage, dance floor, PA system, dressing rooms

Actors and Directors Lab   **(212) 695-5429**
(Theater Row)   Contact: Jane MacPherson,
412 West 42nd Street   Manager
New York, NY 10036
2 theaters, rehearsal studios, reception area
Capacity: 90/110
Proscenium stage, dance floor, complete lighting facilities
Suggested uses: concert, class, lecture, meeting, performance

Actors Institute   **(212) 924-8888**
48 West 21st Street (4th fl.)   Contact: Twila Thompson,
New York, NY 10010   General Manager
2 rehearsal studios
Capacity: 23' x 43' with stage/23' x 40' without stage; 23' x 20'
   in smaller studio
Rental fee: $18 per hour for larger studio; $15 per hour for
   smaller studio
Pianos

Actor's Playhouse   (212) 741-1215

100 Seventh Avenue South   Contact: Jack Ross or
(Bleecker & Grove)   Charles Timm, Producers
New York, NY 10014

Auditorium
Capacity: 165
30' x 28' proscenium stage, piano; food may be served
Suggested uses: concert, class, lecture, meeting, party, performance, promotion, off-Broadway play

and

Playhouse 91   (212) 831-2001

316 East 91st Street
New York, NY 10028

Theater
Capacity: 299
25' x 50' stage, piano, large lobby and mezzanine
Suggested uses: concert, class, meeting, party, performance, promotion, off-Broadway play, film location

---

The American Mime Theatre   (212) 777-1710

24 Bond Street   Contact: Paul J. Curtis,
New York, NY 10012   Director or Jean Barbour,
    Administrator

Studio/rehearsal space
Capacity: 50 in 25' x 80' space
Inner stage
Suggested uses: class, lecture, meeting, rehearsal

American Theatre of Actors   (212) 581-3044

314 West 54th Street   Contact: James Jennings
New York, NY 10019

3 indoor performance spaces, 1 outdoor performance space
Capacity: 40 in 20' x 18' space; 70 in 23' x 23' space; 99 in 45' x 22' space
Proscenium or three-quarter stages, professional sound and lighting equipment, dimmer board

---

Apple Corps Theatre Company   (212) 929-2955

336 West 20th Street   Contact: John Raymond,
New York, NY 10011   Artistic Director or Neal
    Arluck, Managing Director

Theater, meeting room
Capacity: 175 in fixed seat theater; 30 in meeting room
Stage, sound system, piano
Suggested uses: concert, class, lecture, meeting, performance

---

Bouwerie Lane Theatre   (212) 677-0060

330 Bowery   Contact: Stewart Russell,
New York, NY 10012   General Manager

Auditorium/theater, rehearsal space, reception area
Capacity: 140 in auditorium
30' x 16' x 25' proscenium stage
Space is a landmark listed in the National Register of Historic Places.
Suggested uses: auction, concert, class, lecture, meeting, party, performance, film location

CSC: Classic Stage Company   (212) 677-4210

136 East 13th Street   Contact: Ellen Novack,
New York, NY 10003   Managing Director

Theater
Capacity: 180 (flexible seating)
1000 sq. ft. black box stage with 20' grid height, sound and lighting equipment, large lobby, dressing rooms
Suggested uses: concert, class, performance, lecture, meeting, reception, party

---

Calderon Productions Studios   (212) 262-9878

1628 Broadway (50th Street)   Contact: Mr. Des
New York, NY 10019   Calderon or Andrea Bocca

2 studios
Capacity: 200 in 400 sq. ft. and 1300 sq. ft. spaces; 2500 sq. ft. in total
Rental fee: hourly rates
Mirrors, barres
Suggested uses: rehearsal, audition, class

Charas/New Assembly Performance Space   (212) 982-0627 (212) 533-6835

350 East 10th Street   Contact: Emily Rubin or
New York, NY 10009   Chino Garcia

Theater, Terraza room/theater, classroom
Capacity: 390 in theater; 100 in 28' x 45' Terraza room; 21' x 21' of space available in classroom; 25' x 45' of space available in hardwood floor gymnasium
Rental fee: $8 to $10 per hour (excluding lighting equipment) day or evening; extended use negotiable
25' x 30' proscenium stage, upright piano, sound and lighting equipment, 12' ceilings minimum, kitchen; food may be served
Suggested uses: class, social or professional dance, meeting, performance, benefit

and

La Terraza

360 East 10th Street
New York, NY 10009

Cabaret-style theater
Capacity: 100
Flexible stage, piano, sound and lighting equipment, bar; food may be served
Suggested uses: performance, rehearsal

Chez White Mask Theatre Corporation   (212) 683-9332

22 West 30th Street (3rd fl.)   Contact: Doloris Holmes,
New York, NY 10001   Director

Theater in the round/rehearsal space/classroom/exhibit space
Capacity: 50/74
Piano, organ, dance floor
Suggested uses: all special events are possible, especially an art or health-related workshop, except an auction, banquet, fair or reception

Circle In the Square (Uptown)

(212) 307-2700

1633 Broadway (50th Street)
New York, NY 10019

Contact: Paul Libin,
Producing Director

Theater in the round
Capacity: 680
Suggested uses: concert, corporate meeting, dance, fashion show
Note: Space is only available on dark nights.

and

Circle In The Square (Downtown)

159 Bleecker Street
New York, NY 10012

Contact: Theodore Mann,
Artistic Director and Owner

Theatre in the round, rehearsal space
Capacity: 299

City Center 55th Street Theater

(212) 247-0430

131 West 55th Street
New York, NY 10019

Contact: Bill Sensenbrenner,
Assistant Director of Theater Operations

Built in 1923 by the members of the Ancient Accepted Order of the Mystic Shrine, this unique performance space looks like a Moorish temple. Presently this center is renowned as a national performing arts institution and a premiere dance theater.

In addition to its grand performance space, this facility also offers a 42 ft. x 36 ft. Studio with a 13 ft. ceiling.

Capacity: 2731 in Orchestra, Mezzanine, 1st and 2nd Balcony; 75 in Studio
Suggested uses for Studio: rehearsal, workshop, audition, meeting
Note: Special rental rates for non-profit groups.

Comedy Elite & First Amendment Improvisation Company

(212) 677-1409

Contact: Barbara Gray

2 Bond Street (Broadway & Lafayette)
New York, NY 10012

Capacity: 100 seated/200 for a party in 2000 sq. ft. space
25' x 10' stage, piano, long bar
Suggested uses: all special events are possible
Note: Space is not available on Friday or Saturday evenings.

Courtyard Playhouse

(212) 765-9540

39 Grove Street
New York, NY 10014

Contact: Bob Stark

Theater
Capacity: 75
18' x 22 ½' stage, fully equipped
Suggested uses: performance
Note: Space only rents on a month-to-month basis.

Creative Space

(212) 645-1630

134 Fifth Avenue (18th Street)
New York, NY 10011

Contact: Sherry Nehmer

Studio, lounge
Capacity: 150 in 1000 sq. ft. studio
Piano, oak floors, mirrors
Suggested uses: rehearsal, performance, meeting, reading, exercise class, showcase, party

Cubiculo

(212) 265-2139

414 West 51st Street
New York, NY 10009

Contact: Mark Barreiro,
Administrative Director

2 theaters
Capacity: 74 in 24' x 48' theater; 50 in 24' x 40' theater
Sound system, theatrical lighting
Suggested uses: performance, rehearsal, lecture, audition

Dan Wagoner and Dancers

(212) 334-1882

476 Broadway
(Broome & Grand, 4th fl.)
New York, NY 10013

Contact: Karen Kooster,
Company Manager

Rehearsal studio
Capacity: 24' x 50' of space is available
Piano, 24' x 50' Marley dance floor, mirrors, 2 dressing rooms, 12' ceilings

Dance Center

(212) 737-7536

(West 50's)
New York, NY

4 studios
Capacity: 300/400 maximum; 50/100 in each studio
Sound system, piano, hardwood floors, film projection and video equipment
Suggested uses: performance, fashion show, party
Note: Space is only available on weekdays after 7:30 p.m. and after 5 p.m. on Saturday and Sunday.

Dance Concepts Studio

(212) 757-1941

231 West 54th Street
New York, NY 10019

Contact: Ms. Eval

3 studios
Capacity: 70 in 25' x 60' studio; 30 in 18' x 35' studio; 150 in 25' x 60' studio with 18' ceiling with skylights on top floor
Pianos, mirrors, sound equipment
Suggested uses: rehearsal, performance, meeting, party, location shoot

Dance Notation Bureau

(212) 807-7899 (receptionist)
(212) 674-4979 (Allison)

33 West 21st Street
New York, NY 10010

Contact: Receptionist or
Sharna Allison (after 6 p.m.
and weekends)

Studio
Capacity: 24 x 40 sq. ft. of space is available
Piano, 2 dressing rooms
Suggested uses: rehearsal

Dance Space, Inc.

(212) 777-8067

622 Broadway (Houston, 6th fl.)
New York, NY 10012

Contact: Michelle Miller
or James Garvey

5 studio spaces
Capacity: 150 on 2 floors in studios ranging from 20' x 16 to 80' x 50'
Hardwood triple sprung floor, piano, windows, mirrors

Dance Theater Workshop, Inc.　(212) 691-6500

Bessie Schonberg Theater　Contact: Michelle Miller,
219 West 19th Street (2nd fl.)　Business Manager
New York, NY 10011

Black box theater, dance studio

Capacity: 100 in theater; 31' x 35' of space is available in studio

25' x 32' performing area with wings in place (25' x 48' without wings), piano, dance floor, theatrical lighting, sound equipment, wood floor in studio

Performance space books fairly far in advance. Applications accepted as of January 1st are applied for following performance year. Class and rehearsal space available on shorter notice.

Suggested uses: dance performance, rehearsal, dance class, exhibit, theater or music event, audition, showing

Danse Mirage Theatre/Elinor　(212) 226-5767
Coleman Dance Studio　Contact: Marie Tinsley or

153 Mercer Street (2nd fl.)　Elinor Coleman
New York, NY 10012

Performance/rehearsal studio

Capacity: 50 seated on folding chairs plus 30 on floor mats for performance in 60 x 20 sq. ft. space

Rental fee: $8 to $10 for a rehearsal; $15 to $40 for a class or workshop; $150 for a dance or music performance

Sprung oak floor, 14 ft. ceiling, dressing room, stage lights, lightboard, mirrors, portable dance barres

Donnell Library Center　(212) 621-0613

20 West 53rd Street　Contact: Philip Gerrard
New York, NY 10019

Auditorium, exhibit space

Capacity: 278

Rental fee: varies with profit-making or non-profit group

26½' x 12' proscenium stage, piano, 16mm motion picture projector, sound equipment

Douglas Fairbanks Theater and　(212) 564-3643
Studio Complex　Contact: Gail Bell

432 West 42nd Street
New York, NY 10036

Theater, studio, courtyard

Capacity: 199 in off-Broadway theater; 45 in studio

Proscenium stage (in theater), piano, dance floor; food may be served

East Harlem Arts & Education　(212) 427-2244
Complex　Contact: Robert North or

The Heckscher Building　Clarence Wilkins
1230 Fifth Avenue (104th Street)
New York, NY 10029

Theater, rehearsal/dance space, classrooms, conference room, exhibit space, reception area, gymnasium, outdoor roof

Capacity: 667 in theater; 10/50 in classrooms; 100 in Conference Room 201; 200 in reception area; 200/300 in gymnasium; 1000 on outdoor roof

40' x 30' proscenium stage, wood dance floor, murals, kitchen; food may be served

Suggested uses: all special events are possible

Edison Theatre　(212) 302-2255

240 West 47th Street　Contact: Doris Buberl
New York, NY 10036

Theater, rehearsal space, lounge, dressing rooms

Capacity: 500

34' x 20' stage, piano, motion picture projector and screen; food may be served

Suggested uses: lecture, sales meeting, fashion show, industrial conference, audition

Note: Space is only available during the day. An additional rehearsal space is also available.

Elisa Monte Dance Company　(212) 982-4264

39 Great Jones Street　Contact: Susan Jagendorf,
New York, NY 10012　General Manager

Rehearsal studio

Capacity: 24 x 36 sq. ft. of space is available

Sprung maple floor, barres, mirror

Note: Space is only available weekdays from 10 to 6 p.m.

Elizabeth Streb Dance Studio　(212) 966-6923

309 Canal Street (3rd fl.)　Contact: Peter Larose
New York, NY 10013

Dance studio

25' x 60' wood floor with Marley surface, mirrors, windows, 12' ceiling

Rental fee: $8 per hour

Suggested uses: rehearsal

First Run Studios　(212) 760-9310

306 West 40th Street　Contact: Joe Lanteri or
New York, NY 10018　Dan Wolgemuth

4 studios; lounge/reception area

Capacity: 20 in 24' x 13' space; 30 in 24' x 18' space and 25 in 35' x 16' space; 50 in 48' x 18' space; 40 in lounge

Mirrors, pianos, sound system

Suggested uses: rehearsal, audition, class, party

Foundation for the Advance of Dance　(212) 989-2250

55 Bethune Street (630A)　Contact: Deborah Shears
New York, NY 10014

Rehearsal space

Capacity: 30' x 35' of space is available

Dance floor, mirrors, barres

Overlooks the Hudson River

Suggested uses: rehearsal, small performance, class

Foundation for Vital Arts Inc. (212) 475-1065
Eleo Pomare Dance Company (212) 475-1297
33 East 18th Street Contact: Minet Garcilazo
New York, NY 10003
4 dance studios, performance space
Capacity: 20/30 in 2 smaller studios; 30/50 in 2 larger studios; 100 in performance space; a total of 15,000 sq. ft. of space is available
Wood floors, dressing rooms, professional sound and lighting equipment
Suggested uses: class, rehearsal, casting

French Institute (212) 737-7536
(East 60's)
New York, NY
Well situated between Madison and Park Avenues, this location offers two spaces which are particularly suited for a performance, dance, concert, film or lecture.
Capacity: 120 seated in auditorium; 400 seated in Florence Gould Hall
Stand-up receptions are allowed when connected to a performance or lecture.

Gene Frankel Theatre Workshop, Inc. (212) 777-1710
Contact: Manager
24 Bond Street
New York, NY 10012
Theater, rehearsal space
Capacity: 77 in 23' x 80' theater space; 40 in 23' x 60' rehearsal space
2 pianos; 20 ft. ceiling in performance space
Suggested uses: performance, class, workshop

Harlequin Rehearsal Studio (212) 819-0120
203 West 46th Street Contact: Desk Manager
New York, NY 10036
13 rehearsal rooms, conference rooms
Capacity: 2/30
Platform, pianos, dance floor; food may be served
Suggested uses: all special events are possible except a banquet, reception or wedding

Harry (212) 334-1910
476 Broadway (Broome & Grand) Contact: Dominik Balletta
New York, NY 10012
Studio
Capacity: 25 x 55 sq. ft. of space is available
Rental fee: $9 per hour; long term discounts
Maple dance floor

Hunter College Central Reservations (212) 772-4869
695 Park Avenue (67th Street) Contact: Reservations
New York, NY 10021
Assembly hall, playhouse
Capacity: 2185 in assembly hall; 692 in playhouse
Rental fee: $2,500 for assembly hall; 1,500 for playhouse (technical assistance costs are included)
Stage, piano

Irish Arts Center (212) 757-3318
553 West 51st Street Contact: Kurt Wagemann
New York, NY 10019
Rehearsal space
Capacity: 85
20' x 20' stage, platform, dance floor
Note: Space is only available Monday through Friday during the day.

The Isadora Duncan Dance Foundation (212) 691-5040
Contact: Lori Belilove or Jaxon Flores
Lori Belilove Dance Studio
141 West 26th Street (3rd fl.)
New York, NY 10001
Rehearsal studio
Capacity: 75 seated/125 standing in 30' x 40' space
Rental fee: $12 to $25 per hour
Piano, sound system, dressing rooms, hardwood floor, kitchen, 800 sq. ft. landscaped terrace
Suggested uses: rehearsal, workshop, exercise class, social function

Jacob Riis Houses Amphitheater (212) 228-2400
454 East 10th Street Contact: Manager
New York, NY 10009
Amphitheater
Capacity: 800 plus 100/500 standees
Rental fee: none
Note: Space is only available to non-profit community groups, not of a religious or political nature, especially during the summer.

James Weldon Johnson Community Centers, Inc. (212) 860-7250
Contact: Nicole Brisbon, Receptionist or Barbara Skinner, Executive Director
2205 First Avenue (114th Street)
New York, NY 10029
Auditorium, outdoor recreation area
Capacity: 300 in auditorium; 500 in outdoor recreation area
Stage, platform, dance floor; food may be served
Suggested uses: all special events are possible except a promotion

Joy of Movement   (212) 260-0453

400 Lafayette Street   Contact: Diane Grumet,
New York, NY 10003   Art Director

Rehearsal space, exhibit space, reception area, 5 studios
Capacity: 17,000 sq. ft. of space is available; 15,000 sq. ft. of
  studio space
Piano, dance floor; food may be served
Soho loft environment
Suggested uses: auction, banquet, concert, class, exhibit, lecture,
  meeting, party, promotion, reception, wedding

The Joyce Theater   (212) 691-9740

175 Eighth Avenue (19th Street)   Contact: Martin Wechsler,
New York, NY 10011   Booking Manager

Auditorium, rehearsal space, conference room, reception area
Capacity: 474 in auditorium; 15 in conference room
Suggested uses: dance, theatrical performance

Kraine Club   (212) 982-7118

85 East 4th Street   Contact: Denis Woychuk
New York, NY 10003

Capacity: 60 seated or standing upstairs; 125 seated or standing
  in 2000 sq. ft. main hall
Piano, hardwood floors, kitchen

Laban Institute for Movement   (212) 689-0740
Studies   Contact: Rental Office

31 West 27th Street
New York, NY 10001

3 studios, body work/therapy room
Capacity: 600 sq. ft., 1150 sq. ft., 1400 sq. ft. of space is available
  in the studios; 100 sq. ft. in body work room
Upright piano, Marley wood floor, dressing room, portable ballet
  barres
Suggested uses: rehearsal, class, workshop

Lamb's Theater   (212) 997-0210
   (212) 575-0300

130 West 44th Street
New York, NY 10036   Contact: Stephen Nebgen,
   Business Manager

2 professional theaters, ballroom, board room, library, restaurant
Capacity: 99/350 in theaters; 220 in ballroom; 20 in board room;
  60 in library; 125 in Sanctuary Restaurant
Stage, platform, piano, fireplace, kitchen; catering is available
  or bring your own
Suggested uses: banquet, theater performance, fundraiser, loca-
  tion shoot
Note: Alcoholic beverages and smoking are not allowed.

Latin American Theatre Ensemble   (212) 246-7478

175 East 104th Street   Contact: Margarita Toirac
New York, NY 10029

Theater
Capacity: 75 in 2000 sq. ft. space (flexible seating)
Rental fee: $100 per night; $12 for a rehearsal
Proscenium stage
Suggested uses: performance, meeting, party

Lucille Lortel Theatre   924-2817

121 Christopher Street   Contact: Ben Sprecher,
New York, NY 10014   General Manager

Theater
Capacity: 299
Rental fee: negotiable
22' x 24' thrust stage, electronic dimmer boards
Suggested uses: concert, lecture, performance, promotion

and

Promenade Theatre   (212) 580-3777

2162 Broadway (76th Street)
New York, NY 10023

Theater
Capacity: 399
40' x 30' proscenium thrust stage
Suggested uses: performance, concert, location shoot

Manhattan Theatre Club   (212) 645-5590

453 West 16th Street   Contact: Assistant Production Manager
New York, NY 10011

4 studios
Capacity: varies from 768 sq. ft. to 2088 sq. ft.
Rental fee: $12 to $20 per hour; $500 to $900 per week
Pianos, air-conditioning
Suggested uses: rehearsal

McGinn/Cazale Theatre   (212) 787-8302

2162 Broadway (76th Street)   Contact: Dorothy Maffei,
New York, NY 10023   Managing Director

Theater
Capacity: 108 in 20' x 30' space
Rental fee: $100 per night; $15 per hour or $2,000 per week
Lighting and sound system, lobby, dressing rooms
Suggested uses: concert, lecture, performance
Note: Access for the handicapped.

Medicine Show   (212) 431-9545

353 Broadway (Leonard & Franklin)   Contact: James Barbosa
New York, NY 10013

Theater, rehearsal space
Capacity: 74; theater has flexible seating
Rental fee: $150 per performance, negotiable depending on
  number of performances and performers involved; hourly
  rentals available
32' x 120' sprung wooden floors, platforms, 2 pianos, professional sound and lighting equipment
Suggested uses: concert, class, professional dance, meeting,
  theater performance

Merce Cunningham Studio   (212) 691-9751
55 Bethune Street   Contact: Alice Helpern
New York, NY 10014

Rehearsal space, concert/dance performance space
Capacity: 125
Rental fee: $165 per performance; hourly rates are available
Piano, dance floor
Suggested uses: concert, professional dance, performance, location shoot

Murphy Center at Asphalt Green   (212) 369-8890
555 East 90th Street   Contact: Director
New York, NY 10128

Theater, classroom, gymnasium, football field
Capacity: 91 fixed seats in theater (capacity for 145); 235 in classroom; 320 in gymnasium/classroom
Proscenium stage
Suggested uses: meeting, performance, concert, play reading, cultural event, etc. in Mazur Theater; football (astroturf), soccer, volleyball, basketball, on football field
Note: Space is a community sponsored cultural/recreation center and is associated with the Fireboat House Environmental Center which holds classes on marine science.

Musical Theatre Works Inc.   (212) 677-0040
440 Lafayette Street (8th Street)   Contact: Rick Louis,
New York, NY 10003   Facilities Manager

Black-box theater
Capacity: 65/75 in 25' x 50' space (flexible seating)
Theatrical lighting, sound equipment
Suggested uses: workshop, audition, showcase, reading

Nat Horne Theatre   (212) 736-7128
440 West 42nd Street   Contact: Mark DeGasperi
New York, NY 10036

Theater, 3 rehearsal spaces, classroom
Capacity: 99 in theater; 23' x 44' of space is available in the 2 largest rehearsal spaces
23' x 24' proscenium stage, 2 pianos, dance floor (masonite and mylar)
Suggested uses: all special events are possible including a rehearsal

New Dramatists, Inc.   (212) 757-6960
424 West 44th Street   Contact: Janet Heller,
New York, NY 10036   Program Associate

Auditorium, rehearsal space, conference room, studio
Capacity: 99 in auditorium; 30 in conference room; 65 in studio
Rental fee: negotiable
Flexible platform, sound system, theatrical lighting, kitchen; food may be served
Suggested uses: lecture, meeting, rehearsal, audition
Note: Space has limited availability especially from October to May.

New York City Mission Society,   (212) 368-8400
Minisink Town House   Contact: Marilyn Nance
646 Lenox Avenue
New York, NY 10037

Auditorium, theater
Capacity: 500 for a dance/716 auditorium-style in auditorium; 150 in theater
Platform, piano, kitchen (minimum charge); food may be served
Suggested uses: concert, dance, meeting
Note: Space is only available Friday and Saturday evenings; Sunday day and evening.

Nikolais/Louis Dance Lab   (212) 777-1120
(Choreospace)   Contact: Richard Biles
33 East 18th Street (7th fl.)
New York, NY 10003

3 studios
Capacity: 90 seated/200 standing in 70' x 34' Studio A; 90 seated/200 standing in Studio B; 40 seated/75 standing in 31' x 31' Studio C. A total of 7000 sq. ft. of space is available.
Rental fee: $20 per hour for Studio A; $25 to $50 per hour for Studio B; $8 per hour for Studio C
Proscenium stage, platforms, theatrical lighting, sound system, video equipment, hardwood floors, elevator
Suggested uses: performance, rehearsal, meeting, fashion show, location shoot, sitdown dinner (Studio A)

Nola Sound Studios, Inc.   (212) 582-1417
250 West 54th Street   Contact: John Ortiz
New York, NY 10019

6 rehearsal spaces
Capacity: 50/75
Steinway Grand piano in each space
Suggested uses: class, lecture, meeting, piano instruction and practice, singing, play rehearsal, fashion or television show
Note: Space is not available on Sundays.

Off Center Theatre   (212) 929-8299
436 West 18th Street   Contact: Abigail McGrath
New York, NY 10011

Theater, rehearsal space, reception area, cabaret (2nd floor)
Capacity: 50/100
25' x 20' proscenium stage, platform, piano, dance floor, bar, kitchen; food may be served
Suggested uses: all special events are possible

Ohio Theatr   (212) 966-4844
66 Wooster Street   Contact: Robert Lyons
New York, NY 10012

Theater
Capacity: 4000 sq. ft. space with flexible seating
Rental fee: $600 per day; $1,600 per week
Platform, hardwood dance floor; food may be served
Suggested uses: conference, performance, benefit, party

One Astor Place
(212) 575-0725

1515 Broadway (45th Street)
New York, NY 10036

Contact: Minskoff Rehearsal Studios

8 studios/rehearsal spaces
Capacity: 25/100
Pianos, floor-to-ceiling mirrors
Suggested uses: meeting, party, reception, rehearsal, audition

Orpheum Theatre
(212) 460-0990

126 Second Avenue
New York, NY 10003

Contact: Alan Perry, General Manager

Theater
Capacity: 299 (fixed seating)
Stage
Suggested uses: performance, concert, lecture, meeting

Pelican Studio
(212) 730-2030

750 Eighth Avenue (48th Street)
New York, NY 10036

Contact: Eric Kramer

Studio
Capacity: 60 seated; 1200 sq. ft. of space is available
Lighting equipment, dressing room; 15 ft. ceiling
Rental fee: $15 per hour for a rehearsal
Note: Space is primarily available during the day.

Performance Space 122
(212) 477-5288

150 First Avenue (9th Street)
New York, NY 10009

Contact: Mark Russell

2 theaters
Capacity: 50/150 in each (flexible seating)
Rental fee: $8 to $10 per hour
Sound system, hardwood floors
Suggested uses: rehearsal, meeting, dance performance

Perry Street Theatre
(212) 255-7190

31 Perry Street
New York, NY 10014

Contact: Ingrid Nyeboe, General Manager

Capacity: 103
Rental fee: negotiable
Flexible stage
Suggested uses: concert, class, professional dance, lecture, meeting, performance

Port Authority of New York & New Jersey
Contact: Manager's Office

625 Eighth Avenue
2nd fl., North Wing
New York, NY 10018

Groups may perform at Port Authority Bus Terminal's north wing (between 41st and 42nd Street on Eighth Avenue) some Thursdays for 2 hour performances between 4:30 and 6:30 p.m. Dance performance should fit into a 20' x 30' space.
Payment is possible.
Applications must be made in writing.

Primary Stages Company
(212) 333-7471

584-86 Ninth Avenue
(42nd Street, 2nd fl.)
New York, NY 10036

Contact: Herbert O'Dell, Producer

Rehearsal studio, 2 theaters
Capacity: 40 in 1000 sq. ft. rehearsal studio; 65 in one theater; 99 in other theater
Piano, end stage
Suggested uses: rehearsal, workshop, reading, auction, concert, class, lecture meeting, performance
Note: The theaters are located at 345 West 45th Street.

Prometheus
(212) 477-8689

239 East 5th Street
New York, NY 10003

Contact: Fred Fondren

Capacity: 40 people in 350 sq. ft. space
Proscenium stage, sound equipment, dimmer board
Suggested uses: performance, rehearsal, lecture, poetry reading

Richard Allen Center for Culture & Art
(212) 281-2220

Contact: Shirley Radcliffe

Church of the Intercession
155th Street & Broadway
New York, NY 10032

Performance space, classroom
Capacity: 99
Suggested uses: concert, class, exhibit, lecture, meeting, performance, reception

Larry Richardson's Dance Gallery
(212) 685-5972

242 East 14th Street
New York, NY 10003

Contact: J. Anthony Siciliano, Manager

Performance space/gymnasium
Capacity: 260 in 50' x 70' x 20' space
Rental fee: $150 during the evening
Proscenium stage or in the round, piano, theatrical lighting, sound equipment, dressing rooms, velours (can be made into a black box); food may be served

Roundabout Theatre Company's Christian C. Yegan Theatre
(212) 420-1360

Contact: Ellen Richard, General Manager

100 East 17th Street
New York, NY 10003

Theater
Capacity: 500
Proscenium stage, sound and lighting system, bar area
Suggested uses: concert, professional dance, lecture, meeting, performance, promotion
Note: This theater is available for a maximum of ten-day periods. It is newly renovated to state-of-the-art specifications.

and

continued on next page

Roundabout Theatre Susan Bloch Theatre
307 West 26th Street
New York, NY 10010
Three-quarter arena theater
Capacity: 152
Lighting equipment, 18 dimmer lighting board, large lobby area, dressing room; food may be served
Suggested uses: all special events are possible including a party

St. Clement's   (212) 246-7277
423 West 46th Street   Contact: Douglas Williams
New York, NY 10036
Theater, rehearsal space
Capacity: 99 in theater; 55 in rehearsal space
45' x 45' stage, masonite over wood Marley dance floor, 2 speakers, reel-to-reel tape deck, amplifier, turntable, dressing rooms
Suggested uses: meeting, staged reading, etc.

St. Mark's Studio   (212) 777-3055
94 St. Mark's Pl.   Contact: Michael Schulman
New York, NY 10009
Studio
Capacity: 40 seats on risers
Raised stage, piano
Suggested uses: class, reading, backer's audition

Sandra Cameron Dance Center Inc.   (212) 674-0505
439 Lafayette Street   Contact: Larry Schulz
(Astor Pl. & 4th St., 2nd fl.)
New York, NY 10003
3 studios
Capacity: flexible seating in 25' x 25' of space in each studio; 25' x 53' of space if 2 studios combined
Rental fee: $15 per hour or $25 when 2 studios combined; monthly rates available
Piano, sprung maple dance floor, mirrors, ballet barres, sound system
Suggested uses: exercise class, rehearsal, workshop

Sanford Meisner Theater   (212) 206-1764
164 Eleventh Avenue (22nd Street)   Contact: Robert Coles
New York, NY 10011
Theater
Capacity: 74
Rental fee: hourly, single night or full weeks
Piano, light and sound system
Suggested uses: performance, rehearsal, audition, occasional party

School for Creative Movement   (212) 929-0929
20 West 20th Street   Contact: Jack Wiener,
New York, NY 10011   Director
Studio
Capacity: up to 150 in 25' x 50' x 11' 6" space
Rental fee: $12 per hour for a rehearsal/$19 per hour for a class/$40 per hour for a performance
Piano, wood floors, ballet barres, dressing room, track lighting, windows on two sides
Suggested uses: rehearsal, class, workshop, party

Soho Repertory   (212) 925-2588
80 Varick Street   Contact: David Waggett
New York, NY 10013
Rehearsal studio
Capacity: 32 ft. x 32 ft. of space is available
Rental fee: reasonable; day or evening
Piano
Suggested uses: rehearsal or audition

Spaceplace   (212) 677-8075
303 Park Avenue South   Contact: Myra Hushansky
New York, NY 10010
2 studios
Capacity: 15 in one; 40 in the other
Marley floor and wood floor
Note: Space is only available to dance teachers for classes or to dance companies for rehearsals.

TaDa!   (212) 627-1732
120 West 28th Street   Contact: James Learned
New York, NY 10001
Theater
Capacity: 99
Rental fee: reasonable; by hour, day, week or month
Piano, lights, dressing room
Suggested uses: performance, rehearsal, class audition, party

Theater In Action   (212) 431-1317
46 Walker Street   Contact: Drew Dix
New York, NY 10013
Theater, studio
Capacity: 106 in theater upstairs; 30 in studio downstairs
Professional light and sound system
Suggested uses: class, exhibit, lecture, meeting, dance or theater rehearsal

The Theater of the Open Eye   (212) 769-4141
270 West 89th Street   Contact: Adrienne Brockway
New York, NY 10024
Theater
Capacity: 100
Open stage
Suggested uses: dance, theater, music performance

Theatre, Opera, Music Institute, Inc.   (212) 787-3980
(Tomi, Inc.)   Contact: Lisa Bottalico,
23 West 73rd Street (16th fl.)   Office Manager
New York, NY 10023
2 theater/meeting/classrooms, reception area, terraces
Capacity: approximately 75/150 in 25' x 40' space
Rental fee: varies from $7 to $20 per hour; weekly and monthly rates are available
24' x 36' thrust stage, platform, 4 pianos, theatrical lighting, dressing rooms
Panoramic view of New York City

Theatre Row   (212) 736-7932

422 West 42nd Street   Contact: Darren Lee Cole
New York, NY 10036

Numerous theatrical groups are housed in 7 buildings containing
  performance spaces and studios
Capacity: varies from 99/299
Proscenium stages, platforms, pianos, dance floors, complete
  lighting facilities; food may be served
Suggested uses: concert, class, professional dance, lecture, meeting, performance, rehearsal, trade show

Theatre at St. Peter's Church   (212) 935-2200

619 Lexington Avenue at   Contact: Edmund Anderson
Citicorp Center (54th Street)
New York, NY 10022

Theater
Capacity: 199
30' x 33' stage, lighting and sound equipment

Theatre 22   (212) 243-2805

54 West 22nd Street   Contact: Sidney Armus,
New York, NY 10010   Owner

Theater, rehearsal room, classroom
Capacity: 74 in 2000 sq. ft. loft (can be divided); 30' x 20'
  performing area; 23' x 20' rehearsal room
Rental fee: $75 per performance in theater; $5 to $10 per hour
  for rehearsal room
Piano, dance floor, dressing room, 12' ceilings, kitchen; food
  may be served
Space is a loft.
Suggested uses: concert, class, social or professional dance,
  lecture, meeting, party, performance

13th Street Theatre   (212) 675-6677

50 West 13th Street   Contact: Edith O'Hara
New York, NY 10011

Theater, rehearsal space, lobby
Capacity: 75 in theater; 15' x 25' of rehearsal space is available;
  30 in lobby
Rental fee: $200 weekend; $150 for weekday evening show in
  theater; $15 per hour for stage ($10 extra per hour with lights);
  $10 per hour for rehearsal space
18' x 24' stage, platform, piano, snack bar; food may be served
Suggested uses: all special events are possible including a children's birthday party

Tribeca Studio   (212) 966-1997

83 Leonard Street   Contact: Laura Segal
New York, NY 10013

Dance studio
Capacity: 22' x 44' of space is available
Wood floor, 12' ceiling
Suggested uses: rehearsal, class, workshop

Two Village Cabaret Theaters   (212) 737-7536

(Bleecker Street)
New York, NY

2 cabaret theaters, enclosed sidewalk cafe lounge
Capacity: 300 upper level/450 lower level; 80 in lounge
Fully equipped stages, pianos, dance floor, complete sound and
  lighting equipment, kitchen; food may be served by space or
  caterer of your choice
Suggested uses: concert, rehearsal, private party, off-Broadway
  presentation, location shoot, press conference, backers' audition, benefit
Note: As of fall '89 there will be an additional location on West
  114th near Columbia University. Three separate rooms will
  accommodate 100 to 140 people. Dance floor, sound system,
  piano and catering will also be available.

UBU Repertory Theater   (212) 683-6639

15 West 28th Street   Contact: Ingrid Nyeboe,
New York, NY 10001   Administrator

Theater, rehearsal hall/dance studio
Capacity: 100 in theater; 60 in rehearsal hall
Proscenium stage, platform, piano

University Settlement   (212) 674-9120 ext. 156

184 Eldridge Street   Contact: Alice Kearney
(Delancey & Rivington, 2nd fl.)
New York, NY 10002

Performance/rehearsal studio
Capacity: 275 maximum/200 seated on folding chairs in 1152
  sq. ft. space
Rental fee: $8 to $10 per hour for a rehearsal; $12 per hour for
  a class
544' stage, wood floor, many windows
Suggested uses: rehearsal, performance, class, workshop

Vandam Theater, SoHo   (212) 242-2519

15 Vandam Street   Contact: Dorothy Ames
New York, NY 10013

Auditorium/theater, rehearsal space, conference room, exhibit
  space, reception area
Capacity: 199 in auditorium; 70 in conference room
Stage, platform, dance floor; food may be served
Suggested uses: auction, concert, class, exhibit, lecture, meeting,
  performance, screening, live theater

Westside Arts Theatre   (212) 246-6351

407 West 43rd Street   Contact: Ms. C. Swann
New York, NY 10036

2 theaters, cabaret stage
Capacity: 249 in Downstairs Theatre; 290 in Upstairs Theatre;
  74 in cabaret
Rental fee: varies with production needs
Proscenium stage, platform, piano
Suggested uses: class, lecture, meeting, performance, reading

Westside Dance Project (212) 580-0915
220 West 80th Street Contact: John DeBlass or
New York, NY 10024 Maria Zannieri
3 dance studios
Capacity: 700 sq. ft., 800 sq. ft., and 1000 sq. ft. of space is available
Suggested uses: rehearsal, class, audition, party

Brooklyn

The Brooklyn Academy of Music (212) 737-7536
Brooklyn, NY
Opened in 1861, America's oldest performing arts center currently leads the world with dance presentations. Theatrical performances under the directorship of Peter Brook will also make headlines because of its recently restored Majestic Theater which won the 1988 Municipal Art Society's Certificate of Merit. "More a revelation than a restoration, its long proud history is writ in painted layers both old and neo-old. Is the plaster crumbling or the eye superbly tricked? Director Peter Brook's vision has been brought to fruition by masters." (From *The Livable City*, June 1988, a publication of the Municipal Art Society).
Capacity: 550 in Leperq Space; 901 in Majestic Theater; 1,011 in Carey Playhouse; 2,086 in BAM Opera House
Note: The Leperq Space, a multi-purpose space with flexible seating transformed from an old ballroom, also serves as a banquet room for formal dinners.

Laziza (718) 797-3116
123 Smith Street (Dean & Pacific) Contact: Kathleen Laziza
Brooklyn, NY 11201
Theater
Capacity: 19 x 37 sq. ft. of space is available
Rental fee: $4 to $6 per hour
Maple floor, mirrors, natural light
Suggested use: rehearsal

Spoke the Hub Dancing (718) 596-5250
295 Douglass Street Contact: Narta Warshaw-Chu
(south of BAM between 3rd &4th Avenues) or Felice Long
Brooklyn, NY 11217
Dance studio
Capacity: 60/80 on bleachers in 60' x 40' space
Note: A 2-hour birthday party for up to 25 children is also offered.

Queens

Black Spectrum Theater (718) 723-1800
Roy Wilkins Park of Southern Queens Contact: Carl Clay,
119-07 Merrick Blvd. Executive Director
Jamaica, NY 11434
Theater, piano lounge
Capacity: 425 in theater (flexible seating); 75 in piano lounge
Sound board, computerized lighting system, projection screen, dressing rooms, lobby, ticket booth; fully equipped kitchen
This former Naval Officer's Club is available as a performance space as well as for social functions.
Suggested uses: performance, dinner theater, social, etc.

Long Island

Inter-Media Art Center, Inc. (516) 549-9666
370 New York Avenue Contact: Michael Rothbard,
Huntington, NY 11743 Executive Director
Theater, meeting room/gallery/lobby
Capacity: 650 in theater; 100/300 in meeting room
85' x 50' proscenium stage, full 21' overhead lighting grid, multiple camera TV production facilities in ¾" and ½" formats
Lobby serves as visual arts gallery and meeting room.
Suggested uses: performance, videotaping, location shoot
Note: Non-profit groups and independent artists are particularly welcome.

Also see: AUDITORIUMS (Seating 500 or more)
CHURCHES
DISCOS/SUPPER & VIDEO CLUBS
Heart of Broadway
LIBRARIES
MEETING ROOMS/CONFERENCE ROOMS/ AUDITORIUMS (Seating 499 or less)
PARKS & PLAZAS
PERFORMANCE SPACES (CONCERT/ RECITAL)
Theater/Studio Loft
Three Versatile Floors
Y's

PIERS

*T*he following department has responsiblity for a number of waterfront sites available for short term recreational use by special permit. Contact in writing:

N.Y.C. Department of Ports & Trade
Property Management
Battery Maritime Building
Foot of Whitehall Street
New York, NY 10004
Attn: Ronald Trinchetto, Asst. Commissioner of Property
    Management

New York City Passenger Ship   **(212) 466-7985**
Terminal   Contact: Edward Peters
711 Twelfth Avenue (52nd Street)
New York, NY 10019
3 piers, exhibit space, reception area

Capacity: 2000 for each pier; 65,000 sq. ft. of pier space per pier
    is available
Open rooftop parking
Overlooks the Hudson River
Suggested uses: all special events are possible particularly trade shows

---

Pier 11   **(212) 732-0414**
South & Wall Streets   Contact: Joe Giovani or
New York, NY 10005   Arthur Tisi
Capacity: 10,000 on 60' x 550' pier
20' x 40' stage, 28 international food stalls
View of Brooklyn Bridge and Statue of Liberty. Performance
    area is at water's edge.
Suggested uses: dance, cultural event, corporate party, social
    function, location shoot
Note: Mailing address is Plaza Cafe & Catering Corporation, 133
    Mulberry Street, New York, NY 10013.

Pier 16   **(212) 669-9400**
South Street Seaport Museum   Contact: Debra Dillon
East River and Fulton Street
New York, NY 10038
Capacity: approximately 2000 persons may be accommodated
    occasionally for private functions on 23,000 sq. ft. pier
Parking is available nearby.

Also see: Large Private Party and Meeting Facility
                Overlooking Harbor (Pier 17)

POETRY READING PLACES

*T*he following places offer poetry reading space on a regular basis:

ABC No Rio   **(718) 596-6532**
56 Rivington St.   **(before noon or after 6 p.m.)**
(Clinton & Suffolk)   **(212) 254-3647**
New York, NY 10002

Back Fence   **(212) 475-9221**
155 Bleecker St.
New York, NY 10012

Books & Company   **(212) 737-1450**
939 Madison Ave. (74th St.)
New York, NY 10021

Dixon Place   **(212) 673-6752**
37 East 1st St.
New York, NY 10003

Ear Inn, Inc.   **(212) 226-9060**
326 Spring St.
New York, NY 10013

Endicott Booksellers   **(212) 787-6300**
450 Columbus Ave. (81st St.)
New York, NY 10024

Fashion Moda   **(212) 585-0135**
2803 Third Ave.
Bronx, NY 10455

Guggenheim Museum   **(212) 360-3503**
1071 Fifth Ave. (89th St.)
New York, NY 10128

The Kendall Gallery   **(212) 477-6552**
152 Forsyth Street (Chrystie & Delancey)
New York, NY 10002

Henry Lindenbaum Jewish   **(212) 595-7929**
Community Center   **(212) 595-7087**
270 West 89th Street
New York, NY 10024

Poet's House   **(212) 627-4035**
351 West 18th Street
New York, NY 10011

St. Mark's in the Bowery   **(212) 674-0910**
Poetry Project
131 East 10th St.
New York, NY 10003

Woodside on the Move   **(718) 476-8449**
Poetry Committee
58-14 Roosevelt Ave.
Woodside, NY 11377

Also see: **LIBRARIES**
                  PERFORMANCE SPACES (DANCE
                  /THEATER)

RACEWAYS

Aqueduct   **(516) 488-6000**
Rockaway Boulevard & 110th Street   **(718) 641-4700**
Ozone Park, NY 11417   Contact: Marge Fearon
3 dining/meeting areas
Capacity: 25/500 in Equestris; 250 in Kelso Room or Lexington
    Room
Suggested uses: lunch, dinner, meeting
Note: Mailing address is New York Racing Association, Inc.,
    P.O. Box 187, Jamaica, NY 11417.

Belmont   **(516) 488-6000**
Hempstead Turnpike & Plainfield Avenue   **(718) 641-4700**
Elmont, NY 11003   Contact: Marge Fearon
Dining/meeting area, outdoor terrace
Capacity: 450 indoors
Suggested uses: luncheon, meeting
Note: Mailing address is New York Racing Association, Inc.,
    P.O. Box 187, Jamaica, NY 11417.

The Meadowlands   (201) 460-4378

Giants Stadium
New Jersey Sports & Exposition Authority
East Rutherford, NJ 07073

Contact: Ray Kasyan, Events Coordinator

Capacity: 1050 in Stadium Club; 550 in dining room (475 with dancing); 250 in bar area; 250 in buffet room
Dance floor, sound system
Suggested uses: meeting, conference, dinner dance, trade show, etc.

Yonkers Raceway   (914) 968-4200

Yonkers, NY 10704

Contact: Group Sales Director

2 dining/meeting facilities
Capacity: 1200 seated in Empire Terrace Dining Room; 800 seated in Good Times Room
Sound and lighting system, dance floor
Largest dining facility in Westchester
Suggested uses: all special events are possible

REHEARSAL PLACES

Abraham Goodman House
Actors Institute
Actor's Playhouse
American Academy and Institute of Arts and Letters
American Association of University Women
American Mime Theatre
Bloomingdale House of Music
Bouwerie Lane Theater
Bronx House
The Buckley School
C.W. Post Center of Long Island University (Long Island)
Calderon Productions Studios
Cami Hall
Carnegie Hall Corporation
Chez White Mask Theatre Corporation
Circle in the Square
City Center 55th Street Theater
Clark Center for the Performing Arts
Dan Wagoner and Dancers
Dance Notation Bureau
Dance Space, Inc.
Dance Theater Workshop, Inc.
East Harlem Arts & Education Complex
East Side International Community Center, Inc.
Edison Theater
Educational Alliance
Elisa Monte Dance Company
Elizabeth Streb Dance Studio
Ethnic Folk Arts Center
Experimental Intermedia Foundation
Fashion Institute of Technology
Flushing Jewish Center (Queens)
Foundation for the Advance of Dance
Foundation for Vital Arts Inc.
Gene Frankel Theatre Workshop, Inc.
Greenwich House Music School
Gustave Hartman YWHA
Harlem School of the Arts
Harlequin Rehearsal Studio
Harry
Hudson Guild
International House

Irish Arts Center
The Isadora Duncan Dance Center
James Weldon Johnson Community Center, Inc.
La Guardia Community College (Queens)
La Terraza
Laban Institute for Movement Studies
Laziza
Lehman College Center for the Performing Arts (Bronx)
Long Island University (Brooklyn)
Manhattan Theatre Club
Manhattanville Community Centers, Inc.
Marc Ballroom
Marymount Manhattan College
Merce Cunningham Studio
Sam & Esther Minskoff Cultural Center
Nat Horne Theatre
New Dramatists, Inc.
New Lincoln School
New York University/Loeb Student Center
Nikolais/Lewis Dance Lab (Choreospace)
Nola Sound Studios, Inc.
Off Center Theatre
Ohio Theatr Center
One Astor Place
Pelican Studio
Pratt Institute (Brooklyn)
Primary Stages Company
Queensborough Community College
Radio City Music Hall
Rehearsal/Party Site
Riverdale-Yonkers Society for Ethical Culture (Bronx)
Roberto Clemente State Park (Bronx)
Saint Hilda's & St. Hugh's School
St. Mark's Studio
Sandra Cameron Dance Center, Inc.
Sanford Meisner Theater
School for Creative Movement
School of T'ai Chi Chuan, Inc.
Sloane House YMCA
Soho Repertory
Spaceplace
Studios 58 Playhouse, Inc.

Symphony Space
TaDa!
Taller Latino Americano
Thea's Studio
Theater In Action
Theatre 22
13th Street Theater

Tribeca Studio
UBU Repertory Theater
University Settlement
Vandam Theater, SoHo
Workmen's Circle Building

RINKS

Empire Roller Disco   **(718) 462-1400**
Empire Rollerdome   Contact: Gloria McCarthy
200 Empire Boulevard
Brooklyn, NY 11225

2500 people can be accommodated in 2 skating rinks of 30,000 sq. ft.
Rental fee: depends on number of people
Sound equipment, flexible lighting, disco music, snack bar; food may be served
Note: Space is only available Monday, Wednesday and Thursday evenings.

Mineral Springs Skates   **(212) 861-1818**
Mineral Springs Pavilion   Contact: Manager
Sheep Meadow, Central Park
New York, NY 10021

Private parties for up to 50 adults and/or 30 children. Skating in Mineral Springs Pavilion courtyard and on paved roads in Central Park.
Group rates available
Health food concession on premises
Note: Weekends 10 to 12 noon only. Space is closed December through March.

Sky Rink   **(212) 695-6556**
450 West 33rd Street   Contact: Guy Robinson
New York, NY 10011

750 people may be accommodated (600 on rink, 150 in conference room)
Snack bar, kitchen; food may be served
Space is a penthouse ice skating rink atop a 16-story office building.
Suggested uses: banquet, meeting, party, ice skating performance, promotion, location shoot

ICE SKATING RINKS IN NEW YORK CITY PARKS

BROOKLYN

Kate Wollman Rink   **(718) 965-6561**
Prospect Park,   **(718) 946-6535**
East Dr. between Lincoln Rd. & Parkside Ave.
(26,000 sq. ft.)

Abe Stark Rink
Surf Ave. & West 19th St.
(17,000 sq. ft.)

MANHATTAN

Wollman Rink   **(212) 517-4800**
Central Park, East Dr. & 63rd St., north of Pond
(33,000 sq. ft.)

Lasker Rink   **(212) 397-3106**
Central Park, near 110th St. & Lenox Ave.
(26,600 sq. ft.)

QUEENS

World's Fair Ice Skating Rink   **(718) 271-1996**
New York City Bldg., Flushing
Meadows Corona Park
(18,000 sq. ft.)

STATEN ISLAND

Staten Island War Memorial Ice   **(718) 720-1010**
Skating Rink
Clove Lakes Park, Victory Blvd. off Clove Rd.
(28,000 sq. ft.)

SCHOOLS & COLLEGES

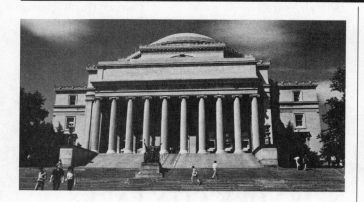

MANHATTAN

Borough of Manhattan Community   **(212) 618-1832**
College   Contact: James Pawlak,
199 Chambers Street   Conference Services
New York, NY 10019
2 theaters, 5 conference rooms, gymnasium, lecture halls,
cafeteria, faculty dining room, game room
Capacity: 1000 in Theater 1, 282 in Theater 2, 25/50 in conference rooms; 25/300 in banquet-style in game room
Note: Space has limited availability.

The Buckley School   **(212) 535-8807**
113 East 73rd Street   **(212) 535-8787 (switchboard)**
New York, NY 10021   Contact: Per von Scheele
Gymnasium
Capacity: 40' x 70' of space is available
Note: Space is only available for sport activities.

City College of the City University of   **(212) 690-6900**
New York   Contact: Laura Greer,
134th Street & Convent Avenue   Associate Producer
New York, NY 10031

Aaron Davis Hall
The Main Stage
Capacity: 750
40' x 24' proscenium stage; 40' x 40' performance sprung space

and

The Experimental Theatre
Capacity: 300 maximum
62' x 62' open space with full grid; sprung floor
Rental fee: negotiable
Note: Space has limited availability.

Columbia University   **(212) 854-6646**
New York, NY 10027   Contact: Suzanne Gold,
                             Assistant Director, Facilities
                             Services, B-230 East Campus
Rental of facilities and locations for filming and photography
such as classrooms, laboratories, athletic facilities, offices,
libraries, cafeterias, auditoriums, lounges, exterior locations,
etc.

Altschul Auditorium   **(212) 854-4469**
School of International Affairs   Contact: Larry Dais,
West 116th Street   Office of Community
New York, NY 10027   Affairs, 301 Low Library
Capacity: 400

Catherine Bache Miller Theater   **(212) 854-1633**
200 Dodge Hall   Contact: Mary Kaye Fletcher,
Columbia University   Theater Manager
New York, NY 10027
This newly renovated space is primarily used as a performing
arts space. It has state-of-the-art lighting and sound.
Suggested uses: concert, dance performance, literary reading
Capacity: 692

continued on next page

Earl Hall Center
(212) 854-6242
(212) 854-1491
117th Street & Broadway
New York, NY 10027
Contact: Space Coordinator

Auditorium/ballroom, rehearsal space, conference room, Room 302, meeting rooms, reception area/lobby
Capacity: 300 in auditorium; 20/25 in conference room and Room 302; 100 in Dodge Room; 30/49 in Schiff Room; 30 in lobby

Ferris Booth Hall
(212) 854-3611
Columbia University
115th Street & Broadway
New York, NY 10027
Contact: Reservations and Conference Coordinator, Room 206, Student Activities Office

Wollman Auditorium, meeting rooms, The Plex (entertainment complex with dance floor and lounge)
Capacity: 748 in Wollman Auditorium; 30/228 in 11 meeting rooms; 400 in the Plex

Horace Mann Auditorium
(212) 678-3707
Columbia University Teachers College
525 West 120th Street, Box 173
New York, NY 10027
Contact: Leila Bright, Director, Office of Room Assignments

Capacity: 650
Stage, piano, organ, PA system, limited stage lighting
Suggested uses: cultural/educational event
Note: Events must conform to the academic purposes of the school.

Millbank Chapel
(212) 678-3707
Columbia University Teachers College
525 West 120th Street, Box 173
New York, NY 10027
Contact: Leila Bright, Director, Office of Room Assignments

Chapel, reception room
Capacity: 200 in chapel; 80/90 in Grace Dodge Room
Food service is available.
Suggested uses: cultural/educational event in chapel; a reception or a wedding is especially suitable in Grace Dodge Room
Note: Events must conform to the academic purposes of the school. The Grace Dodge Room is separate from the chapel.

Nevis Laboratories
(212) (914) 591-8883
Columbia University
136 South Broadway
Irvington, NY 10533
Contact: Howard Millman, Manager, Facility Management Office

A 70-acre park-like site approximately twenty minutes north of New York City.
Backgrounds such as groomed lawns to forest-type scenes are available for photography. Several 100 year-old barns and Mansion House are available for exterior shots.

St. Paul's Chapel
(212) 854-3574
(212) 854-6246
202 Earl Hall
117th Street & Broadway
New York, NY 10027
Contact: Michael White, Assistant Director

Nave, meeting room/lounge, reception area (Red Room)
Capacity: 500 in nave; 112 in Gustavino Room; 125 in Red Room

Cooper Union Great Hall
(212) 353-4195
7th Street & Third Avenue
New York, NY 10003
Contact: Office of Continuing Education

Auditorium
Capacity: 900

Fashion Institute of Technology
(212) 760-7644
227 West 27th Street
New York, NY 10001
Contact: Bette LeVine

Auditorium, rehearsal space, conference room, exhibit spaces, amphitheater
Capacity: 800 in Morris Haft Auditorium; 400 in Katie Murphy Amphitheatre
Rental fee: $850 for 8 hours for Morris Haft Auditorium; $600 for 8 hours for Katie Murphy Amphitheatre
Professional sound and lighting equipment; food may be served only by caterer on premises

Hunter College of the City University of New York
(212) 772-4282
68th Street & Park Avenue
New York, NY 10021
Contact: Banquet Department

Faculty staff dining room and lounge
Capacity: 125 seated
Terrace and view over the Park Avenue Armory
Resident caterer
Suggested uses: reception, dinner, wedding (when not in use)

John Jay College of Criminal Justice
(212) 237-8000 **(switchboard)**
The City University of New York
444 West 56th Street
New York, NY 10019
(212) 237-8601 **(Williams)**
Contact: Yvonne Williams, Office of the President

Auditorium, theater, conference rooms, reception area, gymnasium, cafeteria
Capacity: 250 in auditorium; 180 in theater; 15/20 in conference rooms; 800 in gymnasium; 800 in cafeteria

The Little Red Schoolhouse
(212) 477-5316
196 Bleecker Street
New York, NY 10012
Contact: Hy Krutzel

Theater, gymnasium
Capacity: 140 (movable chairs)
Piano, hardwood dance floor
Suggested uses: meeting, showcase

and

Elizabeth Irwin High School
40 Charlton Street
New York, NY 10014

Auditorium, classrooms, gymnasium
Capacity: 140 in auditorium; 20/25 in classrooms
Cafeteria; food may be served
Suggested uses: meeting, class

Marymount Manhattan College (212) 517-0475
221 East 71st Street (Fleischer)
New York, NY 10021 (212) 517-0545 (Hurtado)
Contact: Mary Fleischer,
Managing Director, theater or
Alida Hurtado, Director of
Campus Events, for other spaces
Theater, auditorium/ballroom, rehearsal space, classrooms,
reception areas, mezzanine, esplanade, swimming pool
Capacity: 250 in theater; 250/400 in Great Hall; 20/60 in class-
rooms; 75 in reception area

New Walden Lincoln School (212) 879-9200
210 East 77th Street Contact: Myrtle L. Steele, Bursar
New York, NY 10021
Rehearsal space
Capacity: 150
Note: Space is not available on weekends.

New York School of Printing (212) 765-1185
439 West 49th Street Contact: Custodian/Engineer
New York, NY 10019
Auditorium
Capacity: 700

New York University (212) 998-4900
Loeb Student Center Contact: Operations Office,
566 La Guardia Place (Washington Square) Room 300
New York, NY 10012
Auditorium, 20 conference/meeting rooms, exhibit space,
lounge, reception room, cafeteria, coffee house, checkroom
Capacity: 726 in auditorium; 12/150 in conference rooms

Pace University (212) 488-1200 (switchboard)
Schimmel Center for the Arts (212) 488-1398 (Knipe)
1 Pace Plaza (212)488-1369 (Ryder)
New York, NY 10038 Contact: Dawn Knipe,
Director, theater or
Marie Ryder for other spaces
Theater, conference room, reception area, meeting rooms, dining
room, cafeteria
Capacity: 392 orchestra/276 balcony in theater; 150/200 in other
spaces

Parsons School of Design (212) 741-8959
Exhibition Center Contact: Margo L. Turnquest
560 Seventh Avenue (40th Street)
New York, NY 10018
Auditorium, exhibit space, reception area, classrooms, coatroom
Capacity: 50/500
Proscenium stage, runway, platforms, lighting grid, control
booth, screen, electrical/audio technicians
Suggested uses: catered breakfast, luncheon, dinner, cocktail,
stockholders' meeting, fashion show, film shoot, rehearsal,
performance, press party, dance, commencement, testimonial

PUBLIC SCHOOLS

Space in Public School buildings:

*A*nyone wishing to use a classroom, auditorium or gym of a
public school after school hours should get in touch with
the Custodian of a specific school and request a permit application. (All public schools are listed in the telephone directory.)
Rates will be quoted by the Custodian from the schedule of rates
approved by the Board of Education. Alcoholic beverages are
not allowed. For additional information contact:

Director of Plant Operations (718) 706-3802
Division of School Buildings
2811 Queens Plaza North
Long Island City, NY 11101

*Especially large and/or functional public school
auditoriums listed in order of capacity:*

The Charette School
P.S. 3
490 Hudson Street
New York, NY 10014
Capacity: 400

P.S. 41
116 West 11th Street
New York, NY 10011
Capacity: 431

Norman Thomas High School
111 East 33rd Street
New York, NY 10016
Capacity: 750

High School of Art & Design
1075 Second Avenue (57th Street)
New York, NY 10022
Capacity: 800

Martin Luther King Jr. High School
122 Amsterdam Avenue (65th Street)
New York, NY 10023
Capacity: 984

Bronx High School of Science
75 West 205th Street
New York, NY 10468
Capacity: 1000

Truman High School
750 Baychester Avenue
Bronx, NY 10475
Capacity: 1151

Stuyvesant High School
345 East 15th Street
New York, NY 10003
Capacity: 1172

Julia Richman High School
317 East 67th Street
New York, NY 10021
Capacity: 1502

Washington Irving High School
40 Irving Pl.
New York, NY 10003
Capacity: 2500

Fashion Industry High School
225 West 24th Street
New York, NY 10011
Capacity: 3000

St. Hilda's & St. Hugh's School   **(212) 666-9645** ext. 13
619 West 114th Street   Contact: Mrs. Berger,
New York, NY 10025   Secretary to the Headmaster
Auditorium/gymnasium, rehearsal space, 2 classrooms, activities room
Capacity: 500 in auditorium; 10/20 in classrooms; 50 in activities room
Note: Space is not available during the day.

School of T'ai Chi Chuan, Inc.   **(212) 929-1981**
47 West 13th Street (5th fl.)   Contact: Axel Schwolow,
New York, NY 10011   Administrator
Rehearsal space, classroom
Capacity: 50/75 in 60' x 20' rehearsal space; 20/35 in 30' x 18' classroom
Rental fee: $15 to $30 per hour
Dance floor; food may be served in classroom
Suggested uses: class, professional dance, lecture

Tobe-Coburn School for Fashion   **(212) 460-9600**
686 Broadway (4th Street)   Contact: Carol Rivera,
New York, NY 10012   Building Manager
Semi-circular auditorium, 5 classrooms
Capacity: 250 (fixed seating); 40 in each of 3 classrooms; 20 in each of 2 classrooms
Rental fee: $150
Note: Space is only available weekday evenings after 5 p.m.

Village Community School   **(212) 691-5146**
272 West 10th Street   Contact: Rudy Christian,
New York, NY 10014   Building Custodian
Auditorium, gymnasium
Capacity: 250

York Preparatory School   **(212) 628-1220**
116 East 85th Street   Contact: R. Stewart
New York, NY 10028
Classrooms/meeting rooms
Capacity: 110 in largest room
Note: Entire school is available for long-term evening rental.

BRONX

Bronx Community College   **(212) 220-6260**
West 181st Street & University Avenue   Contact: Elaine Gordon
Bronx, NY 10453   or Richard Julius
Playhouse, 3 conference rooms
Capacity: 375 in Hall of Fame Playhouse; 15/120 in each conference room
Proscenium stage, pianos, professional sound and lighting equipment; food may be served in spaces other than Playhouse
Suggested uses: banquet, concert, exhibit, lecture, meeting, performance
Note: Space is usually only available to community groups.

Fordham University   **(212) 579-2453**
Rose Hill   Contact: Martin Zwiren,
Bronx, NY 10458   Director of Conferences
& Special Events
Auditorium, theater, rehearsal space, ballroom, classrooms, conference room, 5 lecture halls, reception area, parade grounds, recreation center, fields
Capacity: 600 in Pope Auditorium; 250 in Collins Auditorium (professional theater) (can be divided); 500 in ballroom; 250/500 in lecture halls; up to 2000 people may be accommodated
Stage, platform, piano, dance floor, audio-visual equipment, kitchens; food may be served only by resident caterer
90 acres of grounds; parking for 1500 cars
Suggested uses: all special events are possible

Lehman College Center for the   **(212) 960-8232**
Performing Arts   Contact: Andrea Rockower
Bedford Park Boulevard West
Bronx, NY 10468
Concert hall (auditorium), theater, experimental theater, rehearsal space, conference room, exhibit space, reception area, dining hall
Capacity: 2310 in concert hall; 500 in theater; 200 in experimental theater
2 proscenium stages, piano, dance floor, complete fly system for scenery and lighting equipment
Parking for 1000 cars
Suggested uses: all special events are possible

Also see: College of Mount St. Vincent

BROOKLYN

Adelphi Academy   (718) 238-3308
8515 Ridge Boulevard   Contact: Rose Kuchinsky
Brooklyn, NY 11209

Auditorium, gymnasium, classrooms, cafeteria
Capacity: 200 in auditorium; 20/30 in each classroom
Note: Space has limited availability except during the summer, evenings and weekends.

Long Island University —   (718) 403-1002 ext. 3464
Brooklyn Center
      Contact: Sally Castiglione,
1 University Plaza   Special Events
Brooklyn, NY 11201

Auditorium, theater, classrooms, gymnasium, athletic field, exhibit spaces, reception area, lecture halls, dining rooms
Capacity: 550 in auditorium; 90/150 in lecture halls; 60/250 in dining rooms

Pratt Institute   (718) 636-3771 (Payne)
Brooklyn, NY 11205   (718) 636-3517 (Moretta)
    (718) 636-3777 (Stone)
Contact: Joan Payne (gym),
Eleanor Moretta (exhibit space),
Andy Stone (all other spaces)
Auditorium, rehearsal space, 2 exhibit spaces, gymnasium/open space, classrooms, lounge, 2 dance studios, Activity Center
Capacity: 500 in auditorium; 50/150 in exhibit spaces; 200 in lounge; 4000 in Activity Center
PA system
Suggested uses: exhibit, meeting, conference, athletic event, demonstration

QUEENS & LONG ISLAND

C.W. Post Center of Long Island   (516) 299-2781
University
      Contact: Peg Larsen
P.O. Greenvale, NY 11548

Theater, 2 auditoriums, rehearsal space, conference rooms, exhibit space, Interfaith Chapel
Capacity: 2700 in Concert Theater; 40/500 in other spaces

Hofstra University   (516) 560-5446
Hempstead, NY 11550   Contact: Dr. Donald H. Swinney,
      Director of Playhouse
Auditorium (John Cranford Adams Playhouse)
Capacity: 1132

LaGuardia Community College   (718) 482-5056
City University of New York   Contact: Arlena Claire-Black,
31-10 Thomson Avenue   Events Coordinator
Long Island City, NY 11101

Auditorium, rehearsal space, conference room, exhibit space, reception area, classrooms, gymnasium, faculty dining room, terrace
Capacity: 250 in auditorium; 35 in conference room; 15/80 in classrooms

Queens College   (718) 544-2996 (Mallalieu)
Long Island Expressway &   (718) 520-7974 (Grogan)
Kissena Boulevard   (718) 520-7215 (Wettan)
Flushing, NY 11367   (718) 544-1445 (Dunn)
Contact: Steven Mallalieu, Facilities Manager, Office of Space Management, for Colden Center and QC Theater; Barbara Grogan, Office of Space Management, for recital hall and lecture halls; Richard Wettan for gymnasium and athletic fields; Jimmy Dunn, Manager, for dining hall
2 theater spaces, recital hall, 8 lecture halls, gymnasium, athletic fields, dining hall
Capacity: 2143 in Colden Center; 476 in QC Theatre; 200 in Rathaus Recital Hall; 100/300 in dining halls

Queens College Student Union (718) 520-7800 ext. 7831
152-45 Melbourne Avenue   Contact: Audrey Grimm,
Flushing, NY 11367   Reservations
Ballroom, 14 conference rooms, exhibit space, lounges, underground parking
Capacity: 850 in Grand Ballroom

Queensborough Community College   (718) 631-6321
56th Avenue & Springfield Boulevard   (Carobine)
Bayside, NY 11364   (718) 631-6228 (Lundenberg)
Contact: Tony Carobine, Director of Performing Arts or Arnold Lundenberg, Campus Planning
Auditorium/theater, rehearsal space, conference room, exhibit space, reception area, plaza, 2 dressing rooms
Capacity: 875 in auditorium
Rental fee: $1000 per performance
40' x 30' x 21' proscenium stage, platform, piano, complete sound and lighting equipment
Suggested uses: performance, auction, concert, class, lecture, meeting, reception

STATEN ISLAND

The College of Staten Island (718) 390-7948
Sunnyside Campus Contact: Dorothy Zarrilli
715 Ocean Terrace
Staten Island, NY 10301
Theater, quadrangle, sports field, parking lot
Capacity: 918 in Williamson Theatre
Stage, platform, piano; space's cafeteria food only may be served

and

St. George Campus
130 Stuyvesant Place
Staten Island, NY 10301
College hall
Capacity: 175
Stage, platform, piano; space's cafeteria food only may be
    served

Eltingville Lutheran School (718) 984-8830 (before 2)
300 Genessee Avenue Contact: Church Office
Staten Island, NY 10312
Church parlor, playground
Capacity: 150

Wagner College (718) 390-3221
631 Howard Avenue Contact: Wagner Union Staff Office
Staten Island, NY 10301
Auditorium, conference rooms, exhibit space, reception area,
    gymnasium, cafeteria
Capacity: 320 in auditorium; 14/85 in conference room; 1650 in
    gymnasium; 400 in Main Cafeteria
Note: Dormitories with 400 beds can be used during summer for
    conferences; 75 beds are available during rest of year.

Also see: **AUDITORIUMS (Seating 500 or more)**
    City University of New York Graduate Center
    CONFERENCE CENTERS
    Hunter College of the City University of New
        York

SCREENING ROOMS

Eleonora (212) 765-1427
117 West 58th Street Contact: Mrs. Joseph Lyttle,
New York, NY 10019 Proprietor
Film and TV cassette screening room
Capacity: 20
Space's own food and drink must be served

Magno Preview One/Magno Preview (212) 302-2505
Two Contact: David Friedman
729 Seventh Avenue (49th Street)
New York, NY 10019
2 screening rooms, party room
Capacity: 68 in Preview 1, 33 in Preview 2
16mm, 35mm and 70 mm screening with Dolby stereo, video
    screening

and

Magno Preview Four/Magno Preview Nine
1600 Broadway (48th Street)
New York, NY 10019
Preview Four offers screening rooms on 4th floor; party
    room/lounge in Preview Nine on 9th floor

Capacity: 69 in screening rooms; ¾", ½" and 1" video screen-
    ing in Preview Nine; 67 in party room/lounge

and

Magno Sound and Video
729 Seventh Avenue (49th Street)
New York, NY 10022

Mixing, transfers, stripping, codings, voice recording, sound
    effects, video

Also see: Department of Cultural Affairs
    Museum of Broadcasting
    PERFORMANCE SPACES (DANCE/
        THEATER)
    Seaport Experience Theater

SOCIAL HALLS

Finnish Aid Society Imatra (718) 438-9426
740 40th Street Contact: Mauno Laurila,
Brooklyn, NY 11232 President
2 ballrooms, yard
Capacity: 250 in main ballroom upstairs; 125 in downstairs
  ballroom; 100 on main floor
Rental fee: $400 to $500 upstairs; $275 to $300 downstairs
Stage, dance floor, bar, kitchen; food may be served
Suggested uses: all special events are possible including an
  ethnic fair, birthday or wedding
Note: Space does not have air-conditioning.

Greek Cultural Center of Astoria (718) 726-7329
27-18 Hoyt Avenue South Contact: Panteleimon
Astoria, NY 11102 Melissinos
Hall
Capacity: 120
Piano, sound system, theatrical lighting; food may be served
Suggested uses: meeting, performance, party, ethnic festival

Also see: CHURCHES
  Former Farm/Now Beer Garden and Social Hall

STADIUMS

John J. Downing Stadium (212) 860-1828
Randall's Island, Manhattan
Capacity: 21,000

Giants Stadium (201) 935-8500 ext. 4387
New Jersey Sports Exposition Authority
East Rutherford, NJ 07073
Capacity: 76,981

Madison Square Garden Center (212) 216-2000
4 Pennsylvania Plaza (33rd Street) Contact: Mark Allin
New York, NY 10001
Felt Forum-amphitheater seats 4600
Madison Square Garden— major sport event, convention, enter-
  tainment spectacular; seats 20,000
Penn Plaza Club— Dining area and cocktail lounge
Rotunda— 50,000 sq. ft. exposition area
Bowling Center, Press Club

Food may be served by space or bring your own.
Suggested uses: anniversary, screening, sales meeting, exposition, commencement program, symposium, alumni gathering, clinic, dining, etc.

Nassau Veterans Memorial Coliseum   (516) 794-9300
Mitchel Field Complex   **(516) 794-3555** (caterer)
Uniondale, NY 11553   Contact: Lloyd Fraizer,
Director of Booking or
Hillary Hartung, Director of Public Relations;
Harry M. Stevens, Inc. for kitchen and food
Arena/auditorium, exhibit hall
Capacity: 17,500 maximum in arena
Rental fee: $10,000 or 17½% of gross ticket receipts plus expenses, whichever is greater, per event, for arena; $2,400 minimum per day, plus expenses, for exhibit hall
Proscenium stage, platform, kitchen; food may be served only by caterer on premises
Suggested uses: banquet, concert, exhibit, consumer or trade show

Rice Stadium   (212) 822-4363
Pelham Bay Park, Bruckner Blvd. & Middletown Road, Bronx
Capacity: 4500

Shea Municipal Stadium   (718) 699-4220
Flushing Meadows, Corona Park, Queens
Capacity: 55,000

South Mountain Arena   (201) 731-3829
560 Northfield Avenue   Contact: Jack Sheik,
West Orange, NJ 07052   Manager
Meeting/conference room
Capacity: 2640 permanent seats/1400 folding chairs in 248' x 148' building with a 60' ceiling
In-house organ, theatrical lighting, large parking lot, a 200' x 85' indoor ice skating rink (surface can be converted), fully equipped PA system, control booth, locker rooms and luncheonette. Additional personnel are available. Suitable for all special events including a circus, tennis exhibition, sports competition, trade show, convention or horse show.
Located one hour from New York City.

U.S. Tennis Association National   (718) 592-8000
Tennis Center
Flushing Meadow Park, Queens
Capacity: 19,000

Van Cortlandt Park Stadium   (212) 822-4335
West 241st St. & Broadway, Bronx
Capacity: 3600

Yankee Stadium   (212) 992-1634
River Ave. & 161st St., Bronx
Capacity: 55,000

Also see: SCHOOLS & COLLEGES

STEPS

In a formal sense, steps leading to public buildings can be used for public ceremonies and press conferences. Informally, they serve as places for sunbathing, people watching, impromptu concerts and rendezvous perches for meeting friends. Some of the best steps for these purposes are those of the Low Memorial Library at Columbia University, the Metropolitan Museum of Art, St. Thomas Church, St. Patrick's Cathedral, The New York Public Library at Fifth Avenue and 42nd Street, City Hall and Federal Hall.

STUDIO SPACES (For Artists at Work)

Bronx Council on the Arts
(212) 842-5659
1738 Hone Avenue
(212) 931-9500
Bronx, NY 10461
Contact: Fred Wilson

This community arts council makes available 2 studio spaces on a six-month basis to artists who apply by resume and work samples.
Gallery space is available for exhibition.

Department of General Services
(212) 566-4593
Division of Real Property
Contact: Amilda Burgos,
2 Lafayette Street
Director of Community Leasing
New York, NY 10007

Any non-profit group in search of permanent studio and/or workshop space may write to the above address and contact person. The letter should give proof of the group's non-profit status and intended use of property. A letter of support from the Community Board where property is located will be requested; if a cultural group, a letter of support from Department of Cultural Affairs; if a one-time event or outdoor festival, a letter of approval from Police Precinct commander having jurisdiction where property is located. A certified financial statement detailing funding and demonstrating, when a structure is involved, capability to provide for maintenance and operating expenses should also be submitted.

All city-owned property, such as police and fire stations, vacant school buildings, etc., may be leased to a service-oriented, non-profit group on a month-to-month lease agreement. The group must provide its own insurance, pay utilities, and be prepared to move out of the premises if and when a city agency wants occupancy. If a group is not certain as to whether a specific space is city-owned, Director Burgos will check its availability.

Institute for Art and Urban Resources
(718) 784-2084
Contact: Karen Ott
c/o Project Studio One (P.S. 1)
46-01 21st Street
Long Island City, NY 11101
Auditorium, 15 exhibition spaces, 20 studios

Capacity: 4200 sq. ft. of space is available in auditorium; 25,000 sq. ft. of exhibition space; 25,000 sq. ft. of studio space
Rental fee: Applicable only when studio/workspace is rented for a period of a year. There is no rental fee for use of exhibit or performance space.
Performance space and special project space is given by submission of a proposal in writing. All exhibition areas are curated.
Space was a 19th century school building which has been converted into an experimental work center for artists.

Jamaica Arts Center
(718) 658-7400
161-04 Jamaica Avenue
Contact: Carol Bourne
Jamaica, NY 11432

Exhibit space, meeting rooms, performing and visual arts studio space
Capacity: 150
Rental fee: approximately $25 during the evening; negotiable flat fee for regular use
Piano; food may be served
Note: Collection and admission charges are usually not allowed.

Multi-use of Public School Buildings
(718) 706-3882
2811 Queens Plaza North
Contact: Geraldine Prishivalko,
Long Island City, NY 11101
Section Chief, Site Acquisition & Building Inventory

When a school facility is under-utilized by the school at the time the school is in session, space may be available under terms and conditions set by The Board of Education to qualified non-profit, educational and service-oriented groups.

Organization of Independent Artists
(212) 929-6688
201 Varick Street, Box 146
Contact: Annette Kuhn,
New York, NY 10014
Executive Director

This organization facilitates visual art exhibitions such as painting, sculpture and photography in public spaces throughout the New York City area. Public parks and hospital grounds are used for large outdoor sculpture shows.
Information on the use of federal properties for cultural purposes and the Public Building Cooperative Use Act is available.

The Writer's Room
(212) 807-9519
153 Waverly Pl. (5th fl.)
Contact: Renate Rizzo-Harvi,
New York, NY 10014
Executive Director

This 10-year-old urban writers colony makes 30 desks available to any writer with a serious commitment to writing. Open 7 days a week, 24 hours a day. An application must be submitted.
Rental fee: $165 per quarter year

Writer's Studio   **(212) 755-6710**
The Mercantile Library   Contact: Library Director
17 East 47th Street
New York, NY 10017

This non-profit, private lending library, which was founded in 1820 by a group of merchant philanthropists to serve as a library and evening reading room for their clerks, makes available 17 spaces on its sixth floor where serious writers can work. A formal application must be made and will be reviewed by a selection committee.
Rental fee: $200 for each 3 month rental period

For TOWNHOUSES see:
      PARTY PLACES/GREATER NEW YORK
      PARTY PLACES/NEW YORK CITY

For WEDDINGS & WEDDING RECEPTIONS see:
      BALLROOMS
      BOATS & BARGES
      CHURCHES
      CLASSIFIED (New York City & Environs)
      DISCOS/SUPPER & VIDEO CLUBS
      HORSE-DRAWN CARRIAGES & WAGONS
      HOTELS
      PARKS (ceremonies only)
      PARTY PLACES/GREATER NEW YORK
      PARTY PLACES/NEW YORK CITY

WORKSHOP/SEMINAR SPACES

*A*ll of the following lofts and studios are suitable for workshops and seminars. For more elegant or formal lofts see *LOFTS FOR PARTIES* in *PARTY PLACES/NEW YORK CITY*. Call (212) 737-7536 for updates.

Adjacent To Carnegie Hall   **(212) 737-7536**
(West 57th Street)
New York, NY

Situated in the historic Carnegie Hall building, this studio emanates the atmosphere of a century's devotion to dance and music. With 20 ft. high ceilings, mirrors and windows facing West 57th Street, this softly hued space nobly carries its tradition into the present.
Capacity: up to 60

Calligraphy School and Recording   **(212) 737-7536**
Studio in Noho
(Bond Street)
New York, NY

Blending traditional arts with modern technology, this Japanese center was founded in 1972 as the New York branch of the Japan Calligraphy Education Foundation.
As a cultural center, it promotes worldwide exchange and communication between East and West as well as world peace. As a recording studio it offers state-of-the-art video and audio facilities such as recorders, play back units, dubbing machines, synchronizers, and a studio console.
Capacity: up to 100 in Kampo Hall; additional space on 5th floor

Caribbean Cultural Center   **(212) 307-7420**
408 West 58th Street   Contact: Marta Vega or
New York, NY 10019   Laura Moreno

4 floors in a brownstone
Capacity: approximately 50 seated on each floor
Cultural and educational groups are particularly welcome.
Suggested uses: lecture, meeting, performance

Dick Shea's   **(212) 677-5690**
100 East 16th Street (2nd fl.)   Contact: Dick Shea or
New York, NY 10003   Adrienne Melissen
Dance loft with reception area
Capacity: 260
Piano, professional sound system and lighting grid, hardwood floors, video equipment, windows

continued on next page

Suggested uses: rehearsal, workshop, party
Note: Smoking is not allowed on the dance floor. Space rents weekdays after 7:30 p.m., Fridays and Saturdays from 7:30 till 10 p.m. and Sundays from 1 p.m.

Ethnic Folk Arts Center   (212) 620-4083
179 Varick Street   (212) 691-9510
New York, NY 10012   Contact: Rental Manager
Capacity: 250 seated in 35' x 65' space
Dance floor, professional sound system
Suggested uses: performance, rehearsal, seminar, workshop
Note: Smoking is not allowed.

Experimental Intermedia Foundation   (212) 966-3367
537 Broadway (Prince & Spring)   Contact: Amy Axelrod
New York, NY 10012
Concert space, rehearsal space, classroom, exhibit space
Capacity: 80/100
Rental fee: $100 per performance; per hour rental available
Piano, dance floor, lighting grid
Suggested uses: concert, class, professional dance, meeting, performance (non-play), video and film, taping and screening

Loft on Broome Street   (212) 737-7536
(Soho)
New York, NY
This 1500 sq. ft. open space artist's loft has a 13' high tin ceiling and floor to ceiling windows. Air-conditioned.
Capacity: 40/60
Kitchen
Suggested uses: seminar, workshop, artistic/informal wedding reception

MAGI Studio   (212) 737-7536
(Soho)
New York, NY
This light and airy loft offers 20 windows and center skylight.
Capacity: over 200 in 5000 sq. ft. space on top floor
Maple floors, 25 ft. mirrored wall
Suggested uses: dance performance, workshop, photo and film shoot

Self-Awareness Loft   (212) 737-7536
(East 91st Street)
New York, NY
Capacity: over 200 standing/400 theater-style in 4500 sq. ft. space
Restored concert grand pianos from the 19th and 20th centuries serve as backdrop in this 2nd floor gallery-like setting or they can be removed.

Reception room, raised platform, oak floor, white walls, freight elevator for wheelchair access
Space is especially appropriate for meetings and workshops by self-awareness and spiritual groups. Also suitable for a concert, art exhibit, seminar or non-alcoholic party. Dancing is permitted.

Soho Photo Studio   (212) 737-7536
(Broadway & Prince Streets)
New York, NY
Capacity: 70 maximum in 1200 sq. ft. L-shaped Studio A
Light and airy, good wood floors
Suggested uses: bridal shower, wedding reception, birthday party, etc.
Note: Space is only available after 6 p.m. on weekdays; day and evening on weekends.

Studio 505   (212) 431-7748
39 Walker Street (top floor)   Contact: Marc Kaczmarek
New York, NY 10013
Capacity: approximately 45 x 45 sq. ft. of space is available
Light refreshments may be served.
Suggested uses: dance, photography, Tai Chi and other workshops

Waverly Place Loft   (212) 737-7536
(Village)
New York, NY
This living loft with brick walls is available for meetings, seminars and workshops.
Capacity: 60 in 1500 sq. ft. space
Rental fee: $35 per hour

The Works   (212) 737-7536
(16th Street & Fifth Avenue)
New York, NY
Exercise studio
Capacity: approximately 150 in 2500 sq. ft. space
Sprung wood floor, windows along one wall
Suggested uses: class, workshop, sweet 16, children's birthday party

Yoga Center   (212) 925-6578
78 Grand Street   Contact: Peentz Dubble
(2nd fl., Wooster & Greene)
New York, NY 10013
Capacity: 45 on floor/100 meeting-style in just under 2000 sq. ft. space
50 chairs; kitchen
Suggested uses: healing, lecture or massage workshop (without shoes)

Y's

MANHATTAN

92nd Street Y   **(212) 427-6000** ext. 220
1395 Lexington Avenue   Contact: Linda Greenberg
New York, NY 10128
Auditorium
Capacity: 916

Sloane House YMCA   **(212) 760-1707**
356 West 34th Street   Contact: Yvonne Mayers,
New York, NY 10001   Program Department
Auditorium, rehearsal space, conference rooms, lounge, exhibit
    space
Capacity: 200 in auditorium; 15/80 in conference rooms

Vanderbilt YMCA   **(212) 755-2410**
224 East 47th Street   Contact: Nancy Scalafani,
New York, NY 10017   Membership Program Director
Conference rooms
Capacity: 12/100
Movie projector; food may be served only by caterer on premises

---

Westside YMCA   **(212) 787-4400** ext. 105
5 West 63rd Street   Contact: Carmen Urbina,
New York, NY 10023   Business Office
5 conference rooms, 12 classrooms, cafeteria
Capacity: 12/150
Rental fee: $130 for a full day; $45 for a half day

YMCA, McBurney Branch   **(212) 741-9229**
215 West 23rd Street   Contact: Tom Bynum
New York, NY 10011
Auditorium, conference room, 7 meeting rooms, gymnasium
Capacity: 225 in auditorium; 120 in conference room; 25/70 in
    meeting rooms

YWCA   **(212) 755-4500**
610 Lexington Avenue (53rd Street)   Contact: Elaine Quinn
New York, NY 10022
Auditorium
Capacity: 225
Note: Space is only available to non-profit groups.

BRONX

YM-YWHA   **(212) 548-8200**
5625 Arlington Avenue (256th Street)   Contact: Director's
Riverdale, NY 10471   Office
Professional theater, multi-purpose room, gymnasium, pool, 2
    outdoor terraces
Capacity: 245 seated in theater; 300 seated in multi-purpose
    room; 300 seated on terraces
Note: Catering must be Glatt Kosher.

BROOKLYN

Brooklyn YWCA   **(718) 875-1190**
30 Third Avenue   Contact: Fran Stokes
Brooklyn, NY 11217
Auditorium (Memorial Hall); 2 ballroom/conference rooms;
    exhibit space, gymnasium, pool
Capacity: 438 main floor/167 balcony in auditorium
Rental fee: $400 for 4 hours in auditorium; $25 for kitchen

QUEENS

Central Queens YMCA   **(718) 739-6600**
89-25 Parsons Boulevard   Contact: Membership
Jamaica, NY 11432   Marketing Director
6 meeting rooms, 2 gymnasiums, large swimming pool
Capacity: 70 in each meeting room; 40 in pool
Piano
Suggested uses: class, dance, exhibit, lecture, meeting, church
    service

Gustave Hartman YM-YWHA   **(718) 471-9600**
1800 Seagirt Boulevard   **(516) 239-1029**
Rockaway, NY 11691   Contact: Room Rental
Auditorium, rehearsal space, conference room, exhibit space,
    lounge, gymnasium, game room, playground, 2 Olympic-size
    pools, parking lot
Capacity: 300 in auditorium

Also see: **PERFORMANCE SPACES (DANCE/
             THEATER)**

GREATER NEW YORK METROPOLITAN REGION

(NEW JERSEY, CONNECTICUT, HUDSON VALLEY & LONG ISLAND)

NEW JERSEY

Albemarle   (212) 737-7536
Princeton, NJ

The Gerard D. Lambert mansion is presently the home and school of The American Boys choir, one of the finest boy choirs in the world. Most social occasions, including weddings, are welcome.

Guest capacity: 200 seated/250 standing in three rooms

The Art Center of Northern New Jersey   (201) 599-2992
250 Center Street   Contact: Mrs. Joan Studer,
New Milford, NJ 07646   Executive Director

Located in Bergen County, this renovated church/now art gallery and school is suitable for meetings, weddings, showers and other social events. Kitchen facilities; bring your own caterer. Approximately 60 miles from New York City.

Charming Women's Clubhouse   (212) 737-7536
Englewood, NJ

Just a few minutes drive from the George Washington Bridge, this delightful clubhouse is available for all manner of special events and wedding receptions. Its french doors open onto a lovely terrace, lawn and trees.

Guest capacity: 120 seated/150 standing

Colonial Clubhouse   (212) 737-7536
Glenridge, NJ

This attractive women's clubhouse accommodates guests on two levels.

Guest capacity: 300 seated in Williamsburg Room; 85 seated on mezzanine

Grand piano, fireplace

Colonial Inn (212) 737-7536
Princeton, NJ

Built prior to the Revolutionary War in the heart of Princeton, this late Georgian Colonial Revival house with high dormers and big front porch is rife with the history of an emerging United States, of New Jersey and of Princeton University to which it became affiliated in 1911. Students such as F. Scott Fitzgerald and Bertrand Russell have spent time there, as did Albert Einstein.

Guest capacity: 110 seated/250 cocktails in Dining Room; 500 cocktails in entire house; separate small private rooms are also available accommodating 35 overnight in 17 guest rooms, each decorated in its own style

The Encampment at Morristown (212) 737-7536
Morristown, NJ

The area where in 1779 Washington's army survived the worst winter of the century is now a National Historical Park which is administered by the National Park Service of the Department of Interior.

The area surrounding the main building of an estate on the park site, called the Cross Estate, may be used for special functions, and occasional use of the large downstairs rooms of the estate may also be made.

Guest capacity: 150 for outdoor weddings with use of main indoor rooms

Note: Available May through October. All receptions on grounds must end at 8 p.m. Amplified music is not allowed.

Environmental Center and Planetarium (212) 737-7536
Lyndhurst, NJ

Opened in the winter of 1983 among the tall grasses and murky waters of the Hackensack River, this attractive educational and scientific resource facility is part of the 19,730-acre Hackensack Meadowlands District.

The solar heated Visitors Center, which is perched on stilts over the Kingsland Creek Marsh, offers a glass-enclosed octagonal room with tables, chairs, couches and a spectacular view of the Meadowlands and the Manhattan skyline.

The adjacent Planetarium has been marvellously conceived by craftsman Victor Haeselbarth.

Guest capacity: 200 seated at tables/250 lecture-style in Visitors Center (75 seated in conference room, 60 classroom, 50 lecture room); 288 in fixed seat auditorium; 200 seated lecture style/100 at tables in Museum

Former Church/Now Cultural Center (212) 737-7536
Upper Saddle River, NJ

This small white 19th century church has transformed itself into a cultural center and opened its doors to special functions and wedding receptions.

Guest capacity: 100/150 in Fellowship Hall; 100 in Sanctuary (meeting or lecture)

Stage, small kitchen

Note: Limited smoking; hard liquor is not allowed.

Georgian Mansion (212) 737-7536
Morristown, NJ

Built in 1912 by the Van Rensselaer/Thorne family, this gracious mansion with gardens and lawns is available for weddings with one stipulation—the bride and groom must be willing to repeat their vows on the premises.

Guest capacity: 150 seated; additional numbers possible in summer

Gill-St. Bernard's School (201) 234-1611
St. Bernard's Road Contact: Paul Lowe
Gladstone, NJ 07934

Built in 1894 by George Post, this Victorian structure surrounded by forty acres of landscaped grounds was the home of John Dryden, founder of the Prudential Life Insurance Company. The property, which is now a private school, makes seven rooms available for private parties.

Guest capacity: 200 maximum

Baby grand piano; food may be served by in-house caterer only

Note: Space is available only evenings and weekends except for the summer when it is available during the week.

Gorgeous Gazebo and Garden in the Garden State
(212) 737-7536

West Orange, NJ

This large colonial-style house set on a twenty-two-acre estate offers a garden and gazebo as well.

Guest capacity: 130/600

Suitable for weddings, dinner/dance parties, luncheons, bar mitzvahs, seminars and corporate events.

Located approximately thirty miles from New York City.

Lodge on Lake
(212) 737-7536

Rockaway, NJ

This mansion offers one room which is available from Labor Day to Memorial Day for all manner of functions, including weddings.

Guest capacity: 200 seated in club room

Working fireplace, patio, lawn, lake

Morris Museum
(201) 538-0454

6 Normandy Heights Rd.   Contact: Judy Boyd

Morristown, NJ 07960

This local art museum offers a theater as well as conference rooms and a caterer's kitchen.

Guest capacity: 312 seated in theater; small groups in several conference rooms

Proscenium stage, audio-visual equipment, film and slide projection capacity.

Suitable for corporate and organizational meetings, seminars and receptions.

Old Monroe School House
(201) 827-4459

c/o Hardyston Heritage Society

R.D. 1, Box 599

Hamburg, NJ 07419

Situated in Sussex County of northern New Jersey, this is one of the few hand-hewn stone school houses still in existence. Built in the early 1800's, it has recently been restored with the help of local and federal funds and is listed on both the State and National Registers of Historic Places.

Complete with pot-belly stove, hand slates, wooden desks, etc., this one-room school house is open for children's parties.

Guest capacity: 25 children indoors; 300 adults and children outdoors

Outdoor area is suitable for picnics, crafts fairs, etc.

Private Luncheon Club
(212) 737-7536

Roseland, NJ

This recently built club is available for private functions, including weddings on weekends.

Guest capacity: 200 seated/400 cocktails in Atrium; 100 in special room for ceremony; 60 in each of two smaller rooms

Resident caterer

Reeves Reed Arboretum
(201) 273-8787

165 Hobart Avenue   Contact: Director

Summit, NJ 07901

Within its twelve-and-a-half acres, this arboretum and nature center combines native woodlands with formal public gardens and rolling lawns, including a rose garden, an herb garden and a front lawn which is a spring setting for thousands of daffodils. Created in 1889 by Mr. and Mrs. John Hornor Wisner, who also built the present Colonial Revival house, this property is less than an hour's drive from New York City.

Guest capacity: 100 seated/150 standing

Suggested uses: luncheon, tea, meeting

Note: Wedding receptions and alcohol are not allowed. Food and tents are not allowed outdoors.

Simon Van Wickell House   (201) 873-2500
1289 Easton Avenue
Somerset, NJ 08873

Surrounded by eight acres of nature trails and gardens, this eighteenth century Dutch farmhouse also provides access to the Delaware and Raritan Canal for fishing and boating. It is available for weddings, wedding receptions and parties.

Guest capacity: 60 seated or standing

Skyland Manor   (201) 962-6201
Box 1304 R.D.
Ringwood, NJ 07456

Located in northern New Jersey at the very edge of New York State is the site where, with the formation of the Ringwood Company, America's iron industry started in 1740. These forges and furnaces were of great importance to the colonies during the American Revolution and Robert Erskine, manager of the Ringwood mines, was also the Surveyor General for the American Army at that time. He prepared maps at Ringwood which aided General Washington in his military campaigns and many of Washington's horses were shod at the Ringwood blacksmith shop. When Robert Erskine died, he was buried on the property overlooking the lake and General Washington and his wife planted a tree there in 1782.

Subsequently, a family named Ryerson came into possession of the property, but in 1853 Ringwood was purchased by the New York philanthropist Peter Cooper, known as the founder of Cooper Union Institute. Within a few years, the property passed on to Abraham S. Hewitt, considered America's foremost nineteenth century iron master. It so happened that Mr. Hewitt, as a young man, tutored one of the Cooper family's sons and, while doing so, fell in love with the young man's sister, Amelia. They were married in 1855 and made Ringwood their country residence. Over a period of many years, the complete landscaping of Ringwood was due to Mrs. Hewitt's efforts, for she oversaw the transformation from a location of iron mines into a six hundred acre park-like setting.

Garden wedding ceremonies are permitted on the grounds. Most suitable locations are: The Italian Garden, which contains columns which came from the New York Life Insurance Building when it was demolished to make room for the present one. Mr. Hewitt placed them there to provide the Classical atmosphere of the garden and Colonnade Row which is comprised of cast iron Torcheres taken from Lafayette Place in New York City.

Note: Application for a wedding ceremony permit must be made.

Special Functions in Georgian Mansion   (212) 737-7536
Shrewsbury, NJ

Located forty-five miles from New York City on twenty acres of formal gardens with fountains, arbors and agate trees, this Georgian mansion is now entirely devoted to special functions.

Guest capacity: 130 in each of several rooms/600 maximum

Tudor-Style Mansion   (212) 737-7536
South Orange, NJ

A spacious home originally built in 1903 for Ira A. Kip, a stockbroker, it is currently owned by a Jewish congregation. Its high ceilinged, wood panelled social rooms can accommodate guests of any denomination.

Guest capacity: 100 seated

Two Houses in One   (212) 737-7536

Ho-Ho-Kus, NJ

A Gothic Revival villa and a Victorian home were owned by four
  generations of the Rosencrantz family. Adjacent to each other,
  they are but a thirty minute drive from New York City.

Guest capacity: 125 on tented patio of the Victorian house; 50
  for ceremony only in Gothic Revival villa

Two Nature Park Sites   (201) 768-1360

c/o Palisades Interstate Parks Commission
Alpine, NJ 07620

Administered by the Palisades Interstate Park Commission and
  overlooking the Hudson River, these two historic nature parks
  offer rustic environments for special events.

The Alpine Boat Basin is an open air covered stone and wood
  pavilion on a river bank. Wooden floor is particularly service-
  able for square dancing. All special events are possible including weddings, parties, concerts, dances and picnics.

The Visitor's Center in Fort Lee offers a forty-foot x ten-foot
  stage, screen and sound system. It is suitable for meetings,
  lectures, concerts, recitals and theatrical productions. There
  is an outdoor patio.

Guest capacity: 100/200 at picnic tables in Alpine; 204 in Fort
  Lee Visitor's Center

Unusual Stone Mansion   (212) 737-7536

Englewood, NJ

This 130 year-old Gothic stone mansion surrounded by two acres
  of land offers indoor formality with signed French murals on
  its walls coupled with a swimming pool and two deck areas
  for indoor/outdoor sociability.

Guest capacity: 150 maximum; 18 seated in formal dining room

Also see: Aviation Hall of Fame
  New Jersey Corporate Picnic Site
  The U.S.S. Ling
  Where Front Porch Rocking is an Art

CONNECTICUT

WESTERN CONNECTICUT/ NEAR NEW YORK STATE

Avant-Garde Museum in Colonial   (212) 737-7536
Setting

Ridgefield, CT

Located in a two hundred year-old landmark known as "Old
  Hundred" on the main street of a town which has maintained
  a genuine bygone American character, this two-floor Colonial
  house, now contemporary art gallery, will rent out for weddings, receptions, etc.

A three-story glass atrium serves as an entry foyer to the new
  gallery/auditorium; a covered terrace and garden are also
  available.

Guest capacity: 250 in atrium if foyer, gallery, terrace and
  sculpture garden are used; 100 indoors in Colonial house;
  many more in Sculpture Garden

Country Estate of Ruth and Skitch   (212) 737-7536
Henderson

New Milford, CT

Located in Connecticut's Litchfield Hills, this 200-acre Hunt
  Hill Farm property houses a country kitchen store, gallery and
  cooking school in former stables and dairy barns.

Private functions may be created around food and cooking
  demonstrations with guest teachers, cookbook authors and

chefs. Receptions and celebrations can also take place around current exhibits in the Gallery which is the former hay loft.

Guest capacity: up to 90 in Gallery; 30 in country kitchen

Suggested uses: shower, pre-wedding party, anniversary, corporate affair

Early Golden Age Mansion   (212) 737-7536
Norwalk, CT

One of the country's first millionaires, LeGrand Lockwood bought land in his boyhood town of Norwalk in 1863 with the express purpose of building a manor house that would be unequaled anywhere in America. Being the Treasurer of the New York Stock Exchange and also involved in the railroad and steamship business as well as in the promotion of the sale of Civil War bonds, LeGrand Lockwood could well afford to materialize his dream. He engaged the services of one of the foremost architects of the time, Detlef Lienau, who introduced a style of building which later— with the famous Vanderbilt homes in Newport and New York— became characteristic of the Golden Age.

Artists and artisans were brought from Europe. The stonemasons and woodworkers arrived from Italy on the decks of the ships which transported the rare woods and marble in their holds, yet when the grand manor house containing fifty rooms was completed, LeGrand Lockwood would only enjoy it for four years. He died suddenly from pneumonia. Money was owed, the estate was foreclosed and the family of Charles Drelincourt Mathews, a New York importer, lived in the mansion from 1876 to 1938. The city of Norwalk bought the property in 1941 and sold land to make way for turnpikes. The sites of the greenhouses were used for parking lots. Faced with the threat of the mansion's demolition, a citizen's group was formed to preserve it, and thanks to its undaunted efforts, the mansion is now being completely restored. Its fragile glass conservatory, which had been destroyed by a falling tree, has had its original French plate glass decorated with a blue fleur-de-lis pattern copied exactly in acrylic materials.

Guest capacity: 100 seated in each of several rooms; 450 standing on first floor

Note: Smoking is not allowed. Weddings and other private functions are not allowed. The mansion's dining room, billiard room and rotunda are presently only available to non-profit organizations and corporations for special functions.

Former Country Club   (212) 737-7536
Westport, CT

This former country club, now a conference center and wedding site, offers a ballroom and overnight accommodations. It overlooks the Sound.

Guest capacity: 300 in ballroom; 14 overnight

Former Governor's Mansion   (212) 737-7536
Ridgefield, CT

Built in 1896 as a replica of the Connecticut State Building at the World's Columbian Exposition, Chicago 1893, by Phineas C. Lounsbury, a former governor of Connecticut, this property is now used for all manner of functions, including weddings.

Guest capacity: 180

Garden House   (212) 737-7536
Ridgefield, CT

Set in formal gardens enclosed by brick walls, this eighty-year-old garden house, built by Cass Gilbert, a neo-classical architect, offers French doors on three sides and a fireplace.
A reflecting pool and fountain grace the sunken portion of the garden.
Guest capacity: 90

Holly Barn   (212) 737-7536
Greenwich, CT

This nineteenth century barn is preserved by the Historical Society of the Town of Greenwich.
Guest capacity: 75

Meadowlands   (212) 737-7536
Darien, CT

This former private home, now community center, offers fine spaces both indoors and out.
Guest capacity: 130 seated/250 reception in Garden Wing; 185 reception in Library and Foyer; 50 seated/115 reception in Assembly Room; 30 seated/60 reception in dining room; 22 seated/45 reception in East Room; 250 seated/500 reception in whole house

Penny Arcade Barn   (212) 737-7536
Greenwich, CT

A natural shingle 1790's barn, featuring a forty-foot open beam ceiling, hand painted Portuguese tile floor and a Jacobean-style fireplace from the 1800's, houses a valuable collection of one thousand antique penny arcade games, music machines and circus memorabilia. Antique mechanical banks, 1920's nickelodeons, and other objects are also exhibited in the kitchen and in smaller nooks and crannies.

The large but cozy granery features an eighteenth century New England hearth, a pine floor and picture windows which look out onto a tranquil Connecticut countryside.
Guest capacity: 72 seated in granery
Suggested uses: surprise birthday party, etc.

Public Park and Manor House   (212) 737-7536
New Canaan, CT

This three hundred-acre estate overlooking Long Island Sound was formerly the gentlemen's farm and summer residence of wealthy New York City families, primarily the Thomas W. Hall's and the Lewis H. Lapham's who, during the period of 1895-1939, had their breakfast eggs, produce and freshly cut carnations delivered to their New York City townhouses from this Connecticut farm. They played polo on their private field and later erected an airplane hangar so young Jack Lapham could land his open cockpit plane from oil fields in Texas. After World War II the operation of everything came to a stop.
The property and English-style manor house which was designed in 1912 by W. B. Tubby is now publicly owned by the Town of New Canaan.
Guest capacity: 180 seated indoors; a tent may be erected on the grounds

Rose-Colored Summer Cottage   (212) 737-7536
Woodstock, CT

This cottage with its bright pink exterior reflects the interest in Gothic Revival architecture and evokes the tradition of rose plantings and purple-to-rose colors with which the exterior has always been painted.
Henry C. Bowen (1813-1896) commissioned the English-born architect Joseph Collins Wells to design a summer residence in the region where he was born and where his father had kept a country store and post office. Young Bowen left his home town at age twenty-one to seek his fortune in New York City.
After five years as a clerk to a dry goods merchant, whose daughter he later married, Bowen formed a partnership with one of his co-workers. Their business prospered, but the economic turbulence of the late 1850's forced him into bankruptcy. Undefeated by this setback, Bowen then directed his energies to *The Independent*, a congregational weekly publication espousing abolition, congregationalism, patriotism and the Republican Party. Thus, when the Bowen family was in residence in its rose-colored cottage, they entertained prominent literary and political figures. Henry Ward Beecher and Presidents Ulysses S. Grant, Rutherford B. Hayes, Benjamin Harrison and William McKinley were guests there at one time or another.
The cottage is the central building in a complex of structures, including a 35' x 60' carriage barn with windows on all sides

lying close to the *parterre* garden with one of the earliest surviving interior bowling alleys, an ice house and an aviary. The grounds reflect the idea of picturesque landscaping found in the writings of A. J. Downing. The *parterre* garden has survived since 1850 when it was laid out with six hundred yards of dwarf edging. The property is presently preserved and managed by The Society for the Preservation of New England Antiquities.

Guest capacity: up to 100 in tent; 150 in carriage barn

CENTRAL CONNECTICUT/ NEAR HARTFORD

Carousel and Pavilion   (212) 737-7536
Hartford, CT

Created in 1914 by the artistic carousel company Stein & Goldstein of Brooklyn, New York, which also made the slightly larger carousel in Central Park, it is one of the few hand-crafted carousels which still exists.

Featuring forty-eight brightly painted horses, two ornate Lovers' Chariots, eight hundred light bulbs, bevelled mirrors, plus music on the Wurlitzer Band Organ, the carousel is housed in a stained glass pavilion which can accommodate all manner of events including birthdays and weddings.

Guest capacity: 250 indoors

Connecticut Historical Society   (212) 737-7536
Hartford, CT

Founded in 1825, this historical society's mansion is situated on eight acres of landscaped grounds in Hartford's West End. It offers an Auditorium whose walls are lined with antique Connecticut tavern signs; a panelled, portrait-lined Board Room with large windows, a fireplace and gold leaf ceiling; and a Fountain Room with tiled floor, a working fountain and plants.

The Ballroom, Hallway, plus Fountain Room form a fine unit for receptions with an easy flow from room to room.

Guest capacity: 250 seated in Auditorium; 150 in Board Room, Hallway and Fountain Room combined; 50 seated in basement Lecture Room; 18 seated around Board Room table

Note: Available only to organizations and corporations; private functions are not allowed.

Gillette Castle State Park   (203) 526-2336
67 River Road
East Haddam, CT 06423

William Hooker Gillette, the noted actor, director and playwright who was best known for his portrayals of Sherlock Holmes, built an eccentric twenty-four-room fieldstone castle along the east bank of the Connecticut River in 1913.

Although private functions are not allowed inside the castle, the State Department of Environmental Protection sanctions the use of the grounds for weddings and provides a dressing room inside the castle for the bride.

Justice of the Peace House   (203) 289-4266
South Windsor, CT   Contact: Muriel A. Mahr

Listed in the National Register of Historic Places and located in a historic district of town, this Victorian home was built in 1851 by Commodore Charles Green. Its current owner is a lady Justice of the Peace, who performs the ceremony and stays on to coordinate the reception. Her fifteen well-appointed rooms and spacious outdoors with gazebo and pool make this a warm place for weddings.

Guest capacity: 50 buffet; 250 outdoors
Tenting is permitted.
Located ten miles northeast of Hartford.

Mark Twain Carriage House   (212) 737-7536
Hartford, CT

Built to house the coachman, horses and carriages of the Samuel Clemens family, the carriage house stands adjacent to the home in which Mark Twain lived from 1874 to 1891, his

continued on next page

happiest and most productive years. The house and carriage house were designed in High Victorian Gothic-style by the noted Victorian architect Edward Tuckerman Potter.

Guest capacity: 50 seated dinner/60 lecture/85 reception in Carriage House

A small kitchen is available.

The ground floor and exhibit area of the Mark Twain home can be visited during the function.

Note: Available only to clubs and business organizations, not to private individuals.

Norman Manor House on the Connecticut River   (212) 737-7536

Middletown, CT

Built in 1902 by architect Sidney Algernon Bell for Howard Taylor, a successful lawyer, this manor house was modeled in part after the Inn of William the Conqueror of Divers and the Chateau of Langais in France.

The actual construction of the house involved many Italian immigrants whose careful craftsmanship is evident in its masonry and woodwork. Most of the woodwork was done in chestnut, which was a plentiful and nearly indestructible hardwood available until the chestnut blight took its toll in 1908. However, a double row of chestnut trees still grace the mansion's driveway.

In 1969, the estate was transferred by the Taylor family to Wesleyan University.

Since then its Great Hall with working fireplaces has been the setting for many meetings, seminars, parties and wedding receptions.

Guest capacity: 65 seated/100 standing; additional capacity outside if tented

Oldest State House in the Nation   (212) 737-7536

Hartford, CT

Designed in 1796 by Charles Bullfinch of Boston, this brownstone and brick building is one of the greatest surviving examples of Federal architecture and the oldest State House in the nation. It may be rented for all manner of social occasions such as banquets, dinner dances, meetings and weddings.

Grand staircase in Great Hall is especially suited for tossing wedding bouquets.

Guest capacity: 120 seated banquet style/200 for a meeting in Court Room; 300 standing in Great Hall and Court Room

Turn-of-the-Century Opera House   (212) 737-7536

East Haddam, CT

Built on the banks of the Connecticut river by William H. Goodspeed, a local businessman who loved opera, and completed in 1876, the building included a theater with excellent acoustics as well as Mr. Goodspeed's shipping business, professional offices, a bar, a steamboat passenger terminal and a general store.

For a quarter of a century this opera house flourished featuring shows that travelled by steamboat from New York City, but after 1920 it stood idle. By 1958 it was marked for demolition, but preservationists came to its rescue and created a foundation which, together with the cooperation of the State of Connecticut and many private donors, saved the opera house and restored it to mint condition. Presently, it is the only theater in America entirely dedicated to the American musical.

Guest capacity: 399 in theater

The opera house may be rented for benefits. Dining arrangements may be made in a tent outdoors or at the Gelston House restaurant next door. The opera season runs from April to November and benefit performances must be arranged far in advance, particularly if these involve the entire theater.

Arrangements can also be made for guests to arrive by boat.

Webb-Deane-Stevens Museum   (212) 737-7536
Wethersfield, CT
Located south of Hartford, this one hundred year-old barn in a
    quiet historic district, is owned and operated by the Colonial
    Dames of America. It is available once a week from mid-May
    to mid-October for special functions, including weddings.
Guest capacity: 140
Kitchen may be used only to warm up food by professional caterers.
Note: Fundraising, tents, smoking and candles are not allowed.

Majestically perched on the shoreline, this mansion-style inn
    was recently transformed from a family-run operation to a
    combination inn/convention center and time-share con-
    dominium complex.
Still maintaining its intimate appeal, its public areas look out through
    wide expanses of glass to sweeping visions of sea and sky.
Guest capacity: 200 seated in ballroom; 100 seated in dining
    room; 100 on terrace; 45 in two-tiered lounge with private
    terrace; 5 conference areas; 30 overnight rooms and suites
Suggested uses: wedding, corporate reception, conference, meeting

EASTERN CONNECTICUT/
NEAR RHODE ISLAND

**Shingle/Stone Mansion at the Water's   (212) 737-7536
Edge**
Westbrook, CT

New Haven: Auditoriums, Halls & Meeting Rooms (by capacity for special functions)

New Haven Colony Historical Society   (203) 562-4183
114 Whitney Ave. 80/130
Long Wharf Theatre   (203) 787-4284
222 Sargent Dr. ....(reception)100/400
Peabody Museum of Natural History   (203) 432-5099
170 Whitney Ave. 150/400

THE HUDSON VALLEY

(WESTCHESTER, ROCKLAND, DUTCHESS, ORANGE, PUTNAM AND ULSTER COUNTIES)

America's Oldest Winery   (212) 737-7536
(Orange County)
Washingtonville, NY
Almost 150 years ago Jean Jacques, a French emigre and Pres-
    byterian elder, began to produce wine in the Hudson Valley
    for church purposes. Making wine for churches helped this
    thirty-five-acre winery survive the Prohibition in 1919 and
    continue its prosperous operation even today.
Under new ownership since 1987 and dramatically renovated,
    this winery offers a landmark stone building for large parties
    and a manor house for small parties, meetings and conferen-
    ces. All functions may be combined with tours of the under-
    ground cellars as well as large outdoor areas.
Guest capacity: up to 250 in stone building; 100 in manor house;
    additional capacity outdoors

At the River's Edge   (212) 737-7536

(Westchester County)
Garrison, NY

The famous gazebo which featured so prominently in the film *Hello Dolly* is available for wedding ceremonies. Adjacent river front green may be obtained for receptions.
Guest capacity: over 125

Charming Historical Society   (212) 737-7536

(Westchester County)
Bedford Village, NY

Formerly a New England meeting hall, this eighteenth century white building with green shutters lends itself for gracious weddings.
Guest capacity: 100 seated indoors; 200 seated indoors and out

---

The Claddagh   (212) 737-7536

Cold Spring, NY
(Dutchess County)

A Mariner thirty-two-foot ketch whose captain, Jackie Ring, is one of a handful of women U.S. Coast Guard captains on the Hudson River. Fresh flowers hang in a green basket in the galley, books on the Hudson and pamphlets of local interest are on the shelves, and the strains of classical music and sea chanteys can by heard below in the main cabin.
A full keel and total weight of thirteen thousand pounds make Claddagh a very stable vessel. Its name derives from the ancient part of the city of Galway in the Irish Republic and from Claddagh Ring, which symbolizes love, trust and loyalty and is sometimes worn as a wedding ring.
Thus, the Claddagh is a charming vessel for a small wedding party or honeymoon Hudson cruise.
Guest capacity: 6 under sail
Rental fee: $30 per person for 2 hours including refreshments
Note: Embark from Garrison, one hour and forty-five minutes north of New York City.

Classic Italianate Renaissance Mansion   (212) 737-7536

(Westchester County)
North Tarrytown, NY

Built in 1851 by John Butler Shuck, one of the architects of Grand Central Station, this villa sits on a grassy bluff and overlooks the Hudson River and Tappan Zee Bridge. Elaborately furnished, its Corinthian columns, marble floor, high ceilings and sweeping veranda lend great style to special functions.

Guest capacity: 200 seated/175 with dancing on veranda; 50 seated/100 cocktails indoors
Steinway grand piano

Club House   (212) 737-7536

(Westchester County)
Scarsdale, NY

This Victorian Gothic home offers a Grand Ballroom and french doors leading onto a large front lawn.
Guest capacity; 110 seated/150 cocktails in Ballroom
Small stage, grand piano

Colonial Homestead/Now Inn   (212) 737-7536

(Westchester County)
Purdy, NY

On the stately land of the original owner's descendents, this charming white landmark has been completely restored to its sturdy beams and wood-burning fireplaces. The original owner was a Colonial merchant/Loyalist who traded cotton for tea amongst other goods. A hangman's tree and a large stone used by a portly Colonial family member for mounting his horse are in front of this genuinely charming country house.
Guest capacity: 70; 12 in dining/conference room; 2 in honeymoon bedroom
Resident caterer
Located approximately 70 miles from New York City.
Perfect for small weddings inclusive of ceremony, as well as friendly corporate gatherings and country birthdays.

The Commander   (212) 737-7536

(Westchester County)
Peekskill, NY

This historical vessel built in 1917 is listed on the National and
State Registers of Historic Places. It is available for charter
for cruises on the Hudson River from West Haverstraw,
Westpoint and Peekskill, for excursions through the "Hudson
Highlands" which are considered to be the most scenic part
and are often called the Rhineland of America.
The lower deck is enclosed and offers chairs, tables and benches
plus a small area for dancing. The upper deck is partly covered
with a canopy.
Guest capacity: 125 on entire boat; 100 on enclosed lower deck
Note: Available May 1 through October, it is a one-hour drive
from the George Washington Bridge.

Dutchess County English Country   (212) 737-7536
Estate

Amenia, NY

Fronted by a row of towering sycamores planted in 1835 and
nourished by eleven springs, including a bubbling brook that
splashes across the front lawn, this romantic thirty-one
bedroom English estate is situated two hours and fifteen
minutes from New York City. Its slate roof, winter garden
dining room, fireplaces, tennis court, covered heated pool,
and large outdoor swimming pool make this a favorite of
leading corporations for think tank meetings, as well as
brides for country weddings.
Guest capacity: 100 seated, 125/135 buffet indoors; 250 outdoors in tents

Dutchess County Fairgrounds   (914) 876-4001
Rte. 9   Contact: Manager
Rhinebeck, NY 12572

A bandstand and stage are situated on 140,000 acres of fairgrounds.
Available May through October
Guest capacity: 50,000

Exquisite Hudson River Estate   (212) 737-7536
Grounds

(Dutchess County)
Annandale-on-Hudson, NY

Formerly owned by
two leading
Hudson River
families, the
Livingstons and
the Delafields,
these 434 acres of
tranquil orchards,
fields and lawns
are available for
outdoor private
functions. The
North Pavilion of
the estate's
twenty-three-room
mansion, which is attached to the mansion, may serve as a
location for a bar or band, although the mansion itself is not
available for celebratory purposes, except for tours. The West
Lawn, with its lovely view of the river, is a favorite site.
Guest capacity: over 250 in tent on West Lawn or elsewhere on
grounds
Rental fee: $5,000
Kitchen facilities; ample parking

Former Home of a Russian Prince   (212) 737-7536
(Dutchess County)
Rhinebeck, NY

This thirty-room Queen Anne period stone mansion was the
former home of Prince Serge and Alice Astor Obolensky. It
was built between 1923 and 1926 by architect Mott Schmidt,
using European artisans and craftsmen for its masonry, stone
cutting, marble foyers and maple floors.
Surrounded by spacious parklands with views of the Hudson River
and the Catskill Mountains beyond, its half-mile entrance drive
is bordered by one hundred year-old locust trees.

continued on next page

Suitable for conferences as well as weddings and dinner dances.
Guest capacity: 30 seated/50 cocktails in Hudson Room and Ferncliff Room respectively; 60 seated/100 cocktails in Astor Salon and Prince Obolensky Salon respectively, or they can be combined to seat 90 for dinner; a large white canopy connected to side of ballroom seats 250 with dancing
There are additional rooms on the second floor. A terrace and garden are also available.

Four Hundred Year-Old Samurai Farmhouses/Now Restaurants   (212) 737-7536

(Orange County and Westchester County)
Central Valley and Hawthorne, NY

These two four hundred year-old Samurai (warrior) farmhouses were dismantled in Japan and reconstructed by Japanese carpenters without using nails. Now converted into restaurants, each is surrounded by five acres of lush Japanese gardens with a fishpond, water wheel, waterfalls, teahouses, and Japanese stone statuary.
Guest capacity: over 200 seated in each farmhouse; 130 in each main dining room and 70 upstairs; cocktails and hors d'oeuvres served in bar lounge or garden
Resident caterer
Suggested uses: private party, business meeting, wedding reception
Note: Entire restaurant available Saturday and Sunday, 11:30 a.m. to 4:30 p.m.; seven days a week for smaller parties. Also available for location shoots.

Gothic Revival Hudson River Estate   (212) 737-7536

(Westchester County)
Tarrytown, NY

Designed by A. J. Davis and built in 1838 for William Paulding, a former mayor of New York City, this marvellous example of Gothic Revival architecture later served as the summer home for railroad tycoon Jay Gould.

In 1964, Gould's daughter, Anna, Duchess of Talleyrand-Perigord, left the sixty-seven-acre Hudson River property, complete with original furnishings, to the National Trust for Historic Preservation to be operated for the public as a non-profit historic house/museum. It is the policy of the Trust to allow it to be used for receptions, dinners, meetings and other special uses so long as the user adheres to the guidelines designed to protect such property.
The castle's newly opened Guest House offers "the Great Room" with a cathedral ceiling, working fireplace, leaded windows and river view. This enchanting intimate space is furnished with antiques.
Guest capacity: 150 seated on the piazza; 200 in rose garden; 200 maximum for tented functions on lawn; 35 seated/50 cocktails in Guest House

Hammond Museum   (914) 669-5033

Deveau Road   Contact: Manager
North Salem, NY 10560

A Japanese stroll garden is available for wedding receiving lines by special permission from a small museum that stands on a hill and overlooks farmlands, lakes and woods in Westchester County. Guests may be seated in a Medieval-style hall complete with a fireplace and tapestry, or in an outdoor courtyard.
Guest capacity: 130 seated indoors; 130 seated outdoors
Resident caterer

Hilltop Hudson Valley Mansion   (212) 737-7536

(Westchester County)
Dobbs Ferry, NY

This nineteenth century great house with a two-story central hall, marble double staircase and elaborate twelve-foot fireplace is a thirty minute drive from New York City.

Guest capacity: 250 maximum seated/approximately 300 for a cocktail party; additional guests may be accommodated on outside grounds and porch.
It is particularly suitable for weddings and large parties.
Resident caterer

Historical Society on the Hudson   (212) 737-7536
(Orange County)
Newburg, NY

Built in the 1830's by David Crawford, a prominent businessman involved in Hudson River shipping, this Greek Revival-style home set on a bluff in what is now Newburg's historic district overlooks the Hudson. Its sliding etched-glass doors, flying staircase, chandeliers and yellow and white hues gives this house a soft southern feeling.
Guest capacity: 90 in double parlor
A small garden with sundial is on grounds.
Note: Dancing is not allowed.

Mediterranean Splendor   (212) 737-7536
(Westchester County)
Katonah, NY

A villa of great Mediterranean splendor stands in the center of a forest-like park and gardens in the rolling hills of northern Westchester. Built in the 1930's for Walter Tower Rosen, a New York lawyer and investment banker, to provide a harmonious setting for his stunning collection of European and Chinese art, this exquisite treasure houses entire rooms from European palaces and villas.
Guest capacity: up to 700 in tent in formal garden or canopy in the courtyard; 1700 in venetian garden
Note: Not available Thursday through Sunday last two weeks in June as well as all of July and August. Functions may not take place inside the villa; amplified music is not allowed.

Museum of Art and Science   (212) 737-7536
(Westchester County)
Yonkers, NY

In close proximity to New York City, this Westchester museum of both art and science offers a multiple building complex which spans the old and the new: Trevor Mansion, an 1876 Eastlake-style house, as well as contemporary galleries. The courtyard located between the contemporary wing and the mansion affords views of the Hudson River and the Palisades.
Guest capacity: 60 seated/100 standing in Trevor Mansion; 300 seated/750 standing in Main Exhibition Galleries; 200 seated/400 standing in multi-purpose auditorium with stage, plus terrace; 300 seated/500 standing in courtyard (particularly suitable for weddings).
Note: Facilities may not be used for partisan political gatherings, fundraising events where direct solicitations are made, or commercial affairs where merchandise is sold.

Old Rhinebeck Aerodrome, Inc.   (212) 737-7536
(Dutchess County)
Rhinebeck, NY

continued on next page

Old-time flying machines, dating from 1900 to 1937, in rustic aerodrome hangar settings may be seen, photographed and also rented for special flights.

Guest capacity: 2000 spectators seated/5000 spectators standing

A large picnic area is available.

Suitable for location shoots for TV commercials, films, fashion ads, company picnics.

Place of the Great Spirit   (212) 737-7536

(Putnam County)
Garrison, NY

The name "Manitoga" chosen by the renowned industrial designer of the 30's and 40's, Russel Wright, for his eighty-acre Hudson Highland estate is derived from Algonquin meaning "Place of the Great Spirit." For thirty years, Mr. Wright worked to express "the Great Spirit" in the design of his house, whose main support is a one hundred year-old cedar tree which he found by the brook, whose masonry reflects the stones of the nearby mountainside, whose sunken tub in the bathroom is supplied with water from crevices in the natural rock wall and whose terrace is situated so that the moon rises over it and throws its light across the stones.

Guest capacity: 60 seated/60 cocktails indoors and out; a tent may be used for larger functions

Suggested uses: small conference, workshop, wedding

Rip Van Winkel M/V   (914) 255-6515

Hudson River Cruises
P.O. Box 333
Rifton, NY 12471

This motor vessel may be boarded at Kingston and chartered past Westpoint, historic mansions, Bear Mountain and other sites.

Guest capacity: 350

Brunch, lunch and dinner cruises with dancing.

Resident caterer

Rondout Belle   (914) 338-6280

Hudson Rondout Cruises Inc.
11 East Chestnut Street
Kingston, NY 12401

This passenger vessel is sixty-eight feet long, eighteen-feet wide and twin diesel powered. Charters may include viewing the famed Rondout Lighthouse and the Esopus Lighthouse.

Guest capacity: 90

Brunch, lunch and dinner cruises.

Resident caterer

Sacred Place: From Garbage Dump to Sanctuary   (212) 737-7536

(Orange County)
Warwick, NY

On the banks of the Wawayanda, an overgrown fieldstone ruin of a late eighteenth century water mill inspired Frederick Franck, a Dutch artist, to transform what had become an unofficial garbage dump into an oasis of inwardness. He and a fellow Dutchman, Bert Willemse, began their work in the late 1960's, creating from ruins a work of art outside the art game, a work of faith outside the religious game, and called it *Pacem in Terris* (Peace on Earth).

Open to the public on weekends for concerts, plays, readings and for wedding ceremonies of every denomination, as well as to unaffiliated loners.

Note: Available weekends only, May through September, 11 a.m. to 6 p.m.

Victorian House with Panoramic Views of the Hudson   (212) 737-7536

(Westchester County)
Yonkers, NY

This lovingly restored home and carriage house offers several venues for special functions including weddings. The maroon, pink and beige indoor space is primarily for small affairs. Larger events may take place on the veranda, whose supporting pillars are topped with pink ram horns, as well as on lawn.

Guest capacity: 30 seated indoors; 75 seated/100 on veranda for cocktails

Parking for about twenty cars. Located thirty minutes from New York City.

Note: Smoking and throwing of confetti/rice are not allowed indoors. Music and dancing are allowed on veranda only.

Ward's Castle   (212) 737-7536
(Westchester County)
Port Chester, NY

This castle-like cement structure offers fireplaces in every room.

Guest capacity: 60 seated on two levels

Westchester's Only Winery   (212) 737-7536
North Salem, NY

Located on several hundred acres in the beautiful rolling hills of northern Westchester, this winery is owned by a New York City physician and his wife. It produces some ten varieties of premium local wines in a rustic beamed barn.

Guest capacity: 30 seated/50 buffet in glass and tile Tasting Room; larger functions may be tented outdoors

Suitable for small private dinner parties and wine tastings as well as tented weddings. Ample parking.

Winery with its Own Regional Restaurant   (212) 737-7536
(Dutchess County)
Amenia, NY

The farms that have cultivated the rolling hills of the Hudson Valley provide this contemporary Dutchess County winery

and restaurant with regional culinary treasures. In the belief that one of the best ways to preserve open farm lands and to keep developers at bay is to make sure that farming remains profitable, William Wetmore, the vintner/restaurateur, showcases a great variety of wines, including his own, from the Hudson Valley, Long Island, Finger Lakes and Great Lakes. Also available are regionally produced specialty foods such as cheeses, venison and other game, smoked trout and salmon prosciutto, lamb, veal, fresh fruits, vegetables, herbs and a prize-winning local foie gras.

Guest capacity: 50 seated in dining room; 70 on porch and downstairs; larger numbers maybe accommodated with tents

Winery on the West Bank   (212) 737-7536
(Ulster County)
West Park, NY

This one hundred-acre wine estate specializes in Chardonnay. The charming winery is a 130-year-old former dairy barn. Wedding ceremonies may take place on a hill affording a spectacular view of the Hudson River.

Guest capacity: 125 seated in main room; 45 seated in small room; 250 in tent next to vineyards; 500 outdoors

Resident caterer

Suggested uses: corporate seminar with lunch and dinner service, bar mitzvah, wedding, etc.

Women's Club in Bronxville (914) 337-3252
135 Midland Avenue
Bronxville, NY 10708

Currently being considered for landmarking, this two-story building with high ceilings offers floor-to-ceiling windows, a ballroom and a patio.
Guest capacity: 150
Stage, screen, microphone, projector; resident caterer
Space is not air-conditioned.
Suggested uses: meeting, party, wedding

Woolworth Mansion Replica (212) 737-7536
(Westchester County)
White Plains, NY

Built in 1920 as a replica of Long Island's North Shore Woolworth Mansion, this villa is especially appropriate for tented outdoor parties and weddings. Its landscaped grounds offer specimen trees, a rock garden, a rose garden, a grape arbor, tennis court, flood lights for night events and a veranda for dancing.
Guest capacity: 100 indoors; over 200 in garden

LONG ISLAND

Clark Garden (516) 621-7568
193 I.U. Willets Road   Contact: Ellen Basile
Albertson, NY 11507

This nature center offers a backdrop for bridal photographs. Flower beds, a woodland gazebo, rose garden and a pond are just some of the serene settings.
Note: A permit must be obtained at least two weeks in advance. A fee is charged.

Fifty-Six-Acre Estate (212) 737-7536
(Suffolk County)
Smithtown, NY

This fifty-six-acre estate offers orchards and vineyards, plus a reflecting pond with a gazebo. The grounds also include two outdoor court yards.
Indoor facilities are a 12,500 sq. ft. glass-enclosed pool area and a ballroom in a 5000 sq. ft. Roder pre-span structure which is beautifully appointed, air-conditioned and heated.
Guest capacity: 300 seated/up to 800 cocktails
Resident caterer

Former Movie Theater/Now North Shore Catering Hall (212) 737-7536
(Nassau County)
Glen Cove, NY

This restored ornate former movie theater now serves as a fine new site for meetings and weddings.
Guest capacity: 400 seated
Resident caterer

Former Playhouse/Now Wedding Hall (212) 737-7536
(Nassau County)
Floral Park, NY

This former playhouse and movie theater has been entirely decorated for wedding receptions and other special occasions. It offers a circular dance floor, wall-to-wall carpeting, a gold leaf inlaid ceiling and a bridal room. An elevator accesses the ballroom.
Guest capacity: 350 seated in ballroom; 350 cocktails in cocktail lounge
Air-conditioned; 200-car parking garage and basement
Resident caterer

Former Pratt Mansion (212) 737-7536
(Nassau County)
Glen Cove, NY

Situated on fifty-five rolling acres, this Georgian manor house on the North Shore's Gold Coast can accommodate 300 guests for wedding ceremonies, receptions and cocktail parties. Indoor and outdoor facilities. Overnight accommodations for 200.

Rental fee: $125 minimum per person
Resident caterer; kosher catering also available

Four Hundred Year-Old Samurai Farmhouse/Now Restaurant in Suffolk County   (212) 737-7536

Hauppauge, NY

This restaurant is modeled after a four hundred year-old Japanese farmhouse. Beautiful grounds with Japanese walkway and outdoor patio.

Guest capacity: over 200 seated in entire farmhouse; cocktails and hors d'oeuvres served in lounge or on patio

Suggested uses: private party, business meeting, wedding reception

Note: Entire restaurant available Saturday and Sunday, 11:30 a.m. to 4:30 p.m.; seven days a week for smaller parties.

Long Island Vineyard   (212) 737-7536

(Suffolk County)
Aquebogue, NY

Located in an area of beaches, farmlands and villages, this contemporary winery and tasting room incorporates state-of-

the-art viticulture. Near Riverhead on the North Shore, the Tasting Room is decorated with heavy oak walls and antique fixtures purchased from London's eighteenth century public houses. A spacious, wrap-around deck extends from the Tasting Room out into the vineyards themselves affording a magnificent view of sixty-one acres.

Guest capacity: 40 seated/200 standing in Tasting Room
Located approximately 120 miles from New York City.
Suggested uses: executive outing, fundraiser, employee day trip, alumni gathering, wedding

Nature Preserve/Special Function Site   (212) 737-7536

(Nassau County)
Manhasset, NY

This shingle-style mansion set atop rolling green lawns overlooking Long Island Sound offers two panelled rooms, a large covered porch and spacious lawns for tent parties.

Guest capacity: 100 indoors; more may be accommodated when tent is used outside

North Shore Women's Club   (212) 737-7536

(Nassau County)
Great Neck, NY

This 1938 brick house offers a large hall with a stage and dining room with french doors that open onto a patio and lawns.

Guest capacity: 150 with dancing in large hall; 150 cocktails in dining room

Old Westbury Gardens   (516) 333-0048

P.O. Box 430
Westbury, NY 11568-0430

This former estate of the Philipps family offers a magnificent garden for outdoor wedding ceremonies.

Guest capacity: 70 for corporate dinner, luncheon or meeting; any amount for outdoor wedding ceremony; in case of rain only up to 100 persons can find shelter on the mansion's porch.

continued on next page

Note: Functions inside the mansion are only available to corporate patrons and members. All functions are subject to approval by Board of Trustees. Wedding receptions are not allowed.

Corporate patrons donate $3,000 contribution for a cocktail party or meeting; $6,000 contribution for tent party

Planetarium and Historic House on Long Island   (212) 737-7536

(Nassau County)
Centerport, NY

The forty-three-acre landscaped grounds overlooking Northport Harbor, its elegant mansion and planetarium are part of the William K. Vanderbilt II estate. The sixty-foot tall Sky Theater Planetarium is available for corporate conferences and meetings. It contains all audio-visual equipment needed for corporate presentations. Corporate receptions may be held in the Rose Garden and the Boat House.

Guest capacity: 60 seated indoors; 400 or more if tent is used
Rental fee: $500 to $10,000 for corporate membership
Note: Space is not available for private or non-profit functions.

Planting Fields Arboretum   (516) 922-9206

P.O. Box 58, Planting Fields Road   Contact: Gordon Jones,
Oyster Bay, NY 11771   Director

The Haybarn, a former red brick stable of William Robertson Coe, is available occasionally for fairs and functions of school and educational groups. There are 409 acres of guided walks, conifer trails, lawns and greenhouses available to the public for quiet self-guided tours.

Capacity: 350 seated/600 standing
Note: Weddings are not allowed.

Six-Sided Club House   (212) 737-7536

(Nassau County)
Cold Spring Harbor, NY

Set on four wooded acres, this charming rustic clubhouse offers a 40-foot cathedral ceiling, 18-inch wooden beams throughout, two fireplaces, brick paths and flower gardens.

Guest capacity: 80 seated indoors; 200 in tents outdoors
Note: Space is available anytime in winter; after 7 p.m. in summer.

Also see : CONFERENCE CENTERS
           Former Bread Factory/Now Film Studio
           Long Island City; The New Frontier

LAST MINUTE ADDITIONS

Faculty House   (212) 737-7536
(Upper West Side)
Columbia University
New York, NY

Built in 1923, this large campus structure offers three floors of dining and meeting rooms for small and large functions.
Guest capacity: 250 on each floor; 700 if all three floors are used
Small private dining/meeting rooms are also available.
Suggested uses: all manner of social functions including a wedding, bar mitzvah, conference or dinner meeting
Note: Space is not available in August.

Historic Trading Floor   (212) 737-7536
(Tribeca)
New York, NY

Built in 1884, this 5500 sq. ft. space with tall arched windows and 50-foot high walls was the original trading floor before it became the New York Stock Exchange and moved to Wall Street.
Guest capacity: 500 seated/2000 cocktails
Note: Beautifully restored, commitments for special functions can only be taken three months prior to the event date.

Historic Woman's Club Building /Now   (212) 737-7536
Dramatic Arts School
(East 30's)
New York, NY

Built in 1905 by Stanford White, this graceful six-story townhouse was first built in 1905 for The Colony Club, which was the first woman's club building in New York City.
Now the East Coast headquarters of a renowned school for the dramatic arts, it is still graced with lovely moldings, fireplaces, mirrors, brass chandeliers and a lovely stairway.
Guest capacity: 60 seated/150 cocktails in 6th floor Reception Hall/Library; 160 seated/225 cocktails in 5th floor dining room; 105/163/169 respectively in three separate theaters
Suggested uses: organizational meeting, reception, wedding

Light and Airy Ballroom in a Countrified   (212) 737-7536
Setting
(Westchester County)
Bedford, NY

Located in a Mediterranean-style mansion, a white-washed ballroom offers eight large French windows which open onto a lawn and formal garden.
Guest capacity: 170 seated with dancing; 200 in tent on lawn

Midtown Private Club with Terrace and   (212) 737-7536
View
(East 60's)
New York, NY

Available in the evenings and all day Saturday and Sunday, this contemporary private club offers an exclusive midtown location with views and a charming outdoor terrace. Gazebo on terrace is suitable for wedding ceremonies.
Guest capacity: 55 seated indoors/100 cocktails; 120 with terrace
Resident caterer

New Museum Devoted to the History and   (212) 737-7536
Technology of Film
(Astoria)
Queens, NY

Recently opened as part of the 1920's Astoria Studio complex and newly renovated by the renowned contemporary architectural firm of Gwathmey Siegel, this is the first museum in the United States devoted to the art, history and technology of motion pictures, television and video. It offers more than 60,000 artifacts, including the actual movie set from *Glass Menagerie* which Paul Newman directed, as well as reception areas and one of the most versatile screening facilities in the U.S.
Guest capacity: 60 seated in Screening Room; 200 seated in Theater; 150 seated/250 cocktails in Cafe/Lobby area
Note: The Museum will be fully staffed for evening functions offering lectures and tours to guests. Its surprisingly interesting gift shop may also stay open by special request. Located 20 minutes from midtown Manhattan, transportation via private vehicles may be arranged.

Oh! What a Beautiful View   (212) 737-7536
Long Island City, NY

Two banquet rooms on the water's edge offer glass-enclosed views of the East River and Manhattan, plus open-air terraces fore and aft. It is ideal for weddings.
Guest capacity: 50/250 seated; 50/350 cocktails
Resident caterer

Society's Brownstone   (212) 737-7536
(East 60's)
New York, NY

Built in 1875, this five floor brownstone offers a tasteful third floor dining room decorated with paintings by Maxfield Parrish and Andrew Wyeth plus a separate bar and attached terrace. Two museum spaces are on lower floors.
Guest capacity: 74 seated/90 cocktails in dining room; 250 cocktails on museum floors
Resident caterer

NEW YORK AND ENVIRONS

Some of the advertisers which follow offer services not covered by a single heading, i.e., a caterer may also be a party planner and visa versa, a party planner may also do invitations. It is, therefore, a good idea to scan related headings.

BAKED GOODS

Cakeability
(212) 744-6761

Encore Patisserie
(212) 505-1188
Superb cakes for all occasions. Specializing in gold-opera, raspberry St. Ange, chocolate truffle cakes and fine french pastries. Our wedding cakes are unique in design and flavour.

The Erotic Baker, Inc.
(212) 362-7557
YES, THE EROTIC BAKER does all kinds of cakes, not just erotic ones! We will follow your party theme--company logos, theatre posters or whatever suits your special occasion! We accept most major credit cards and deliver in MANHATTAN.

CATERERS

A Sense of Taste Inc.
(212) 570-2928
Complete party designing for corporate and private events. We'll plan the food, the mood and create the perfect atmosphere right down to the last detail.

A Taste of Paris
(800) 227-9768
(203) 438-5761 (in Connecticut)
"The Innovative Caterer"
Full Service Catering and Event Planning
You just need to make one call!

Alouette Caterers
(718) 784-1167
Exquisite, kicky, precious, hearty, high-tech, opulent...always creative, with a keen eye to detail and a keen ear to appropriateness. We can service your every party need. Let us whet your appetite and stir your imagination. Customized services from 100 to 3,000.

Austin's Regional Fare
(212) 807-7471

Bierman & Carrington Caterers
(212) 249-4594

Black Tie Affair
(212) 892-5079
A complete catering service. We can satisfy all your needs, social or corporate, from the space to the conclusion of your event. Call for an appointment and Thomas Esposito will tell you more about our services.

Bob Goldberg-In Service Caterers
(212) 431-5900

Catering by Steven P. Salsberg, Inc.
(212) 289-8506
Let us also find your party location for less. We specialize in yachts and discos at unbeatable prices. References available on request.

Celebrations Inc.
(212) 684-4070/(201) 656-3500
Celebrations, an award-winning events management and catering company specializes in corporate events, theme parties, meetings, and extravaganzas throughout the U.S. Parties from 50 to 5,000. Decor, transportation, entertainment, catering, rentals, site selection, invitations. Our experienced staff will handle every detail with finesse and style.

Charlotte's
(212) 732-7939
"Food That Dreams Are Made Of"

Chez Vous Caterers
(718) 720-0900

Clambakes by Jim Sanford
(212) 865-8976

The Cleaver Company
(212) 431-3688
High quality caterers. Private, corporate. Take-out store at 229 West Broadway in New York City. Breakfast, lunch, dinner.

Continental Caterers
(516) 239-4868
Full service gourmet catering at select locations (including country clubs, inns, yachts, temples, mansions, etc.). Profiled in "Who's Who in America's Restaurants". Located at 473 Bayview Avenue in Inwood, New York.

Corporate Cuisine International
(212) 601-3449/(201) 356-7810
Distinctive catering and event management. Private, corporate cocktail receptions to formal dinners. Trained tuxedoed staff. French, Russian, English, American service. Each party is unique unto itself.

Corwin Nove Caterer
(212) 496-2254/(212) 477-1533

Creative Gourmet
(212) 601-1800/(212) 601-1801
Special events planner and full-service caterer. Theme, food, entertainment, decor, staffing, location, rentals, limousine service, etc.

Cynthia Cariseo Catering
(212) 580-1857

Elite Caterers, Inc.
(718) 275-7650
Fine food and pastries deliciously prepared for all occasions. Complete catering service for intimate dinners, corporate breakfasts and lunches, cocktail parties, weddings, etc. We will travel to wherever your next affair takes us.

Epicure Catering
(212) 737-7536
Of course we have exquisite handmade food, stunning presentations, and wonderful sites. But we are also really nice, friendly people who can take the fear out of party planning. We specialize in NEW JERSEY locations. Call us for menu ideas and prices.

Fanfare Inc.
(212) 319-9093
Corporate and private caterers.

Food Fantasies
(212) 315-5115/(201) 484-5227

Food In Motion
(212) 807-8935
Food In Motion engages its clients with sumptuous cuisine, presented with style. We are proud of our creative menus and gracious service — the elements of a perfect party. Call us for full party planning including floral design and decor.

Fred Rothberg Catering Inc.
(718) 852-3673

Heinzerling Catering
(212) 737-7536
Heinzerling Catering is a full service caterer providing elegantly presented fresh foods and professional staff. Based in Park Slope, Brooklyn they work Manhattan and the tri-state area with a competitive edge. Small corporate luncheons to gala receptions. Fully licensed and insured.

Howard's Gourmet Catering
(212) 737-7536
Fine catering for private and corporate occasions. Bar mitzvahs, conventions, party and meeting planning. Kosher-style available.

In Good Taste Ltd.
(212) 534-0825
For banquets, balls, brunches...on a yacht, in the boardroom, or at home...no party's too intimate, no gathering too grand, each occasion is festive and carefully planned. Celebrate...call...IN GOOD TASTE.

Incredible Edibles
(Fran Zaslow Catering)
(516) 747-2540
Former corporate chef. Emphasis on fresh, seasonal ingredients. Home-baked desserts. Complete party planning from 10-1,000. Contact Fran for that personal touch.

Jack Hocks' L'Entourage
(212) 532-9784
Fine, distinctive catering.

Mariner III Catering
(212) 727-7272
By land or sea.

Marquis Caterers
(718) 769-7010
New York's kosher yacht caterer. Distinctive kosher cuisine for weddings, bar mitzvahs, corporate events. Specialist in off-premise catering at offbeat locations.

Maxine Walsky Catering, Inc.
(212) 737-7536
Maxine's provides exquisite and creative menus as well as party planning. Cuisines and locations are individually customized, limited only by a client's imagination. From memorable weddings to unique corporate events, Maxine's has catered to European heads of state while welcoming the most intimate dining occasion.

Mr. Babbington Caterers
(212) 860-1980/(914) 478-4550

New York Parties
(212) 777-3565

Occasions
(212) 727-1587
Fine catering and complete party planning. Innovative, elegant cuisine created by an experienced New York City restaurateur. From intimate dinners for 2 to parties for any number. Let us plan your special occasion.

Panhandlers Catering Service, Inc.
(212) 564-7350
A full-service catering company offering a wide variety of cuisines, flowers, music and entertainment. Beautifully served food with special attention to each client's needs.

Perfect Pear Caterers
(212) 864-1771
Full-service, corporate and private catering. Exceptionally good food, personal service, beautiful presentation. Every party is a memorable event. Catered in your space, private townhouses, or lofts.

Perfect Touch Caterers
(212) 972-0820
Professional off-premises, full-service catering. Party planning, fully insured. Realistic prices. Corporate, weddings, bar mitzvahs, social. Culinary Institute of America-trained chefs serving New York City, Long Island, Westchester.

Philip Stone Caterers
(212) 737-7536
Elegant, imaginative and distinctive catering in New York and LONG ISLAND. Unusual locations. Complete party service and event coordination. New York's finest and most professional staff. Private and corporate.

Randall Gottier Catering
(212) 758-0265
"Applause! Applause!" said Bloomingdales. "I'm Impressed": New York Magazine. Just two of our rave reviews. Cocktails-buffets-sit downs for 2-2,000. Full party planning service — thematic events are a specialty. Food or staff only. Also available— American and Continental cuisines.

Rita Miller Catering
(201) 763-4274
New Jersey's most versatile caterer. Will travel. Creative menus. Exquisite presentation. Call Rita for a personal consultation.

Road to Mandalay, Inc.
(212) 226-4218
Specializing in Southeast Asian cuisine. Also Burmese, Indonesian, Vietnamese and Thai menus as well. On and off-premises catering.

Robert Day Dean's Catering
(212) 755-8300
Private, corporate and cultural events catered by our professional staff with style and expertise.

Rosa Ross' Wok on Wheels
Catering
(212) 777-3420

Simply Divine
(212) 737-7536
Simply the best in kosher catering. Specializing in wedding and life cycle events.

SIMPLY ELEGANT PARTIES, By Beverly
(212) 737-7536
From extravagant soirees to intimate home cooked suppers, we specialize in on-location catering. Only the freshest, all natural ingredients are used in our professionally served gourmet meals. We personally oversee all details of your party from start to finish.

Special Attention
(212) 683-6569

Stephen Kennard Catering
(212) 243-7043
Social and corporate catering.
Personal and imaginative.
Ten years experience in successful entertaining.

Susan Layton Catering Inc.
(212) 737-7536
Susan Layton Catering Inc. has provided personalized catering services to individuals and corporate clients in the Fairfield, CONNECTICUT and WESTCHESTER COUNTY area for 15 years. Our professionally trained chefs, graduates of the Culinary Institute of America, will create classical menus ranging from 12 to 1,000 guests. A glorious selection of bridal and other important occasion cakes are another facet of our services.

Tentation Catering
(212) 353-0070

Terrace II Caterers
(516) 759-9295
Distinctive catering and event planning for our private and corporate clients. Classical and regional American cuisines. Call for personalized attention for your party needs; staffing, tenting, etc.

Total Party Concepts, Ltd.
(914) 353-4466/(212) 861-4869
Creative catering with special detail to presentation— exotic and European floral design— theme environment coordination. Serving the tri-state area.

Umanoff & Parsons, Inc.
(212) 219-2240
Bakers and caterers. Our desert specialties are mud cake, fresh fruit pies, carrot and cheese cakes. We also create beautiful birthday and wedding cakes.
Our full-service catering offers personal service and delicious menus.

Very Very Gourmet
(212) 737-7536
Creative catering. Elegant cuisine. Specializing in weddings, dinner and cocktail parties, corporate and special occasions! Let us plan a party for your personal taste and budget.

Vincent Minuto Caterers
(212) 903-4975
Corporate and private dinners, buffets and cocktail parties. Menus are arranged according to clients needs and taste. Accompanied by New York's finest staff. New York, Southampton, Greenwich.

William Poll
(212) 288-0501
First in gourmet luxuries and catering. Choose from our selection of prepared take-out foods—appetizers, dinners, desserts—and the finest caviar and smoked salmon. Services include rentals, staffing, music, flowers.

FLORAL DESIGNERS

Castle & Pierpont
(212) 737-7536
"Where the World of Art and Nature Meet" Hard to find European floral specimens. Personalized and coordinated festive floral service to express your individual self.

Growingthings
(212) 737-7536
Well known in Park Slope and Brooklyn Heights, these "gardeners with a storefront" gather the freshest flowers and arrange them with their fullest, most natural expression in mind.
Feature Victorian and romantic floral designs.

Surroundings
(212) 737-7536
Surroundings is a full service florist that can handle anything from a small dinner party to a gala event.

INVITATIONS/ PAPER GOODS

Gemini Paper Goods, Ltd.
(718) 768-5568
Imprinted and personalized napkins, gift towels, matches, escort cards, informals, totebags, gift ribbon, etc. A total party accessory company.

Fancy That
(212) 838-1201
Unique custom and catalog invitations for all occasions. Party accessories too— place cards, printed paper goods, centerpieces, favors, etc. From traditional to avant garde, with your creativity and/or ours, we bring the theme together. Party and entertainment coordination services and calligraphy available also.

Invitations Plus
(212) 548-3900
America's most exquisite invitations, announcements, stationery, and party accessories including kipot, benchers, kitubot, placecards, matches and more at DISCOUNTED prices. Mont Blanc and Cross pens. Calligraphy available.

LIGHTING

Stortz Associates/Event Lighting
(212) 473-6802
Special event lighting of all kinds. "The most beautiful lighting of a party that I have ever seen." Suzi, "New York Post," 1988.

LIMOUSINES

American Dream Transportation
(212) 737-7536
NY's most unique fleet of vehicles. Our VIP limo bus comfortably seats 23 passengers with on-board hostess, VCR, color TV's, stereo, snacks and beverages, deluxe restroom. For groups up to 10 travel in "NY's largest luxury limousine" with indoor jacuzzi, color TV's, three moon roofs, plus leather interior. Complete packages available.

Shaw Limousines
(212) 737-7536
Affordable elegance. Stretch limousines and luxury sedans. Personalized and reliable service for all occasions.

MUSICAL ENTERTAINMENT

Anne Harris Music
(212) 927-6836
A comprehensive music service featuring dance bands, classical music and swing. Audition our bands on videotape!

Disc Jockey-Alan Fleishman
(718) 638-4404

Lisa Goodman Ensembles
(212) 489-1641
A highly personalized and complete music service. We offer the finest swing, jazz and contemporary groups for listening and dancing as well as a wide variety of classical ensembles.

Mark Sonder Music, Inc.
(212) 876-3500/(212) 996-4815 FAX
The right music for any gathering!
We will arrange all of your musical needs...so the music will be there, ready for you and your guests to enjoy!

Masterwork Music
(212) 737-7536
Masterwork Music provides the ultimate in entertainment. Society, jazz, swing, contemporary, rock or classical music. Preview our ensembles on video at either our midtown Manhattan or Westchester, White Plains office.

Paul Gary Music
(212) 320-0010
BAND/CHAMBER PACKAGE:
Virtuoso String Quartet plays for ceremony, cocktails. Alternates with great Society/Contemporary band.
PLUS: GOLDEN HARP TRIO, smooth jazz/ Rock, Violins, ALL AT SENSIBLE VOLUME

PARTY PERFORMERS/ ARTISANS

Corporate Caricaturist-Phyllis Rudenjak
(212) 772-2813
Dazzling caricatures for your party, corporate event, meeting, convention, anniversary, promotion, financial closing, ice breaker, gift.
Light up your event by making every guest a "star"!

Ellen Devens
(212) 674-0538
Harlequin-shaped masks on nightsticks covered with fabric, lace, stones, findings and feathers. Masks are feminine, fantasy, artsy and surreal. Custom-designed to match your gown, room or party. Corsages too.

Friends in High Places
(212) 737-7536
Stilt-dance experts in special events and parties! From ballet to ballroom, the duos elegantly costumed and choreographed repertoire combines spectacle, skill and humor (minimum ceiling height 11 feet)!

Goodfriend Productions
(212) 737-7536
We create and perform exciting mystery shows for any situation, any place, and most any budget. Corporate events, trade shows, conventions, private parties.

Guest Stars, The Talent Agency
(212) 472-3030
Extraordinary performers for private/corporate parties including authentic rock bands, jazz greats, Broadway stars, cabaret singers, classical musicians, comedians, dancers, unique ethnic music.

Jon Steinfeld-Magician Extraordinaire
(212) 228-2967
Grand illusions.
As seen in "TV Guide," "Omni," and "Rolling Stone."

Rod Young Puppets
(212) 929-1568

Scottish/Irish Piper-Duncan Robertson
(212) 737-7536
Scottish/Irish piper in full regalia. For all kinds of special events, celebrations.

PARTY RENTALS

Broadway Famous Party Rentals, Inc., The POSH PARTY
(212) 269-2666
Where service is silver, glass is crystal and china is porcelain. Where the ambiance fulfills the promise of good taste, whether complementing hors d'oeuvres or a full gourmet dining experience.

PHOTOGRAPHY & VIDEO

Belle Image Photography and Video
(718) 591-1616
Belle Image offers an unobtrusive and imaginative approach to capture the unique feeling and spirit of your event. We offer personalized high caliber photographic and video service for your wedding, corporate and special event.

Dianne Baasch Maio, Photographer
(212) 724-2123

Focus On New York
(212) 683-6323
In Focus Productions
Video documentation for all occasions: corporate functions, private gatherings, festive parties (with special effects).
Gift specialty: "A day in the life of... ."
Unobtrusive, experienced, professional.

Paule Epstein, Photographer
(212) 777-5177

Laurie Leifer
(212) 737-7536
Laurie Leifer takes a documentary approach to public relations events and weddings. Her photo journalistic style lets the event unfold without artificial stage management. This non-traditional method relies on being unobtrusive, enabling the warmth and excitement of the event to be expressed through candid images.

Sarah Merians
(212) 737-7536
Photography with a creative and elegant approach unique for each client's need. Unobtrusive video as well. Also engagement portraits.

Steve Greenberg Video Productions
(212) 737-7536
For your wedding or your business...when you want the very best for any occasion. Choose the experienced professional!

Totally Informal Photos
(718) 728-7180

White Light Studios Inc.
(718) 728-7180
Photography/Video.
We shoot the event to suit your personal style. We capture your event as it happens to preserve memories for a lifetime. Fifteen years of experience. Tri-state area. Flexible rate.

SPECIAL EVENT PLANNERS & PARTY PLANNERS

Adriane Kutner Productions, Inc.
(201) 762-0036

All That Glitters
(212) 744-6228
Let us turn your fantasy party into a spectacular reality. Unique invitations and party accessories, complete party planning and referral service. By appointment only.

Chargé d'Affaires, Inc.
(212) 627-3545

Claster and Company, Inc.
(212) 633-0970/(212) 633-1034 FAX
Capture your corporate statement with our custom corporate event planning services and coordinated gift programs and gift baskets.

Claudia A. Hilbert
(914) 337-5942
Special events consultant. Personalized events planning. Create, plan and organize fundraising galas, corporate meetings and functions, private parties and weddings.

Come Party With Us
(516) 482-6066
Custom and discount invitations.
Party planning and all accessories.
Complete referral services.
Entertainment.
Corporate and private.

Corporate Promotions Group
(212) 972-0230
Corporate and association special events. Off-site, sales meetings, incentive trips, annual meetings, conference and seminars including international receptions, hospitality suites and trade show support. Your successful event anywhere starts with a phone call to us.

Details II Special Events
(201) 662-9190
Innovative event-production designed to develop and promote corporate identity. Personalized themes, resources and service are tastefully combined to meet your budget with an eye TO DETAILS!

Entirely Yours, Inc.
(212) 772-9835
Special event planning on a project-by-project basis. Additional brain and hands-on manpower at no additional cost to you! We meet your budget! Call us!!

Eventfull Inc.
(212) 570-7483/(203) 255-8875/(416) 440-4103
New York, Connecticut, Toronto
Event management for corporations, non-profit organizations and private individuals. International and domestic.

Executive Events Unlimited, Inc.
(212) 986-3355
Planners of corporate special events. Meetings, conferences and parties.

Fitzgerald Associates International Inc.
(203) 661-8157
A firm known and respected for its dedication to excellence, quality, freshness, style and effectiveness in producing all aspects of gracious special events. Meetings, company parties and special celebrations.

Halberg-Kroll Associates Inc.
(212) 369-4008
Complete custom-designed event services for corporate and private clients. Events produced with flair and dignity — for a small group or a cast of thousands.

Helping Hands Network Inc.
(718) 984-4840
Professional event planning for busy people. Let us plan your next corporate or social event! We have the experience you need to plan your party the way you would!

Hudson Affairs, Inc.
(201) 656-6361
A special events planning and management firm located in northern New Jersey. Each event is custom-designed to meet the needs of the individual client.

International Meeting Services, Inc.
(203) 454-2259
Organize and produce corporate meetings and special events.
Design and implement promotional programs.
Source premium and gift items.

It's Your Party, Inc.
(800) 458-7396

Judy Paulen Designs
(201) 871-1335
Party consultants, event planning.
Custom invitations, table accessories.
Room decoration, catering rentals.
Music and entertainment.

Le Clique. . .The Merchants of Fantasy
(212) 936-2525
Le Clique produces special events/parties with a unique and impeccable flair. The hallmarks of Le Clique blend administrative, theatrical and musical services.
Excellence is within reach.
Press kit/videos upon request to Stewart R. Feinstein.

Lovin' Oven Celebrations
(516) 271-3561
Premier party planning. Exclusive locations.
Full special event services.
Elaborate cocktail parties, press lunches, employee morale boosters, movie sets, mobile kitchens.
Call for press kits.

Lucullus World Event Management Inc.
(212) 974-9704
Lucullus World Event Management sees to all aspects of your party planning: premises, entertainment, catering, audio-video, party help. Your party wishes are our command. Unusual needs our specialty. Trains, yachts, balloons, etc.

Manhattan Party Planners, Inc.
(212) 753-8750
A New York company which will handle every aspect of entertaining in the English country house-style, from a simple tea party to a grand wedding. Addressing, forwarding and checking invitations. Supplying food, flowers, furnishings, staff and security.

Marcy L. Blum Associates Inc.
(212) 688-3057
Special event design and production firm established in 1984. Has been featured in "Women's Wear Daily", "Wall Street Journal", "Time Magazine" and "New York Magazine" for their innovative touches.

New Idea
(718) 633-1774
Party/event planning from ice to entertainment.
For busy offices and busy individuals in need of proper event orchestration. Free brochure/consultation. Call today and take the stress out of your event.

Party Artistry
(212) 628-9555/(201) 762-2240
Extraordinary floral and room designs since 1973. From caterers and musicians to extensive linen selections and entertainment. We are the single point of contact for all your event needs.

The Party Box Inc.
(212) 362-1800

Party Panache Ltd.
(516) 482-6111
Complete party planning service for corporate and private events.
Custom designed invitations and party accessories. By appointment only at The Atrium, 98 Cutter Mill Road, Great Neck, New York.

The Personal Touch, Inc.
(212) 752-2345
A leading design studio and product promotion firm, founded 1964, offering a total service including planning and design, invitations, catering, place cards, centerpieces, decor, entertainment, etc., all coordinated to make your special event memorable. Located at 156 West 56th Street in New York City.

PROMoceans Ltd.-The Prom Company
(212) 289-8506

Saved By The Bell Corp.
(212) 874-5457/(201) 585-8660
You're planning a party, you know who and when. Now call SAVED BY THE BELL to arrange where, what and how. Our work will reflect your personal or corporate identity. Place the details of your party in competent, reliable hands. Let SAVED BY THE BELL make your life easier.

Singer & Engelhardt, Inc.
(212) 586-2820
New York/Palm Beach
Special events for corporations, not-for-profit organizations and private clients since 1979. We are there for the details — to make your event THE event you need it to be — on budget, on target, on time.

Successful Affairs
(212) 683-7574
Specializes in discovering and uncovering the finest in party facilities. Conveniently plan your entire affair without making another call. Let us arrange all your future events to be successful affairs!

The Total Affair
(201) 522-0261

Viewpoint International
(212) 355-1055
Special Event Management is what we do with all the creative resources and the places too.

Wunderman Productions, Ltd.
(516) 868-1795
Great events don't just happen...they are borne out of weeks of meticulous planning, research and creative thought. Our staff of experienced production professionals take pride in their work and pay close attention to every detail. Some of the many services we provide: themed environments and decorations, centerpieces, name artists, full shows and revues, variety acts, live music and d.j.'s, ethnic entertainment, costumed walk-around performers, dancers, celebrity look-alikes, lasers, lighting, staging & sound systems. Call today for your free brochure and event planning kit.

THEME DECORATORS

S. Michael Ereshena
(718) 965-1625
If it's a veranda in Newport or the ruins of Pompeii, our services include a unique transformation of your space. Linens, flowers, props and lighting create an atmosphere of your choice.

Wunderman Productions, Inc.
(516) 868-1795
From Buckingham Palace complete with costumed horsemen and coaches, decorative knights, heralding trumpeters, royal look-alikes, etc., to 2001 space odyssey with futuristic dancers, shooting laser beams, portable robots and full-scale space ship with control bridge--we have just the theme for you. From design to execution, we provide full production services plus performers, live music, technicians & stage managers. Call our design specialists for free consultation. (See ad under Party Planners.)

WEDDING APPAREL

Genesis III Wedding Center
(212) 868-0626
Di Willis Fashions.
For "The bride who chooses to be different." Custom designs and one-of-a-kind wedding gowns, veils and accessories. Restorations. Tuxedos too.

LIAISONS OUTSIDE OF THE NEW YORK AREA

PLACES continuously scours regions outside the New York area for representatives who are familiar with locations in their specific locale. These caterers/special event planners have proven themselves to be reliable and courteous as well. They offer a broad range of helpful services and welcome inquiries. However, if you are only interested in finding a place, and do not wish to work with a caterer or special event planner, **PLACES** will provide you with the direct phone numbers of the sites themselves. Call (800) 284-7028 (from outside New York City, New York State, Connecticut and New Jersey), or (212) 737-7536 (in the New York area) to reach our liaisons.

ARIADNE CLIFTON *(Metropolitan Boston and environs)*
Elegant entertaining. Full service catering. Corporate and private.

BOLD IDEAS *(Chicago area)*
Specialists in event planning for corporate and non-profit organziations only.

BRAUN'S FINE CATERERS
(Washington, DC and environs)
A full-service caterer serving the Washington area for 40 years. Providing all styles of food, service, personnel and equipment.

CHIEF EXECUTIVE EVENTS
(Chicago and out-of-state)
Chief Executive Events acts as consultants to corporate executives for the design and production of special events and off-site meetings. Board meetings, top client conferences, and corporate staff retreats are creatively managed for Fortune 1000 clients. Yachts, mansions, inns, ranches and railroad cars are utilized discreetly all over North America.

EVENTDESIGNS *(Northern California)*
Eventdesigns offers complete event planning, combining style, creativity and service. We are committed to your success from theme development to site selection, from menu design to entertainment. We take care of every aspect to make your event a success. Conferences, theme parties, weddings and private events are done with careful attention to detail.

FINE DINING *(Washington, DC, Northern Virginia, Maryland)*
Caterer for special events of both a personal and public nature.

FLORENTINE LILY *(Georgia as well as most of the South, i.e., Alabama, Florida, North Carolina and South Carolina)*
We provide catering and/or special event and party planning for both private and corporate events.

GEORGE JEWELL CATERING SERVICES, LTD. *(Chicago and all suburban areas as well as surrounding states, i.e., Indiana and Wisconsin)*
We have worked hard to develop the reputation in both food and service that is a must for both private and corporate events. Our services range from a gourmet dinner for two to the grand opening of the Chicago Bloomingdales for 2300 people. Our catering services can be customized to any location.

INNOVATIVE EVENTS & WEDDINGS *(Texas)*
We are receptive to all your special event needs, weddings as well as corporate events, anywhere in Texas.

MARILYN JENETT LOCATIONS
(Southern California and major convention cities)
Famous event location service offering the most complete and unique selection of locations for events nationwide. Mansions, castles, historic landmarks, museums, film studios, etc. Finest event coordination available.

PANACHE & SPECIAL EVENTS
(New Orleans as well as all of the Southeast, from the Florida panhandle, through to Texas and Alabama)
New Orleans' premiere caterer--custom corporate and social event planner. Floral design, transportation, theme events, location assistance.

RIDGEWELLS *(Philadelphia, Washington, DC, Virginia, Maryland, Delaware)*
In business for over 70 years. Full service off-premise caterer who takes pride in designing customized menus for each client. We have equipment, linen and a staff of service personnel for any size function and have the resources available to assist in arranging everything from flowers, limousines, tents or special props. Our client base covers the corporate, social and political spectrum. We have offices based in Philadelphia and Washington, DC and know the unique sites in these cities and the cities surrounding them. We will travel wherever our services are requested.

BOSTON/CAMBRIDGE & ENVIRONS

PARTY PLACES

BOSTON/CAMBRIDGE

Back Bay Mansion with French-Style Ballroom   (800) 284-7028
Boston, MA

One of the most beautiful ballrooms in Massachusetts was added on to a five-story Edwardian mansion by Walter Baylies, a textile broker, for his youngest daughter's debut in 1912. The 26 x 50 ft. room has Versailles-like crystal chandeliers and gold leaf touches which still maintain their original luster.

Designed by architect William Peters of Peters and Rice, the ballroom lobby and music room are available for all manner of special functions including weddings.

Guest capacity: 100 seated, 200 buffet/cocktails

Boston Public Parks
City Hall Plaza, Room 816
Boston, MA 02201

Contact: Commissioner of Parks and Recreation

Numerous public parks in Boston, such as Jamaica Pond and the Public Garden, are lovely settings for wedding ceremonies. Receptions, however, must be held elsewhere. To use a Boston park for a wedding ceremony, write to the above address. There are no charges other than a nominal fee to cover the attendance of a grounds supervisor. The standard time period for a wedding ceremony is about thirty minutes.

Boston Tea Party   (800) 284-7028
Boston, MA

Brig Beaver II, a full-size working replica of one of the three original Tea Party ships, is permanently moored at Griffin's Wharf, the exact spot where on December 16, 1773 tea was dropped into the Boston Harbor as a protest against the tea tax and the concept of taxation without representation.

The adjacent small Tea Party museum tells of this historic event. Social functions may be held in the museum and aboard the red ensign-flying tea ship.

Guest capacity: 65 seated/85 cocktails on *Beaver II*; 100 seated/200 cocktails in museum

Note: Tea chests may also be hurled overboard. "Rally Mohawks! Bring out your axes! And tell King George we'll pay no taxes!" (Rallying song of the Tea Party in 1773).

Boston's Tallest Building   (800) 284-7028
Boston, MA

Considered the highest man-made point in New England, this modern location offers a spectacular panorama stretching from the gold- domed Statehouse and gracious townhouses of Beacon Hill to the distant White Mountains of southern New Hampshire.

Guest capacity: 85 seated/150 cocktails

Children's Museum   (800) 284-7028
Boston, MA

Located in a renovated wharf building, the museum consists of five galleries complete with games and dance floor, including a Japanese room for small dinner parties.
Guest capacity: 200 in each gallery; 1000 in entire museum

Civil War Hall/Harvard University   (800) 284-7028
Cambridge, MA

When the Civil War ended, Harvard University saw the need to build a memorial to the sons of Harvard who died defending the Union. A large architectural competition was initiated and the winning design, created by two young alumni, included both a large dining hall as well as a theater for literary festivities.
The Hall is decorated with twenty-eight tablets of the names of those who fell, as well as period paintings. Beautiful stained glass windows decorate the Dining Hall. These were given by alumni classes.

Exuding both dignity and warmth, this Hall was recently chosen by the University as a reception site to honor Prince Charles. It is available for all manner of functions including weddings.
Guest capacity: 500 seated in Dining Hall; 1232 in Sanders Theater

Computer Museum   (800) 284-7028
Boston, MA

Original wooden beams and brick plus the latest in computer technology create a blend of old and new in a renovated warehouse on the Boston waterfront.

Guest capacity: 300 seated/500 standing in auditorium; 1000 in entire museum
Video projection room

Cyclorama Hall   (800) 284-7028
Boston, MA

This round building was originally opened in 1884 to house the cycloramic painting of The Battle of Gettysburg executed by the artist Philippoteaux. It was also the location where Alfred Champion later developed and manufactured the spark plug.
The Hall also offers 25,000 sq. ft. for all manner of special events and exhibits. The diameter of the rotunda is 125 feet and the height from floor to ceiling is 70 feet.
Guest capacity: 200/900

Faneuil Hall Marketplace   (800) 284-7028
Boston, MA

In 1742 a prosperous Bostonian, Peter Faneuil, bequeathed a two-story bronze-domed building to the city of Boston as a public meeting hall and marketplace. As the scene of many spirited political debates and noted historical speeches, the building's upstairs meeting hall became widely known as The Cradle of Liberty. Although the downstairs housed the city's wholesale produce market business, it soon became too small, and a massive domed building comprising three 535-foot long Greek Revival arcades was erected to serve the wholesale food industry. This second building was named the Quincy

continued on next page

Market Building after former Boston mayor Josiah Quincy.

As Boston began to lose its supremacy as the leading Eastern seaport in the 1900's, a decline of the market business ensued. Not until the 1960's, when the nation began looking into the idea of urban renewal, dedicated local interest groups worked to revitalize Boston's downtown area. The restoration of Faneuil Hall and Quincy Market by Rouse Company was a bellwether for similar downtown projects in other cities across the nation.

Guest capacity: 125 seated/200 standing in Alexander Parris Room; 350 standing in Rotunda; 350 seated/450 standing in Great Hall

All manner of special events are possible including weddings.

Resident caterers

Former Police Station/Now Art Museum   (800) 284-7028

Boston, MA

Formerly a police station, now a museum of contemporary art, this recycled Richardsonian building in Boston's Back Bay makes available its galleries for private evening gatherings.

Guest capacity: 150 in auditorium; 350 maximum in galleries

Harvard University Art Museum   (800) 284-7028

Cambridge, MA

Located in a neo-Georgian brick building just east of Harvard Yard, two floors of galleries surround a handsome Italian Renaissance courtyard.

Guest capacity: 200 seated/500 reception

House on Tory Row   (800) 284-7028

Cambridge, MA

Situated on Tory Row, the street so named because its early residents were Loyalists whose sympathies were anti-revolutionary, this handsome eighteenth century house under the care of the Cambridge Historical Society is adorned with rare wallpapers printed by Dufours of Paris, a fireplace closet, a beehive oven and a 12 ft. x 12 ft. chimney.
Guest capacity: 75
Suggested uses: dinner, meeting, wedding

The John Fitzgerald Kennedy Library (800) 284-7028
Boston, MA

This library, which is located only four miles southeast of downtown Boston, was designed by I.M. Pei and dedicated to the memory of John F. Kennedy, thirty-fifth President of the United States.
It is situated on a beautiful ten-acre site on the tip of Columbia Point Peninsula on Dorchester Bay and is made available for special functions from 6 to 10 p.m. to community-based organizations and corporations under the Federal Government's Living Buildings Program.
Guest capacity: 300 seated/700 standing in 115-foot high pavillion
Two theaters are additionally available for organizational programs.

La Bibliotéque Française (800) 284-7028
Boston, MA

This home away from home for people who love French culture, with its grand Louis XV chandelier, wood-paneled salons, elegant spiral staircase and wrought iron fence was donated in 1961 by the wealthy Bostonian sculptor Katherine Lane Weems.
Guest capacity: 50 seated in small salon; 70 seated in Theatre Room; 200 cocktails in both rooms
Resident caterer

Loft Soho Style (800) 284-7028
Boston, MA
This raw space has a wall of windows.
Guest capacity: up to 200
It is suitable for dance parties and photo shoots.

McKim, Mead and White Classical (800) 284-7028
Mansion
Boston, MA

This back bay house of white limestone, the home of an international institute, offers handsome spaces for special functions.
Guest capacity: 50 seated/70 standing in Dining Room; 60 seated/90 standing in Living Room; 80 seated/100 standing in Ballroom

Museum which Delights the Senses (800) 284-7028
Boston, MA

Built at the turn-of-the-century in the style of a Venetian palace, this exceptional museum is the achievement of Isabella Stewart Gardner (1840-1924), the wife of John L. Gardner. Mrs. Gardner formed the art collection, built the museum and ultimately endowed it.
Light from a glass roof four stories above fills a central courtyard (Fenway Court), where flowering plants thrive amid ancient sculpture, a Roman mosaic and a Venetian fountain. Overlooking the courtyard are galleries in which Mrs. Gardner herself arranged a distinguished collection of paintings by Italian and Dutch masters as well as sculpture, furniture, ceramics and textiles.
Guest capacity: 50 seated/250 standing in Fenway Court
Note: Available only to corporate benefactors and non-profit organizations.

New England Aquarium (800) 284-7028
Boston, MA

This modern addition to Boston's renovated Central Wharf offers a setting for large special events. Indirect lighting, blue neon waves and giant tanks with sharks, sea turtles and other marine creatures create a sense of being under water in the Main Building.

The Marine Mammal Pavilion, Discovery, adjacent to the main building, overlooks Boston Harbor and offers a setting for sunset dinner parties and dances.

During the summer months, The Harbor Terrace offers views of passing ships and harbor activities and is an additional location for a formal party or informal clambakes.

Guest capacity: 288 in auditorium for lectures, meetings and presentations; 200 seated/400 cocktails in Harbor View Room; 350 seated/1000 cocktails in Main Building; 700/1200 in tents for clambakes, etc.

Skywalk (800) 284-7028
Boston, MA

On the 50th floor of the Prudential Tower, this unique location has the only 360 degree view of Boston and beyond.

Guest capacity: 300 in Full Deck; 150 in One-Half Deck; 65 in One-Quarter Deck

Symphony Hall (800) 284-7028
Boston, MA

The home of the Boston Symphony Orchestra offers a magnificent music hall and three separate private function rooms.

Guest capacity: 250 seated in each private room; 2500 in music hall

U.S.S. Constitution Museum (800) 284-7028
Boston, MA

This elegant nineteenth century brick building in the Boston Harbor, with heavy beamed ceilings and naval artifacts dating back to the War of 1812, has the U.S.S. Constitution *Old Ironsides* moored two hundred yards away. It boasts one of the best views of the Boston skyline.

Guest capacity: 250 standing; seating capacity varies

GREATER BOSTON AREA

Castle Museum (800) 284-7028
Gloucester, MA

This medieval castle built in 1926 by John Hays Hammond, Jr. is now a non-profit institution open to the public. It's Great Hall features the nave of a cathedral and a fifteenth century fireplace, stained glass windows reproduced from the Chartres Cathedral and a magnificent organ whose pipes rise eight stories.

Guest capacity: 110 seated/150 buffet/225 cocktails

Charleston Mansion Transported (800) 284-7028
Beverly, MA

The elaborately carved mantels, cornices and doorways of this Federalist-style house designed by architect Philip Richardson, which were part of a house in Charleston, South Carolina, so impressed Ellery Sedgwick, the former editor of the Atlantic Monthly, that he had them shipped by schooner to embellish his summer home outside of Boston. This 114-acre property is also widely renowned for its gardens. In 1979 the estate was given to The Trustees of Reservations, an independently administered non-profit organization in the state of Massachusetts, to preserve for the public beautiful and historic places. The property rents out for special functions, formal gatherings and weddings. Its Chinese Fence, an ornately carved Chinese-motif garden structure, is an especially appropriate spot for outdoor wedding ceremonies.

Guest capacity: 150 indoors

Note: Space is only available April 15 through November 15.

Codman Carriage House (800) 284-7028
Lincoln, MA

Located in a park-like setting of sixteen landscaped acres which also includes a formal Italian garden, this newly renovated Carriage House features one thousand square feet of carpeted special event space and a modern kitchen. A guided tour of the adjacent eighteenth century main house, which was lived in by the Codman family, may be included.

Guest capacity: 65

Note: Space is only available May through October.

Concord Art Association   (617) 569-2578

Lexington Road
Concord, MA 01742

A 38 ft. x 27 ft. gallery loft upstairs with glass ceiling and skylight, plus three smaller galleries downstairs and a garden with a large waterfall, make this a charming site for receptions.
Guest capacity: 80 maximum
Preferred caterer on premises
Note: Space is only available to persons who join the Association.

Contemporary Art Museum in   (800) 284-7028
Castle-like Building

Lincoln, MA

This Romanesque-style former private country ouse sits high on a hilltop surrounded by rolling lawns, ornamental shrubs, a spacious sculpture park, pond and terrace.
Guest capacity: 120 seated/175 cocktails; 200 on tented terrace
Approved list of caterers
Suitable for corporate and non-profit events as well as weddings.

Country Seat of a Gentleman   (800) 284-7028
Waltham, MA

Theodore Lyman (1753-1839), a wealthy Boston merchant and enthusiastic horticulturalist, commissioned Samuel McIntire to build what is presently considered to be one of New England's finest examples of a Federal period country estate. Surrounded by thirty acres of pleasure grounds, lawns, wooded areas, garden beds and magnificent rhododendrons, the estate remained in the hands of the Lyman family from 1793 until 1952.

As the founder of the Massachusetts Society for the Promotion of Agriculture, Mr. Lyman also built numerous greenhouses which are still in operation today: a Grape House which produces black Hamburg grapes grown from cuttings of vines at Hampton Court in England, the Camellia House which is one of the few remnants of Boston's heritage as a center for camellia culture, and a greenhouse for cut flowers.
Presently owned and managed by the Society for the Preservation of New England Antiquities, its Federal ballroom, dining rooms and three parlors provide ample space for corporate meetings and private social affairs.
Guest capacity: 20/175

Eighteenth Century New England   (800) 284-7028
Meeting House

Amesbury, MA

This genuine eighteenth century New England Meeting House

with pulpit and pews is under the protection of the Society for the Preservation of New England Antiquities. It can be rented for simple wedding ceremonies.

Guest capacity: 120 seated
Note: Smoking is not allowed.

French-Style Carriage House   (800) 284-7028
Brookline, MA

This many-turreted 1888 Carriage House modeled after a French castle is listed on the National Register of Historic Places and serves to exhibit classic cars.

Situated on spacious grounds, it is a unique location for both corporate receptions as well as weddings, indoors and out.

Guest capacity: 80 seated indoors when space is shared with classic cars, up to 150 may be seated when cars are not present; any amount of guests may be accommodated under tents outdoors

A video theater, oversize movie screen and stereo system are on the premises.

Note: A classic limousine service is available to transport guests to and from the museum.

Great House on Ipswich Bay   (800) 284-7028
Ipswich, MA

A Stuart baronial mansion designed by Chicago architect David Adler in 1927 is surrounded by 1352 acres of landscaped gardens and natural seashore. Its use for public benefits and special social functions as well as conferences, seminars and a variety of special events can be arranged.

Guest capacity: 20/200 for a seminar, 300 for a wedding; up to 1500 with canopies

Rental fee: approximately $2,400 for six hours

Suitable for weddings, concerts, seminars, dances, exhibits, reunions, incentive parties and clambakes.

Hall for Mechanics, Presidents and   (800) 284-7028
Brides
Worcester, MA

Built in 1857 by the Worcester County Mechanics Association to train apprentices, hold exhibitions and social functions, this award-winning facility became a cultural center in the late nineteenth and early twentieth centuries. Presidents have used

it as a forum and Enrico Caruso, Charles Dickens, Mark Twain, Paderewski and Arthur Rubinstein performed on its stage. Though considered a white elephant in the 1930's, it was authentically restored in 1977 and is now considered one of the largest and finest concert halls remaining from the mid-nineteenth century.

In addition to the acoustically famous Victorian Great Hall, this multi-use facility offers spaces for every type of social and educational function, from weddings to antique fairs.

Guest capacity: 50 tables for trade shows/500 banquet (with dancing)/800 banquet (without dancing)/1700 theater-style in Great Hall; 25 tables for trade shows/300 banquet/500 theater-style in Washburn Hall; 70 banquet/100 theater-style in Boyden Salon; 35 in Board Room

Modern sound booth for broadcasting, film and slide presentations. Modern light board for theatrical events.

Catering areas

Nature Center Near Boston   (800) 284-7028
Belmont, MA

Thirty-five acres of a formal garden, including a rose garden and a wild flower garden, surround a Lincolnshire-style house.

Guest capacity: 100 maximum indoors and/or outdoors

Old Ship Church and Meeting House   (800) 284-7028
Hingham, MA

Built in 1681, this Elizabethan Gothic church and New England meeting house features a roof structure of axe-hewn curved frames resembling the hull of a ship. Known always as a people's church for broadly welcoming persons of every diverse outlook, it is also one of the few places in America where one can hear English change ringing—bell ringing based on constantly shifting mathematical patterns.

Guest capacity: 160 in Hall behind Parish House; 300 in Meeting House

On the Highlands Overlooking the Sea (800) 284-7028
Gloucester, MA

Leslie Buswell, a young Englishman who came to the U.S. as a juvenile actor in 1913, accomplished some astounding things. Early on, he became associated with the Hammond Radio Labs in Gloucester. While in France during the First World War, he was involved in the formation of the American Field Service, writing about his experiences in a book called Ambulance No. 10. Returning to the U.S., he selected a spectacular site for his permanent residency, constructing an English Manor house, whose Great Hall became the home of New England's first summer stock theater.

Now, half a century later, this fine estate has re-opened for performances, concerts, conferences, private parties and receptions.
Guest capacity: 14 seated in formal dining room; 200 seated in Great Hall; additional rooms, terraces and grounds available including a Guest house with overnight accommodations

Richardsonian Mansion   (800) 284-7028
Waltham, MA

Constructed of fieldstone and cedar shingle, this fine house is the last large Richardsonian mansion available intact in the country. Set on conservation land it offers a grand staircase, a Great Hall, a summer parlor, fireplaces and back patio. Historically authentic decor throughout.
Guest capacity: 100 seated with dancing/150 buffet
Note: Tenting is not allowed. Smoking is only allowed on the back porch.

Russian-Mirrored Ballroom in the   (800) 284-7028
Town Where Witches Burned
Salem, MA

Political animosity between Salem's two leading commercial families, the Crownshields and the Derbys, resulted in the 1805 construction of a historic assembly hall and showpiece for the renowned local architect and woodcarver Samuel McIntire. Greatly influenced by the English architects, Robert and James Adam, and an ally of the Derbys, McIntire's *piece de resistance* is the second floor ballroom replete with a musican's gallery, elaborately mantled fireplaces and two large mirrors imported from Russia, plus its famous spring floor which is renowned to make dancing extremely pleasant.
Guest capacity: 225 seated/350 cocktails; two historic smaller rooms are available as well
Working kitchen with brick hearth and large ovens

WESTERN MASSACHUSETTS

Estate Hotel in the Berkshires   (800) 284-7028
Lenox, MA

Though this Renaissance palace has noble proportions, it never loses its intimacy and is a perfect setting for large and small gatherings such as weddings, retreats and family reunions.
Guest capacity: 50 day meeting/150 seated/200 cocktail buffet; 17 rooms for overnight, many suitable for double occupancy
Tennis courts, swimming pool, 21 wooded acres

Norman and Shingle-Style Summer   (800) 284-7028
Mansion in the Berkshires
Stockbridge, MA

Designed by Stanford White in 1886 for Ambassador and Mrs. Joseph Hodges Choate, this twenty-six-room former summer mansion, now museum, also boasts one of the loveliest gardens in America. Fitted to a steep and difficult site, the gardens were first planned by Nathan F. Barrett, a pioneer in landscaping. Later Fletcher Steele, a Boston landscape architect, extended Mr. Barrett's original ground plans.
In addition to the garden's gentle slopes lined with hemlock hedges, grassy glades, white oaks, groves of shimmering white birches, a topiary promenade, Linden walks and marble chip pathways, it is unusual for its inclusion of many oriental plantings such as Gingko trees. The addition of a Chinese pagoda, a Chinese garden and many stone Buddhas, lions, dogs and other figures and carvings are the result of travels to the Orient in the 1930's by Mrs. Mabel Choate.
Guest capacity: 50 on grounds

continued on next page

Suitable for wedding ceremonies, the site is the property of the Trustees of Reservations, a private non-profit conservation organization. In the event of inclement weather, the rear porch of the museum will be made available.

Note: Available primarily on weekends from Memorial Day to Columbus Day and daily from last week of June through Labor Day.

Pleasant Valley Trailside Museum   (413) 637-0320

472 West Mountain Road   Contact: Mr. Rene Laubach
Lenox, MA 01240

This rustic barn with large fireplace, antique tools and kitchen is part of the Wildlife Sanctuary at the Massachusetts Audubon Society.

Guest capacity: 100

Note: Rents for special functions from late Spring to early Fall. Alcohol and music are not allowed.

Summer Home of the First Woman to   (800) 284-7028
Win the Pulitzer Prize

Lenox, MA

Edith Wharton and the Boston architect, Ogden Codman, Jr., built this American classical house in 1902 on the precepts set forth by them in their co-authored book, *The Decoration of Houses*. While in residence there, Ms. Wharton wrote *Ethan Frome* and *The House of Mirth*, among others. The Pulitzer prize was bestowed upon Mrs. Wharton in 1920 for *The Age of Innocence*.

Weddings, birthdays, dinners, receptions, film location shoots and salon concerts are suitable.

Guest capacity: 160 seated/200 reception; 130 on terrace

Note: Space is not available June, July or August.

Summer Home and Studio of a   (800) 284-7028
Sculptor

Stockbridge, MA

This property of the National Trust for Historic Preservation is the former summer home and studio of sculptor Daniel Chester French, creator of the seated Lincoln for the Lincoln Memorial in Washington, DC. Located 130 miles north of New York City, this 128-acre estate features many free-standing pieces of sculpture and an outdoor setting overlooking the Berkshire hills. There are three period buildings, gardens, grounds, nature walks and splendid vistas.

Guest capacity: 75 maximum in Barn Sculpture Gallery; 75 on terrace or mansion; many more guests may be accommodated for tented functions outdoors

Suitable for weddings, meetings and concerts.

Boston: More Auditoriums, Halls & Meeting Rooms *(by capacity for special functions)*

The Lyric Stage Theatre   (617) 742-1790
54 Charles St. ....*(reception)* 114

Shubert Theatre   (617) 426-4520
265 Tremont St. .... *(reception)* 400

Museum of the National Center   (617) 442-8014
of Afro-American Artists
300 Walnut Ave. 100/500

Wang Center for the Performing Arts   (617) 482-9393
268 Tremont St. 330/600

John Fitzgerald Kennedy Library   (617) 929-4557
Columbia Pt. .... *(seated/reception)* 300/700

Museum of Fine Arts   (617) 267-9300
465 Huntington Ave. 350/1000

The Opera House   (617) 426-5300
539 Washington St. 250/1000

Boston Center for the Arts   (617) 426-5000
539 Tremont St. 40/1800

The Orpheum Theatre   (617) 482-0651
1 Hamilton Pl. ....*(meeting)* 2829

Museum of Science and Hayden   (617) 723-2500
Planetarium
Science Park 600/3000

RHODE ISLAND

Chinese Teahouse
(800) 284-7028

Newport, RI

On the grounds of Marble House, this teahouse is probably the only Chinoiserie building of its kind in the eastern U.S. Built in 1913, it has a beautiful view of other Newport mansions and the Atlantic Ocean.

Guest capacity: 60 seated; 80 maximum

Continental Sloop Providence
(800) 284-7028

Newport, RI

Nicknamed *The Lucky Sloop* by the British and commanded by John Paul Jones, she was the first ship of the U.S. Navy in 1775. Her true name was The Providence. Faithfully reproduced and commissioned in 1976 as a Bicentennial project, this grand vessel sails up and down the Eastern seaboard, trains young people, and is available for special events.

Guest capacity: 40 sailing; 100 on board dockside

Famous Newport Casino/Now International Tennis Hall of Fame
(800) 284-7028

Newport, RI

The Casino Building was designed by McKim, Mead and White for James Gordon Bennett, Jr., publisher of *The New York Herald* in 1880. The building complex is an outstanding example of the Shingle period of American architecture and has been designated a national landmark.

Guest capacity: 300 in Horse Shoe Piazza; 300 in Hall of Fame USTA Wing; 450 theater-style in Casino Theater

Food may be served by caterer of your choice.

Suitable for weddings, private parties, meetings, lectures and dramatic productions.

Happy Woodland Estate That Overlooks Narragansett Bay
(800) 284-7028

Bristol, RI

This is the former turn-of-the-century summer residence of A. S. Van Wickle, a coal mine owner from Hazelton, Pennsylvania who sailed regularly on Narragansett Bay. Encompassing thirty-three waterfront acres, the estate is best known for its magnificent gardens: rock garden, rose garden with a moon gate entrance, water garden as well as a woodland which is a cool retreat even on the warmest summer day. There is also a gracious mansion styled after a seventeenth century English country manor, with rooms, terraces and porches that command sweeping views of the bay.

Guest capacity: 50 seated/100 standing; a tent for over 100 guests

Suitable for weddings, receptions, parties and business meetings.

Summer White House
(800) 284-7028

Newport, RI

This twenty-eight-room shingle-style house was built in 1887. Landscaped by Frederick Law Olmstead, this estate was the site of the 1953 wedding reception of Jacqueline Bouvier and John F. Kennedy.

Guest capacity: 180 maximum for a buffet in the Deck Room with enclosed patio, Living Room and Foyer; 700 maximum indoors and outdoors

Suitable for weddings, parties and clambakes.

Versailles
(800) 284-7028

Newport, RI

This magnificent mansion was designed by Stanford White in 1902 after the Grand Trianon at Versailles. Its royal French ballroom with chandeliers and French doors opening onto a terrace was the scene of brilliant social entertaining.

Guest capacity: 500 maximum

154

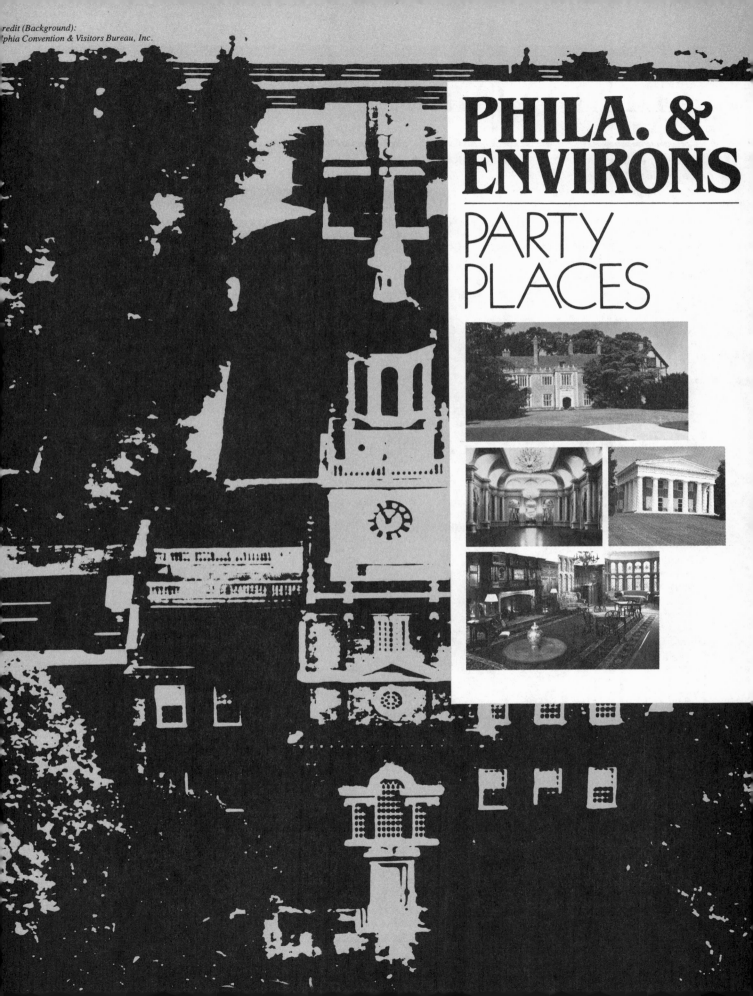

PHILA. & ENVIRONS

PARTY PLACES

PHILADELPHIA

Academy of Music   (800) 284-7028
Philadelphia, PA

Styled after the Versailles Hall of Mirrors, the Grand Ballroom of the Philadelphia Academy of Music, with its gold and white crystal chandeliers, is available for social and civic functions as well as lectures.

Guest capacity: 200 for a sitdown dinner/250 reception/400 auditorium-style

Note: Weddings are not allowed.

Academy of Natural Sciences   (800) 284-7028
Philadelphia, PA

The nation's oldest natural science museum offers several of its spaces for special event rental.

Guest capacity: up to 2000; 415 seated in auditorium; 25/100 in conference rooms; 140 sitdown dinner/200 reception in North American Hall; 100 sitdown dinner/200 cocktails in African/Asian Hall; 250 reception in Dinosaur Hall

Note: Space is only available to corporate and non-profit groups.

Albert M. Greenfield Conference   (215) 242-9100
Centers of Temple University
Bell's Mill Road & Germantown Avenue
Philadelphia, PA 19118

Overlooking the Wissahickon Valley, Sugarloaf, a forty-four-acre estate, comprises three buildings for banquets and lodging. Greenfield House is a contemporary-style building with dining room, floor-to-ceiling windows, a paneled library, grand piano and french doors that open onto a terrace. Adjacent to Greenfield is a three-story Victorian mansion from an 1875 farm estate. Wyncliffe has a drawing room and a wraparound porch. The Eleanor Widener Dixon House has a James I drawing room with massive fireplace, eighteenth century furniture and seventeen guest rooms.

Guest capacity: 75 minimum; 60 seated/100 cocktails in Wyncliffe; 70 seated/125 cocktails in Eleanor Widener Dixon House; 150 seated with dancing/225 stand-up reception/34 overnight accommodations in Greenfield House

Resident caterer

America's Oldest Botanic Garden   (215) 729-5281
Philadelphia, PA

An eighteenth century stone farm house and stable situated on the Schuykill in what is now an industrial park of Philadelphia was the home of botanist/gardener John Bartram (1699-1777).

Presently administered by the Fairmount Park Commission and the John Bartram Association, both the house and stable are available for private events.

During the winter, a fire will be burning in the hearth of the eighteenth century kitchen and candlelight tours may be arranged. From mid-May through October, events can be scheduled in the stable and under adjacent grape arbor where George Washington sat.

Guest capacity: 25 in John Bartram House; 50/150 in stable

Archeological/Anthropological: (800) 284-7028
The University Museum
Philadelphia, PA

Since its founding in 1887, the University Museum of the University of Pennsylvania sponsored over three hundred expeditions and is one of the leading institutions in the study of ancient peoples and traditional cultures.

Gallery tours may be combined with social functions.

Guest capacity: 50 seated/100 standing in Mosaic Gallery; 90 seated/150 standing in Lower Egyptian Gallery; 248 seated in Rainey Auditorium; 450 seated in Chinese Rotunda; 350 seated/800 standing in Upper Egyptian Gallery; 800 seated in Harrison Auditorium

Note: Available only to corporate and educational organizations. Private parties and dancing are not allowed.

Art Alliance   (215) 545-4302

251 South 18th Street   Contact: Emily B. Schilling,
Philadelphia, PA 19103   Public Relations

This historic Rittenhouse Square mansion is honeycombed with galleries rentable by non-members for small affairs. There are two galleries and two dining rooms downstairs and four galleries plus a roomy landing where a bar and music can be set up on the second floor.

Guest capacity: 50 in The Dietrich Gallery, 25 in additional gallery, 45 in each of two dining rooms downstairs; 200 stand-up in modern gallery on second floor; three additional galleries are available for buffets only

Grand staircase

Resident caterer

Note: Space is closed in August.

Atwater Kent Museum   (800) 284-7028

Philadelphia, PA

This history museum has gallery space available for cocktail parties and receptions.

Guest capacity: 60 seated in second floor gallery; 250/300 on two floors and in five separate gallery areas; up to 500 in garden

---

Belmont Mansion   (800) 284-7028

West Fairmount Park, PA

This twenty-room mansion offers a spectacular view of the Philadelphia skyline. The circa-1684 house has ornate Georgian ceilings and eighteenth and nineteenth century furnishings.

Guest capacity: 125 seated/150 cocktails among first and second floor rooms

In warm weather, a 62 x 32 ft. canopy may be erected.

Resident caterer

College of Physicians   (800) 284-7028

Philadelphia, PA

This 1909 modified Jacobean-style building designed by Stewardson and Page is available for special events including weddings.

Guest capacity: 250 seated for a dinner dance/300 for dinner/375 theater-style in Mitchell Hall Ballroom; 2 smaller rooms are also available

The Medical Garden may be used for wedding ceremonies.

Conversation Hall   (215) 686-6213
City Hall   (212) 686-2876

Philadelphia, PA 19107

Approval of the Mayor is needed before events may be held under the hand-painted ceiling of Conversation Hall. Private and corporate dinners, luncheons and receptions are allowed.

Guest capacity: 100 seated/200 standing

Note: Space has no kitchen facilities. A letter requesting permission for use of space must be addressed to the Chief of Staff at City Hall.

Franklin Institute   (215) 448-1165

520th & The Parkway   Contact: Richard Newton,
Philadelphia, PA 19103   Special Events Coordinator

This venerable institution offers innovative surprises for private parties and special functions in a variety of settings, i.e., giant walk-through heart, planetarium show, etc. Also staff members will perform entertaining science demonstrations such as man-made lightning, chemical magic, etc., if requested.

Guest capacity: 300 in U Gallery (250 with adjacent Electricity/Electronics exhibit); 200 in Shipbuilding on the Delaware (400 when combined with adjacent Mechanics Hall); 350 in Fels Planetarium (with after dinner cordials); 100 seated/800 standing in the Benjamin Franklin National Memorial (for candlelight dinners)

Graceful Family Mansion in Germantown

(800) 284-7028

Philadelphia, PA

Completely furnished with family items, this lovely home which has been lived in by more than five generations since it was built in 1801 by Thomas Armat, a civic-minded Philadelphia merchant, also boasts the only original early nineteenth century kitchen in all of Philadelphia.

Guest capacity: 40/50

Wedding receptions are welcome.

Horticulture Center

(800) 284-7028

Philadelphia, PA

Opened in 1979, this new Horticulture Center is a modern greenhouse facility built on the exact site of the 1876 Horticultural Center which at that time had been erected for the nation's Centennial Exhibition in Fairmount Park.

Comprising a twenty-two-acre protected arboretum, the Center has numerous indoor areas which are available for meetings, parties and weddings.

Guest capacity: 75 seated in meeting room; 150 seated indoors in Display House; 150 seated indoors in Tropical Garden; 300 seated indoors in Hibiscus Garden; 150 seated indoors in Tropical Garden; 1000 standing in last three areas named above

The Reflecting Pool area may be rented in conjunction with the first three indoor areas named above.

The Manor with a Tudor Rose

(800) 284-7028

Philadelphia, PA

Modeled after the sixteenth century English manor, Sutton Place, and designed by Philadelphia architect Robert McGoodwin, the unique character of this marvellously maintained University of Pennsylvania property is due to the fact that its floors, woodwork, tiles and glass were carefully collected over many years from historic buildings in England. The reassembled intrinsic artifacts emanate a feeling of history and the time of Queen Elizabeth I which no copy could.

Already the tone is set upon entering the grounds of the estate, where the drive leads past a small cottage which was at Guildford, England in the 1500's. The five hundred year-old Willoughby Gateway which stood in the garden of Parham Old Hall, is the first entrance to the house. The interior is reached through a great oak door which has seen one thousand years of comings and goings.

In the large living room, the huge stone fireplace which came from Cassiobury Hall, was owned by Lord Essex who was the reputed lover of Queen Elizabeth I. The Queen's Tudor Rose is preserved in the leaded glass window as proof that she had actually been there. Other artifacts of this extraordinary house are the stone slabs worn smooth by the passage of 850 years and the pacing of prisoners held captive in Warwick Priory, an iron campaign chest that once belonged to the Revolutionary War General Mad Anthony Wayne, a four hundred year-old pendulum clock, as well as the entire room in which Alexander Pope penned his Essay on Man.

Guest capacity: 100 seated/150 buffet-style in three different rooms

The manor house is available for conferences, seminars, receptions and dinners.

Mansion on Laurel Hill

(800) 284-7028

Philadelphia, PA

Formerly the home of affluent Philadelphians, this yellow and white Georgian-style mansion built circa 1767 stands on a hill overlooking the Schuykill.

Its octagonal room was added in the nineteenth century. Owned by the city since 1900, it stood vacant until 1976 when Women of Greater Philadelphia, a volunteer organization, assumed responsibility for restoration and operation under an agreement with the Fairmount Park Commission.

Large porch at the rear is used for summer receptions and concerts.

Guest capacity: 60 seated/80 standing in Octagonal Room

Memorial Hall   (800) 284-7028
Philadelphia, PA

This colossal Beaux Arts building was erected in 1876 to house the
Art Museum for the Centennial Exposition of the United States.
Guest capacity: 100 reception-style in front vestibule; 500 seated
with dancing/1500 cocktails in Great Hall

Museum Celebrating New Years   (800) 284-7028
Philadelphia, PA

This unique museum was designed and constructed as a permanent
display of the history and traditions of Philadelphia Mummery—
a product of Northern European, British and Black American
heritage dating back to pre-colonial times. Informal merrymak-
ing and customs to celebrate and welcome in the New Year were
fully incorporated into the city-sponsored parade in 1901.
It is available for weddings, private and corporate parties as well
as fundraisers.
Guest capacity: 250 seated

National Register Building in   (800) 284-7028
Germantown
Philadelphia, PA

This fine example of Federal-style architecture was built on the site
where George Washington fought the 1777 Battle of Germantown. Furnished with authentic period furniture, the mansion is
available for weddings, parties and corporate events.
Guest capacity: 125 seated; 150 in entire house

Oasis in Germantown   (800) 284-7028
Philadelphia, PA

Surrounded by six acres of century-old trees, this mansion was
the scene of the Battle of Germantown during the American
Revolution. Presently owned by the National Trust for Historic Preservation and operated by Cliveden, Inc., the property was the home of Benjamin Chew, a successful lawyer
whose descendants lived there for two hundred years. The
lovely site, within the bustling Germantown section of
Philadelphia, is available for receptions, dinners, meetings
and other special uses.
Guest capacity: 100 seated/125 standing in Carriage House
Note: Smoking and amplified music are not allowed.

Perfect Mansion on the Delaware   (800) 284-7028
Philadelphia, PA

This Italianate villa-style summer home of Charles MAcalester,
financial advisor to eight U.S. presidents, was built on the
banks of the Delaware in 1850. Formal gardens, a gazebo,
carriage house, boathouse, gatehouse and stone water tower
may all still be found along the paths of this eighteen-acre
estate. The mansion has twenty-five ornamented high-ceilinged rooms filled with antiques, plus a grand stairway dap-
pled with light from a forty-foot high domed stained glass
skylight. Glass-enclosed sun porch is perfect for dancing and
viewing the Delaware River.
Guest capacity: 150 in formal dining room; larger groups may
rent a tent and portable dance floor for use on the grounds; 35
overnight accommodations
A Haskell pipe organ and vintage Steinway grand piano are also
available.

Philadelphia Maritime Museum   (800) 284-7028
Philadelphia, PA

Philadelphia is the city where the United States Navy was
founded in 1775, the first steamboat was built and the first
atomic powered vessel launched. This great maritime
museum is filled with maritime art, ship models, ship-build-
ing tools, navigational instruments, scrimshaw, weapons and
figure heads as well as a fine library.
Guest capacity: 60 seated dinner/120 lecture-style/200 reception-style
Note: Private functions are not allowed.

Philadelphia Zoo   (800) 284-7028
Philadelphia, PA

The treehouse is the main attraction here where special events are held under a forty-foot high fiberglass ficus tree surrounded by tall arched windows.

Guest capacity: 120 seated/220 cocktails; up to 6000 in entire zoo which includes the Rare Animal House, Impala Fountain and The Children's Zoo; additional persons may be accommodated when the lawn is used as well

Playful Museum   (800) 284-7028
Philadelphia, PA

Filled with exhibitions of costumes, puppets, games and toys, this colorful museum for young children also rents out for every kind of event for adults.

Weddings, for example, take place in the atrium on a circular ramp with a multi-colored dragon suspended from the ceiling. Space is suitable for birthday parties for children and adults, performances, recitals, lectures, workshops, seminars, office parties, rehearsals and weddings.

Guest capacity: 12/250 in various areas; 350 in entire building

Polish Hall   (800) 284-7028
Philadelphia, PA

Formerly an ethnic social hall built in the early 1900's, this facility has been recently renovated.

Guest capacity: 225 downstairs; 350 upstairs

Kitchen on each floor

Residence of an Eighteenth Century Mayor   (800) 284-7028
Philadelphia, PA

Built in 1765, this Georgian-style townhouse is considered the most beautiful of its style still extant in Philadelphia. It was the residence of Samuel Powel, the last mayor of Philadelphia under the British crown and the first mayor under the new United States republic.

Mrs. Powel was one of the city's most brilliant hostesses. George Washington, the Marquis de Lafayette, foreign ministers and other persons of importance were her frequent guests.

Guest capacity: 40 to 50 seated/70 standing in the ballroom

Owned and maintained by the Philadelphia Society for the Preservation of Landmarks.

Weddings are welcome.

An eighteenth century garden is adjacent to the house.

Seventeenth Century Swedish Manor House   (800) 284-7028
Philadelphia, PA

Three hundred and fifty years ago Christina, the young Swedish queen, assisted in sending a group of hardy explorers to take possession of the American east coast. They left Gothenburg harbor in 1637 and were responsible for planting the Swedish flag over the territories south of Trenton, New Jersey to Wilmington, Delaware. This New Sweden (1638-1655) lives on regally in the form of a seventeenth century manor house in South Philadelphia. Modeled after Eriksberg Castle, it is complete with a European-style copper roof. Most of its rooms were designed and constructed in Sweden, some as recently as 1938, i.e., the art deco-style John Ericsson room in memory of the Swedish-born inventor of the American Civil War steel battleship, the *Monitor*. Other rooms depict memorabilia of the women's rights activist and one of Sweden's most important novelists, Frederika Brenner, as well as Jenny Lind, etc.

The manor house, which serves as a historical society and museum, offers a grand staircase and numerous special function rooms.

Guest capacity: 75 standing in Main Hall; 150 seated in rustic Viking Room

A small tent may be erected in the garden.

Society Hill House   (800) 284-7028
Philadelphia, PA

This four-story square brick house and its walled garden comprise one third of a city block. Formerly owned by Dr. Philip Syns Physick, the "Father of American Surgery," the residence is filled with antiques. The drawing room has a twelve- foot high ceiling adjoining a formal dining room with a candelabra which may be lit.

Guest capacity: 50 seated/75 standing
There is a small garden which contains eighteenth century plants and classical sculpture.
Note: Smoking and dancing are not allowed.

Victorian Library   (800) 284-7028
Philadelphia, PA

Designed in 1845 by John Notman in the Italianate Revival-style, this painstakingly restored reference library offers lofty ceilings, marble columns, gaslight fixtures, polished brass and richly grained woodwork.
Guest capacity: 110 with dancing/150 seated/300 cocktails
Note: Space is only available to corporations and non-profit organizations.

Philadelphia: More Auditoriums, Halls & Meeting Rooms *(by capacity for special functions)*

Germantown Theatre Guild   (215) 561-8715
4821 Germantown Ave. ....(reception) 70

Freedom Theatre   (215) 765-2993
1346 No. Broad St. .... (reception) 100

Afro-American Historical and   (215) 574-0380
Cultural Museum
7th & Arch Sts. ....(reception/meeting) 200

Pennsylvania Academy of the Fine   (215) 972-7627
Arts at the Peale Club
1819 Chestnut St. 250/300

Museum of American Jewish History   (215) 923-3811
55 No. 5th St. 100/500

Annenberg Center   (215) 898-6683
80 Walnut St. 300/1000

Philadelphia Museum of Art   (215) 763-8100
26 St. & Benjamin Franklin Pkwy. 400/1000

GREATER PHILADELPHIA (BUCKS, CHESTER, DELAWARE, MONTGOMERY AND NORTHAMPTON COUNTIES)

Academy for Military Training   (800) 284-7028
(Delaware County)
Wayne, PA

Georgian brick buildings on the grounds of this 170-acre military academy near Valley Forge rent for weddings, dinners and receptions. Picnic grounds, playing fields, pools, gymnasium and a chapel are also available.
Guest capacity: 180 seated in dining room overlooking ballroom; 50 seated in second dining room with outdoor terrace
Resident caterer

Ashton   (800) 284-7028
(Bucks County)
Swarthmore, PA

This stone house is available for special functions with overnight accommodations.
Guest capacity: 50
Wedding ceremonies may be held in Quaker Meeting House.

Boxwood House   (800) 284-7028
(Chester County)
Coatsville, PA

Twenty miles outside of Philadelphia, this eighteenth century stone plantation house stands amidst eight hundred acres of grounds. The estate includes an enormous eighteenth century boxwood bush and a nineteenth century carriage house and stable. It remained in the Swayne family until the late 1960's and is available for tented functions only.
Guest capacity: 450 seated in tent on grounds

Canals and the Industrial Revolution   (800) 284-7028
(Northampton County)
Easton, PA

continued on next page

In the early nineteenth century more than four thousand miles of towpath canals were dug. Pennsylvania had twelve hundred miles of canals, more than any other state, linking cities, villages, mines, factories and farms.

The Lehigh Canal traverses the length of a 260-acre historic park which together with a museum and restored lockhouse are being preserved as a reminder of these water highways which began the industrial revolution and opened the American frontier. Many nineteenth century industrial ruins also exist within the park.

The *Josiah White*, a mule-drawn canal boat, may be chartered for private parties and the museum may be rented for meetings during the evening.

Guest capacity: 50 in museum; 80 on canal boat; 60/120 at pavilion picnic tables

Catering is available in the pavilions and on canal boat by caterer of your choice.

County Seat of a Leading Family   (800) 284-7028
(Bucks County)
Andalusia, PA

Seven generations of the Biddle family have lived on this idyllic estate which sits high upon the banks of the Delaware River, twenty-five minutes from Philadelphia.

Designed by the eminent architect Benjamin Latrobe in 1806 and expanded in 1834 by Thomas U. Walter, it was Nicholas Biddle, president of the Second Bank of the United States and a man who knew something about everything, including the cultivation of strawberries, gooseberries and currants, who attended to every detail of the estate with a Jeffersonian precision and who imbued this working farm/family estate with the ambiance of a miniature paradise.

The main house, with its thick white Ionic columns, is considered one of the finest examples of domestic Greek Revival architecture in the country.

Guest capacity: 60 seated/125 standing indoors; for larger groups a tent may be erected next to the house and entered through the library or from the portico

Fieldstone House   (800) 284-7028
(Montgomery County)
Radnor, PA

This colonial fieldstone church house predates the signing of the American Constitution by fifty years. Set on thirteen acres,

eight of which are formal lawns and gardens, the house has a covered porch and brick terrace in the back.

Guest capacity: 80 seated/150 cocktails or buffet when both dining room and library are used; over 200 for tented affairs on the grounds

Suggested uses: wedding, small party

Located ten miles west of Philadelphia.

Former Home of Pearl S. Buck   (800) 284-7028
Bucks County, PA

This circa 1835 stone mansion was the home of Nobel Prize-winning author Pearl Buck. Overlooking rolling lawns and gardens, the sixty-acre estate is composed of three buildings: the main house with Oriental paintings and porcelains and the Chinese Windsor desk at which Buck wrote *The Good Earth*; a three-room cottage; and a barn dating from before the Revolutionary War that has been converted into a hall with a high cathedral ceiling, tall windows and stage.

The terrace is suitable for cocktails, wedding ceremonies, etc.

Guest capacity: 75/100 seated in the newly converted barn; functions may also be tented

Gentleman's Country Seat   (800) 284-7028
(Montgomery County)
Havertown, PA

This ten-acre complex comprising a mansion, gardens, outbuildings and woodland reflects the lifestyle of an eighteenth or nineteenth century gentleman. Nevertheless it has undergone numerous changes in its three hundred year history.

The original structure was built in 1700 and later changed from Colonial to English Gothic. It is available for meetings, weddings and parties which take place mostly on the veranda which encircles the house.

Guest capacity: 30 seated/80 cocktails in drawing room; 130 seated on veranda

Note: Space is mainly available between April and October; smaller parties during winter months may be accommodated.

Gristmill Museum   (800) 284-7028

(Delaware County)
Chadds Ford, PA

The largest collection of paintings by one of America's favorite artists, Andrew Wyeth, is housed in this century-old restored grist mill overlooking the Brandywine River. Three floors of gallery space and two glass towers afford views of wildflower gardens.

Guest capacity: 110 seated in museum restaurant; 150 standing on first floor; 120 seated in conference room; 600 in entire museum

Suitable for weddings, parties and receptions.

Located twenty-eight miles outside of Philadelphia.

Harriton House   (800) 284-7028

(Montgomery County)
Bryn Mawr, PA

Situated on over sixteen acres, this Jacobean stone farmhouse dates back to 1704 and was the residence of Charles Thomson, secretary of the Continental Congress. The rooms boast wood paneling, fireplaces and antique furnishings.

Guest capacity: 30 to 35 seated/55 cocktails

Note: Dancing and amplified rock music are not allowed.

Ironmaster's Home   (800) 284-7028

(Chester County)
Wagontown, PA

Thirty miles outside of Philadelphia, this comfortable home of an eighteenth century ironmaster overlooks Brandywine Creek and sits in eight hundred acres of lawn and woodland belonging to Hibernia Park.

Reception areas include a sitting room, a nineteenth century parlor, dining room and a sunroom furnished with wicker furniture. The marble-framed fireplace in the parlor flanked with ferns is a favorite setting for wedding ceremonies.

Guest capacity: 40 seated in dining room; 75 in entire house; unlimited outdoor capacity

Longwood Gardens   (215) 388-6741

(Chester County)   Contact: Marjorie Clark
Kennett Square, PA 19348

Originally the country home of Pierre S. du Pont (1870-1954), this one thousand acre estate reflects both the ambiance of the great eighteenth century European pleasure gardens such as Versailles and Chatsworth, as well as being the ultimate idea of an opulent estate garden of the 1920's. World-renowned for its year-round horticultural displays which keep two hundred employees busy, the Gardens are equally astonishing for their inventive use of water bubbling in small pools, tumbling over rock-strewn waterfalls and shooting from hundreds of fountains whose jets can rise to 130 feet. The one hundred foot long Ballroom in the Main Conservatory offers crystal chandeliers and a pink glass ceiling. An illuminated fountain display choreographed to music may also be requested during the months of May through September in conjunction with the rental of the Ballroom.

It is available for special functions such as dances, musical performances and public dinners.

Guest capacity: 142 in the Auditorium; 250 in the Ballroom; 320 in four rooms in the Terrace Restaurant; 2100 in Open Air Theatre

Resident caterer

Note: Only non-profit organizations whose functions are of direct benefit to the public at large may apply for permission to hold an evening function in the Ballroom/Music Room area or for the use of the Theatre for benefit performances.

Main Line Rambling Country House   (800) 284-7028

(Montgomery County)
Villanova, PA

The approach to this eighteenth century L-shaped property consists of a curving drive through woods, a stone bridge and a waterfall that splashes into a large pond. In addition, a box garden, a terrace lawn and rhododendron glades surround this country house which is owned by the local township and operated and maintained by an excellent house committee fourteen miles from Philadelphia.

Guest capacity: 90 seated/150 standing; 225 in tent outdoors

Manor House in a Rural Setting   (800) 284-7028

(Chester County)
Glenmore, PA

Once owned by nineteenth century capitalist George Bartol, this spacious 1833 country manor house is surrounded by a three hundred-acre farm which still operates today.

The reception area includes a 463 sq. ft. main hall and a 520 sq. ft. music room which is suitable for dancing. A serving room and two meeting rooms are also available. Working fireplaces, detailed woodwork and hardwood floors are characteristic of each room.

For wedding ceremonies, guests are seated in the main hall which permits a fine view of the bridal procession down the hall stairway.

Guest capacity: up to 225 in downstairs rooms; additional capacity with use of wide veranda; many more may be accomodated with canopy tents at the front of the house

Merion Tribute House   (800) 284-7028

(Montgomery County)
Merion Station, PA

Built in 1924 as a tribute to the Merion community's war veterans, this English castle-style house overlooks ten acres of rolling lawns and a formal azalea garden.

Guest capacity: 200 seated with dancing in ballroom; smaller groups in Legion Room

Stage, fireplace and stone terrace

Music/Ballroom and Arboretum   (800) 284-7028
of a Great Former Publisher

(Montgomery County)
Wyncote, PA

During the 1876 Centennial in Philadelphia, many distinguished visitors were entertained on this estate by its original owner, Abraham Barker, a banker.

One of these visitors was Alexander Graham Bell, who was seeking financial backing for his new telephone device. Mr. Barker invited a group of his banker friends to attend the demonstration, and a telephone line was strung between his home and the home of Mr. Barker's brother, Wharton, a quarter of a mile away. However the bankers' verdict was that the device was an interesting novelty with no practical value.

In 1890 this estate was bought by Cyrus H. K. Curtis, publisher of the *Ladies Home Journal, The Saturday Evening Post, The Philadelphia Inquirer, The New York Post,* and other publications. Its Music Room boasts a fabulous oramented ceiling and sky-high Palladian doors that open onto a slate terrace where the cocktail bar is usually set up.

Guest capacity: 120 with dancing/150 cocktails in Curtis Hall; 200 in tented patio

Large stage for orchestra or d.j.

All around the historic stone building are small terraces with vistas of grassy hills and ancient trees. A natural backdrop for wedding ceremonies is a long wisteria arbor.

Note: Sponsorship by a township resident is necessary.

Old-Fashioned Mule Barges   (800) 284-7028

(Bucks County)
New Hope, PA

The Delaware Canal, built in 1832, runs parallel to the Delaware River and is now a national historic landmark. In the 1860's some three thousand boats and barges pulled by teams of mules were travelling the Canal.

Private parties aboard these barges embark from New Hope. They are decorated with flowers and suitable live music may also be arranged. Daily one-hour excursions are also available. Food may be served on the barge or at a secluded picnic area along the way by barge's own caterer or by caterer of your choice.

Guest capacity: 80 maximum in each of four boats

Note: Rentals are only available from April through mid-November.

Old Mill House   (800) 284-7028

(Delaware County)
Media, PA

A thirty-five-foot cathedral-like ceiling and huge stone fireplace are special features of this two hundred year-old former flour and grist mill, now banquet hall

Guest capacity: 250 seated/400 cocktails; larger groups may choose one of the two courtyards which can be tented

There is a full kitchen and air-conditioning.

Quaker Manor House   (800) 284-7028

(Bucks County)
Morrisville, PA

This seventeenth century Quaker manor house, home of William Penn, first governor of Pennsylvania, looks out over the Delaware River. Formal gardens and orchards comprise this twenty-seven-acre estate.

Guest capacity: 200/250 seated, many more for cocktail receptions
Parties and weddings take place under tents; indoor events are not allowed.

The 1716 House
(800) 284-7028

(Delaware County)
Upland, PA

A formal dining room, recently added solarium, ballroom, drawing room and bride's room are featured in this eighteenth century Colonial mansion which has been recently restored and furnished with period antiques. Honeymoon and guest suites are also available. Grand piano. Landscaped grounds.

Guest capacity: 150 in entire house; 60 seated in ballroom; 75 for dinners in formal parlor and dining rooms; 50/75 in atrium-style solarium

Located twenty minutes from Philadelphia.

A Spanish Mansion
(800) 284-7028

(Delaware County)
Wayne, PA

This Spanish twenty-two-room mansion perched on a hilltop offers first floor rooms and a spacious solarium. Sliding glass doors open onto the terrace which is filled with azaleas. A Belgian brick courtyard is a perfect site for wedding ceremonies.

Guest capacity: 150 seated

Thomas Leiper House
(800) 284-7028

(Delaware County)
Wallingford, PA

This 1785 Federal-style summer home of Thomas Leiper, a Revolutionary War patriot and railroad pioneer, narrowly escaped demolition when the expressway designed to run through its site was re-routed. The house with its remaining four outbuildings overlooks Crum Creek.

It is available for private functions such as teas, small parties and wedding receptions.

Guest capacity: up to 75
Rental fee: $150 per party

WESTERN PENNSYLVANIA/ PITTSBURGH

Hartwood Acres Park
(412) 321-4302

c/o Allegheny County Parks & Recreation Dept.
Buhl Science Center, Allegheny Square
Pittsburgh, PA 15212

This 629-acre estate park includes a stately sixteenth century-style mansion designed in 1929 for John and Mary Flinn Lawrence. Since Allegheny County acquired the property in 1969, several works of sculpture by internationally known artists have been placed on the estate.

Guest capacity: 250 maximum outdoors or under tent

Horse-drawn hay rides or sleigh rides are also available to groups.

Note: Weddings and other private parties may be held outdoors only.

Pittsburgh: More Auditoriums, Halls & Meeting Rooms (by capacity for special functions)

Pittsburgh Zoo
(412) 441-6262
Highland Park.. 50/100

Carnegie Music Hall
(412) 622-3360
4400 Forbes Ave. 400/500

Stephen Foster Memorial Theatre
(412) 624-0466
Forbes Ave. 250/500

Heinz Hall for the Performing Arts
(412) 392-4841
600 Penn Ave. 500/1000

Soldiers and Sailors Memorial Hall
(412) 621-4253
5th Ave. & Bigelow Blvd. 800/1000

Syria Mosque
(412) 621-8700
4423 Bigelow Blvd. .... *(seated/reception)*1000

Carnegie Museum of Natural History
(412) 622-3289
4400 Forbes Ave. 800/2000

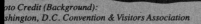

WASHINGTON D.C. & ENVIRONS

PARTY PLACES

WASHINGTON, DC

America's First Museum of Modern Art   (800) 284-7028
Washington, DC

Founded in 1921, this elegant non-governmental museum is located in a Georgian Revival building designed by Hornblower & Marshall.

Guest capacity: 100 lecture or conference, 110 seated/150 standing in Music Room; 250 in annex for seated dinner; 600 reception in main building with annex

The museum has a sophisticated sound system as well as standard projection equipment.

Note: Dances, weddings or political functions are not allowed.

Available for rental by individuals and organizations with the approval of the museum director Tuesdays through Saturdays after 5 p.m., Sundays after 7 p.m., and all day and evening on Mondays.

Beaux Arts-Style Library   (800) 284-7028
Washington, DC

The lobby of this nineteenth century library is a grand interior hall with a marble floor and a swirling double staircase under a skylight roof. Ideal for receptions, banquets, award ceremonies, municipal functions and weddings.

Guest capacity: 300 seated/400 standing in interior hall; 150 seated in downstairs community room

Capital Children's Museum   (800) 284-7028
Washington, DC

Formerly a convent, this high-ceilinged museum is available for special functions and offers themes on Communications, Caves, the Environment and Mexico for both children and adults.

Guest capacity: 100/1000 in entire museum; 150 in auditorium

Note: Space is only available for fundraisers or organizational parties.

Carriage House Two Blocks From the White House   (800) 284-7028
Washington, DC

At the site of where 1812 Naval hero Stephen Decatur stabled his horses, a modern and spacious meeting facility covering 2100 sq. ft. has been newly constructed. French doors lead to a private garden and brick-paved courtyard. Tours of the adjacent Decatur House Museum may be arranged as part of any private function.

Guest capacity: 90 meeting or theater-style/120 seated/250 cocktails in Carriage House; 250 seated/500 cocktails in Carriage House and tented garden

The Christian Heurich Mansion   (800) 284-7028
Washington, DC

Built in 1894, for Christian Heurich, a prominent Washington brewer and philanthropist, this thirty-room mansion is now owned and operated as a house museum by the Columbia Historical Society which preserves the history of the city.

Architecturally, the mansion represents an assertive and flamboyant period. It was probably the first single-family Washington residence built in poured concrete with virtually no structural use of wood and it documents the very significant role of the German-American building trades community in the nineteenth century development of Washington and other large American cities.

Although there are seven first floor rooms plus a medieval foyer, it is the Conservatory with a terra-cotta and turquoise tiled floor, red paned windows and a small fountain, which is used most frequently for events. The museum's exceptionally authentic Victorian interior, largely unchanged since the late nineteenth century, makes this a memorable setting for special events and meetings.

Guest capacity: 40/60 for meetings; 50 seated/65 buffet/100 reception in Conservatory (200 with tenting in Conservatory and garden); 150 garden party; Note: Weddings are not allowed. Smoking is only allowed in the garden and the Conservatory.

The Corcoran Gallery of Art
(800) 284-7028

Washington, DC

This eminent gallery offers a two-story temple-like hall which acts as a double atrium and is the site for receptions and banquets with fluted columns rising forty feet from the marble floor to the skyline ceiling. Famous for its extensive collection of American masterpieces, the museum's galleries may also open for browsing. A particularly charming walnut-paneled room called Clarks Landing is additionally available.

Guest capacity: 193 in Frances and Armand Hammer Auditorium; 400 seated/1000 cocktails in gallery space

Note: Commercial, political or fundraising events are not allowed. Red wine and dancing are also not allowed.

"Down Under" Embassy
(800) 284-7028

Washington, DC

This brick and glass open space with outdoor terrace and garden is made available to outside groups by the New Zealand embassy.

Guest capacity: 200 seated/300 cocktails

Note: Weddings are not allowed.

The Former Home of Mrs. Turner A. Wickersham
(800) 284-7028

Washington, DC

This four-story mansion built in 1913 houses a collection of paintings, antique furniture and decorative artifacts from all periods of American and European art and hosts some of Washington's most elegant events. Mrs. Wickersham was a socialite who is said to have brought the Christian Science movement to Washington.

Guest capacity 10/150 in eleven art-filled rooms

Note: Amplified music is not allowed.

Former Iranian Embassy
(800) 284-7028

(Massachusetts Avenue N.W.)
Washington, DC

Presently owned by the Department of State, this former embassy still sparkles with mirrored tiles on its sky blue ballroom ceiling and a mosaic fountain splashes in its courtyard.

Guest capacity: 120 seated in ballroom; 220 cocktails in ballroom and lobby; 210 seated/450 cocktails in ballroom and courtyard

Resident caterer

Courtyard may be tented. Parking for 150 cars.

Note: Weddings are not allowed.

Former Pension Building
(800) 284-7028

(Judiciary Square N.W.)
Washington, DC

Called "the most breathtaking room ever created by the U.S. government," this Great Hall has been the site of eleven Presidential Inaugural Balls and many other elegant social events since it was built by architect Montgomery C. Meigs a century ago.

Located in what was formerly the Bureau of Pensions, the spectacular Great Hall is lined with long arcades and its center is crossed with the eight largest Corinthian columns in the world. Each of the marbleized columns is eight feet in diameter and seventy-five feet high. This powerful space also has a fountain in the middle.

Guest capacity: 135 in auditorium; 140 in conference room; 140 in Presidential Suite; 1600 in the Great Hall

**General Services Administration
Departmental Auditorium &
Conference Rooms**
Contact: Rene Walker,
Facilities Reservation
Assistant

12th & 14th Street and Constitution Avenue
Washington, DC 20407

An auditorium and three conference rooms are available.
Guest capacity: up to 35 in conference rooms; 800 for dinner/1325 seated auditorium-style
Suggested uses: fundraiser, dance, political speech, performance
Note: Space is only available to non-profit groups having events which are open to the public. Alcohol and smoking are not allowed. Application for use must be made in writing to Triangle Field Office, 1200 Pennsylvania Avenue, N.W., Rm. 1315, Washington, DC 20004.

Georgetown Mansion
(800) 284-7028
Washington, DC

Conceived during the last years of the eighteenth century, this Adamsesque Federal-style museum house with garden is available for private and corporate functions.
Guest capacity: 200 in entire house and garden; smaller groups in separate rooms
Resident caterer

Gracious Ballroom
(800) 284-7028
Washington, DC

Pale yellow is the delicate hue of this 54 ft. x 45 ft. ballroom which boasts a forty-foot high ceiling and is flanked by two living rooms at either side. These are furnished with Williamsburg antiques, have working fireplaces and chandeliers. The ballroom was originally used to hold tea dances during the 1940's and is equally popular today for all manner of special functions.
Guest capacity: 110 seated/350 cocktails

Hall of Dazzling Arrivals and Departures
(800) 284-7028
Washington, DC

There is probably no building in Washington as emotionally charged as Union Station with memories of loved ones going off to war, of newly elected presidents and dazzling arrivals and partings. Its original construction in 1908 was headed by architect Daniel Burnham, who also created the grand plan for the park system of Washington.
Serving as a rail passenger station for the first sixty years, the station was unsuccessfully converted into a National Visitor's Center when rail travel declined in the late 1960's. A new redevelopment, however, was completed in 1988, and this great historic station is once again the "noble portal for travelers that every city deserves."
Modeled after the public baths of Diocletian of Rome, the Main Hall has barrel vaulted coffered ceilings which soar 100-feet above the polished Italian marble floors. The East Hall is renowned for its skylights which produce splendid natural lighting and make it a fine setting for receptions and black-tie dinners. The Columbus Club is a completely private and secluded versatile site for informal functions.
Guest capacity: 1650 seated/3500 cocktails in Main Hall; 450 seated/900 cocktails in East Hall; 225 seated/440 cocktails in the Columbus Club

Hexagon Called the Octagon
(800) 284-7028
Washington, DC

Designed at the turn of the eighteenth century for Col. John Tayloe III of Virginia by Dr. William Thornton, a versatile man of letters, medicine and architecture, this unusually shaped house was one of the finest residences of its time. It is an excellent example of the American Federal period with a circular entrance hall, oval staircase and diagonally placed rooms. "The Octagon" also played a significant role in the early life of the capital as a meeting place for individuals who shaped the country's future. It is presently owned by the American Institute of Architects Foundation.

A special room is located on the third floor. It is perfectly round, painted yellow and blue, and offers a grand view of the city.

Guest capacity: 30 luncheon in third floor "Mrs. Ogle's" parlor; 150 cocktails inside; 150 seated/200 cocktails in tented garden

Note: Available only to non-profit organizations and business groups.

Historic Home on the Waterfront   (800) 284-7028
461 N Street, S.W.
Washington, DC 20024

This Federal period mansion sits back on a wide lawn overlooking the Potomac in Southwest Washington. Built in 1794 by Robert Morris of Morris, Nicholson and Greenleaf. Mr. Morris is known as the financier of the American Revolution and John Nicholson was the Comptroller General of the Continental Congress.

In the spring of 1796, Thomas Law, Esq., an aristocrat who made a fortune in India, leased this mansion as a temporary home for himself and his bride, Eliza Parke Curtis, a granddaughter of Martha Washington. It is enhanced by brass fixtures, Greek Revival fireplaces, oak floors, and terrace views of Washington's monuments. It is currently available for all manner of special functions, including weddings.

Guest capacity: 75 seated, 150 cocktails/buffet; 300 outdoors
Resident caterer

The John F. Kennedy Center   (202) 634-4152
for the Performing Arts   (800) 424-8504 (Group Sales)
Washington, D.C.   Contact: Special Events Office

Ticket-holding theater patrons may have use of several spaces for their special events.

Guest capacity: 50 seated/70 standing in Chinese Room; 60 seated/80 to 100 standing in one of two Foyers; 100/400 standing in Atrium; 350 seated/500 standing in Atrium including Foyers

Underground parking
Resident caterer

Mississippi River Boat on the   (800) 284-7028
Potomac
Washington, DC

This recently designed sternwheeler is elegantly appointed for private entertaining with high tin ceilings, ceiling fans, brass chandeliers and sconces, etched glass and solid mahogany woodwork. Powered solely by two paddle wheels, this river

boat takes leisurely cruises on the Potamac and in the bays and harbors of the region.

Guest capacity: 200 seated/cocktails

Monroe and Macfeely Houses   (800) 284-7028
Washington, DC

Two connecting nineteenth century townhouses form an art gallery featuring the work of Washington artists. This spacious facility includes a ballroom as well as two fine banquet rooms furnished with antiques and Waterford-crystal chandeliers. French doors lead to a tree-shaded patio surrounded by a sculpture garden. A library and drawing rooms are on the second floor.

Guest capacity: 125 seated/300 reception; 300 in garden
Resident caterer

Mule-Drawn Canal Boats   (800) 284-7028
on the Chesapeake and Ohio Canal

Two mule-drawn canal boats representative of the boats used in the 1870's are available for group rides for up to two hours. Both offer costumed National Park Rangers who tell stories about life over a century ago when the waterway was in its heyday. The *Georgetown* departs from Lock 3 in Georgetown and passes by many historic buildings, townhouses and chic shops.

The *Canal Clipper* departs from Great Falls Park, near Potomac, Maryland, and travels through the quiet countryside.

Guest capacity: 60 on each boat
Note: Rents primarily during spring and summer.

Museum for the Women's Movement   (800) 284-7028
Washington, DC

The significance of this house, which was built in 1840, is its historical association with Alice Paul, founder of the National Woman's Party, whose militancy was indispensable to the passage of suffrage for women and the 19th Amendment to the Constitution. The house was designated as a national historic landmark in 1972, as it was the only house left standing in the U.S. from which the contemporary women's movement went forward. It is currently a national museum on the history of women's fight for equality.

Guest capacity: 50 seated/125 cocktails in house; 400 under tent in garden

Note: The garden's brick terrace may be used for dancing. Wedding ceremonies and smoking are not allowed. Caterers must be selected from approved list.

National Park Service   (202) 485-9660

Ohio Drive S.W.
Washington, DC 20242

For those who don't mind gambling on the weather, weddings
  and receptions may be held by the Lincoln Memorial, Jefferson Memorial, or in one of dozens of the District's national
  parks free of charge.

National Press Club   (202) 662-7515

14th & F Streets, N.W.   Contact: Catering Manager
Washington, DC 20045

This 50,000 sq. ft. club occupies the thirteenth and fourteenth
  floors of the totally renovated National Press Club Building.
  It so impressed newsman Eric Severeid, that he described it
  as "the only hallowed place I know that's absolutely bursting
  with irreverence."
The club offers four meeting rooms, each named after a distinguished American journalist. Three of the rooms may be
  joined. Its main lounge is furnished with overstuffed sofas and
  a working fireplace flanked on either side by dark wood bars.
  Its ballroom may be partitioned into separate sections and has
  two large balconies.
Guest capacity: up to 500 for a banquet or conference/up to 1500
  for a reception; 150 cocktails on terrace

Old Town Trolley Tours   (202) 269-3020

3150 V Street
Washington, DC 20018
Contact: General Manager

A trolley car may be chartered to transport guests to a particular
  location or to offer a private sightseeing tour. Music, food,
  beverages and special decorations are available as well as
  customized tour routes and stops.
Guest capacity: 42

Pavilion at the Old Post Office   (800) 284-7028

Washington, DC

Having twice cheated the wrecker's ball, this imposing neo-
  Romanesque structure, which served as the first federal post
  office, was saved by preservationists such as local architect
  Arthur Cotton Moore, who in 1977 won a competition to
  modify the building for commercial use on its lower floors
  with government offices above.
The building's most exciting space is its multi-storied Cor-
  tile/Pavilion which rises 215 feet and is topped by a huge
  skylight. The old post office's clock tower, rising 350 feet,
  offers one of the best views of Washington.
Guest capacity: 550 seated/3500 standing
Performing arts stage and lighting
Resident caterers

Private Rooms in One of   (800) 284-7028
Washington's Oldest Restaurants

Washington, DC

Around the corner from the White House is one of the oldest
  restaurants in Washington.
Guest capacity: 50 seated/80 reception in Cabinet Room; 130 in
  Atrium

Spectacular Recent Restoration/   (800) 284-7028
Now Museum

Washington, DC

A former Masonic
  hall, then movie
  theater, has been
  turned into a spec-
  tacular museum
  featuring works
  of art by women.
  It also functions
  extremely well
  for conferences,
  meetings, lunches
  and dinners.
Beige and rose are
  the predominantly
  soothing colors
  reflected in the
impressive marble interior of its Great Hall with marble stairs
that truly ensure the grand entrance. The immensely attractive
pink marble was brought over from Turkey and laid down by

Turkish workers. This home for women's art is a work of art by itself.

Guest capacity: 20 in boardroom; 200 seated in state-of-the-art auditorium; 120 seated/325 cocktails in third floor gallery; 450 seated/900 cocktails in Great Hall

Catering kitchen

Textile Museum   (800) 284-7028
Washington, DC

Elegantly housed, this is the pre-eminent museum in the Western Hemisphere focusing exclusively on the study of historic and handmade textiles and carpets.

Founded by George Hewitt Myers, the heir of the Bristol-Myers fortune, the museum operates out of two adjacent mansions: the original home, designed by John Russell Pope, architect of the Jefferson Memorial; and the adjoining building designed by Waddy Wood, architect of the Woodrow Wilson House.

A garden offers a fountain set in a lily pond, pebbled paths and a pavilion.

Guest capacity: 60 reception in two rooms and foyer of the Pope mansion; 125 reception when galleries are open

Two Contrasting Mansions   (800) 284-7028
Washington, DC

The Meridian House, designed by John Russell Pope, architect of the Thomas Jefferson Memorial and the National Gallery of Art, is considered to be one of the finest examples of eighteenth century French urban architecture in the U.S. Presently serving as a reception center, world affairs council and art gallery, the house is available for conferences, meetings and receptions by its affiliates, by corporate benefactors and by non-profit and private institutions with compatible international objectives. Also appropriate for TV and still photography.

The adjacent White-Meyer house is a Georgian-style mansion which belonged to Ambassador White and then to the Meyer family. It is available for small intimate functions as well as large galas.

Guest capacity: 80 seated in drawing room, 90 seated in dining room, 1500 in garden in the Meridian House; 60 seated in dining room; 40 seated in adjacent library; 100 seated/300 cocktails when both rooms are joined; 200 on terrace in White-Meyer House

Note: Space is not available for weddings and purely social occasions.

Washington Boat Lines   (202) 554-8000
Pier 4, Sixth & Water Sts., S.W.
Washington, DC 20024

Private charter Potomac River cruises for business meetings, fundraisers, receptions and weddings.

Guest capacity: 300 on *Spirit of Mt. Vernon*; 415 on *Spirit of Washington*

Year-round operation.

Washington Doll's House & Toy Museum   (800) 284-7028
Washington, D.C.

This museum collection of carefully researched, primarily Victorian, antique doll's houses, toys and games is dedicated to the proposition that doll's houses of the past comprise a study of architecture and decorative arts in miniature, and that toys of the past reflect social history.

An Edwardian waitress in starched apron and cap conducts a tour of the museum and serves refreshments amidst potted palms; a carousel whirls a tinkly tune; a tin weight lifter lifts "one hundred pounds" with his tin teeth; and a fuzzy bear performs astonishing feats.

Guest capacity: 100 cocktails indoors; 300 with tent for a cocktail reception; 24 seated indoors; 150 seated with tent

Note: Smoking is not allowed in the museum. Available from 5 p.m. to midnight and all day Mondays.

The Woodrow Wilson House   (800) 284-7028
Washington, DC

As the only former President to make his home in the nation's capital, Woodrow Wilson retired to this elegant red brick Georgian Revival townhouse in 1921 and reflected upon his long scholarly and political career. After his death, his widow continued to live there for thirty-seven more years and she carefully preserved their furnishings and varied mementos.

Presently owned and managed by the National Trust for Historic Preservation, the house is open for social functions year-round.

Guest capacity: 36 seated/75 cocktails in house; 100 seated/300 cocktails in house and garden

Resident caterers

Note: Smoking in the interior of the house is not allowed. Dancing and amplified music indoors are not allowed.

Also see: Art Deco Private Railroad Cars (New York City and Washington, DC)

District of Columbia: More Auditoriums, Halls & Meeting Rooms

(by capacity for special functions)

Lafayette   (202) 223-8788
1020 16th St., N.W. ....50 seated/reception

H.H. Leonards Fine Arts Mansion   (202) 659-8787
2020 O St., N.W. ....60 seated/100 reception

Sam Pardoe's House   (202) 828-7000
2804 Q St. ....34 seated/100 reception

American Society of Association   (202) 626-2799
Executives Conference Center
1575 Eye St., N.W. ....75 seated/150 cocktails

Fondo del Sol   (202) 483-2777
Visual Art and Media Center
2112 R St., N.W. ....60 seated/150 reception

Daughters of the American   (202) 628-1774
Revolution Museum
1776 D St., N.W. 100/200

Thompson Boat Center   (202) 333-9543
Rock Creek Pkwy. & Virginia Ave., N.W. ..200 seated/reception

The National Aquarium   (202) 377-2826
U.S. Dept. of Commerce Bldg.
14th & Constitution Ave., N.W. ....150 seated/300 reception

Capitol Hill Club   (202) 484-4590
300 1st St., S.E..................................... 240 seated/400 cocktails

The Folger Shakespeare Library   (202) 544-7077
201 East Capitol St., S.E. 250/400

Touchdown Club   (202) 223-1542
2000 1 St., N.W. .... 280 seated/400 cocktails

Jefferson Auditorium   (202) 447-2911
Dept. of Agriculture Bldg.
14th & Independence Ave., S.E.. 480

U.S. Dept of Agriculture Patio   (202) 447-8482
14th St. & Independence Ave., S.W.
(at the Mall) ....350 seated/600 reception

SUBURBAN WASHINGTON/ MARYLAND

Armory Place   (301) 585-5564
925 Wayne Avenue
Silver Spring, MD 20910

This fortress-like building offers eight rentable areas of which seven are primarily classroom-style spaces. The eighth measures 96 ft. x 58 ft. and is a fine space for any purpose including banquets with dancing.

Guest capacity: 25 to 600 for meetings; 320 seated/700 cocktails in large hall

---

Belgian Nobelman's Mansion   (800) 284-7028
Riverdale, Prince George County, MD

Baron Henri Joseph Stier, who fled to the U.S. during the French Revolution, built this home in 1801 as a copy of the Chateau du Mick, the home he had left behind in Antwerp. Because of its vicinity to Washington, DC, the house has subsequently been lived in by numerous statesmen, including Henry Clay in the 1850's, Senator Hiram Johnson of California from 1916 to 1929, and Senator Thaddeus Caraway of Arkansas and his wife Hattie, who in 1932 became the first woman in history to be elected to the U.S. Senate.

The mansion, which is presently owned and managed by the Maryland National Capitol Park and Planning Commission, also has lovely grounds. It is located about fifteen miles from downtown Washington.

Guest capacity: 80 in music room; 105 seated/165 cocktails in three interconnecting salons

Belmont Conference Center　　　(301) 796-4300

6555 Belmont Woods Road
Elkridge, MD 21277

This eighteenth century mansion located on 365 acres of rolling fields and woods offers both sleeping and meeting facilities.

Guest capacity: 35 seated; 150 in the garden; 25 overnight

Resident caterer

Capital Club　　　(301) 350-3111

Harry S. Truman Drive
Landover, MD 20785

Located within Washington's premiere sports/entertainment facility, this special function space is rented in conjunction with major entertainment performances going on at the Capital Centre.

Guest capacity: 350 seated/700 cocktails

Resident caterer

English Boxwood Garden Mansion　　　(800) 284-7028

(Prince George County)
Laurel, MD

The land where this mansion now stands was originally included in a 1076-acre land grant deeded to Richard Snowden who came from Wales in 1669 and who established one of the earliest ironworks in Maryland. Considered to be one of the finest examples of a five-part Georgian house in America, it was built by Mr. Snowden in the mid-eighteenth century.

In subsequent years, the house passed through many hands until it was purchased in 1928 by the Honorable and Mrs. Breckenridge Long, a career diplomat, who served as Assistant Secretary of State under Presidents Woodrow Wilson and Franklin Roosevelt. It was Mrs. Long who particularly supervised the care and maintenance of the mansion's English boxwood gardens and the boxwood-lined pathway which runs through the garden to the summer house. The latter is the only original eighteenth century summer house extant in

Maryland and may be one of only two still in existence in America.

The estate is presently owned and managed by the Maryland National Capitol Park and Planning Commission and is situated near Washington, DC.

Guest capacity: 100

Home of Sumner Welles　　　(800) 284-7028

(Prince George County)
Oxon Hill, MD

This neo-Georgian brick mansion was designed in 1929 by the Washington architect Jules Henry de Sibour for Sumner Welles, who served under President Franklin Roosevelt in various positions. A wide brick terrace runs along the back of the house and an enormous lawn slopes down towards the Potomac. Five first floor rooms are available indoors. The home is presently managed by the Oxon Hill Manor Foundation, Inc., and is situated near Washington, D.C.

Guest capacity: 300 inside; 800 tented

Suitable for receptions, business dinners and meetings.

Note: Not available during February for rentals.

Mount Airy Plantation　　　(301) 856-1860

Box 1008, Rosaryville Road
Upper Marlborough, MD 20772

Poised on a summit in the woods, this is a comfortably restored house that offers seven rooms plus two suites for overnight. Main dining room is glass topped with French doors leading to the estate's lawn.

Guest capacity: 30 to 80 meeting-style; 200 seated throughout the house; 250 in the garden

Resident caterer

National 4-H Center　　　(301) 961-2809

7100 Connecticut Avenue
Chevy Chase, MD 20815

This former campus of the Chevy Chase Junior College offers thirty conference rooms plus overnight accommodations.

Guest capacity: 25/650 meeting-style; 650 overnight

Resident caterer

Navy Commander's Dairy Farm (800) 284-7028
(Prince George County)
Mitchellville, MD

Constructed in the 1930's, this 585-acre estate of Captain Newton H. White USN, the first commander of the U.S.S. Enter-
prise, was developed by him into a successful dairy farm.
Full-length windows are hung with balloon curtains. Crystal
chandeliers light the ballroom and bleached pine paneling,
instead of the usual dark wood, lends its own accent here.
Now owned by the Maryland National Capital Park and
Planning Commission, the mansion provides a setting for
numerous functions including weddings, business meetings
and conferences.
Guest capacity: 80 seated in one room; 120 seated/200 cocktails
throughout the first floor

Prince George's Ballroom (800) 284-7028
Landover, MD

Situated inside the Capital Beltway, the Prince George's
Ballroom was formerly known as the old Prince George's
Country Club.
Guest capacity: 320 seated/reception in 85 ft. x 40 ft. Ballroom
There is an adjacent lounge area in front of a copper covered
fireplace and french doors that lead to a long sun porch.
Suitable for business meetings and private functions, food may
be served by caterer of your choice.

Rockville Civic Center Mansion, (301) 424-3184
Theater and Social Hall
603 Edmonston Drive
Rockville, MD 20851

This stone plantation house situated on one hundred acres offers
a conservatory, dining room, lounge and library on its first
floor. It also houses the F. Scott Fitzgerald Theatre and a
social hall on its lower level.
Guest capacity: 50 buffet/60 for meetings/225 cocktails in plantation house; 235 seated/250 cocktails in social hall; 250 in
social hall; 500 in theater

Rockwood Manor Park (301) 585-5563
1101 MacArthur Boulevard
Potomac, MD 20854

Situated in a private park maintained by the Maryland National
Capital Park and Planning Commission, this renovated
former Girl Scout camp offers a rambling brick manor house
with seven multi-purpose rooms, eight guest bedrooms and
five overnight cabins.
Guest capacity: 8/132 meeting-style, 89 seated/150 standing in
two rooms; 129 overnight
Caterer must be selected from approved list.

Rustic Mill Near Washington (800) 284-7028
Adelphi, MD

Built around 1796,
the mill is a three-
story thick walled
stone building
with exposed
beams and bare
hardwood floors.
Great for square
dancing.
Guest capacity: 150
seated/cocktails

Strathmore Hall Arts Center (301) 933-7422
10701 Rockville Pike
Rockville, MD 20852

This turn-of-the-
century red brick
mansion with
columned porticos
and patio offers
serenely furnished
eight first floor
rooms.
Guest capacity: 70
seated in one
room; 120 seated
on first floor

Woodend   (301) 652-9188

8940 Jones Mill Road
Chevy Chase, MD 20815

This stately red brick mansion is headquarters for the
Audubon Natural Society which operates the forty-acre es-
tate as a wildlife sanctuary and nature education center. Its
Great Hall is a large open reception area. In addition there
is a dining room, meeting room and lounge.
Guest capacity: 100 seated/125 cocktails indoors; 150 with tent
Resident caterer

WOODEND   J.R. SCHROEDER

Woodlawn Manor House   (301) 585-5564

16501 Norwood Road
Sandy Spring, MD 20860

This Georgian brick manor house surrounded by wide open
pastures was built around 1800 by a Quaker family. It offers
three downstairs rooms and two upstairs sitting rooms for
private functions.
Guest capacity: 75 seated/125 cocktails inside; 1000 on grounds
Caterer must be chosen from approved list.
Note: Tents are not allowed.

Baltimore: More Auditoriums, Halls & Meeting Rooms (by capacity for special functions)

Babe Ruth's Birthplace/ Maryland   (301) 727-1539
Baseball Hall of Fame Museum
216 Emery St.............................(reception/meeting) 60

The Peale Museum   (301) 396-3523
225 Holliday St. 25/200

Baltimore Maritime Museum   (301) 396-5528
Pier 5, Pratt St. .... 75 on Lightship "Chesapeake"
250 on U.S. Coast Guard Cutter"Taney"

Memorial Stadium   (301) 396-7113
1000 East 33rd St. ....(dining/reception) 250

George Peabody Library of the   (301) 659-8179
Johns Hopkins University
17 East Mt. Vernon Pl. ....200 seated/350 cocktails

Westminster Hall   (301) 328-2070
500 West Baltimore St. ....250 seated/350 cocktails

The Maryland Historical Society   (301) 685-3750
201 West Monument St.......................................250/500

The Walters Art Gallery   (301) 547-9000
600 No. Charles St. 300/500

The Baltimore Museum of Art   (301) 396-6320
Art Museum Dr. ....220 seated in Fox Court/
350 seated Fox Court and Schaefer Court;
363 in auditorium; 800 cocktails when spaces are combined

Maryland Jockey Club /Pimlico   (301) 542-9400
Race Course
Hayward & Winner Aves................................. 400/1491

National Aquarium in Baltimore   (301) 576-3833
501 East Pratt St., Pier 3 ....700 seated/1500 cocktails
on two levels; 300 on terrace

Lyric Opera House   (301) 685-5086
148 West Mt. Royal Ave. 350/1883

Joseph Meyerhoff Symphony Hall   (301) 727-7300
1212 Cathedral St. ....50 seated/80 cocktails in Green Room;
165 in recital hall; 2400 in auditorium

The B & O Railway Museum and   (301) 237-2387
Roundhouse
901 West Pratt St...............................850 seated/2400 cocktails

Maryland Science Center   (301) 685-2370
and Davis Planetarium
601 Light St. 500/2500

Baltimore Civic Center   (301) 837-0903
201 West Baltimore St. 75/3000

P.T. Flaggs   (301) 244-7344
601 East Pratt St. ....3000 in 4 areas

SUBURBAN WASHINGTON/ VIRGINIA

Boyhood Home of Robert E. Lee   (800) 284-7028
Alexandria, VA

John Potts built this early Federal-style house in 1795. It has stood for the better part of two centuries on a tree-lined street.

From its upper windows, one can see the Potomac River as once did Robert E. Lee.

Guest capacity: 100

Caterers may be brought in with approval of staff.

Note: Smoking is not allowed.

Collingwood-on-the-Potomac   (703) 765-1652
8301 East Boulevard Dr.
Alexandria, VA 22308

Originally part of George Washington's river farm, this Federal Palladian structure which George Washington built for one of his farm managers is directly on the edge of the Potomac. Ninety acres of sloping lawn meet the river's edge. Both floors also serve as a museum on Americanism.

Guest capacity: 75 seated/150 cocktails; over 150 in garden

Fairfax County Park Authority   (703) 941-5000
4030 Hummer Road
Annandale, VA 22023

The Fairfax County Park Authority has more than 14,000 acres of park land upon which numerous historic buildings are available for special function rental.

CABELL'S MILL
Built c. 1820

G. MATTHEWS

Some of these properties are:

Cabell's Mill   (703) 631-9566
Eleanor C. Lawrence Park, 5040 Walney Road, Centreville, VA
Guest capacity: 150

Colvin Run Mill   (703) 759-2771
Colvin Run Mill Park, 10017 Colvin Run Road, Great Falls, VA
Guest capacity: 150 indoors; 150 on grounds on this restored grist mill for country weddings, candlelight suppers, etc.

Dranesville Tavern   (703) 759-2771
Leesburg Turnpike, Annandale, VA
Guest capacity: 90 in this former roadside inn

Frying Pan School House   (703) 437-9101
2709 West Ox Road, Herndon, VA
Guest capacity: 100 in this four-room schoolhouse

Great Falls Grange Hall   (703) 759-6037
9818 Georgetown Pike, Great Falls, VA
Guest capacity: 200 in main hall; 180 in basement; outdoor picnic area, ball fields, etc.

Green Spring Farm   (703) 941-6066
Green Spring Farm Park, 4601 Green Spring Road, Annandale, VA
Guest capacity: 50 in this eighteenth century farmhouse now an art and exhibition center

Hunter House   (703) 938-7532
9601 Court House Road, Vienna, VA
Guest capacity: 50; 125 with canopy in this former private residence and winery

Stoneybrooke Mansion   (703) 768-1777
3900 Stoneybrooke Drive, Stoneybrooke, VA
Guest capacity: 35 for meetings/50 buffet in this former eighteenth century residence of Commodore Walter Brooke

Sully Plantation   (703) 437-1794
Sully Road, Chantilly, VA
Guest capacity: 300 in selected areas of the gardens and grounds

---

Flour and Grist Mill   (800) 284-7028
Berryville, VA

This stone and clapboard building was built in 1782 and operated as the flour and grist mill of Lt. Col. Nathaniel Burwell and Brig. Gen. Daniel Morgan.

During the War Between "The States," flour and feed from the Mill were sold to both armies. Presently restored with wooden gears dating from 1750, its great wheel turns under the splash of waters and its stones grind as they did over two hundred years ago.

Outside grounds are landscaped by the Garden Club of Virginia.

Guest capacity: 100 seated indoors

Gift from George Washington   (800) 284-7028
Mount Vernon, VA

George Washington set aside two thousand acres from his Mount Vernon estate as a gift to his foster daughter, Eleanor Parke Custis, and his nephew Lawrence Lewis who were married there in 1799. Designed by Dr. William Thornton, the first architect of the U.S. Capitol, construction of the Potomac River mansion began in 1800. Until it finally came under the public ownership and protection of The National Trust for Historic Preservation, the estate had to be saved numerous times from public sale, hurricane damage and neglect.

Presently in mint condition, its interior remains true to its early days. Its grounds are traversed by nature trails designed by The National Audubon Society and its gardens, which include a collection of old-fashioned roses, are designed and executed by The Garden Club of Virginia.

Guest capacity: 100 seated/125 standing; a tent must be used if the guest list exceeds the capacity of the house

Caterers may be chosen from approved list.

Home of Thirty-Five Lees of Virginia   (800) 284-7028
Alexandria, VA

Built in 1785 by Phillip Richard Fendall, Director of the Potomac Canal Company, the house was occupied by thirty-five Lees for 118 years. The last resident owner was labor leader John L. Lewis who lived there from 1937 to 1969.

The house and large garden with massive magnolia, old chestnut trees, rose garden and boxwood paths may be rented for special occasions. The property is on the National Register of Historic Places and is owned by the Virginia Trust for Historic Preservation.

Guest capacity: 100

Hounds and Hunt Museum Estate   (800) 284-7028
Leesburg, VA

Surrounded by twelve hundred acres of woods and pastures, this stunning white mansion offers a Renaissance Great Hall as its main private function room, a Jacobean dining room, a French drawing room and Flemish tapestries covering seventeen-foot high walls.

Guest capacity: 50 seated for a meeting in Trophy Room; 50 seated/150 cocktails in Renaissance Great Hall; 400 seated/2500 cocktails outdoors

Hunt Country Mansion   (800) 284-7028
Leesburg, VA

Located in the heart of northern Virginia's hunt country, this Classical Revival mansion and 261-acre property was built in the early 1800's by George Carter, a descendant of a notable Virginia family.

Set amid formal terraced gardens, with boxwood, magnolias, statuary, a gazebo and specimen trees, the mansion has a central three-story section flanked by two-story wings, a large portico with hand-carved mas-sive capitals and an octagonal draw-ing room.

After the Civil War, the fortunes of the Carter family de-clined and the family was forced to take in boarders. By the turn-of-the-cen-tury, the buff-colored mansion was in disrepair and its gardens overgrown. With the intention of returning the house and garden to their original beauty, the property was purchased by Mr. and Mrs. William Eustis in 1903. Mrs. Eustis, who restored the garden, was the daughter of Levi P. Morton, who was Vice President under President Benjamin Harrison. Mr. Eustis, the grandson of the founder of the Corcoran Gallery of Art, was a distinguished sportsman and one of the founders of the Loudon Hunt.

This beautifully restored property is now owned by the National Trust for Historic Preservation and administered by Oatlands, Inc.

Guest capacity: 75 seated/200 for a buffet in Main House; tents with dance floors may be used on the lawns

Montpelier   (800) 284-7028
Orange, VA

The National Trust for Historic Preservation acquired the peach-colored stone mansion that was once the home of James and Dolly Madison from members of the duPont family. It is a 2677-acre estate.

Guest capacity: several hundred guests may be accommodated in tents on lawn

Note: The mansion itself may not be used for the special event.

Old Town Hall   (703) 385-7976
3999 University Dr.
Fairfax, VA 22030

A popular social center, this ninety-year-old imposing building offers a wide open first floor light-filled space.

Guest capacity: 175 seated/200 cocktails

Plantation Game Preserve and   (800) 284-7028
Nature Sanctuary
Lorton, VA

George Mason, Father of the Bill of Rights, created during the 1750's this exquisite brick house on the Potomac River near

Mount Vernon. He brought master craftsman William Buckland from England to design the superb interior carvings. Buckland later worked on many houses in Virginia and Maryland, but Mason's home is considered to be his masterpiece and its Palladian Room, or formal parlor, boasts some of the most beautiful hand-carved woodwork in America. It also shows the elegance reached in colonial times.

Situated twenty miles from Washington, DC, its remaining 550 acres of formal gardens, deerpark, woods and streams serve today as a nature sanctuary. The property is considered ideal for meetings, seminars, luncheons, dinners and wedding receptions. Such functions are held in a modern building near

the plantation house. The meeting room has a cathedral ceiling and glass doors facing a brick paved courtyard with a fountain.

Guest capacity: 150 seated/200 for a meeting or seminar/350 for stand-up reception; 2000 in tent on grounds

Schooner Alexandria   (703) 549-7078
Alexandria Seaport Foundation
120 North Street
Alexandria, VA 22314

This three-masted topsail schooner was built in Sweden in 1929 and remodeled for passengers in the 1970's. Sporting seven thousand sq. ft. of red sails, this 125-foot long vessel is luxurious inside.

Guest capacity: 12 seated in Main Salon; 100 on deck

Scottish-Style Stone House   (800) 284-7028
Alexandria, VA

This mid-Georgian stone manor house, completed in 1753, was first the home of the Scottish merchant John Carlyle and later used by British General Edward Braddock as his headquarters in 1755. It was there that Braddock summoned five colonial governors to discuss the strategy and funding of the French and Indian War.

Bought in 1970 by the Northern Virginia Regional Park Authority and open to the public as part of the Bicentennial celebration, the house, which is lit by candles, is available for rental seven nights a week.

Guest capacity: 100 in house; 150 in house plus back terrace (April 15 through October 15)

Selma Plantation   (800) 284-7028
Leesburg, VA

Situated on a hill whose winding road promises a fine view, this Classic Revival structure was built in 1900 by a wealthy banker. Its Great Hall offers an open staircase that spirals to a landing overlooking the Hall. A dining room, two living rooms and a study are all handsomely furnished and offer working fireplaces.

Guest capacity: 175 seated/250 cocktails; 350 in the garden

Shenandoah Valley House and Farm   (800) 284-7028
Middletown, VA

Surrounded by the fertile farmland of the northern Shenandoah Valley, this National Historic Landmark is at once an eighteenth century plantation, a working farm and a center for regional crafts.

Built in 1794 for Major Isaac Hite, with the guidance and advice of Thomas Jefferson, the history of this grey limestone house is linked with the fortunes of the Shenandoah Valley. Both the plantation and the valley prospered from the richness of the land, and both suffered from the Civil War through the devastation of the land and the decline of wealth. The house also served as Union General Philip Sheridan's headquarters during the decisive Battle of Cedar Creek.

Recognizing the historical and architectural importance of this property, Francis Welles Hunnewell, the last private owner, bequeathed the house and one hundred acres of farmland to the National Trust for Historic Preservation in 1964. The house functions as a museum house and the land is operated as a working farm.

Guest capacity: 60 seated/125 standing in Manor House; many additional guests may be accommodated on grounds

Torpedo Factory Arts Center   (800) 284-7028
Alexandria, VA

This interesting construction houses eighty-five studios where artists make, exhibit and sell their art, as well as five cooperative galleries. A multipurpose room is available for meetings, lectures, chamber music recitals and small receptions.

Guest capacity: 50 in multi-purpose room; 1000 in Main Hall

Two Handsome Eighteenth Century   (800) 284-7028
Barns
Vienna, VA

Weathered boarding, hand-cut timbers, polished pine floors are the carefully reconstructed interiors of a German and English barn which were dismantled from New York State farms and brought to the Virginia countryside close to Washington DC.

The German barn is also a theater with a fully equipped stage, lighting and sound system and a balcony with fixed seating. The adjoining English barn features a bar and lobby. An inner brick courtyard abuts both barns.

Guest capacity: 225 seated/400 cocktails

Note: Functions may also be booked in conjunction with performances at nearby Wolf Trap Filene Center.

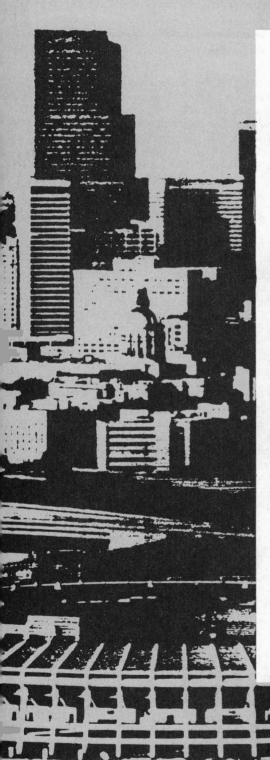

ATLANTA
& ENVIRONS
PARTY PLACES

ATLANTA

Atlanta Market Center

The Academy of Medicine   (800) 284-7028
Atlanta, GA

This neo-classic building surrounded by beautifully landscaped grounds also features the Czechoslovakian crystal chandelier which was part of the movie set for *Gone With The Wind*.

Authentic period furnishings lend elegance to business, civic, cultural and social events.

Guest capacity: 15 in Gold Room; 20 in Dining Room; 40 in Library; 254 in Auditorium and Rotunda

Atlanta Botanical Garden   (800) 284-7028
Atlanta, GA

This garden site is available for banquets, weddings, meetings and conferences.

Guest capacity: 300 seated/600 cocktail reception in Cecil B. Day Hall, a five thousand sq. ft. room overlooking the Rose Garden; 250 standing in James Cox Courtyard, an outside area with fountain; 100 standing in J. Hicks Lanier Terrace, an outdoor space overlooking the Garden; 30/100 for workshops and meetings in the various rooms of the Garden House

Atlanta Market Center   (800) 284-7028
Atlanta, GA

The Atlanta Market Center is a 6.3 million sq. ft. new international trade/convention facility encompassing the Atlanta Merchandise Mart, Apparel Mart and INFORUM. INFORUM is the information processing and telecommunications marketplace for the Southeast.

Atlanta Women's Club   (800) 284-7028
Atlanta, GA

Built in 1895 as a replica of an old French mansion, this granite structure is now run by the Atlanta Women's Club and is the last of its kind left on Peachtree Street in the heart of midtown Atlanta. It offers an oval dining room, sun parlor, drawing room and ballroom.

Guest capacity: 175 seated/300 standing in ballroom with grand piano and small stage; 400/500 in entire house

Suggested uses: reunion, corporate reception, wedding

Callanwolde Fine Arts Center   (404) 872-5338
980 Briarcliffe Rd., N.E.
Atlanta, GA 30306

This Tudor-style, 27,000 sq. ft. mansion, built in 1920 as the home of Charles Howard Candler, the eldest son of Coca Cola founder Asa G. Candler, was designed by Henry Hornbostle. Almost all the rooms adjoin the great halls located on each floor, and the entire mansion is centered around a large courtyard. The mansion's most unique feature is its music system which consists of a 3,752-pipe Aeolian organ with outlets to every major room.

Located in Druid Hills, a section of Atlanta which was originally planned by Frederick Law Olmsted, the father of Central Park, its twelve acres of lawns and gardens are now tended by various civic groups as well as the DeKalb County Parks Department.

Guest capacity: 50 seated/75 cocktails in Library; 50 seated/75 cocktails in Dining Room; 175 seated/200 cocktails in covered Courtyard; 200 seated/300 cocktails in Great Hall

The Fabulous Fox   (404) 892-5685

The Fox Theatre   Contact: Director of Marketing
660 Peachtree St., N.E.
Atlanta, GA 30365

Listed in the National Register of Historic Places, this 1929 Moorish/Egyptian art deco fantasy boasts one of the world's great auditoriums plus three ballrooms for social functions. The Auditorium was conceived as an open courtyard in an ethereal Moorish city, with twinkling stars in an azure sky overhead.

Its famous Egyptian Ballroom is decorated with reliefs of Ramses II.

Guest capacity: 300 seated in Spanish Room; 400 seated in Grand Salon; 1000 seated with dancing in Egyptian Ballroom; 4000 seated in Auditorium
Resident caterer

Floyd Building/Twin Towers   (404) 656-3850

2 Martin Luther King Jr. Dr., S.W.   Contact: Special Events
Atlanta, GA 30334   Coordinator, Georgia Building Authority

This modern building offers numerous spaces. On its 20th floor, the Empire Room affords a fine view of downtown Atlanta.

Guest capacity: 800 seated/1000 reception in Cafeteria; 520 seated/700 cocktails in Floyd Room; 150 seated/400 cocktails in Empire Room; 80 seated/100 reception in Conference Room
Resident caterer

Georgia Plaza Park and Garden   (404) 656-3850

85 Mitchell Street   Contact: Special Events Coordinator,
Atlanta, GA 30334   Georgia Building Authority

In addition to fountains and an outdoor plaza, this municipally-owned downtown location also offers four indoor special function rooms.

Guest capacity: 100 seated/120 cocktails in Capitol City Room; 200 seated/300 cocktails in Fireplace Room; 200 seated/300 cocktails in Waterfall Room; 200 seated/400 cocktails in Montage Room; 900 seated/1100 cocktails when three rooms are combined
Resident caterer

Georgia Railroad Depot   (404) 656-3850

Central & Martin Luther King Jr. Dr.   Contact: Special Events
Atlanta, GA 30334   Coordinator, Georgia Building Authority

Built in 1869, this restored depot is an attractive location for special functions offering 8254 sq. ft. in the Freight Room and 1175 sq. ft. in the Blue Room.

Guest capacity: 150 seated in Blue Room; 1000 seated in Freight Room
Resident caterer

High Museum

Atlanta, GA

(800) 284-7028

Opened in the Fall of 1983 and designed by Richard Meier, this unusual museum structure offers a five thousand sq. ft. atrium which functions as a central core and serves as an excellent space for receptions and special functions.

Guest capacity: 225 seated/1000 standing in 5000 sq. ft. Atrium; 225 seated in Walter C. Hill Auditorium

Houston Mill House

849 Houston Mill Rd., N.E.
Atlanta, GA 30329

(404) 727-7878
(404) 321-0530

Presently owned by Emory University, this fieldstone country house on a quiet wooded hillside less than a mile from the university campus, is popular for organizational meetings,

receptions and wedding ceremonies. A huge stone fireplace and an outdoor gazebo embellish the site.

Guest capacity: 70 for luncheons and dinners; 100 for meetings/seminars; 250 for receptions and weddings; 2 overnight guest rooms; outdoor functions may be held on landscaped lawns

Resident caterer

New Georgia Railroad

The Georgia Building Authority
1 Martin Luther King Jr. Dr.
Atlanta, GA 30334

(404) 656-0769

Volunteers from the Atlanta Chapter of the National Railway Society operate a restored steam locomotive and vintage passenger cars, a business car, a dining car and lounge. Departing from Zero Milepost in Atlanta, the train makes the loop around Atlanta's historic district (ninety minutes), or the trip to Stone Mountain Park and Village (one hundred and fifty minutes).

Guest capacity: up to 900 for a private charter
Resident caterer

Rhodes Hall

Atlanta, GA

(800) 284-7028

The former castle/home of A.G. Rhodes, a well-known Atlanta businessman and humanitarian, reflects the architectural, cultural and social richness of Atlanta at the turn of the century. Built in 1903 by Willis F. Denny, its design was inspired by the castles on the Rhine.

Guest capacity: 80 seated/225 standing/300 with the use of porch and front yard

Rupert's   (404) 266-9834
3330 Piedmont Road
Atlanta, GA 30305

Unabashedly glitzy, this huge nightclub is a hot spot featuring live entertainment in its multi-tiered movie set interior.
Guest capacity: 1100

The Swan House   (404) 261-0636
3130 Slaton Dr., N.W.   Contact: Coach House
Atlanta, GA 30305   Restaurant Manager

Built in 1928 and situated atop a series of gentle terraces, this former private mansion, now museum, makes its Georgian/Palladian-style garage and servants' quarters available for special events.
Receptions are held in a series of period rooms or on a canopied terrace that opens onto twenty-six acres of gardens and woodlands.
Guest capacity: 85 seated/200 standing
Resident caterer

Trolley Barn   (800) 284-7028
Atlanta, GA

This 4800 sq. ft. building was a trolley barn for twelve trolleys in the early part of this century. It now serves as a first rate meeting and social space.

Located in Inman Park, a Victorian-era suburb, two miles from downtown Atlanta, its spacious 2800 sq. ft. room has a 25 ft. ceiling and handsomely refinished beams. French doors open onto a brick patio. Mesquite wood floor is suitable for dancing.
Guest capacity: 250 seated/400 cocktails

Wrens Nest   (404) 753-7735
1050 Gordon St., N.W.
Atlanta, GA 30310

This is the historic home of Georgia author and journalist Joe Chandler Harris, who chronicled the exploits of Br'er Rabbit, Br'er Fox, Tar Babies and other Uncle Remus characters. Named for a family of wrens that nestled in the mailbox, the house contains original furnishings and memorabilia.
Guest capacity: 20 seated/300 standing
Note: Available for corporate and organizational functions; weddings and other private functions are not allowed.

Atlanta: More Auditoriums, Halls & Meeting Rooms (by capacity for special functions)

Center for Puppetry Arts   (404) 873-3089
1404 Spring St., N.W. .... (seated/reception) 400

Peachtree Playhouse   (404) 252-8960
1150 Peachtree St., N.E. 125/400

Robert W. Woodruff Arts Center   (404)898-1111
1280 Peachtree St., N.E. 600/1500

Atlanta Civic Center   (404) 523-6275
395 Piedmont Ave., N.E. 5000/8000

SAVANNAH

Gazebo in Whitfield Square

P.O. Box 1027
Savannah, GA 31401

Contact: Park and Tree
Commission

Both wedding ceremonies and receptions are allowed in Savannah's many parks and squares, some of which have gazebos. The most popular gazebo is situated in Whitfield Square, between Taylor and Gordon Streets. It has been the site of some of Savannah's finest weddings. Requests for the use of Whitfield Square and/or any other of Savannah's squares are directed to The Park and Tree Commission. There is no charge for the permit which can be obtained by writing to the address above.

Note: Commercial events, cars lining the streets, or debris left on site after the event are not allowed.

Gingerbread House

(800) 284-7028

Savannah, GA

Built in 1899 for Cord Asendorf, a German immigrant who prospered in the grocery business, this family home is considered one of the most outstanding examples of Steamboat Gothic gingerbread carpentry in the U.S. The recently completed five-year restoration includes ten Victoriana rooms, pink marble baths, a caterer's kitchen and an 1862 burled-walnut grand piano.

Guest capacity: 125 indoors; 175 in courtyard

Food may be served by caterer of your choice.

Old Fort Jackson

1 Fort Jackson Road
Savannah, GA 31404

(912) 232-3945
Contact: Director

Georgia's oldest standing fort overlooks the Savannah River, three miles from downtown Savannah. Here, the Confederate vessel *Savannah* fired on Union troops who occupied the Fort

in 1865. Within its moat-enclosed brick walls special functions, including weddings, may be held.

Guest capacity: 200 seated in air-conditioned room; 400 seated in covered pavilion; additional capacity for outdoor cookouts and picnics

Specialties are oyster roasts and shrimp boils. Every group is greeted by a Civil War garrison. Cannon firing may be arranged.

Outstanding Regency House

(800) 284-7028

Savannah, GA

Designed by William Jay and built in 1819 for William Scarbrough, a wealthy merchant, the house is one of the most outstanding examples of Regency architecture in the country. Its magnificent atrium and third story skylight make it an elegant setting for weddings, receptions, social functions, meetings and art exhibitions.

Guest capacity: 150 seated/200 for cocktails indoors; 200/300 in recently restored garden and pavilion

Southern House Built by a Rhode Island Master Builder

(800) 284-7028

Savannah, GA

This outstanding example of American Federalist architecture was completed in 1821 by a Rhode Island master builder who had come to Savannah to make his career and who made this house his home. By the 1930's however, the house had become a tenement. In 1955 speculators, wanting to sell its precious old brick and make way for a new parking lot, threatened demolition. A group of outraged citizens stepped in, saved the building and established the Historic Savannah Foundation. Completely restored and furnished with period furnishings from America and England, the house is both architecturally important and invitingly personal.

Guest capacity: 150 in garden

NEW ORLEANS & ENVIRONS
PARTY PLACES

NEW ORLEANS

Audubon Zoo
(800) 284-7028
New Orleans, LA

In addition to the Louisiana Swamp Exhibit, which is a favorite for Cajun Fais Do Do parties, the Audubon Zoo has four other areas available for evening functions.

Guest capacity: 300 in Miller Beer Garden; 400 in Louisiana Swamp Exhibit; 1000 in Sea Lion Pool; 3500 in Odenheimer-Hibernia Pavilion; 5000 in Diana Pool

Note: In the Fall of 1990, the Zoo will be opening a world-class Aquarium of the Americas on the banks of the Mississippi River in the French Quarter. The Zoo and the Aquarium will be linked by an eighteen-minute hydrofoil ride on the Mississippi. Both facilities will be available for private functions.

Board of Trade Building
(800) 284-7028
New Orleans, LA

After more than a century of commodities exchange, this award-winning architectural structure featuring a columned arcade entrance and a hand-painted mural dome, which overlooks the former trading floor, has been graciously transformed into a *grand salle a manger*.

Guest capacity: 25 seated/60 cocktails in The Patio; 40 seated/70 cocktails in The Arcade; 60 seated/150 cocktails in The Plaza; 100 guests on the Terrace level/160 seated on The Trading Floor

Note: The Trading Floor may also be used for seminars and meetings.

Cajun Queen, Creole Queen, and River Rose
(800) 284-7028
New Orleans, LA

The *Cajun Queen* is New Orleans' newest river boat. *The Creole Queen* is a newly built paddlewheeler. Both are in the style of a bygone era. *The River Rose* is a Gothic river boat passenger vessel.

Guest capacity: 600 on the *Cajun Queen*; 950 on the *Creole Queen*; 90 seated/150 cocktails on the *River Rose*

Elms Mansion
(800) 284-7028
New Orleans, LA

Designed by Lewis E. Reynolds in 1869, this fine example of Italianate-style architecture provides grandeur to the Garden District. Surrounded by lovely gardens and patios, its interior offers such decorative touches as hand-carved Carrara marble, ornamental plaster cornices, twenty-four carat gold sconces and a forty-eight-foot Grand Ballroom lined with jewelled windows.

Guest capacity: 150 in Garden Room; 350 in entire house; 1000 in house and on grounds

French Colonial Plantation House
(800) 284-7028
New Orleans, LA

This house, which was built in the last quarter of the eighteenth century, was typical of the cool and comfortable West Indies-style mansions that lined each side of the Bayou St. John at the time. Rooms run the depth of the house, opening through french doors onto jalousied galleries, to assure a refreshing sweep of air throughout the building.

In 1962, when this important house was threatened with demolition, it was rescued by the Louisiana Landmarks Society and moved to a neighboring site. After painstaking restoration, it appears today as it must have on any pleasant day when its original owner, a French judge and New Orleans' first mayor, came home from court to join his family in what was then the "country."

Guest capacity: 50 seated/75 cocktails indoors; 150 in downstairs rooms, galleries and garden

Gallier Hall
(800) 284-7028
New Orleans, LA

Modelled after the Erechtheum in Athens and designed by architect James Gallier, Sr., this noble structure is one of the finest examples of Greek Revival architecture in the U.S. Its portico is supported by ten Ionic columns.

In 1853, the seat of New Orleans city government was moved from the Cabildo to this Hall where it remained for over one hundred years.

Guest capacity: 70 seated/125 cocktails in Mayor's Parlor; 125 cocktails in Dining Room; 175 cocktails in Council Chamber; 230 seated/350 cocktails in Ballroom

Garden District Mansion   (800) 284-7028
New Orleans, LA

This pre-Civil War mansion of Greek Revival and Italianate architecture has traditional second floor iron work on the outside. Its ornate interior features gold leaf cornices, Florentine mirrors, crystal chandeliers from one of the imperial palaces of St. Petersburg, stained glass windows and a signed fresco by Tojetti on the ceiling of the Music Room. An awning on the front veranda may be dropped for a quasi-outdoor feeling. Members of the Women's Guild will act as hostesses and, if desired, will wear the antebellum dresses worn at the time the house was built.
Guest capacity: 100 seated/300 cocktails

Great City-Estate Garden   (800) 284-7028
New Orleans, LA

This grand city-estate was the home of the late philanthropists Edgar B. Stern and his wife Edith Rosenwald Stern, the Sears heiress. It is fashioned after the great country houses of England and surrounded by picturesque gardens and fountains. The Greek Revival mansion has fine collections including antiques, art and porcelain. The gardens are centered around the Spanish Court, a formal garden reminiscent of the Generalife Gardens of Granada, Spain.
Guest capacity: 30 standing in the guest cottage (Whim House); 64 seated/150 standing in the Playhouse; 300 seated/500 standing in the Tennis Court Pavilion; 2000 on grounds

Hi-Tech Club   (800) 284-7028
New Orleans, LA

Located on the site of the "Italian Village" of the 1984 World's Fair, this renovated 10,000 sq. ft. warehouse space creates a dramatic backdrop for corporate or social entertaining.
Guest capacity: 750; additional guests in tented areas
Offers video-theatrical lighting and a quality sound system.

House with the Magnificent Staircase   (800) 284-7028
New Orleans, LA

Designed in the free Renaissance-style by James Freret, this mansion was constructed in 1872 by Bradish Johnson, a young man of wealth whose family fortune was based on sugar plantations.
An outstanding feature of this fine building is the winding staircase which rises at the rear of the marble-floored entrance hall. It has been frequently honored as a masterpiece of design and craftsmanship. Also, one of the many magnolia trees on the grounds was declared to be the most magnificent specimen in the U.S.
Situated in the Garden District, this grand building is now one of the outstanding private schools for girls in the South.
Guest capacity: up to 200 indoors; 500 outdoors and on grounds

London Lady   (800) 284-7028
New Orleans, LA
This is a sixty-five-foot motor yacht.
Guest capacity: 40

Louisiana Children's Museum   (800) 284-7028
New Orleans, LA

This museum will provide staff members to operate the Bubbles Exhibit, Miniature Television Studio, Animation Workshop, and its Miniature Supermarket to bring out the child in any adult.

Guest capacity: up to 350

Mardi Gras Theme Party   (800) 284-7028
New Orleans, LA

The builders of the famous Mardi Gras floats make their studios available for private functions. Guests are surrounded by huge floats, dragons, eight-foot parrots, twelve-foot elephants and more.

Guest capacity: 50/5000

New Orleans Museum of Art   (800) 284-7028
New Orleans, LA

Located on the lagoons of City Park, the entire museum can be made available for private functions in exchange for a contribution.

Guest capacity: 225 seated in auditorium; up to 1000 in entire museum

The Presbytere   (800) 284-7028
New Orleans, LA

The Presbytere, or priests' residence, was designed in 1791 by Gilberto Guillemard. It offers numerous exhibits of paintings, decorative arts, furniture, costumes and the arts of Louisiana's silversmiths.

Guest capacity: 150

Romantic French Quarter House that   (800) 284-7028
Almost Became a Macaroni Factory
New Orleans, LA

This fascinating French Quarter house, one of the most romantic in New Orleans, was built in 1826 for Joseph Le Carpentier, a well-to-do auctioneer. In 1865, General Pierre G. P. Beauregard returned to New Orleans and lodged in it for eighteen months. By 1925 however, the house, which had had many owners, was to be demolished by its present owner for a macaroni factory.

But the fact that General Beauregard had once lived there aroused the interest of patriotic ladies who saved it from demolition. In 1944, Frances Parkinson Keyes, the novelist, rented and later bought the house as a winter residence. While writing half a dozen novels there, she also supervised its expert restoration.

Guest capacity: 18 in small dining room; 80 seated in ballroom; 200 in entire house including courtyard

Spring Fiesta Mansion   (800) 284-7028
New Orleans, LA

This gracious home in the Vieux Carre district is furnished with early 19th century and Victorian pieces. It provides a fine setting for weddings, receptions and corporate functions.

Guest capacity: 30 seated in double parlor; 125 cocktails in whole house; 200 cocktails inside house and on patio

U.S. Mint

(800) 284-7028

New Orleans, LA

Designed by William Strickland, this first major branch of the U.S. Mint began in 1835 during the presidency of Andrew Jackson. In 1861 the Mint served as the only mint of the Confederate States of America. In the 1930's the building was used as a Federal Detention Center and later as a Coast Guard warehouse.

The building has recently been restored and today is a beautiful example of the blending of the Classical Revival and Victorian tastes. In the rear courtyard, nestled among the myrtle trees, rests the *Streetcar Named Desire*. The Jazz and Carnival Museums are located on its second floor.

Guest capacity: 300/500 reception-style in auditorium; 500 reception-style when all three floors are used

Suggested uses: reception, business meeting, lecture, dinner

Vieux-Carré Townhouse

(800) 284-7028

New Orleans, LA

Located in the heart of New Orleans' Vieux-Carre, this historic house is an outstanding example of the most affluent period in New Orleans history, the 1830's through 1860's, known as the Golden Era.

Originally built by a wealthy German merchant in 1831, it was later lived in by several generations of the family of Judge Felix Grima. Presently owned and restored by The Christian Woman's Exchange of New Orleans, the property offers evening corporate receptions.

In case of inclement weather, guests have access to upstairs Board Rooms.

Guest capacity: 300

Where Tennessee Williams Stayed

(800) 284-7028

New Orleans, LA

This classic Greek Revival house was bought by a German-American family in 1925 and still remains in the family's hands. Historically, the house was Tennessee Williams' introduction to New Orleans in the 1940's when he briefly lived on its third floor as a friend of the family. While there, he received the inspiration for his Garden District plays. The solarium of this house is the setting for his play, *Suddenly Last Summer*.

Guest capacity: 125 seated/150 buffet downstairs; 350 cocktails on two floors; 500 with tent in back of house

New Orleans: More Auditoriums, Halls & Meeting Rooms *(by capacity for special functions)*

Saenger Performing Arts Center

(504) 525-1052

143 No. Rampart...(reception) 150

Toulouse Theatre

(504) 522-6484

615 Toulouse St. 100/225

Le Petit Theâtre du Vieux Carré

(504) 522-9958

616 St. Peters St. ....(reception) 350

Contemporary Arts Center

(504) 523-1216

900 Camp St.. (seated/reception) 700

New Orleans Museum of Art

(504) 488-2631

Lelong Ave., City Park 100/1000

(504) 522-0592

New Orleans Cultural Center

1201 St. Peters St. 2000/5000

Louisiana Superdome

(504) 587-3663

1500 Poydras St. 10,000/20,000

PLANTATION COUNTRY

Asphodel   (504) 654-6868
Rte. 2, Box 89   Contact: Ellsworth Kemp,
Jackson, LA 70748   Caterer

Located one hundred miles from New Orleans, this stately
mansion was built in the 1830's and named after Homer's
Asphodel Meadow of Vast Extent in the Fields of Elysium. It
is now a restaurant surrounded by other historic houses, some
of which have been moved to the site to form a historic village.
Guest capacity: 60 seated in dining room; 100 in dining room
and parlor; 250 on wrap-around porch and patio; overnight
accommodations available

Facing Sleepy Bayou Lafourche   (800) 284-7028
Napoleonville, LA

Built in 1846 by Col. Thomas Pugh, this twenty-one-room
white-columned Greek Revival mansion was designed by
Henry Howard, a noted architect from Cork, Ireland. The
facility includes the mansion's ballroom, which can be used
for wedding ceremonies, the mansion's Center Hall, which is
available for the receiving lines, the ground floor of Charlet
House, as well as large grounds.
Guest capacity: up to 250
It is situated 74 miles from New Orleans.

Glencoe Plantation   (504) 629-5387
P.O. Box 178   Contact: W. Jerome Westerfield, Jr.,
Wilson, LA 70789   General Manager

Situated on 1038 acres of land, this house, which was first
constructed in 1870 and reconstructed in 1903, is a tremen-
dous trove of Victorian embellishments and is considered one

of the finest examples of Queen Anne-style Victorian Gothic
architecture in the state of Louisiana.
From its wide gingerbread-bedecked galleries, to its former oak
panelled living foyer and double parlors, it is a house made
for entertaining.
Guest capacity: 50 seated in double parlor; 300 in courtyard and
on three levels of bannister; 12 overnight rooms
Resident caterer

Headquarters of a Yankee General   (800) 284-7028
New Iberia, LA

Overlooking the Bayou Teche, this Greek Revival plantation
house which was built in 1857 is of the raised cottage-style
common to Louisiana during the eighteenth century and on
up to the Civil War. During the latter period, a skirmish was
fought on the grounds of the plantation and it became headquarters for General Alfred Lee, the "Kansas judge turned
warrior."
The property gradually deteriorated and was slated for demolition when it was purchased by its present private owner in
1976 and was restored to its former elegance inside and out.
Guest capacity: 150 for a reception in covered area; up to 500 on
grounds

Inspired Re-creation   (800) 284-7028
Brittany, LA

Situated forty-five miles from New Orleans, this impressive
Greek Revival structure is not a restored plantation home, but
a new location that owner-poet James Ellis Richardson pieced
together using architectural and structural elements salvaged
from forty-six demolished Louisiana plantations. The house
has twenty-eight massive white columns reaching from
ground to roof and enclosing the galleries which surround the
house on the ground and second floors.

One of the South's most extensive collections of Victorian Rococo furnishings, porcelains, crystals and *objets d' art* embellish the interior.

Guest capacity: 70 seated in indoor dining room; 300 outdoors; overnight accommodations are available

Milbank Plantation   (800) 284-7028
Jackson, LA

Located in Feliciana Parish, an area famous for palatial homes, this Greek Revival plantation house, which features twelve thirty-foot Doric columns, is situated in the center of town and once served as the old bank building.

Completely furnished with museum quality antiques, this stately mansion may be rented for weddings and other receptions.

Guest capacity: 40 seated in ballroom; 500 with tents; 5 overnight rooms

Plantation with 250 Year-Old Oak Trees   (800) 284-7028
Vacherie, LA

Sixty miles above New Orleans, a French sugar planter built this plantation home between 1837 and 1839 for his bride. Almost a century later, this romantic home became one of the first of the Great River Road plantations to be fully restored.

Furnished just as its last owners had left it, house tours are still conducted by their personal servants.

Luncheon featuring local menus is served in an old slave quarter building. The Plantation restaurant also caters outdoor picnics.

Guest capacity: approximately 300 may be accommodated in Main House (larger numbers by special arrangement); blacksmith's shed accommodates 150 for seated meetings; four quarter-houses offer overnight accommodations

Suitable for corporate parties, weddings and honeymoons, the estate is both a non-profit foundation and a National Historic Landmark.

South's Largest Plantation House   (800) 284-7028
White Castle, LA

With fifty-three thousand sq. ft. under its original slate roof, this great home was built in 1859 in a blend of Greek Revival and Italianate styles. Saved from total destruction during the Civil War through the kind act of a Northern gunboat officer who had been a former guest at the mansion, it is presently in mint condition.

Originally designed by renowned nineteenth century architect Henry Howard for John Hampdon Randolph, a wealthy sugar planter, this American castle offers great views of the Mississippi River, century-old live oaks, a pond and an island with Canadian geese and ducks.

Guest capacity: 200 for a wedding in the White Ballroom (the most famous of its sixty-four rooms); up to 30 guests may avail themselves of the overnight accommodations

It is suitable for receptions, conventions, weddings and other functions.

Candlelight dinners and Planters Breakfasts are also available. This plantation is air-conditioned.

It is located sixty-nine miles north of New Orleans.

Tezcuco Plantation Village   (504) 562-3929
Rte. 1, Box 157
Convent, LA 70723

continued on next page

Located sixty miles from New Orleans, this antebellum raised cottage plantation house is constructed of cypress cut on the property and bricks from the plantation's own kiln. The recently restored main house is surrounded by other restored buildings, a chapel, a country store, and former slave quarters which now serve as overnight cottages.

Guest capacity: 150 seated/250 cocktails in restaurant; 250 seated/400 cocktails in Bringier Hall; unlimited capacity on grounds; 14 overnight rooms

Resident caterer

Townhouse on a Bayou   **(800) 284-7028**
New Iberia, LA

Set in the lush, semi-tropical Cajun country of southern Louisiana, 150 miles west of New Orleans, this white pillared manor house overlooking the Bayou Teche was built in 1834 for a wealthy planter, David Weeks. It served as plantation headquarters and social center for the Weeks family before the Civil War.

The house and gardens were restored by the builder's great grandson, William Weeks Hall, in the 1920's. Once described as "the last of the Southern gentlemen," he used this National Historic Landmark to revive the tradition of genteel hospitality. The complex includes antebellum period rooms, meeting spaces, and the garden. Presently the property belongs to the National Trust for Historic Preservation.

Guest capacity: 300 standing in garden

Note: All functions must take place in the garden; however, tours of the house may be combined with outdoor functions.

A Special "Places" Place in the South....

Cameo Caught in Amber   **(800) 284-7028**
Rembert, SC

This plantation, now conference center/sanctuary, was built in the early 1880's by a gentleman who wanted the opulence of Victorian city life and the solace of a forest. Its nine hundred acres of forest and farm land, its forty-acre black pond, its bridle paths and historic outbuildings, grist mill, general store, pigeon house and its exquisite interior decor, Hepplewhite chairs, Duncan Phyfe sofas and gilded clocks and cornices have been totally undisturbed by protective family members.

The great-great grandson of the original owner is presently making this "cameo caught in amber" available to corporations and organizations in need of renewal. Technical as well as gastronomical support are available: Limousine and car service to and from nearest airport (Columbia), audio-visual and secretarial services. Fine Southern fare.

Guest capacity: 30 in four meeting rooms; 9 overnight accommodations in Shiloh Guest Cottage

Heated and air-conditioned

CHICAGO & ENVIRONS

PARTY PLACES

CHICAGO

First Planetarium in the Western Hemisphere

The Auditorium   (800) 284-7028
Chicago, IL

In 1886 Ferdinand Park, a devout music lover and successful businessman, wished to give Chicago a grand opera house. He went to those who controlled the purse strings of the day — Marshall Field, Nathaniel Fairbank, Martin Ryerson. Three short years later, Chicago's elite turned out by the thousands to be the first to catch a glimpse of Dankmar Adler's and Louis Sullivan's glittering architectural masterpiece: a multi-purpose structure offering retail and office space, a 400-guest room hotel and a 4200-seat acoustically perfect theater.

This one hundred year-old building was threatened with demolition, but the sturdiness of its structure made demolition more costly than the value of the land which saved it from the wrecker's ball. However, it did become a soldier's canteen in

World War II. Today it is considered, again, one of Chicago's timeless treasures after extensive restoration.
Guest capacity: 300 on stage; 350 seated/500 cocktails in one of two lobbies; 3982 in Auditorium

Chicago Athletic Assocation   (800) 284-7028
Chicago, IL

Located on Michigan Avenue and overlooking the lake, this many storied club building offers all the amenities for meetings and social entertaining.
Guest capacity: up to 400
State-of-the-art studio visual equipment and secretary service. Location may be used for weddings.

Field Museum of Natural History   (800) 284-7028
Chicago, IL

Established in 1893, this world famous natural history museum offers opportunities for large social gatherings amid classic fountains and stately Ionic columns, plus private viewings of permanent and/or travelling exhibits.
Guest capacity: 1500 seated/2000 standing in Stanley Field Hall

First Planetarium in the Western   (800) 284-7028
Hemisphere
Chicago, IL

Founded in 1930 by philanthropist Max Adler, a senior officer of Sears Roebuck and Company, this great planetarium sits at the end of a half-mile long peninsula which juts out into Lake Michigan providing one of the best vantage points for viewing the Chicago skyline.
In recognition of its world-renowned collection of early scientific instruments, sculptor Henry Moore created a thirteen-foot high bronze sundial which sits on the planetarium's plaza. Special sky shows may be arranged followed by cocktails and dinner.
Guest capacity: 200 seated/400 cocktails; 450 seated in auditorium

Gatsby-Style Former Country Club (800) 284-7028
Chicago, IL

Located on Lake Michigan's south shore, this palatial former country club, adjacent to a nine-hole golf course, was designed by Marshall & Fox, architects of such other Chicago landmarks as the Blackstone and Drake hotels. It offers twenty-five-foot ceilings and vast, recently restored, accommodations.

Guest capacity: 150 seated in solarium; 350 seated in dining room; 750 seated in ballroom; 1500 seated/2000 cocktails in entire facility

Resident caterer

Gift from Daddy (800) 284-7028
Chicago, IL

So as to properly entertain her friends, Gwentholyn Jones, who was then a young art student, received this house in 1914 as a gift from her father, a member of the Armour family.

Designed by the architectural firm of Holabird and Roche, this house, which is one of Chicago's architectural treasures, resembles a Tuscan villa. Marvellously suited for entertaining, its gracious drawing room is connected to the dining room by an expansive tea room. In addition, there is a ballroom, various sitting rooms, and tall windows open onto a Byzantine courtyard.

Guest capacity: 500 in whole house; 120 seated in ballroom
2 grand pianos

Grand Old Lady of 111th Street (312) 785-8181
Hotel Florence Contact: Historic Pullman
11111 South Forrestville Foundation
Chicago, IL 60628

Railroad sleeping-car magnate George Pullman planned the nation's first industrial community in Chicago where executives lived in houses with as many as ten rooms, managers in smaller frame houses, skilled laborers in tight row houses, and unskilled single men in crowded tenements and boarding houses. In the 1880's the most handsome of all the community buildings was the Hotel Florence where Mr. Pullman played host to government leaders and vaudeville stars. The four-story red brick structure is a Victorian gem which still stands today. Now owned by the Historic Pullman Foundation, it serves guests as a museum and restaurant.

Guest capacity: 150
It is available for weddings.

Historic Water Tower and Pumping Station (800) 284-7028
Chicago, IL

This facility, which since 1869 supplies fresh water to half a million Chicagoans, was built and designed by William W. Boyington, a nineteenth century Massachusetts architect who designed many of Chicago's important buildings. Much importance was given to the design of the Pumping Station and its 138-foot high water tower at the time because some of Chicago's most prominent families were building mansions in its immediate neighborhood.

continued on next page

Having survived numerous demolition threats and still pumping seventy-two million gallons a day, this landmark location is also available for corporate meetings, sales presentations and sitdown dinners.

Guest capacity: 200 seated/500 standing; 200 seated in each of two multi-media theaters; observation deck also available

House of a Brewery Owner   (800) 284-7028
Chicago, IL

Completed in 1896, this European-stylethree-floor mansion was the collaborative effort of architect Adolph Cudell, who had built the Cyrus H. McCormick mansion, and Arthur Hercz, who specialized in the interiors of the Hotel Plaza in New York and the Fairmont in San Francisco. A hand-wrought iron staircase, stained glass windows, marble fireplaces, indoor fountain wishing well and English courtyard are some of the ornate highlights.

Guest capacity: 125 in ballroom; 500 in entire house and English courtyard

Ideal Setting for Corporate Functions   (800) 284-7028
Chicago, IL

This world class art institute offers amongst its many treasures the famous Stock Exchange Trading Room. Designed by Dakmar Adler and Louis Sullivan, it was moved to the Institute from its original location and is one of the celebrated interiors of the Chicago School of Architecture.

Guest capacity: 50 seated/275 cocktails in the McKlintock Court Garden; 50/500 seated in 3 Dining Rooms; 400/600 cocktails in the Trading Room; 949 in Arthur Rubloff Auditorium (additional auditoriums available)

Library/Cultural Center   (800) 284-7028
Chicago, IL

The elaborate "beaux arts" style of this Chicago Public Library building built in 1897 was renovated in the late 1970's to serve as a cultural center. An architectural showcase of bronze, marble, mosaic and stained glass, it offers spectacular public areas. Its grand staircase and walls are constructed of Carrara marble and medallions of rare dark green marble from Connemara, Ireland are set into the balustrades. The staircase leads to Preston Bradley Hall with its magnificent dome and hanging lamps designed by the House of Tiffany.

Guest capacity: 50 in each of two meeting rooms; 294 maximum in Theater; 300 standing in the Grand Army of the Republic Rotunda; 360 seated/700 maximum standing in Preston Bradley Hall

Note: Use of the facilities is restricted to civic, educational and cultural nonprofit organizations.

Municipal Pier   (800) 284-7028
Chicago, IL

Extending more than three thousand feet into Lake Michigan, this former Municipal and Navy Pier is now metamorphosing into a multi-use facility where large trade shows and major entertainments can take place. Its semi-circular Auditorium with a stage ringed by a balcony is ideal for banquets, convocations, conventions, exhibits, dancing and dining.

Guest capacity: 3000 maximum; 1700 seated dinner

Orchestra Hall   (312) 435-8122

220 South Michigan
Chicago, IL 60604

This gracious building was designed by famous Chicago architect Daniel Burnham, father of the "Chicago Plan," in the Adamsesque style. It contains an oval ballroom that is perfect for receptions, seated dinners and small recitals.

Guest capacity: 220 seated/400 cocktails in Ballroom; 2600 in Concert Hall for performances

Renovated Warehouse Owned by Two   (800) 284-7028
"Chicago Bears"

Chicago, IL

This two-floor loft with a view offers 11,700 sq. ft. of versatile space. Theme parties are particularly popular here such as speakeasy parties, 50's parties and, of course, sports oriented parties. Unique to this location is the "automobile party" where sports cars race on a raceway by remote control.

Guest capacity: 50 seated/75 cocktails in private room; 250 seated/1500 cocktails in entire space

Sound and lighting system, video equipment and a prep-kitchen area are on the site as well. Available seven days a week.

The 95th   (312) 787-9596

John Hancock Building
875 North Michigan
Chicago, IL 60611

A focal point on the Chicago skyline was designed by the world famous architectural firm of Skidmore, Owings & Merrill. The building features a restaurant on its top, 95th floor, which commands a panoramic view of the city.

Guest capacity: 40 seated in Wine Room; 130 seated/300 cocktails in main dining room

Resident caterer

Chicago: More Auditoriums, Halls & Meeting Rooms (by capacity for special functions)

Historic Pullman Foundation   (312) 785-8181
11111 So. Forrestville Ave. ....(seated/reception)100

Chicago Academy of Sciences   (312) 549-0606
Museum of Ecology
2001 No. Clark St. ....(seated/reception) 150

ArchiCentr   (312) 326-1393
330 So. Dearborn St. 100/200

The Renaissance Society   (312) 962-8670
5811 So. Ellis Ave. 75/200

The Goodman Theater   (312) 443-3808
200 So. Columbus Dr. 15/300

Chicago Botanic Garden   (312) 835-5440
Lake-Cook Rd. (Glencoe) ....(seated) 500

Drury Lane Theatre South   (312) 422-8000
2500 West 95th St.
Evergreen Park .... (seated/reception) 1000

Museum of Science & Industry   (312) 684-1414
57th St. & Lakeshore Dr. 50/1500

Arie Crown Theatre   (312) 791-6190
23rd St. & Lakeshore Dr. 25/5000

SUBURBAN CHICAGO

Armour Mansion   (800) 284-7028

Lake Forest, IL

This Italian Renaissance mansion built by J. Ogden Armour, the second son of the founder of this famous meat packing family, rents its Great Hall for private functions.

Guest capacity: 300 seated/300 cocktails in Great Hall and several adjacent rooms

Resident caterer

Frank Lloyd Wright Home and Studio (800) 284-7028
Oak Park, IL

Designed and built by Frank Lloyd Wright between 1889 and 1898 for his bride, Catherine Tobin, this extraordinary house gave expression to the original and distinctive American design which revolutionized architectural design around the world and was known as the Prairie School. Conceived when Mr. Wright was only twenty-two years old and constantly remodeled until 1911, its free flowing spaces, interweaving of interior and exterior, ground-hugging horizontals marked by long bands of windows, and the use of natural materials changed the nature of the American home.

In 1974, the Frank Lloyd Wright Home and Studio was founded as a non-profit corporation to preserve the building in partnership with the National Trust for Historic Preservation.

Guest capacity: 20 seated/60 cocktails

Note: This location is made available upon a corporate or private donation of $2,500 or more. Weddings are not allowed.

Nineteenth Century Women's Club (312) 386-2729
178 Forrest Avenue
Oak Park, IL 60301

Guest capacity: 180 seated in South Room; 500 seated in Auditorium

The North Room is used for dancing.

Dusty rose and white linens are provided. Also silver candelabras for skirted head-table.

Resident caterer

Note: All the food is homemade, right down to the rolls.

Prairie School Mansion (800) 284-7028
Oak Park, IL

This thirty-three-room mansion was built in 1913 by Charles White, a noted Prairie School architect who had also worked with Frank Lloyd Wright. Situated on several acres of grounds, this historic site is available for corporate meetings and receptions as well as social functions such as weddings.

Guest capacity: 100 seated/150 cocktails on ground floor; more guests may be accommodated when patio and tented grounds are used

A greenhouse is also available.

MIDWEST: ADDITIONAL CITIES

INDIANA

Indianapolis: Auditoriums, Halls & Meeting Rooms (by capacity for special functions)

President Benjamin Harrison Memorial Home (317) 631-1898
1230 No. Delaware St. 65/100

Clowes Memorial Hall (317) 283-9696
4600 Sunset Ave. 125/160

Morris-Butler Museum of Victorian Decorative Arts (317) 636-5409
1204 No. Park Ave. 50/200

Indiana Theatre (317) 635-5277
140 West Washington St. ....(seated/reception) 250

Indiana State Museum (317) 232-1637
202 No. Alabama St. 225/900

Indianapolis Zoological Society (317) 547-3577
3120 East 30th St. 60/2000

Murat Theatre (317) 635-2433
502 No. New Jersey St. ....(seated/reception) 2000

MICHIGAN

Fair Lane: The Henry Ford Estate   **(313) 593-5590**
The University of Michigan/Dearborn
4901 Evergreen Road
Dearborn, MI 48128

Completed in 1915 at a cost of two million dollars, this Scottish
    baronial mansion was named for the road which Henry Ford's
    father, William, was born on in County Cork, Ireland and was
    the final home of Henry and Clara Ford.
Thoreau's paraphrased quote: Chop your own wood and it will
    warm you twice, is inscribed on one of its cypress wood
    mantels, no doubt a favorite motto of Henry Ford himself.
The adjoining six level powerhouse, still complete with original
    machinery, combined the genius of Ford and Edison and made
    Fair Lane self sufficient in power, heat, light and ice in the
    early twentieth century.
Guest capacity: 200 conference-style/300 seated/400 cocktails
Resident caterer

Detroit: Auditoriums, Halls & Meeting Rooms (by capacity for special functions)

Orchestra Hall   **(313) 833-3362**
3711 Woodward Ave. ....*(reception) 100*

Detroit Science Center   **(313) 577-8400**
5020 John R St. *75/200*

Historic Fort Wayne   **(313) 297-9360**
6325 West Jefferson Ave. *150/250*

Music Hall Center for the Performing   **(313) 963-7622**
Arts
350 Madison Ave. *150/400*

The Scottish Rite Cathedral Theatre   **(313) 832-7100**
500 Temple Ave. *850/1500*

Ford Auditorium   **(313) 224-1030**
1 Auditorium Dr. ....*(reception) 2000*

Henry Ford Museum and Greenfield   **(313) 271-1620**
Village
20900 Oakwood Blvd. *500/2000*

Masonic Temple   **(313) 832-5900**
500 Temple *5000*

MINNESOTA

Minneapolis: Auditoriums, Halls & Meeting Rooms (by capacity for special functions)

Minneapolis Planetarium   **(612) 372-6644**
300 Nicollet Mall ....*(seated/reception) 150*

African American Museum of Art   **(612) 332-3506**
and History
2429 So. 8th St. *75/300*

The Guthrie Theatre   **(612) 377-2224**
725 Vineland Pl. *100/400*

University Art Museum   **(612) 373-3421**
84 Church St. *200/400*

Orpheum Theatre   **(612) 338-7968**
910 Hennepin Ave. *150/500*

Minneapolis Institute of Arts   **(612) 870-3140**
2400 Third Ave. *200/600*

Children's Theatre Company   **(612) 874-0500**
2400 Third Ave So. ....*(reception) 850*

Walker Arts Center   **(612) 375-7600**
Vineland Pl. *100/1000*

Orchestra Hall   **(612) 371-5633**
1111 Nicollet Mall *50/2543*

St. Paul: Auditoriums, Halls & Meeting Rooms (by capacity for special functions)

Minnesota Museum of Art   **(612) 292-4338**
St. Peter at Kellogg *125/200*

Landmark Center   **(612) 292-3230**
75 West 5th St. ....*(seated/reception) 500*

Chimera Theatre   **(612) 292-4321**
30 East 10th St. *175/1000*

continued on next page

The Science Museum of Minnesota   **(612) 221-9400**
30 East 10th St. 180/2000

Landmark Center St. Paul-Ramsey   **(612) 292-3272**
75 West 5th St. 600/2500

MISSOURI

Richardsonian House   (800) 284-7028
St. Louis, MO

This forty-two-room Romanesque mansion was designed by the architect Thomas Annon, who was greatly influenced by H. H. Richardson. Built for Samuel Cupples, a nineteenth century self-made businessman who dealt in woodware, this house, its twenty-two fireplaces, woodcarvings, iron work and stained glass cost $500,000 in 1890 currency. Presently owned by St. Louis University, its rooms decorated in period furniture, including The Musicians Gallery between the first and second floor, are open to the public.
Guest capacity: 125 seated/150 standing
Suitable for dinners, meetings, receptions, concerts, recitals, rehearsal dinners.
Resident caterer

Kansas City: Auditoriums, Halls & Meeting Rooms *(by capacity for special functions)*

Kansas City Museum   **(816) 483-8326**
3218 Gladstone Blvd. 60/350

Uptown Theatre   **(816) 531-0011**
37th & Broadway .... (seated/reception) 700

Center for the Performing Arts   **(816) 363-4300**
4949 Cherry St. 140/1000

Folly Theater   **(816) 842-5500**
300 West 12th St. 250/1000

Nelson-Atkins Museum of Art   **(816) 561-4000**
4525 Oak St. 250/1200

Midland Center for the Performing Arts   **(816) 421-7500**
1228 Main St. 200/2700

Kansas City Auditorium Complex   **(816) 421-8000**
301 West 13th St. 7500/15,000

St. Louis: More Auditoriums, Halls & Meeting Rooms *(by capacity for special functions)*

Loretto Hilton Center   **(314) 961-0644**
130 Edgar Rd. .... (seated/reception) 150

McDonnell Planetarium   **(314) 535-5810**
5100 Clayton Rd. Forest Park .... (seated/reception) 200

Missouri Botanical Garden   **(314) 577-5119**
4344 Shaw Blvd. 200/500

Westport Playhouse   **(314) 878-7538**
600 Westport Plaza .... (seated/reception) 1000

Opera House   **(314) 241-1010**
1416 Market St. 600/1500

The St. Louis Art Museum   **(314) 721-0067**
Forest Park 240/2000

OHIO

Cincinnati: Auditoriums, Halls & Meeting Rooms *(by capacity for special functions)*

Showboat Majestic   **(513) 241-6550**
Ft. of Broadway .... (reception) 100

Cincinnati Playhouse in the Park   **(513) 421-5440**
962 Mt. Adams Circle .... (seated/reception) 125

The Taft Museum   **(513) 241-0343**
316 Pike St. 75/200

Contemporary Arts Center   **(513) 721-0390**
115 East 15th St. 100/200

Cincinnati Music Hall   **(513) 621-1919**
1241 Elm St. 300/500

Zoological Society of Cincinnati   **(513) 281-4701**
3400 Vine St. 75/500

Taft Theatre   **(513) 621-4829**
5th & Sycamore ....*(seated/reception) 550*

Cincinnati Art Museum   **(513) 721-5204**
Eden Park *200/1000*

Cincinnati Museum of Natural   **(513) 621-3889**
History
1720 Gilbert Ave...*200/1000*

Cleveland: Auditoriums, Halls & Meeting Rooms (by capacity for special functions)

Shaker Historical Museum   **(216) 921-1201**
16740 So. Park Blvd.
(Shaker Heights) *40/50*

Karamu House Art Gallery   **(216) 795-7070**
2355 East 89th St...*150/200*

The Cleveland Playhouse   **(216) 795-7000**
8500 Euclid Ave...................................*(reception) 350*

Beck Center for Cultural Arts   **(216) 521-2540**
17801 Detroit Ave...*200/400*

The Cleveland Metroparks Zoo   **(216) 661-6500**
Brookside Park *350/450*

The Cleveland Center for   **(216) 421-8671**
Contemporary Art
11427 Bellflower Rd. *50/500*

History Museum   **(216) 721-5722**
10825 East Boulevard..*400/800*

Cleveland Museum of Natural History   **(216) 231-4600**
Wade Oval, University Circle *500/1000*

Cleveland Convention Center   **(216) 348-2229**
1220 East 6th St...................................*(reception) 3000*

WISCONSIN

Grain Exchange   **(800) 284-7028**
Milwaukee, WI

Built in 1879 and located in what was the original Milwaukee Chamber of Commerce Building, this 60 foot x 115 foot hall was until 1910 the largest cash grain market in the world. Designed in 1879 by architect Edward T. Mix, the three story room is Italian Renaissance in form and Victorian in ornament: marble murals, frescoes, friezes, gold leaf, stained glass, elaborate columns and huge skylight. Suitable for all manner of functions, including weddings.
Guest capacity: 425 seated

Milwaukee: More Auditoriums, Halls & Meeting Rooms (by capacity for special functions)

Melody Top Theatre   **(414) 353-7700**
7201 West Good Hope Rd....................................*(reception) 400*

Charles Allis Art Museum   **(414) 278-8295**
1630 East Royall Pl. *60/500*

Milwaukee Art Museum   **(414) 271-9508**
750 No. Lincoln Memorial Dr..........................*300/500*

Milwaukee County Zoological Gardens   **(414) 771-3040**
10001 West Bluemound Rd. *250/500*

The Mitchell Park Horticultural   **(414) 649-9830**
Conservatory
524 So. Layton Blvd. ....*(reception) 500*

Milwaukee County War Memorial   **(414) 276-8533**
Performing Arts Center
929 No. Water St. *500/1000*

Milwaukee Public Museum   **(414) 278-2750**
800 West Welles St........................................*300/2000*

DALLAS/HOUSTON & ENVIRONS

PARTY PLACES

DALLAS/HOUSTON

DALLAS

Dallas Garden Center   (800) 284-7028
Dallas, TX

Located in Fair Park, which was the site of the Texas Centennial Exhibition, this Garden Center is a National Historic Landmark.
Guest capacity: 300 seated for dinner/500 seated for meetings or performances in auditorium
Stage

Dallas Museum of Art   (214) 922-0220
1717 North Harwood   Contact: Richard Suttman,
Dallas, TX 75201   Director of Catering

This museum's galleries and courtyards are made available to corporate/patron events.
Guest capacity: 100/1500 in seven locations

Hall of State   (800) 284-7028
Dallas, Texas

Designed as the centerpiece of the Texas Centennial Exposition in 1936, this glorification of Texas history, industry, flora and fauna is also one of America's finest examples of art deco architecture.

Guest capacity: 400 in auditorium; 350 seated/500 standing in Great Hall
Suggested uses: reception, banquet, meeting, wedding

Mansion in an Arboretum   (800) 284-7028
Dallas, TX

Latin, Colonial, English Regency and Art Deco styles are harmoniously combined in this 1930's mansion designed by Texas' most famous residential architect, John Staub.
Overlooking White Rock Lake, the mansion is part of the Dallas Arboretum and Botanical Society and is available for all manner of social functions, including weddings.
Guest capacity: 200; 250 if terraces are included

South Fork Ranch   (214) 231-2088
P.O. Box 863773   Contact: Pamela J. Dobson,
Plano, TX 75086   Tour Administrator

This number one tourist attraction in Texas was chosen by the producers of the TV series *Dallas* as its filming site when this popular series first began. Outdoor scenes are still filmed there.
Owned by Terry Trippet, whose own family was in residence there, the ranch was later sold to a real estate developer who redecorated its interior and built party pavilions, one open air and one heated and cooled. Both the home, now called the Mansion, and all other pavilions and entertainment areas are designed for private and corporate luncheons, dinners, picnics, wedding receptions, auctions, concerts, fashion shows, proms, etc.
Guest capacity: 2000 in Convention Center; 500 in small party pavilion; 150 in the Mansion indoors; more on patio and poolside
Hayrides, stagecoach rides, rodeos and picnics may be incorporated in a special event.

Dallas: More Auditoriums, Halls & Meeting Rooms (by capacity for special functions)

Dallas Zoo   **(214) 946-5155**
621 East Clarendon Dr. .... *(seated/reception) 100*

Planetarium/Southwest Museum of   **(214) 428-8351**
Science & Technology
Fair Park *100/200*

Dallas Repertory Theatre   **(214) 369-8966**
North Park Shopping Center .... *(seated/reception) 215*

Majestic Theatre   **(214) 880-0137**
1925 Elm .... *(meeting) 1568*

HOUSTON

Houston Museum of Fine Art   **(713) 639-7577**
P.O. Box 6826   Contact: Alice Collette,
Houston, TX 77265   Development Office

The Bayou Bend Mansion is an outstanding location which belongs to this museum. It is famous for its decorative arts collection. Several other museum locations are also available for special functions in addition to the mansion's garden.
Guest capacity: 200 cocktails in the Lillie and Hugh Roye Cullen Sculpture Garden; 200 cocktails in the Glassell School of Art; 300 cocktails in the gardens of the Bayou Bend Mansion; 800 in entire museum
Note: Only corporate/patron events are allowed.

Rainbow Lodge   **(713) 861-8666**
1 Birdsall   Contact: Jonathan Kessing,
Houston, TX 77007   Manager

Once a private home built in 1935 for a Houston doctor, it now serves as the main entrance and cocktail area for this three-story restaurant/lodge. A glass-enclosed dining room overlooks the bayou, a duck pond, a lake with a gazebo and two and one-half acres of landscaped grounds with waterfalls.
Guest capacity: 40 in upstairs private dining room; 150 in three-level dining room
Resident caterer

Regal Ranch   **(713) 499-9651**
P.O. Box 21172
Houston, TX 77226

This frontier-style ranch is available for large theme parties: barn dances and fiestas.
Guest capacity: 450 seated in barn; 350 on patio; more may be accommodated in tents outside

Houston: More Auditoriums, Halls & Meeting Rooms (by capacity for special functions)

Alley Theatre   **(713) 228-9341**
615 Texas Ave. *70/200*

Houston Zoological Gardens   **(713) 520-3209**
1513 Outer Belt Dr. .... *(reception) 300*

Astrodomain   **(713) 799-9873**
Kirby Dr. *500/1000*

Houston Museum of Natural Science   **(713) 526-5273**
1 Hermann Circle Dr. *500/1000*

LOS ANGELES & ENVIRONS

PARTY PLACES

LOS ANGELES AND LOS ANGELES COUNTY

Above Sunset Boulevard   (800) 284-7028
Hollywood, CA

Located in the hills above Sunset Boulevard, this residence offers a spectacular view of Los Angeles.
Guest capacity: 30 seated indoors/just under 100 when combined with outside grounds

Airplane Hangar   (800) 284-7028
Van Nuys, CA

This twenty thousand sq. ft. airplane hangar will provide jet planes, bi-planes, bearcats and the like to set the mood.
Guest capacity: 1200

Art Deco Palace   (800) 284-7028
Los Angeles, CA

Re-opened as a performing arts center in 1985, this 1920's theater has been designated by the National Register of Historic Places and declared a Historic-Cultural Monument by the City of Los Angeles.
Guest capacity: 1288 in Orchestra; 306 in Loge; 692 in Mezzanine; additional capacity in upstairs cafe and bar

Chewing Gum Magnate Mansion   (800) 284-7028
Avalon, CA

Built on a mountain top in 1921 by chewing gum magnate William Wrigley, this terraced Georgian mansion/inn overlooks Avalon Harbor.
Guest capacity: 50 seated indoors; 150 when combined with outside grounds; overnight accommodations are also available

Dallas House   (800) 284-7028
Los Angeles, CA

Used as Pamela Ewing's home on the television show *Dallas*, this beautiful New England Georgian Colonial residence has a large backyard and pool area as well as a covered patio.

Guest capacity: 125 indoors; 150 seated/250 buffet in large backyard, covered patio and pool area

Note: An official "J.R." look-a-like is also available.

Dutch Castle in Beverly Hills   (800) 284-7028
Beverly Hills, CA

Perched high above Beverly Hills with a spectacular view of mountains, city and sea, this fairy tale Delft blue and white house is built in the style of a Dutch castle. Multi-tiered lighted fountain in courtyard, competition-size tennis court, Hollywood pool.

Guest capacity: up to 50 seated indoors; more can be accommodated outdoors

Former Estate/Now Campus   (800) 284-7028
Los Angeles, CA

The former estate of Edward L. Doheny, in the heart of Los Angeles, offers elegantly preserved Victorian mansions and gardens. Its Tiffany glass domed Pompeiian Room is a grand setting for receptions, dances and concerts.

Guest capacity: 465 in auditorium; 200 in conference room; 100 in Pompeii Room

Note: It is primarily available to non-profit groups.

Frank Lloyd Wright House   (800) 284-7028
Los Angeles, CA

This architectural masterpiece, designed in 1924, is graced with exquisite stained glass, iron work, and thousands of red-brown seventeen-inch concrete blocks carved with geometric Mayan designs. These rise in pillars up to twenty-two-foot high ceilings flanking a long marble hallway which stretches from one end of the house to the other and leads out to the terrace garden and ornamental pool. Spectacular view of Los Angeles.

Guest capacity: up to 125 indoors; slightly larger numbers may be accommodated outdoors

Fraternal Facility   (800) 284-7028
Los Angeles, CA

Located half-way between downtown Los Angeles and Beverly Hills, this facility is available for a variety of functions in its Banquet Hall and Theater/Auditorium.

Guest capacity: 800 seated in Banquet Hall; 1737 in fixed-seated Auditorium

Suggested uses: meeting, concert, exhibit, banquet

From Mediterranean to Martian   (800) 284-7028
Universal City, CA

Any party theme from Classic Western to Martian can materialize in this motion picture studio from its on-location props and costumes.

Guest capacity: 25/40 in Private Dining Room; 200 in Celebrity Room; 300/500 in Studio Room; 700 when combined with lobby and patio area; larger numbers may be accommodated on the studio's theme lots

continued on next page

Note: VIP tours through the movie studios may be arranged as part of the special event.

Futuristic Entertainment Complex   (800) 284-7028
Culver City, CA

The dramatic impact of this center's spectacular facade is heightened by its Grand Atrium which offers a soaring ninety-foot canopy of glass and has become a gathering spot for "the rich and famous" in Hollywood. It includes a stage as well as broadcast-quality sound and lighting and a big screen television projection system.

Guest capacity: 800 seated/1200 reception-style in Grand Atrium

Historic Carousel   (800) 284-7028
Santa Monica, CA

Of the eighty-nine carousels manufactured by the Philadelphia Toboggan Company between 1903 and 1934, only thirty-nine still exist as whole operating units.

Affectionately nicknamed "PTC #62," in accordance with the Philadelphia Toboggan Company's numeric cataloging, its forty-four horses are hand-carved out of basswood in the style

established by one of the company's master carvers, John Zalar.

The sixteen horses on the outside row are stationary, they are called "standers". The twenty-eight horses on the inner rows are called "jumpers" as they are lifted up and down and to and fro by turning devices called "cranks." Two double chariots are available for a more sedate ride.

The Carousel is the centerpiece of the National Landmark Hippodrome Building which overlooks the Pacific Ocean.

Guest capacity: 250 seated/550 cocktails/1200 with adjacent decks

Hotel Queen Mary   (213) 435-5671
P.O. Box 8, Pier J   Contact: Banquet Sales
Long Beach, CA 90801

This is a floating four hundred-room hotel with twelve special events rooms for parties and wedding receptions. Complete convention facility on lower deck.

Guest capacity: 10/1000

Note: Howard Hughes' Spruce Goose is the largest wooden flying boat ever built. Its wing span is longer than a football field. Special events may be held for up to 2000 people in the aircraft's hangar adjacent to the Queen Mary. Telephone: (213) 435-3511

Italian Renaissance Villa   (800) 284-7028
Los Angeles, CA

This 1926 villa designed by architect Gordon Kauffman features a thirty-eight-foot banquet room and a twenty-one-foot high ceiling with hand-stenciled walls. An inner flagstone courtyard surrounds the pool.

Guest capacity: 80 seated/over 200 for a reception indoors; up to 300 outdoors

John Wayne's Yacht   (800) 284-7028
Long Beach, CA

Formerly belonging to John Wayne, this converted World War II
   mine sweeper is now a 140-foot yacht in mint condition. All his
   belongings are aboard as he left them including a green felt
   covered poker table and upholstered leather chairs in main salon.
Fuel capacity for thirty-five hundred miles.
Guest capacity: 150 for parties with dancing along Long Beach
   Harbor; sleeps 11 plus crew for cruises
Resident caterer and crew

Malibu Ranch   (800) 284-7028
Malibu, CA

Breathtaking scenery includes horse arena, emus and llamas,
   plus pool and cabana with dressing areas. Ideal for formal
   affairs and corporate picnics.
Guest capacity: 100 to over 500

Mediterranean Villa Overlooking the   (800) 284-7028
Rose Bowl
Pasadena, CA

Pink stucco and Moorish tiles set off this 1920 Rudolf Valentino-
   style house. Shaded by tall eucalyptus trees and overlooking
   Pasadena's Rose Bowl, it makes a fine setting for garden
   parties and wedding receptions.
Guest capacity: 200

Wattles Mansion   (800) 284-7028
Hollywood, CA

This 1905 Mission Revival house with panelled rooms rents its
   first floor and terraced gardens.
Guest capacity: 125 seated/200 cocktails

Los Angeles: More Auditoriums, Halls, & Meeting Rooms (by capacity for special functions)

Variety Arts Center   **(213) 623-9100**
940 So. Figueroa *50/100*

Coronet Theatre   **(213) 651-0491**
366 No. La Cienega Blvd. ....(reception) 150

Wilshire Theatre   **(213) 468-1700**
8440 Wilshire Blvd. *75/150*

Greek Theatre   **(213) 665-5887**
Griffith Park *100/160*

California Museum of Science &   **(213) 744-7483**
Industry
Exposition Park *120/200*

Huntington Hartford Theatre   **(213) 462-6666**
1615 Vine St. ....(reception) 300

Los Angeles Municipal Art Gallery   **(213) 485-4581**
4804 Hollywood Blvd. .... (seated/reception) 300

Pantages Theatre   **(213) 468-1700**
6233 Hollywood Blvd. ....(reception) 300

Hollywood Bowl   **(213) 856-5400**
2301 No. Highland Ave. ....(seated) 400

Embassy Theatre   **(213) 623-3261**
851 So. Grand *350/800*

George C. Page Museum of La Brea   **(213) 857-6301**
Discoveries
5801 Wilshire Blvd. *600/1100*

Natural History Museum of Los   **(213) 744-3414**
Angeles County
900 Exposition Blvd. *500/1500*

Griffith Observatory   **(213) 664-1181**
Griffith Park *600/2000*

The Music Center   **(213) 972-7211**
135 No. Grand Ave. *1000/2000*

Hollywood Palladium   **(213) 466-4311**
6215 Sunset Blvd. *2400/3000*

Shrine Auditorium   **(213) 748-5116**
649 West Jefferson Blvd. *2000/3800*

SAN FRANCISCO & ENVIRONS
PARTY PLACES

SAN FRANCISCO

The California Academy of Sciences   (800) 284-7028
San Francisco, CA

Located in Golden Gate Park, this museum complex, the oldest
scientific institution in the West, makes its halls: the
Aquarium, the Planetarium, the Laserium, the Hall of Man,
the Earth and Space Hall, the African Hall and Annex, the
(Wild California) in Meyer Hall, Fossil Hall, Mineral Hall,
Insect Hall and Botany Hall available for special functions.

Guest capacity: 400 seated in Morris Auditorium; up to 400 in
individual halls; 3000 in entire museum

California Culinary Academy   (415) 771-3500
625 Polk Street
San Francisco, CA 94102

This conversion from a 1912 social club hall and theater into a
thriving culinary academy offers a lovely dining room with
glassed-in kitchens as center stage.

Guest capacity: 350 seated/500 cocktails

Resident caterer

Club DV8   (800) 284-7028
San Francisco, CA

In the style of "Post Moderne," which signifies contrasts—
Renaissance and Pop Art, candlelit candelabra and
state-of-the-art theatrical lighting, polished concrete and
faux marble, exposed beams and gold veined ceilings, large
areas and intimate spaces— that's the mix which makes
this 20,000 sq. ft. two-floor club chic and multi-functional.

Guest capacity: 50 to 1500 in eight rooms

Stage, runway, three dance floors, sound system, remote video
camera, projection video screens

Resident caterer

Former Residence of the Archbishop   (800) 284-7028
of San Francisco
San Francisco, CA

Built in 1904 in the style of a grand country manor of the Second

French Empire,
this stately
house, which
hosted popes
and survived
the Great
Earthquake, is
completely and
magnificently
restored in the
La Belle Epo-
que style.

Featuring a three-story open staircase, a sixteen-foot glass dome,
floor-to-ceiling fireplaces, painted ceilings and located near
the San Francisco Opera House, this residence names its
rooms after 19th century operas: *La Boheme, Der
Rosenkavalier, Don Giovanni,* etc. and features dining, reception and conference rooms for special events as well as
thirteen overnight suites.

Guest capacity: 25 seated/250 cocktails

Former Shirt Factory and Auto Part   (800) 284-7028
Supply Outlet/Now Gallery
San Francisco, CA

This multi-textured, two-floor contemporary gallery has many
homey touches and interconnecting rooms.

Guest capacity: 75 in first floor Central Gallery; 175 in second
floor Textile Room; 250 in second floor Veranda Gallery; 500
in Main Gallery

Suitable for colloquiums, professional meetings, as well as
fundraisers, performances and social events.

Fort Mason
(800) 284-7028
San Francisco, CA

Two piers, reaching almost six hundred feet out into the Bay and commanding a sweeping view, plus eight buildings make up the Fort Mason complex. It was the former embarkation point to the Pacific Theater of World War II. This thirteen-acre site offers an excellent location for events of all sizes.

Guest capacity: 5000 on each of two piers; 400 in conference center

Suggested uses: fair, festival, conference, fashion show, performance

Gift Center Pavilion
(800) 284-7028
San Francisco, CA

Rose-toned, art deco interior presents 30,000 sq. ft. of giftware showroom space which surrounds a five story atrium. Full production theater.

Guest capacity: 1500 seated/2500 cocktails; 100 in penthouse

Suitable for weddings, bar mitzvahs, fashion shows, musical presentations, luncheons and receptions.

Golden Sunset
(800) 284-7028
San Francisco, CA

This luxurious seventy-five-foot vessel is comprised of three decks — an open-air wing bridge with wet bar, a spacious salon, and a lower deck housing the galley, master and guest bedrooms.

Guest capacity: 40 seated/100 cocktails

Resident caterer

The Green Room
(800) 284-7028
San Francisco, CA

Originally designed as a lounge for World War I veterans, this 138 ft. long loggia is located on the second floor of the San Francisco Veterans Building. Its twenty-eight-foot high ivory and gold leaf ceiling is graced with five chandeliers.

Guest capacity: 300 seated/500 cocktails

Suggested uses: reception, meeting, conference, dinner, fashion show

Headquarters of the California Historical Society
(800) 284-7028
San Francisco, CA

This massive red Arizona sandstone building was built during the years 1894 to 1896 for William Franklin Whittier, a successful early San Francisco merchant, by San Francisco architect Edward R. Swain. Its solid construction withstood the 1906 earthquake with the loss of only one chimney. It has served as the San Francisco Consulate of the German government prior to World War II and became the headquarters for the Mortimer Adler Philosophical Institute where scholars met to discuss and write about great issues of civilization.

Guest capacity: 75 seated in Supper Room (an elegantly panelled ballroom); 250 for receptions in second floor exhibition galleries

Wedding ceremonies may be held on main floor which houses authentic historic rooms.

Note: Smoking is not allowed inside the house. Ashtrays are provided on front porch.

Ideal for Wedding Parties and Ceremonies

(800) 284-7028

San Francisco, CA

This twenty-four-room house, designed by Julius Kraft, was part of the last wave of mansion building in San Francisco at the turn of the century. Its granite steps are flanked by two greylions and lead to a mosaic and marble vestibule and a pair of oak and plate glass doors. Beyond the vestibule is a two-story Central Hall with columns and panelling of golden oak. The grand staircase rises to the west. Adjacent to the mahogany panelled Dining Room is the mosaic and glass Solarium which is capped with three small Tiffany glass cupolas.

Guest capacity: 50 seated in Dining Room; 175 seated/300 cocktails in entire house

Kunin Mansion

(800) 284-7028

San Francisco, CA

Built before the earthquake of 1906, this private Victorian mansion sits in the center of the Pacific Heights area of San Francisco. The large open rooms have fireplaces, high ceilings and original art work.

Guest capacity: 50 seated/250 cocktails

Mansion of a Silver Baron

(800) 284-7028

San Francisco, CA

In 1912, architects Bliss and Faville chose a classic Italian Renaissance design for the Flood family whose wealth originated from silver mining.

Located in the Pacific Heights section, the house affords a grand view of San Francisco Bay. Its marble entry hall is 140 feet long and its courtyard, which may be tented, still has the fern trees which were brought from Australia for the 1915 Panama Pacific Exhibition.

This formidable townhouse, which is in mint condition, rents out for numerous social functions, including wedding receptions.

Guest capacity: 300 seated/800 for receptions on both floors

Old Mint

(800) 284-7028

San Francisco, CA

This is a monument to the boom days of the California Gold Rush. Left intact and standing virtually alone amidst the rubble of the 1906 earthquake, this Federal Classic Revival building was the only financial institution able to open its doors for business. Restored and declared a National Landmark, it produces special commemorative coins and offers one of the finest gold nugget collections in the world. It comprises several high-ceilinged period rooms painted burgundy and gold and decorated with former gas chandeliers. Its Counting and Receiving Rooms, where miners entered with gold dust, are genuine.

Guest capacity: 500 indoors; 700 when combined with Greek courtyard

Palace of Fine Arts
(800) 284-7028
San Francisco, CA

Created as a Palace of Fine Arts in 1915 for the Panama-Pacific International Exposition by the innovative architect Bernard R. Maybeck at a time when San Francisco was honoring the discovery of the Pacific Ocean and the completion of the Panama Canal. It was also celebrating its own resurrection after the 1906 earthquake. Primarily constructed to achieve mood and located on the San Francisco Lagoon, presently known as the Marina District, close to a group of Monterey cypresses, the architect chose as his theme a Roman ruin, mutilated and overgrown. Roman in style and Greek in decorative treatment, it is the only remaining structure of the thirty-two palaces built for the Fair.

By the closing of the Exposition on December 4, 1915, a movement to preserve the Palace was already underway. Eighteen lighted tennis courts were installed in 1934 and remained for eight years. During World War II the Palace grounds were used for storage of army trucks. By 1964, rebuilding was underway at ten times the original cost.

Thanks to private and public grants and the vision of physics professor Frank Oppenheimer, the reconstructed Museum Hall now functions as a Museum of Science and Human Perception and is available for dinners and receptions.

Guest capacity: 3000 cocktails

Guests may roam freely among more than six hundred interactive exhibits. Tactile parties for smaller groups may also be arranged.

Patrons Room
(800) 284-7028
San Francisco, CA

This elegant and comfortable reception room is the focal point of social activity within Davies Symphony Hall. It is enjoyed by members and their guests for receptions and dinners before the start of every San Francisco Symphony concert and also for some opera performances.

Guest capacity: 100 seated/200 cocktails

Note: Invitations to join this Room are extended to all donors who contribute at least $2,000 annually to the San Francisco Symphony. Annual membership dues are an additional $250.

Queen Anne-Style Mansion
(800) 284-7028
San Francisco, CA

This Queen Anne-Style mansion offers volunteers to circulate at parties and give informal house tours.

Guest capacity: 85 for sitdown dinners/100 for cocktails on lower level (ballroom); 50 for sitdown dinners/125 for cocktails and hors d'oeuvres on main floor

Food may be served only by caterers from approved list.

Note: Mansion is not available for lunches or brunches on Wednesdays or Sundays.

Redwood Club House
(800) 284-7028
San Francisco, CA

Designed in 1919 by Bernard Maybeck, architect of the Palace of Fine Arts, this club house is almost entirely built of redwood and epitomizes the final phase of the American Arts and Crafts movement. The property is surrounded by old pines, cypresses, a terrace and a garden and is maintained by the Forest Hill Association, a non-profit corporation with a membership of seven hundred families.

Guest capacity: 150 seated (100 with dancing)/200 cocktails

San Francisco Conservatory of Flowers
(800) 284-7028
San Francisco, CA

This Victorian greenhouse is a State Historical Landmark and was the first permanent building in Golden Gate Park. It is available for evening rental.

Guest capacity: 100 seated (70 with dancing)/200 cocktails

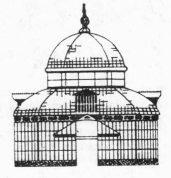

Showplace Square (800) 284-7028
San Francisco, CA

Sixteen square blocks have been redeveloped in downtown San Francisco for commercial show and meeting rooms.

Guest capacity: 3400 in 62,000 sq. ft. San Francisco Concourse; 1400 seated/1800 cocktails in 26,000 sq. ft. Galleria Design Center; up to 2000 in meeting rooms plus 45 permanent showrooms; capacity for up to 600 booths in California Data Mart/High Technology Meeting Center

Soma/Soho Atmosphere (800) 284-7028
San Francisco, CA

Soma is the area in San Francisco which, like early New York Soho, merges artist's lofts and galleries with auto repair and shops and small industrial plants.

Here the space of a former coffee roasting plant has turned into a popular restaurant with potting shed garden room.

Guest capacity: 80

Thirty-Seven-Room Colonial Revival (800) 284-7028 Mansion
Oakland, CA

Built in 1899 by Alexander Dunsmuir, heir to a Scots-Canadian coal mining fortune, for his great love, Mrs. Josephine Wallace, and later owned by I. W. Hellman of the San Francisco Wells Fargo Bank, this grand house with massive Corinthian pillars is nestled in the East Oakland foothills and features a Tiffany-style dome skylight topping the central staircase. Its elaborate gardens have over seventy specimens of trees,

shrubs, camellias and succulents collected from around the world.

Guest capacity: 200 maximum in Carriage House; the downstairs of the main house and grounds are also available

Two Grand Yachts (800) 284-7028
San Francisco, CA

The eighty-three-foot *Pacific Spirit* and the one-hundred-foot *California Spirit* are specifically available for weddings and other special events. In-house catering staff is culinary school trained. The captain is available to perform wedding ceremonies.

Guest capacity: 93 on the *Pacific Spirit;* 149 on the *California Spirit*

Victorian Lighthouse in the San (800) 284-7028 Francisco Bay
Point Richmond, CA

On a rocky island in Marin County near San Francisco, one of the West Coast's earliest lighthouses is still in operation. The station has borne witness to shipwrecks, the passing of clipper ships and the closing of the last whaling station at Point San Pedro. Completely restored, its turn-of-the-century appearance is emphasized by wood-burning stoves, period antiques and old, deep-throated fog horns.

Guest capacity: 300

Boat transportation from Point San Pablo Yacht Harbor.

Diaphone fog horns are used after the completion of a wedding ceremony. Overnight accommodations are offered for honeymoon couples.

San Francisco: More Auditoriums, Halls, & Meeting Rooms *(by capacity for special functions)*

War Memorial Opera House   **(415) 864-3330**
301 Van Ness Ave.......................................(seated) 100

Hellman Hall   **(415) 564-8086**
1201 Ortega St.....................................(reception) 150

Geary Theatre   **(415) 421-4284**
415 Geary St. 100/200

Theatre on the Square   **(415) 236-0562**
450 Post St. 15/200

Club Fugazi   **(415) 421-4284**
678 Green St. 178/300

Herbst Theatre   **(415) 431-5400**
401 Van Ness Ave.. 250/500

Cow Palace   **(415) 469-6085**
Geneva Ave. & Santos St. .... (seated/reception) 550

California Palace of the Legion of Honor   **(415) 750-3678**
Lincoln Park 200/600

National Maritime Museum   **(415) 556-2904**
Hyde Street Pier...300/600

Asian Art Museum of San Francisco   **(415) 558-2993**
Golden Gate Park...385/800

M. H. DeYoung Memorial Museum   **(415) 750-3678**
Golden Gate Park...300/1000

Strybing Arboretum and Botanical Gardens   **(415) 558-3622**
9th Ave. & Lincoln Way 700/1200

Masonic Auditorium   **(415) 776-4917**
1111 California St. 1078/2000

Civic Auditorium   **(415) 974-4000**
99 Grove St. 2000/3000

Natural History Museum Aquarium   **(415) 221-5100**
Golden Gate Park...600/3000

BAY AREA AND BEYOND

Catalonian Winery   **(800) 284-7028**
Sonoma, CA

In 1986, a Catalonian family known for making sparkling wine since the thirteenth century built a multi-million dollar winery in the Sonoma Valley, two hours from San Francisco.

Its Executive Dining Room overlooks man-made wine cooling caves and the Sala de Catadores (Hall of the Tasters) offers lovely views over the vineyards and foothills.

Guest capacity: 40 in Executive Dining Room; 120 seated in Sala de Catadores

It is available for weddings.

Floating Tropical Island   **(800) 284-7028**
Sausalito, CA

Anchored in the San Francisco Bay, this man-made tropical island consists of a 2000 sq. ft. semi-submerged mansion and 1600 sq. ft. of white sandy beach, plus palm trees, flowers and a waterfall cave.

A path behind the waterfall leads to the secret entrance of the underwater mansion complete with a salon, bar, fireplace, concert grand piano, kitchen and three state rooms; all have ports from which to watch sea creatures swim by.

Guest capacity: 50; 8 seated in gazebo

Former Indian Healing Ground/Now Conference Center   (800) 284-7028

Sonoma, CA

A 150-acre private oasis tucked in the serene Valley of the Moon of California's wine country, one hour from San Francisco. Family-owned for three generations, the property offers a large stone fireplace, redwood and adobe housing, meadows, stream and clear water springs, ancient oaks and almond trees, hot tub and sauna.

Guest capacity: 50 for overnight meetings; additional capacity on grounds

Hacienda Winery   (800) 284-7028

Sonoma, CA

A small romantic winery situated on the land where Count Agoston Haraszthy, a Hungarian nobleman, first planted vineyards in 1857. Visitors are invited to picnic under the oaks surrounding this historic landmark. The Sonoma County Historical Society is in charge of Count Haraszthy's villa nearby.

Guest capacity: 100 outdoors

Marin County Victorian Mansion and   (800) 284-7028 Center for Victorian Art

San Rafael, CA

Architect Clinton Day, the designer of San Francisco's City of Paris, built this seventeen room mansion in 1888. In 1974 it was acquired by the City of San Rafael as a direct result of citizen reaction to a developer's proposal to demolish the house. Now it is a highly active and innovative cultural center offering exhibits and events which attract an audience from the entire San Francisco Bay area.

Guest capacity: 75 seated on first floor; 25 on terrace

Eleven acres of formal gardens and wooded hillside are part of the property.

Showplace for a San Francisco Banker   (800) 284-7028

Belmont, CA

This modified Italian villa, which is believed to have been designed by architect Henry Cleveland, was built for William Chapman Ralston (1826-1875), the founder of the Bank of California. Having spent his early days on Mississippi river boats, Ralston incorporated many features of 19th century Steamboat Gothic design into this lavish summerhome, i.e., doors sliding sideways or up into the walls and a promenade deck as a sun parlor.

Ralston devised many financial schemes to develop San Francisco, but rivals broke his hold on the Comstock mines in Nevada and the Bank of California collapsed. A day later, Ralston's body was found in San Francisco Bay.

Presently owned by the College of Notre Dame, its original mirrors and Czechoslovakian chandeliers are still in place in the ballroom, the floor of which is made of hand laid walnut and maple, and the dining room library and various parlors are unaltered.

Guest capacity: 75 seated in dining room; 250 in entire house; several hundred on lawn with fountain

Villa Montalvo   (800) 284-7028
Saratoga, CA

The country home of Senator James Phelan, now an art center, this 1912 Mediterranean-style villa is surrounded by 175 acres of formal gardens and wooded trails.

Guest capacity: under 100 indoors; 200 in Oval Garden outside

Suggested uses: meeting, wedding

Winery for Weddings Near San Francisco   (800) 284-7028
Windsor, CA

One of the very few California wineries which cater to weddings, this modern vineyard is located in the Russian River Valley, 1½ hours from San Francisco. It offers a banquet room, two patios and a theater. The latter is excellent for small sales and business presentations.

Guest capacity: 20/150 seated daytime during the winter in Banquet Room; 20/200 seated daytime during the summer in Banquet Room and patio; 50/200 seated after 5 p.m. in winter; 50/250 seated after 5 p.m. in summer; 400 for receptions after 5 p.m. winter or summer

Suitable for weddings and wedding ceremonies as well as other private celebrations. Business meetings and seminars are particularly welcome.

Tours of the cellars and wine-tastings may be part of the event.

Glossary

Art Deco: a style of decorative art developed originally in the 1920's with a revival in the 1960's marked chiefly by geometric motifs, curvilinear forms, sharply defined outlines, often bold colors and the use of synthetic materials such as plastic.

Baroque: a style of architecture which flourished particularly during the period of 1550-1750. It is characterized by much ornamentation and curved rather than straight lines. The word is thought to stem from the Portuguese barroco, meaning an irregularly shaped pearl.

Colonial: during the Colonial period in the United States, this style, particularly in New England, featured small rooms that could be heated easily and sloping roofs designed to shed rain and snow. Dutch Colonial houses in the middle colonies were often of brick and stone with small windows and shutters.

English Tudor: a style of architecture that prevailed during the reign of the Tudors, 1485 to 1603, which included Henry VII, Henry VIII, Edward VI and Queen Mary. It is characterized by flat arches, shallow moldings and profuse paneling.

Georgian: is the building style used in England and the English colonies during the 1700's and early 1800's, taking its name during the period of George I, II and III. Georgian architecture has symmetry in design and makes extensive use of brick and stone. Most Georgian houses are square or rectangular in shape and are built around a central stair-hall. Imposing main doors and richly ornamented rectangular fireplaces are typical of the style.

Gothic: a style of architecture which spread throughout Europe by the mid-1200's and was primarily known for its achievement of height and pointed arches.

Italian Renaissance: a style of architecture developed in Italy and western Europe between 1400 and 1600 characterized by the revival and adaptation of classical design, harmonious repetition of detail, the use of horizontal lines and delicate carvings.

Romanesque: a style of European architecture of the 11th and 12th centuries, based on the Roman and characterized by the use of low, wide arches and vaults and thick, massive walls. Its outstanding characteristics were strength and heaviness.

Victorian: characteristic of the time when Victoria was queen of England, 1837 to 1901. The style is known for ornately decorated houses and interiors, steeply pitched roofs and gingerbread trim.

INDEX

C

G

O

S

W